# KIDS WORKING
# IT OUT

# KIDS WORKING IT OUT

## Strategies and Stories for Making Peace in Our Schools

Tricia S. Jones
Randy Compton
Editors

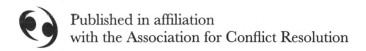

Published in affiliation
with the Association for Conflict Resolution

JOSSEY-BASS
A Wiley Imprint
www.josseybass.com

Lyrics on p. 148 by Carol Johnson are reprinted by permission from the recording "Isn't It Good To Know," Copyright 1982, Carol Johnson, Noeldner Music, BMI. 900 Calvin, SE, Grand Rapids, MI 49506 (www.caroljohnsonmusic.com).

Lyrics on p. 255 by Fred Small are reprinted by permission. Words and music by Fred Small. Copyright 2000 Pine Barrens Music, BMI.

Jossey-Bass books and products are available through most bookstores. To contact Jossey-Bass directly call our Customer Care Department within the U.S. at 800-956-7739, outside the U.S. at 317-572-3986 or fax 317-572-4002.

Jossey-Bass also publishes its books in a variety of electronic formats. Some content that appears in print may not be available in electronic books.

**Library of Congress Cataloging-in-Publication Data**
Kids working it out : strategies and stories for making peace in our
schools / Tricia S. Jones, Randy Compton, editors.— 1st ed.
     p. cm.
Includes bibliographical references and index.
  ISBN 0-7879-6379-8 (alk. paper)
  1. School violence—United States—Prevention—Case studies. 2.
Conflict management—Study and teaching—United States—Case studies.
I. Jones, Tricia S. II. Compton, Randy.
  LB3013.32 .K53 2002
  371.7'82—dc21

                              2002015275


Printed in the United States of America


FIRST EDITION
*PB Printing*  10  9  8  7  6  5  4  3  2  1

# CONTENTS

To my son, Alexander.
May peace bless your life and be your contribution.
—*T.S.J.*

To my father and grandfather, who instilled in me
the passion for achieving a peaceable and just world.
—*R.C.*

# FOREWORD

The high school teacher grabbed the masked gunmen's shirt, forcing him to stop. Slowly, the young killer pulled off his mask so that the gray-haired history teacher could recognize him.

"Robert?" the sixty-year-old teacher, Rainer Heise, asked incredulously. He could not believe that the person who had just killed thirteen teachers, two students, and a police officer had been one of his students.

"Go ahead and shoot me, Robert," Heise said. "But first, look me in the face."

*Kids Working It Out: Stories and Strategies for Making Peace in Our Schools* is written by adults who are "looking in the face" of the next generation. But the contributors to this book are not waiting until violence breaks out and the TV news helicopters begin their vigil in the sky above our children's schools. They are creating programs that *prevent* violence.

German television would later report that it was a "fearless teacher" who stopped the massacre at Johann Gutenberg High School in Erfurt, Germany. But of course that is not true. Rainer Heise was certainly afraid. But what enabled him to overcome his fear and to risk his life dramatically demonstrates the importance of this book. He did not end the worst bloodshed in Germany since World War II with more violence. He did not end it by installing metal detectors, by giving pompous speeches at school assemblies, or by posting the Ten Commandments on classroom walls. He ended it by looking directly into the eyes of his student. His courageous, nonviolent strategy worked because he had a relationship with this dangerously troubled young man—a relationship that was stronger than hate and rage and vengeance. Instead of becoming the fourteenth teacher shot that day, Rainer Heise stopped Robert Steinhaeuser in his tracks. He stopped him because they had a *connection*.

"That's it for today, Herr Heise," the young man said, addressing his teacher with the formal language that indicates respect. He then dropped his gun to his side and momentarily dropped his guard. Heise took the opportunity to escort the student into a nearby classroom and then quickly lock the door behind him. Trapped in the classroom and able to take stock of the carnage he had committed, the nineteen-year-old student ended his own life.[1]

Fortunately for us and our children, the stories in this book are not so bloody. But one of the reasons that the stories in this book are less fatal, and less fatalistic, is precisely because of the conflict resolution education (CRE) programs that the distinguished contributors describe here. Although no school intervention can guarantee safety, the programs in this book come close. They ensure that all students, at some point during their school week, will "look in the face" of an adult who cares about them and who is addressing their inner lives and how they handle conflict. No one knows if such a program would have stopped Robert Steinhaeuser's rampage, or any of the other school massacres. But from his reaction to Rainer Heise's face, it is possible that he could have been reached before he pulled the trigger.

The following chapters are about educators and students who are willing to confront the challenge of conflict. They are "making peace in our schools" because they know that if they don't, many others will be hurt, and some will die. If these tragedies occur, it will not be because they were unavoidable. It will often be because we failed to teach our children the arts of peace.

For the first time in human history, often beginning at a tender age, today's children watch more than one hundred thousand acts of violence before they enter high school. This fictional violence, which is dramatically portrayed on their television sets and in movie theaters, is depicted with all the literary and high-tech gifts that the "entertainment" industry can muster. (Among the violent videos and computer games found in Robert's bedroom was music with the lyrics, "Shoot down your naughty teachers with a pump gun!") With the real-life violence on the evening news, young people today do not need to conjure up images of mayhem from their imaginations. On the contrary, when it comes to committing violence, we have, unfortunately, taught them very, very well.

Even if the consequences are not life-and-death, the stakes are still staggeringly high. As Randy Compton makes clear in the opening chapter, an "epidemic" of violence in schools has been growing for more than a decade. Overwhelming percentages of high school students (80 percent) and fourth through eighth graders

(90 percent) describe themselves as having been the victims of bullying. Despite U.S. government reports that suggest that violence in schools may be decreasing, no one disagrees that the current levels are too high.

The standard responses to violence—longer prison sentences, harsher discipline, and a variety of "zero-tolerance" policies—are not working. What *is* working are the kinds of policies and projects described so beautifully in the following pages. CRE, as Tricia S. Jones succinctly points out in Chapter Two, meets many educational needs that go well beyond what its name implies. It not only fosters a safe and constructive learning environment but also enhances students' emotional and academic growth. CRE takes different forms: individual peer mediation, interpersonal "peaceable classroom" methods, whole-school strategies, and community-wide programs. What they all have in common is that *they work*.

*Kids Working It Out* makes a special contribution to this field in a number of ways. First, it provides a comprehensive framework for understanding the *field* of CRE. Instead of pushing one program or one approach, the book gives educators and others who work with young people a broad overview of their options. Second, it showcases specific programs that have proven their value in a wide variety of school settings. Third, it provides not only facts and statistics to inform the mind but also stories that touch the heart. Finally, it includes the voices so often left out of books about educational policy: those of the students themselves.

The fact is, kids *want* to be responsible. When it comes to conflict, they want to do "the right thing." When educators take the time to teach them, they are eager learners. "The teachers can't watch over you every single minute of the day," says one of the many students interviewed in this book. "They have you for class and then you are out of there and you are in passing period and lunch and stuff, and that is where a lot of the put-downs are. They are not watching us over there. They can't enforce it. We have to." Said another succinctly, summarizing the message of this entire book: "Everybody should know this stuff."

This combination of unique features makes this book an essential part of every educator's toolbox. It also confirms beyond a shadow of a doubt Tricia S. Jones and Randy Compton's conclusion: "CRE and related programs are extremely valuable and should be given the attention and resources they deserve."

If programs like those described in the following pages *are* part of the curriculum where you work or where your children attend school, then reading *Kids Working It Out* will help you strengthen them. If they are *not* yet present in your school system, this book will help you understand why they should be and how to make a compelling case for developing such programs. Whether you are an educator, a parent, a concerned citizen, or a young person who wants a safer place to learn, believe me: this book will help.

Our job, however, is not just to *read* it. Our job is to *use* it. At a time when more and more classroom time and teacher energy is being devoted to preparing students to take tests, we need strong voices in every community that will prepare young people for the ultimate test: life itself. This book provides just the tools we need to protect our kids, safeguard our schools and the dedicated educators who work there, create a healthier learning environment, and, perhaps most important, revive the dream of a just, sustainable, and peaceful world.

*September 2002*                                                              Mark Gerzon
*Boulder, Colorado*

# INTRODUCTION

When the opportunity for this book presented itself, we were thrilled with the chance to share the work in conflict resolution education (CRE) with parents, educators, and policymakers who wish for ways to help children learn constructive ways to handle conflict, build positive relationships, and promote just societies. As scholars and practitioners, we have been dedicated to promoting CRE for years. Our colleagues in the field already know about the power of these programs and approaches, but we have often lamented that there still seems so much to do in spreading the word to the larger society.

Hearing all the "bad news" about the problems in our schools, the shortcomings of our children, and the weaknesses of the educational system can leave one with the impression that nothing positive or innovative is happening. Luckily, that is certainly not the case with CRE and related fields. There is a great deal of "good news," and we hope this book speaks to at least some of it.

The design of the volume was inspired by two goals. First, we wanted to hear from expert practitioners in a variety of CRE programs about the best practices and practical advice they would give to educators interested in implementing similar programs and practices in their schools. Second, we wanted to convey the impact of CRE from the perspective of the students and teachers who are living the experiences. Policymakers, practitioners, and educators rarely stop to listen to those who are most involved in these efforts. Thus, in an effort to give voice to the "sometimes silenced" of our schools, we went across the country interviewing students and teachers from elementary, middle, and high schools involved in CRE.

The result is what we hope is a pleasing, entertaining, and informative format for the book. Part One contains introductory chapters focusing on challenges our children face, an overview of CRE, and a discussion of critical classroom management practices that support CRE efforts.

Part Two is the heart of the work. Here, each chapter focuses on a type of CRE, such as peer mediation, negotiation, bullying prevention, social and emotional learning, curriculum infusion, expressive arts and conflict discovery, bias awareness, restorative justice programs, and after-school programs. Each chapter has two parts. The first is the contribution of the practitioner expert—explaining the nature and goals of the programs, how they are best implemented in different educational levels, and how parents can best become involved. The second part, which we call "In Their Own Words," is a summary of interviews with students and teachers. Generously, many schools opened their doors to us and had students and teachers share with us their experiences, hopes, and concerns with CRE. Whenever possible we have presented their thoughts in their own words to honor their intent and thoughtful contributions. In some cases students asked that their real names not be used. In those situations we gave them pseudonyms and put the false name in quotes the first time it is presented.

The last chapter of the book summarizes some of the themes that emerge across the chapters and suggests areas for new work and continuing efforts. The last portion of the book provides resource materials in two appendixes.

◆ ◆ ◆

Throughout the preparation of this book we have been assisted by so many. We were extremely fortunate to gain the assistance of our truly impressive cohort of contributing authors: Carol Miller Lieber, Rachael Kessler, Heather E. Prichard, Jennifer K. Druliner, Richard Cohen, Paul I. Kaplan, Sarah Pirtle, Rachel A. Poliner, Beverly B. Title, Alice Ierley, David Claassen-Wilson, Priscilla Prutzman, and Sandy Tsubokawa Whittall. We are certain you will find their wisdom valuable and their experience inspiring. Mark Gerzon and Amalia G. Cuervo provide the topnote in their insightful Foreword and Postscript. Mark's Foreword poignantly emphasizes the importance of building relationships and creating safe and caring communities in schools. Amalia's Postscript reminds us of the federal government's strong support for CRE. She clarifies that CRE programs are among the programs that are endorsed for funding under the No Child Left Behind Act of 2001. Educators and administrators at the local and state level can and should communicate this endorsement to schools looking for programs and practices to improve their schools.

Amy Scott, our editor at Jossey-Bass, has been a valued member of our team from the very beginning. She was instrumental in developing the idea for this book, making it a reality, and guiding it through to its present form. We can't thank her enough for her insights, recommendations, support, and patience. We also want to thank the rest of the Jossey-Bass team. Lasell Whipple shepherded us through the production process. Erin Jow was very patient as she helped us with marketing issues. And, of course, senior editor Alan Rinzler provided feedback and vision throughout this process.

Our deepest thanks go to the students and teachers who told us about their lives and how they have been improved through CRE. You will meet most of them by name as you read their statements in the book. Some chose to remain nameless, but their words are just as valuable. To the teachers and administrators who work so diligently to improve the lives of students, we say a profound thank you. We would hope that everyone could see your quality as clearly as we have.

Our final comments are for the students. If you are our future, we can rest easy. Your openness, willingness to embrace positive ways of being in community, and honest assessment of the difficulty and importance of constructive conflict management have reenergized us. Your words have made us redouble our efforts to do justice to you. We hope this book helps bring your wisdom and spirit to other children and educators so they may share your accomplishments.

*Philadelphia, Pennsylvania*                                        Tricia S. Jones
*Boulder, Colorado*                                        Randy Compton

# KIDS WORKING IT OUT

# PART ONE

# CONFLICT RESOLUTION EDUCATION
## The Need and the Potential

# CHAPTER ONE

# KIDS AND CONFLICT IN SCHOOLS
## What's It Really Like?

Randy Compton

Being a kid in today's public schools is a challenge. Rumors, fights, cheating, tattling, bullying, humiliation, and isolation all still exist, often with a new twist. Given the changes that have occurred over the last few decades, many of us may not even know what kids face and feel on a daily basis. Many of us may believe that there has been a dramatic increase in foul language, drug abuse, disrespect, depression, and suicide. One thing we know for certain is that much has changed for kids in school in the last century.

Schools are no longer one-room buildings filled with kids of different ages taking precious time out from working in the fields. Schools are no longer places where all children sit quietly in desks neatly arranged in factory-like rows reading in unison from standard and often biased text books. Schools are no longer places where conflicts stop at bloody noses and bruised feelings. The world of Dick and Jane and *See Spot Run* has changed for good. As a direct result, kids, now more than ever, need skills for living and working together in an increasingly interdependent world—skills in such areas as handling conflicts, managing intense emotions, and making wise choices for themselves and their community.

In this chapter, we look at some of the key issues facing kids today—how schools have changed over time, what life at school feels like for kids, and what experts in the field believe about students and schools today—and set the stage for showing why conflict resolution education is such a vital movement for making peace not only in our schools but also in our world. Having a solid understanding of where we have come from and where we are heading will give us a larger, more complete perspective for making the best curricular decisions for our children and for ourselves.

## Our Changing Educational Models

As our society has changed, so have our schools. Early schools were institutions modeled after the designs and influences of the agricultural age. Short and disrupted school years were created to help socialize children and increase basic literacy. Families valued education, but they also had to balance the needs of the field and the farm.

Later schools were modeled after the industrial age, replete with factory-like replicas of educational efficiency, such as desks neatly lined in rows, standard textbooks, and standard norms taught in a mechanical and efficient way. Discipline was often harsh and obedience swift so as to help establish social norms and social control. At the time, the American dream helped forge a generation of individuals interested in progress, freedom, and tolerance. However, much of the racial, ethnic, and religious diversity that existed in our country was molded into predominantly white, middle-class values. American schools were a melting pot for many cultures and many traditions, and for the time being, the melting pot represented the form that public education followed.

But as times changed, our social structures evolved, and so did school life. The clearly demarcated roles that defined parents, principals, teachers, and children began to erode. The old expectations that boys would be naughty and girls would be nice began to dissolve. The efficient, predictable, factory-like structure of life and school began to complexify, and many of our regular ways of doing things began to change. As we know now, our world and our schools have become "cosmopolitan" in nature,[1] and the computer and the evolving nature of families have forever changed our social and educational patterns of interaction.

Today we are a worldly mix of cultural values and gender roles and expectations, engaged in time-efficient and overlapping activities. We have broken down the timeworn boundaries of the past and created interrelated social structures largely influenced by the information age and its scientific advances. Our simple nuclear families and "nuclear" schools—where all children lived in a predictable family unit and all students learned in a predictable classroom experience—changed. Now we live in multiracial families, single-parent families, and nontraditional families determined not only by blood but also by our interests, our geography, and our creativity. We also live with a multitude of choices in public education, from focus schools to charter schools, from home schools to after-schools. During this time, we outgrew the influences of the farm life and the factory line and instead have adopted the computer network as our model. Our lives are filled with cross-generating beliefs and endless streams of information. The scientific-material-information age—and "cosmopolitan" culture—has shaped schools inexorably—and our kids face the conflicts, the choices, and the challenges that the culture brings.

## A Day in the Life

If we are truly to understand what it is like being a kid in today's schools, we can best do so by putting ourselves in their shoes for a day. Consider a day in the life of a "typical" schoolchild; let's name her Carla.

Carla is a seventh grader living in a middle- to lower-class suburb with her mom, who has recently divorced. Carla attends a junior high school typical of other schools in the country: the building has narrow hallways; brick walls on all sides with small, high windows; bathrooms with few amenities and no art; toilets that are often littered with toilet paper; and outdoor landscaping that looks like it could use some financial help.

At 6 A.M., Carla wakes up after some nagging by her mother, spends half an hour dressing, then rushes to make sure she has her books and belongings for the day. Breakfast is on the run, half of it eaten in the car. Carla gets into a conflict with her mom about eating well for lunch and hardly has time to have a real conversation about it because her mom is preoccupied with her own day ahead. By the time she is at school at 7 A.M., she is only half awake and hoping that the conflict that she had yesterday with a friend will go away, that her social life will improve, and that her teacher will notice how much work she did for her project due today.

In the hallway, other students are drifting in. Some arrived before 7 A.M., having been dropped off by their parents who needed to get to work early. Some take advantage of a modest breakfast of white bread French toast loaded with maple syrup provided by the school; others come early to attend a student council meeting or an early morning sports practice session. By the time the buses and parents arrive with the rest of the students, the school starts to hum with activity and the burgeoning social scene. Carla finds her two best friends, Mia and Crystal, and immediately starts talking about her day—the hassle she got from her mom that morning, the assignment she had last night for history, and the overly strict teacher she has to face in math.

Carla drifts from one class to another, each one lasting fifty minutes and separated by a short four-minute passing period. Sometimes her schedule changes

because of advisory period. This is a short morning class meant to bring kids together as a "family," but many teachers don't always use it well, and it often turns
into silent reading time. Carla likes a lot of her teachers because they try to help
her in school, but she doesn't like all the homework they give. All the students have
"time-trackers" in which they keep their class schedule and assignments. More
than once she has forgotten to look at it and missed something important.

The hallways are crowded, and stuff happens there that teachers either overlook or can't see—such as teasing, harassment, "dirty looks," and verbal threats.
Suki and Jasmine are spreading rumors about Valerie for being "loose." Martin is
being harassed again by Jon, Darryl, and Ian. They are calling him "gay" and
laughing at him. Carla sort of hates it but figures it's just part of life. Sometimes
she even says mean things herself, figuring the person really deserves it or that it
doesn't bother him much anyway. Her language arts teacher, Ms. DeWitt, teaches
kids not to use put-downs, and it works in her classroom; but outside her class the
rules are different. And Carla's mother says that this was the way school was when
she was growing up and to just get along because, as she says, "boys will be boys.
You aren't going to change that."

Classes often seem like a blur, with one or two good classes or favorite teachers interspersed throughout her day. Her teachers have many different styles of
teaching; some are old-style and authoritarian, others more willing to listen. She
likes teachers who know how to really listen and who are firm but not mean.
She wishes secretly that there were more like them. At her school, over ten different ethnicities are represented, and more than seven different languages are
spoken at home. The pressure to perform is intense because her school has lower
test scores than other schools in the district. This means lots of homework and not
enough time to spend with her mom when she gets home after school—something
she sort of misses. She has even heard of an elementary school that eliminated recess so that the kids could spend more time on academics. Her mom thinks that
she should do better in school, but Carla doesn't care because none of the subjects interest her except for language arts. The language arts teacher uses really
good books with stories that mean something to her and her life. Too many of the
other teachers just use standard textbooks and give boring tests.

She finds out later in the day that her close friend Jackson got busted for wearing a ball cap in the school. There is a school rule that says no hats can be worn
inside the school. He was walking down the hallway when the science teacher,
Mr. Markowitz, yelled at him from behind, told him to stop, and yanked his hat
off his head. Jackson told the teacher that he would have taken it off if the teacher
hadn't been "such a jerk." That got him sent to the office quick, and he didn't like
going to the assistant principal's office because the assistant principal has a "holier
than thou" attitude while pretending to be friends with the students. Something

the assistant principal said made Jackson blow up in anger, and he got sent to "in-school suspension." Carla doesn't know what the big deal about hats is when there are plenty of other kids doing drugs, having sex, and harassing other students behind teachers' backs. And a few of the teachers do their fair share of humiliating students as well. All of the students are changing physically and emotionally in ways that some of the teachers have a hard time appreciating.

At lunch, Carla gets into a fight with Kristen over something dumb. Kristen always has to be right, and the argument really seemed to be about something else, but the bell rang and everybody starting talking about going to the next class, and the two of them never got it resolved.

Carla is on the soccer team, so after school she spends the next couple of hours in practice. Thankfully she doesn't have to deal with bullies on her way home. They love harassing kids when teachers aren't around. Then she goes home and finds her mom there frantically preparing dinner for her and her older brother, who is in high school. Dinner has to be quick because there is a parent evening at school that they have to attend. Carla decides to stay home and do homework, but ends up talking with her friend on the phone for forty-five minutes before actually sitting down to read her assignments and do her homework. She goes to bed at 9:30 P.M., feeling a little overwhelmed and empty inside.

◆　◆　◆

Carla is only one fictitious student similar to millions of students around the country. Her story is representative of the daily activities and conflicts in her intellectual, social, spiritual, and physical life. Indeed, this story shows only the point of view of the student and lacks many other, sometimes more mature, perspectives and realities. Yet for her there are many daily conflicts that exist in a school modeled after both factory-like education (desks always in rows, classes moving in a predictable and clockwork schedule, and standardized textbook learning) and computer- and cosmopolitan-like education (many ethnicities; busy, overlapping schedules; Internet-based learning).

Life for children in our nation's schools is complex and difficult to manage. They grow up in a fast-paced world where some parents are often too busy seeking the American dream to provide them with the time, the authority, and the attention they so desperately need—or their parents provide them with too much from the American dream, causing the kids to be spoiled and weak in character. It has been said, and is likely true, that children have been a challenge to their elders since the beginning of time. But if we are to create present-day solutions, we have to understand the present-day problems kids are facing: they are rushed; they live in a violent world; they live in a world that is very different from that of their parents; they go to schools that have complex and competing interests; and they live in a world still filled with prejudice, white privilege, and a wide gap between rich and poor.

## Kids in a Rush

Chip Wood, a well-known and respected educator and the author of the recent book *Time to Teach, Time to Learn,* said this about rushing our children: "We need to stop hurrying children. Our school days require time. Time to wonder, time to pause, time to look closely, time to share, time to pay attention to what is most important. In school we must give children the time they need to learn. To hurry the day, to hurry through classes, grades and a timetable of achievements, is contrary to the nature of children and will do irreparable damage to their minds and souls."[2]

The speed of the Internet and the "always open" 24/7 lifestyle that we have created for ourselves in the name of progress has often created lives that move too fast, and we have trouble adjusting to the constant demands and stimulation of input. Simply put, we have trouble setting appropriate boundaries on our time. And the predicted increase in leisure as a consequence of mechanization has not materialized. Instead we have only increased our capacity for wanting more. Our ability to control our drive to have, buy, and be is not yet strong enough to withstand the pressures of speed and created wants and needs. Kids today find themselves rushing to catch up, often at the expense of the slower pace needed for in-depth learning; for the authentic resolution of conflict; and for the development of social, emotional, and ethical intelligence—what some call wisdom.

Our minds may move fast, but our hearts and emotions need time to experience the depth, richness, and complexity of life. As Mary Pipher points out in her book *The Shelter of Each Other,* "There's too much information and not enough meaning."[3] When we lose this time, we lose a part of ourselves, and when we lose this meaning, we lose a part of our souls. Teachers may instinctively know the importance of fostering meaning and connection in students' lives. With the increasing pressures placed on teachers to raise test scores, they have had to cut many experiential activities, and quantitative results take precedent over qualitative results. By focusing on social and emotional learning and conflict resolution, we help create a learning environment in which students and teachers can slow down the pace of life. When we can slow down the pace of our emotional and conflictual situations, we are better able to get at the root cause of them, which is key to using the critical and creative thinking necessary for understanding and resolving life's conflicts.

## Kids in a Violent World

Even though the United States may be one of the most civilized and even generous countries in the world, we remain, unfortunately, one of the most violent and punitive. We have the highest rate of incarceration in the world. Today the United States has approximately 1.8 million people behind bars; we imprison more people than any other country in the world—perhaps half a million more than Communist China.[4] By the end of elementary school, the average child will have watched one hundred thousand acts of violence, despite the fact that media researchers have repeatedly shown evidence linking media portrayals of violence to aggressive behavior.[5] Domestic violence continues to be a significant problem in our culture. In terms of dating violence, one-third of all teenagers report having experienced violence in a dating relationship.[6] Perhaps most telling, our military budget is larger than all other categories of spending combined,[7] showing that we still believe in, and have to live in, a world where violence is a significant strategy for handling conflicts.

Since 1987, the National Center for Education Statistics of the U.S. Department of Education has conducted a study of school problems. Every three school years, the staff asks a representative sample of some fifty thousand public school teachers to rate specific problems in schools depending on the degree to which they occur in their schools. What has risen steadily since 1987 as being serious or moderately serious in their schools are physical conflicts among students, robbery or theft, student possession of weapons, vandalism of school property, and verbal abuse of teachers.[8] Dell Elliot, of the Center for the Study and Prevention of Violence in Boulder, Colorado, refers to the increase in youth violence in our schools and in our communities in the last decade as an epidemic—the social response to which has largely been limited to "increasingly harsh and lengthy sentencing with little evidence that this approach is deterring violence or rehabilitating young offenders."[9]

What many of us know is that the violence of our youth is a response to and reflection of what is happening around them. Our culture has glorified violence in our movies, our games, our heroes, and our values. Being strong is more often equated with being aggressive, bullying, and violent than it is with demonstrating impulse control, emotional honesty, and direct nonviolent communication.

As weapons have become easier to access for young people in the last decade, fights that in earlier years resulted in black eyes and bloody noses now result in serious injury and death. Easy access to guns and knives, a pervasive culture of violence, and inadequate emphasis on the skills of conflict resolution and the means to create safe, caring communities have resulted in the escalation of conflicts to an epidemic level among our nation's youth.

Eighty percent of adolescents report being bullied during their school years; 90 percent of fourth through eighth graders report being victims of bullying at some point in their school experience; and 15 percent of students are bullies or are long-term victims of bullies. Children who have been identified as bullies by age eight are six times more likely to be convicted of a crime by age twenty-four and five times more likely than nonbullies to end up with serious criminal records by age thirty. Students reported that 71 percent of the teachers or other adults in the classroom ignored bullying incidents.[10]

There is evidence suggesting that this epidemic may be overstated, however. A report from the Center for Disease Control studying the period from 1991 to 1997 showed a decline in the percentage of student reports of physical fights on and off school grounds and showed no significant increase in the number of youth who reported feeling too unsafe to go to school.[11] The good news is that school continues to be one of the safest places for children, and youth and school crime rates are declining.[12] Still, the overall rates are too high for a society that prides itself on being a leader in the civilized world. Violence in our society and violence in our schools have the potential for slowing the advancement of civilization and inhibiting the creation of intelligent and compassionate youth. Civilization depends on the advancement of social as well as economic and political progress, and a violent culture denies our ability to handle social problems "in a civilized manner." Violence in our schools, our neighborhoods, and our homes remains a shadow on our greatness that must be addressed, and one of the best places to address it is in schools where students and staff can learn nonviolent ways to resolve conflicts.

## Kids in a Radically Different World

Many factors have contributed to a world that is radically different for our children than it was for those of previous generations. Not only have computers, the Internet, and travel compressed and changed our world and our schools forever, but the core elements that we used to depend on for social stability and civility—such as the extended family structure, respect for elders, and sharing of communal wisdom—have been significantly altered, causing many families and social institutions to lose the basic keys to social survival. At the end of World War II, there was a mass migration from small towns and farm communities into urban and suburban environments, and an entire culture was disrupted. This was largely due to the Industrial Revolution, the G.I. Bill, reaction to the depression, and technology. As close-knit communities broke down, their wisdom dispersed and people became isolated. In this isolation, people covered their feelings of inadequacy and their lack of knowledge about what to do with a false sense of pride in handling their own problems. Guilt, stress, and denial began tearing at parents when they were unable to turn out the superkids that society seemed to expect. Children who were born after World War II started a downward trend in achievement and an upward trend in crime, teenage pregnancy, clinical depression, and suicide.[13] As traditional family life changed, so did children's lives.

Fewer than half of the children in the United States live with both biological parents, and 59 percent of all children will live in a single-parent household before they reach the age of eighteen.[14] The rise in the number of single-parent and working-parent families increases the number of latchkey kids left at home after school, many faced with a TV or computer as a babysitter. However these children spend time after school, it is unsupervised by adults. In the 1970s and 1980s, the divorce rate in America was around 40 percent. At the turn of the millennium, it is now purported to be close to 50 percent.[15] As a result of this and other social and cultural factors, many children have been raised desperately lacking in emotional wisdom and conflict competence.

Yet this is not just an American phenomenon but a global trend. As competition drives down the cost of labor and the dream of a materially rich life becomes the norm, economic forces press on family members and cause them to spend more time working and less time with each other, their community, their schools, and fulfilling their responsibilities for civic engagement. Even though we claim to value youth and say they are the future of our country, the unfortunate fact is that we often neglect their real needs: for safety, belonging, love, and supervision, among others. As the communal fabric of society unravels and reforms itself, we find ourselves faced with increasing pressure to be selfish, violent, and neglectful, if not mean.

All of this desperately calls out for us to counter the trend toward isolationism by exposing our children to more altruism, self-restraint, and compassion. What we are discovering is that some biological parents are unreliable, immature, or too irresponsible to handle this crucial task by themselves and that—more than the family—the extended, meaningful community, or "tribe," is the key to preserving civilization. For those of us concerned with the future of our society, the lack of skills created by an individualist culture is a clarion call for us to heed.

According to Patricia Hersch, author of *A Tribe Apart,* the distinguishing feature of today's youth is not their technological prowess but rather their "aloneness."[16] Teens spend more time alone than any other generation. They lack a coherent sense of community. However, the good news is that kids and families are resilient and increasingly are finding ways to counteract these pressures, often through conflict resolution programs that teach them emotional management, authentic communication, and collaborative problem-solving skills.

## Kids in Schools with Competing Interests

As our social and economic structures have evolved, so have the purposes of education. Do we educate our children to be skilled workforce members fit for economic progress? Do we educate them to be productive citizens in a democracy? Do we educate them to prepare themselves for higher education? According to John Gatto, former New York State and New York City Teacher of the Year and author most recently of *The Underground History of American Education: A Schoolteacher's Intimate Investigation into the Problem of Modern Schooling,* "There are three major purposes that human history has assigned to schooling, in every part of the world. One is to make good people. Another is to make good citizens. The third is to make people their personal best. There is a fourth purpose, which comes in around the turn of the century: to turn people into resources for the disposition of government and the corporations."[17]

In an effort to build one of the world's most powerful economies, we have created schools that overemphasize the productivity of the student to prepare for the workplace, rather than the inner wisdom of the student to prepare for a creative life of diverse purposes. The underlying structure and philosophy of education have a tremendous and sometimes not so subtle impact on kids in schools, especially when it comes down to teaching styles, discipline, and punishment.

The factory-like education of yesteryear provided equal if not biased education to many students, but the instruction from this method was often painfully dull. Teachers standing at the front of the room, commanding attention with strict obedience and harsh punishments, left little room for individual creativity or personal learning styles. Some still believe that school should be a place where order is achieved through social control; others believe it to be achieved through social empowerment; still others believe there should be a mix of the two. The social and educational bias toward social control and obedience has deep roots in Western civilization and a significant impact on school life for children of all countries. One of our country's most eloquent speakers on youth issues, Larry Brendtro, author of the book *Reclaiming Youth at Risk,* explains that unlike Native American traditions of belief in the natural trait of independence, Western civilization built itself on the belief that obedience is natural if not ideal. Obedience is deeply ingrained in our social life. It served as the fundamental bond of the Europeans—vassal obeyed lord, priest obeyed superiors, subject obeyed king, slave obeyed master, woman obeyed man, and child obeyed everybody. Most approaches to child rearing and education were influenced by the predominant belief about obedience.[18]

Although it is essential to have influence over children as they grow and learn, influence need not be in the form of giving orders. Instead, it can be achieved through developing mutual respect. The youth work pioneers of the European tradition as well as the untapped heritage of Native American philosophies have shown that responsibility is not taught by disciplining for obedience. As Brendtro says, "Children who are docile when little grow up to be dupes as adults."[19] Learning how to be responsible, competent participants in a civic society requires experience, natural consequences, peers, and authoritative rather than authoritarian elders.

Parents, policymakers, and educators today often fall into the trap of emphasizing obedience over respect. The guilt that can be born when we avoid strict obedience often allows permissiveness and overindulgence. However, neither of these are part of the balanced approach necessary for learning and growing—especially in a democracy founded on participation and empowerment. Kids today face this ongoing conflict among child-rearing styles daily as it is played out by classroom teachers and school disciplinarians. Some teachers adhere to a strict model of teaching and discipline in which the teacher is in command at all times. Other teachers follow a more permissive approach, seeing students as friends and exercising lax discipline. Still others seek the middle path, seeing students as friends but also setting clear limits and modeling good character. Although each teacher needs to find his or her own style, students can receive mixed messages about relationships, power, and responsibility by having to move from one class to another.

Most conflict resolution programs seek a "both-and" approach that combines a high-control style with a high-nurturance style. This authoritative approach seeks to provide guidance with independence and serves as a component of the empowerment model used by conflict resolution practitioners who work with youth.

The complex and competing interests in schools have created many myths regarding the state of schooling today. Different groups often use these myths to support their own beliefs about the state of education and the need for change according to their own theories. For example, while some traditionalists decry the fall of education since World War II, many facts bear otherwise. Children spend more hours in the classroom than the children in all other G-8 countries except France. Our primary teachers earn more than their counterparts in any G-8 country except Germany. And our fourth graders perform better on international reading tests than fourth graders in all of the other thirty-two countries tested except Finland.[20] Perhaps the problem is that although we have made education available to all children, we have not tried to educate them all equally or individually. As we try to educate them all, we have found that our educational practices need reform, and this is a part of progress—one that can be supported by conflict resolution programs that emphasize diverse, student-centered classroom practices with clear adult guidance.

## Kids in an Increasingly Diverse World

Demographers predict that students of color will make up about 46 percent of the U.S. school-age population by 2020.[21] Approximately six to fourteen million children live in families headed by gay or lesbian family members, and between 10 to 20 percent of school-age youth identify themselves as gay, lesbian, bisexual, or transgendered. Students live with a tremendous array of diversity within their school, although their parents and teachers may not have caught up with the cultural or educational needs of these diverse students. The old way of teaching all children in a standardized pedagogy is quickly receding as the country is willing to teach and reach all children, not just middle-class white ones. Students have become accustomed to increasingly differentiated teaching. The factory-like model of teaching in which teachers stand in the front of the class is giving way to the computer network–like model of teaching in which teachers employ cooperative learning, peer tutoring, and multilevel teaching.

Discrimination and conflicts between racial groups are also a part of everyday life for young people. However, as time goes on, students are increasingly exposed to, if not tolerant of, diverse backgrounds and perspectives. Although we may have had a great deal of diversity in our schools in the past, much of it was subtly and overtly oppressed. Today's youth are learning how to work together in diverse groups, and students are struggling to deal with the natural conflicts between groups that can arise as whites no longer lay claim to being the dominant cultural group with the dominant cultural norm.

## What These Social Changes Mean for Us Today

In this chapter, we have seen that some timeless, inevitable relationship problems among our youth still exist, such as rumors, escalating anger, bullying, and verbal and physical fights. We have seen that our modern, scientific, material, information age has created some life-altering changes in the family, in the school, and in the community. We have seen that students' learning and growing are diminished by a fast-paced world. Students are not fully able to slow down enough to resolve more difficult issues and attend to more complex feelings.

At the same time, parents, teachers, and others place high expectations on students. This often causes conflicts in a student's life, as the support may not exist to meet these expectations. We have seen that exposure to unproductive conflict and overt and hidden violence is damaging and sets up unhealthy and sometimes contradictory models for behavior. We have seen that a lack of adult supervision and personal connection can lead to diminished emotional wisdom and conflict competence; that conflicting child-rearing styles often result in inconsistent and confusing messages for students; and that teacher-student conflicts may increase along with students' frustrations over these conflicting ideals. Finally, we have seen that an increasingly diverse society has added more stress to the school environment and conflicts to the school day. All these factors, and others, make daily life in schools, with all its conflict and choices, a personal challenge for every young person.

Understanding what it is like to be a kid in school today is important. It gives us real-life clues to the changes that may have occurred since we were kids. It gives us greater empathy for the daily struggles children face. It leads us to wiser judgments as we make decisions that affect all young people in schools. We all strive to provide the best education for our youth. If we are to do so, however, we must listen to both our elders and our youth—our elders will tell us some of the best practices from the past, and our youth will tell us how life's changes may require different strategies for handling the problems of the present. Both require us to listen respectfully and find collaborative solutions to raising a generation of youth prepared to make peace in our schools, in our communities, and in our world.

# CHAPTER TWO

# AN INTRODUCTION TO CONFLICT RESOLUTION EDUCATION

## Tricia S. Jones

*Michael, a first grader, often gets into trouble because he can't seem to express himself, especially when he's upset. Instead, he just "blows up" in anger.*

*Rashid and Carrie share a computer console in their middle school library. They are constantly arguing over who should have access to the computer.*

*Trent lives in fear of going to school. Throughout high school he has been a target of the school's worst bully. He'd rather stay home and flunk out than face any more humiliation.*

*Syisha and Raquel have been friends since second grade, but now that they're in middle school, they hang out with different groups. The problem is that the groups don't get along, and their friendship is being ruined.*

*Danielle and Kim are spreading rumors about Sarah and her boyfriend. Sarah's friends are telling her to "take action" and "shut them up." Sarah hopes there's a better way.*

*Since transferring to a new school, Abdullah eats alone and has few people to talk to. His classmates make fun of his clothes, accent, and religion.*

*Fred and Tom are fine in school, but once school's out they have nothing to do but get in trouble. And that's what they do.*

What do these kids have in common? They are having conflicts, but they aren't handling them well. Most school-age children, like most adults, see conflict as something negative that must result in tension, anger, disappointment, or worse. They don't understand how to make conflict a positive element of their lives.

Conflict is a fact of life in general and certainly a fact of life in our schools. When we disagree with someone about what we want to do or how we want to do it, we have a conflict, especially if we need that other person to help us accomplish something or take action. There's nothing bad or good about conflict itself—but there are better and worse ways to manage conflict.

Unfortunately, all too often children see poor models of conflict management when they look to adults and the media for guidance. We have TV shows that glorify poor behavior toward one another—the *Weakest Link* kind of show that makes insulting others and taking advantage of them seem entertaining. These shows, and *Weakest Link* in particular, teach children that being contemptuous of others is important and powerful. Children often see adults arguing, name-calling, becoming violent, acting aggressively—being unable to constructively deal with everyday problems. Children see factions within nations vying violently for resources, and, sadly, they have seen many examples of wars between nations. It's no wonder that children are unsure of more constructive ways to handle their own conflicts.

How can we help children see conflict as an opportunity rather than a crisis? How can we help them manage conflict such that they make good decisions rather than bad ones? Build relationships instead of tear them apart? Build communities of respect rather than cultures of contempt? How can we give our children these life skills that will empower them to be happier, more successful citizens when they grow up?

Conflict resolution education (CRE) programs provide an answer. As Associate Justice Sandra Day O'Connor noted in 1999, "While it is important to identify the causes of conflict in our society, regardless of cause, we must find ways to mend the tears in the social fabric arising from these disputes. . . . It seems only appropriate that the most innovative forms of nonviolent conflict resolution are found in our schools, for who better than our young people to learn non-violent problem-solving skills? After children learn to defuse the conflicts between each other through non-violent means, they can utilize these skills to defuse conflicts between themselves and their teachers, parents and siblings, and throughout their adult lives."[1]

In this chapter we'll answer some basic questions about CRE:

What is CRE?

What are the goals of CRE programs?

How does CRE fit with the larger educational mission?

What program models are included in CRE?

What are the proven benefits of CRE?

What are some basic guidelines for implementing CRE programs?

## What Is CRE?

CRE "models and teaches, in culturally meaningful ways, a variety of processes, practices and skills that help address individual, interpersonal, and institutional conflicts, and create safe and welcoming communities. These processes, practices and skills help individuals understand conflict processes and empower them to use communication and creative thinking to build relationships and manage and resolve conflicts fairly and peacefully."[2]

CRE emerged out of the social justice concerns of the 1960s and 1970s with the work of such groups as the Society of Friends (Quakers). In the early 1980s, Educators for Social Responsibility (ESR) organized a national association that later led to the development of the National Association for Mediation in Education (NAME) in 1984. NAME subsequently merged with the National Institute for Dispute Resolution and its Conflict Resolution Education Network. Most recently, the Conflict Resolution Education Network merged with the Academy of Family Mediators and the Society for Professionals in Dispute Resolution to form the Association for Conflict Resolution.

Now, almost twenty years after beginning, CRE programs are estimated to be in place in 15,000 to 20,000 of our nation's 85,000 public schools. Some cities and states have made impressive strides in institutionalizing CRE. As early as 1991, Morton Inger, of the ERIC Clearinghouse on Urban Education, noted that in New York City more than eighty thousand schoolchildren had experienced CRE; over three-fourths of San Francisco's public schools had student conflict managers; and all public school students in Chicago took a conflict management course in ninth or tenth grade.[3] Today several states, including Ohio, Oregon, New Mexico, and Indiana, have made significant progress on statewide implementation of CRE.

But when we use the term *conflict resolution education,* we should remember that not all of these programs are alike. There are a variety of efforts that fall under the general umbrella of CRE. The next paragraphs explain some of the common elements of these programs. Later we'll review some of the program models and the general relationships between CRE and other similarly oriented efforts, such as social and emotional learning (SEL), character education, and violence prevention programs.

CRE programs focus on developing critical skills and abilities, as Bodine and Crawford have explained.[4] They provide students with a basic understanding of the nature of conflict. Students appreciate that conflict exists whenever there is a disagreement about goals, methods to achieve those goals, or both. They understand the dynamics of power and influence that operate in all conflict situations. Students also become aware of the role of culture in how we see and respond to conflict. Some programs, such as the expressive arts programs discussed by Sarah Pirtle in Chapter Eight, help students see conflict as something to discover rather than as something to fear. Through music, drama, and the arts, children are helped to appreciate conflict and their relationship to conflict.

An awareness of the nature of conflict helps students appreciate the variety of ways that people can manage or respond to conflict—another program component. Students explore a range of conflict styles (for example, competing, collaborating, accommodating, avoiding, and compromising) and consider the advantages and disadvantages of each. As effective conflict managers know, no approach to conflict management works all the time; the key is knowing which approach is best for the situation. However, CRE emphasizes that a violent response to conflict is almost never an appropriate response.

In many CRE programs, because the emphasis is on empowering students to handle their own conflict and help peers handle their conflict, students are taught basic problem-solving processes. As Jennifer K. Druliner and Heather E. Prichard explain in Chapter Five, sometimes it is a negotiation process that enables students to handle their own conflict. Sometimes it is a mediation process in which the student acts as a third party to help peers solve conflict. In their chapters, Richard Cohen (Chapter Six) and Paul I. Kaplan (Chapter Seven) talk about peer mediation programs for regular education and special needs students. And sometimes, as Alice Ierley and David Claassen-Wilson explain in Chapter Ten, the process is even more elaborate, as in the case of restorative justice circles or councils where disputants, school, and family members convene to engage in dialogue about appropriate actions and accountability to remedy a hurtful event.

An extremely important program component involves teaching students the social and emotional skills needed to prevent conflict and to reinforce their use of prosocial strategies in conflict. In this area CRE overlaps with other fields of work, such as SEL, bias awareness, and character education. Some of the skills that students are helped to develop include effective listening, perspective taking, emotional awareness, and emotional control.

# What Are the Goals of CRE Programs?

There are many possible goals for CRE programs, almost as many goals as there are permutations of the programs themselves. What follows are four of the most common goals. Some CRE programs focus on only one or two of them, whereas others attempt to accomplish them all.

## Create a Safe Learning Environment

In the 1990s, one of the National Education Goals stated that "all schools in America will be free of drugs, violence and the unauthorized presence of firearms and alcohol, and will offer a disciplined environment that is conducive to learning."[5] In response to that goal, Congress passed the Safe and Drug-Free Schools and Communities Act of 1994, which funded the Safe and Drug-Free Schools unit of the U.S. Department of Education. Since its inception, that office has sought to develop, implement, and monitor initiatives that can help create safe learning environments in our schools. Among those initiatives are CRE programs. Programs that emphasize this goal are interested in the following kinds of outcomes:

- Decrease in incidents of violence
- Decrease in conflicts between groups of students, particularly intergroup conflicts based on racial and ethnic differences
- Decrease in suspensions, absenteeism, and dropout rates related to unsafe learning environments

CRE programs that emphasize creating a safe learning environment overlap with violence prevention efforts. Violence prevention programs often include a CRE component, but are more likely to include increases in safety and security techniques pertinent to the prevention of serious violent behaviors that are, luckily, still quite rare in schools. Violence prevention efforts seek to decrease serious risk behavior, including violence. CRE is focused more on the development of important life skills that help students find nonviolent ways to handle their problems, and it may thereby decrease violent behavior.

It is understandable that people are concerned with school violence. In light of the tragedies in too many of our schools, we are all very aware that senseless attacks and killings can and do occur. Yet the vast majority of American schools do not have violent incidents as common occurrences. Instead, the kinds of "safety issues" that are occurring are more appropriately dealt with by using CRE programs than by bringing in metal detectors. In the 1990–1991 and 1996–1997 school years, the U.S. Department of Education surveyed principals about the violence and discipline problems in their schools.[6] The three issues most frequently rated as serious problems by principals were student tardiness, student absenteeism, and physical conflicts (without weapons) among the students.

One area of work that is quite germane is anti-bullying programs, such as those discussed by Beverly B. Title in Chapter Eleven. These programs are an excellent example of efforts that improve the safety of the school environment and teach students (as well as adults) the importance of intervening in destructive conflict situations.

## Create a Constructive Learning Environment

Teachers and administrators know that learning cannot take place unless you nurture a constructive learning environment for students. What is a constructive learning environment? In Chapter Three, which discusses effective classroom practices, Carol Miller Lieber points out that a constructive learning environment is one in which children feel that there is a positive climate and effective classroom management. As Rachael Kessler adds in Chapter Four, which discusses emotional intelligence in the classroom, a constructive learning environment is also a respectful and caring environment where children feel safe to share ideas and feelings.

Teachers often wrestle with classroom management and classroom discipline. One of the first motivations for CRE was teachers' need to have better discipline so that they could spend class time teaching content rather than correcting inappropriate behavior. Some early studies estimated that as much as 40 to 60 percent of class time was devoted to discipline rather than instruction.[7]

When a CRE program creates a constructive learning environment, expected outcomes include

- Improved school climate
- Improved classroom climate
- A respectful and caring environment
- Improved classroom management
- Reduced time spent on disciplinary problems in the classroom
- Increased use of student-centered discipline

## Enhance Students' Social and Emotional Development

At the heart of all CRE is the hope that we are helping our children develop as better people—helping them become more socially and emotionally competent so that they can lead happier lives and contribute more positively to society. If this is achieved, the logic is that other goals of CRE will also be accomplished.

One way to think of this goal is in terms of critical abilities that students gain through their involvement in CRE. Bodine and Crawford argue that students can gain

1. Orientation abilities to develop values, beliefs, and attitudes which promote nonviolence, empathy, fairness, justice, trust, tolerance, self-respect, respect for others, and appreciation for controversy
2. Perception abilities to understand how oneself and others can have different, yet valid, perceptions of reality
3. Emotional abilities to manage and effectively communicate a range of emotions, including anger, fear, and frustration
4. Communication abilities to improve active listening skills, speaking to be understood and listening to understand
5. Creative-thinking abilities to construct cognitive models and to perceive and solve problems in new ways
6. Critical thinking abilities to contrast and compare data, predict and analyze situations, and construct and test hypotheses[8]

It is in the pursuit of enhancing social and emotional development that CRE programs most often overlap with SEL programs. Some people suggest that CRE encompasses SEL and adds an emphasis on understanding and managing conflict. Others see SEL as the larger initiative into which CRE falls. Whichever frame you believe is more accurate, the truly important point is that both CRE and SEL programs support the belief that we should help students develop certain emotional, cognitive, and behavioral competencies.

Conflict resolution educators heartily endorse the following suggested competencies articulated by the Collaborative for Academic, Social and Emotional Learning. In the emotional domain, students should learn to identify emotions, control anger, manage frustration, and respect others' feelings. In the cognitive domain, students should develop the ability to take the other's role or perspective, problem solve, set goals, and cooperate. In the behavioral domain, students should build interpersonal skills necessary for positive social interaction, including the abilities to negotiate disputes, take responsibility for actions, manage time, respect others' space, and appreciate social norms.[9]

It is also in this goal area that CRE overlaps most obviously with character education. Although character education is more focused on teaching students certain core values of citizenship, it—like CRE—teaches skills of cooperation, participatory decision making, and social perspective taking.[10]

Overall, when CRE is effective, the benefits should include the following out-comes:

- Increased perspective taking
- Increased problem-solving abilities
- Improved emotional awareness and emotional management
- Reduced aggressive orientations and hostile attributions
- Increased student use of constructive conflict behaviors in schools and in home and community contexts

## Create a Constructive Conflict Community

As a society, we have turned more and more to our schools to help "raise" our children. Our schools are no longer "just" places of learning; they are places where students, families, and community members obtain a variety of resources. Our schools are becoming more integrated into our communities. Thus, what happens in our schools reflects the community and affects the community. The converse is also true; it is rare to see a healthy school maintain itself over a long period when it exists in the middle of a beleaguered community.

Creating a constructive conflict community entails several things. First, it means developing a sense of social justice and advocating for social justice as a cornerstone of a healthy and enriched society. CRE is integrally linked to issues of social justice. Injustice is often the result of perceptions that the "other" is lesser or inferior in some way. Injustice and oppression go hand in hand, often accompanied by a tendency to blame the target of oppression. Through bias aware-ness programs, such as those discussed by Priscilla Prutzman in Chapter Twelve, educators can help children face their biases and understand how those biases may negatively impact their interpersonal and group relationships.

A constructive conflict community is also one in which there is a shared re-sponsibility for social ills and social accomplishments. In such a community, de-structive conflict is seen as something the community needs to address. This is one of the basic assumptions underlying the notion of restorative justice approaches to CRE, as Alice Ierley and David Claassen-Wilson explain in Chapter Ten. William Ury talks about this idea as "the third side":

> In our societies, conflict is conventionally thought of as two-sided: husband vs. wife, union vs. employer, Arabs vs. Israelis. The introduction of a third party comes almost as an exception, an aberration, someone meddling in someone else's business. We tend to forget what the simplest societies on earth have long known: namely that every conflict is actually three-sided. No dispute takes

place in a vacuum. There are always others around—relatives, neighbors, allies, friends, or onlookers. Every conflict occurs within a community that constitutes the "third side" of any dispute.[11]

Sadly, students may not know how to help create effective internal and external communities. But they do seem to realize this need. Following the massacre at Columbine High School, a CNN poll of 402 teenagers asked "What has gone wrong with America's schools?" Students placed a large part of the blame on themselves: 40 percent identified peer issues as the root of the problem; 18 percent indicated they needed to learn how to get along better; and 18 percent suggested that greater tolerance of differences was necessary before things could get better.[12]

Our schools' responsibilities don't end at the boundary of the playground or campus or when the final bell rings. The school may not always be "in session," but it is always interacting with the host community. This is one of the reasons why CRE does not limit itself only to "in-class" venues. Many CRE programs, such as those discussed by Sandy Tsubokawa Whittall in Chapter Thirteen, occur after school hours when students are out of class but not yet under the watchful eye of parents or guardians.

Creating a constructive conflict community also means actively involving parents and community members in CRE activities. As several of our contributing authors indicate, parents can and should participate actively in CRE—for example, by receiving training, modeling effective skills for their children, and volunteering with program administration. The school can also link with other conflict management and dispute resolution efforts in the broader community—for example, by having student mediators work with community mediators to handle parent-teen conflicts in the community or to help defuse gang conflict in the community.

## How Does CRE Fit with the Larger Educational Mission?

At this point a skeptical teacher might be prompted to ask, "OK, but how does this fit with what we're here to do (and what we're measured on)—how much children learn?" In this age of "teach-to-the-test" pressures, there is no doubt that this is a realistic and important question. As many of our authors know, teachers and administrators feel as though they already have more to do than they can handle. Asking them to take on another task—no matter how valuable—can seem counterproductive or even abusive. I've had teachers say to me, "It's not that learning conflict skills isn't important—it is. But how can I teach them this and also teach them what they need to know to do well on the [insert the name of your standardized test package]?"

Fortunately, there are three answers to this question. The first is that CRE helps children achieve in ways that schools and communities have identified as critical. CRE is tied to key learning objectives. For example, the Maine Department of Education developed a series of "learning results" that all Maine school children should be able to demonstrate by the time they graduate high school. These learning results appear in the list that follows.

Each Maine student must leave school as

- *A Clear and Effective Communicator*
  Uses oral, written, visual, artistic, and technological models of expression
  Reads, listens to, interprets messages from multiple sources
  Uses English and at least one other language
- *A Self-Directed and Life Long Learner*
  Creates career and education plans that reflect personal goals, interests, and skills and available resources
  Demonstrates the capacity to undertake independent study
  Finds and uses information from libraries, electronic data bases, and other resources
- *A Creative and Practical Problem Solver*
  Observes situations objectively to clearly and accurately define problems
  Frames questions and designs data collection and analysis strategies from all disciplines to answer these questions
  Identifies patterns, trends, and relationships that apply to solutions to problems
- *A Responsible and Involved Citizen*
  Recognizes the power of personal participation to affect the community and demonstrates participation skills
  Understands the importance of accepting responsibility for personal decisions and actions
  Knows the means of achieving personal and community health and well-being
  Recognizes and understands the diverse nature of society
- *A Collaborative and Quality Worker*
  Knows the structure and function of the labor market
  Assesses individual interests, aptitudes, and values in relation to demands of the workplace
  Demonstrates reliability, flexibility, and concern for quality

- *An Integrative and Informed Thinker*

    Applies knowledge and skills in and across English language arts and performing arts, foreign languages, health and physical education, science, social studies, and career preparation

    Comprehends relationships among different modes of thoughts and methods associated with the traditional disciplines[13]

In all content areas, Maine educators are expected to prepare students in these areas of competency. What students learn in CRE is strongly related to several of these core learning results, especially in terms of helping a student become a creative and practical problem solver, a responsible and involved citizen, and a collaborative and quality worker.

In a related vein, some educators have developed a list of student "traits" that they believe denote the competencies necessary for students to succeed in the twenty-first century. According to one such list, for example, the *competent* student demonstrates continual academic improvement. The *creative* student utilizes innovative approaches that demonstrate problem solving and original thinking. The *ethical* student displays respect, integrity, and trustworthiness. The *good citizen* demonstrates civic and social responsibility, honors diversity, and participates in positive group interaction. The *healthy* student seeks a well-rounded lifestyle that displays physical, emotional, and social wellness. The *productive* student uses time efficiently and creates quality work. The *successful* student is self-directed and goal-oriented. And the *thoughtful* student develops critical thinking skills and utilizes appropriate decision-making strategies.[14] As is true of the Maine learning results, these competencies for the twenty-first-century student obviously overlap significantly with the skills taught in CRE.

The second answer to teachers' questions about how they can teach CRE and have their students perform well on achievement tests is that CRE programs have been shown to have positive effects on academic performance in students.[15] There are several possible explanations for these findings, two of which are particularly compelling: CRE programs can help create constructive learning environments, enabling teachers to teach and thus making it is easier for students to achieve academically; CRE also teaches critical thinking skills that can help students achieve academically in all subjects.

The third answer for teachers serves as a good bridge to our upcoming discussion of program models. Put simply, some CRE program models are more effective at integrating conflict concepts with ongoing curriculum. As Rachel A. Poliner discusses in Chapter Nine on curricular infusion in CRE, these programs enable teachers to infuse conflict material into the language arts, science, mathematics, or social studies curriculum so that students get both benefits at the same time. In fact, the synergy of the two content areas can be very powerful as a learning tool. Teachers can teach two things at the same time, and in a manner that increases students' ability to integrate content areas. Curriculum infusion also helps students make connections between areas of study as well as connections between their academic work and their lives. Students learn that the information has implications for how they can live better lives.

## What Program Models Are Included in CRE?

In their *Handbook of Conflict Resolution Education,* Bodine and Crawford identify four program models: the mediation program approach, the process curriculum approach, the peaceable classroom approach, and the peaceable school approach.

### Mediation Program Approach

This model is often referred to as the peer mediation program model. These "stand-alone" programs are the most common form of CRE in the United States. A small group of students are trained in mediation so that they can act as third parties in peer conflicts. Once students are trained, the success of the program depends on the extent to which teachers, staff, administration, and students are willing to refer conflicts to the program. In Chapter Six, Richard Cohen provides a wonderful overview of peer mediation programs, explaining basic principles of these programs as well as giving suggestions for optimal program implementation. In Chapter Seven, Paul I. Kaplan eloquently explains how peer mediation programs can be adapted for special education environments.

### Process Curriculum Approach (Also Known as the Direct Skills Instruction Approach)

This model involves a specific curriculum of conflict content; one example is the Workable Peace program, in which students are taught a conflict and negotiation curriculum through a series of case studies and intensive role plays.[16] Although there are a variety of conflict curricula, most address the foundations of conflict and the principles of effective conflict resolution, and introduce some version of a problem-solving process. Depending on the school's needs, the conflict resolution curriculum may be taught as a separate course, as a distinct curriculum outside of regular class time, or as a daily or weekly lesson in a related content curriculum.

## Peaceable Classroom Approach

In the peaceable classroom approach CRE is incorporated into the core subjects of the curriculum and into classroom management strategies. This model includes what others have termed *curriculum infusion*. In addition, the peaceable classroom requires effective classroom management practices that create a constructive and safe learning environment, as several of our contributing authors discuss. Teachers using this approach may do it in conjunction with a larger program, such as cooperative learning.

## Peaceable School Approach

The peaceable school approach is a comprehensive, whole-school methodology that builds on the peaceable classroom approach by using conflict resolution as a system of operation for managing the school as well as the classroom. All members of the school (including parents) learn and use conflict resolution principles and processes. Also called whole-school programs, these efforts often combine peer mediation with additional training and intervention efforts to provide the "whole school" with information to improve conflict behavior and to develop key social and emotional skills. Working from the philosophy that children often model what they see, these programs attempt to improve the ways adults in the schools deal with their own conflicts by training staff (including teachers, nonteaching staff, and administration) in conflict skills.

## Community-Linked Programs

Although this program model was not on Bodine and Crawford's list and is relatively rare, it deserves mention. Community-linked programs are the most ambitious of all. They are usually configured to be the logical extension of a whole-school program; however, they can involve community linkages to peer mediation cadre programs as well. In cadre-linked programs, peer mediators are linked to external community groups, but other members of the school are not similarly involved. For example, the peer mediators may serve as mediation trainers or mediators in a local neighborhood mediation center. This increases the mediators' experience and exposes segments of the community to mediation by youth. However, it is not designed to institute sweeping changes in the community or in the school conflict culture. Peace and Safety Networks involve a number of community members and organizations, linking them with the school's programs and activities. Religious, business, and governmental organizations usually work together with the school to create innovative ways to "spread the word" about mediation and constructive conflict resolution, to increase applications for mediation, and to encourage community members to take part.

## What Are the Proven Benefits of CRE?

During the past several years, there has been a great deal of discussion about whether CRE efforts "work." Our answer is an unequivocal *yes*. However, some educators have been concerned about others' comments that these programs do not work. Let's look more closely at the source of the confusion.

First, let's look at a somewhat troubling comment about the effectiveness of CRE. As many school administrators already know, in 2001 the surgeon general of the United States issued a report on youth violence in which violence prevention programs were reviewed for their effectiveness. In that report is the following statement: "Some educational programs that target universal populations have shown a consistent lack of effect in scientific studies. Peer-led programs, including peer counseling, peer mediation, and peer leaders are among them. In a 1987 review of these interventions, Gottfredson concluded that there is no evidence of a positive effect."[17] In the past year this report has been referenced as "proof" that schools should not implement CRE. This is truly unfortunate and unnecessary.

Why should we be unconcerned about this conclusion of the surgeon general's report? There are three reasons. First, the surgeon general was interested in looking at the "effectiveness" of programs only in terms of whether the program had been proven to prevent serious physical violence (for example, murder, stabbing, and shooting). Although preventing serious physical violence is important, it is not the basic reason for CRE, as we've explained earlier. Those of us in the CRE field strongly recommend that the surgeon general's report (and this specific quotation) not be used without the additional explanation that it pertains only to the standard of preventing serious physical violence. Second, the cited research review, published in 1987, is sorely outdated. In the fifteen years since the publication of this review, there has been a wealth of research on the positive effects of CRE. This research, which we shall mention briefly, suggests there is a great deal of benefit in these efforts. Third, even if Gottfredson's conclusion was valid (then or now), it would apply only to the mediation program model of CRE (for example, peer mediation). It would in no way relate to the process curriculum, peaceable classroom, or peaceable school approaches.

Three sources of information confirm the efficacy of CRE. In "Creating Safe and Drug-Free Schools: An Action Guide," the U.S. Department of Education concludes the following: "The effective conflict resolution education programs highlighted . . . have helped to improve the climate in school, community, and juvenile justice settings by reducing the number of disruptive and violent acts in these settings, by decreasing the number of chronic school absences due to a fear of violence, by reducing the manner of disciplinary referrals and suspensions, by increasing academic instruction during the school day, and by increasing the self-esteem, and self-respect, as well as the personal responsibility and self-discipline of the young people involved in these programs."[18]

In 2001, the Safe and Drug-Free Schools office of the Department of Education published a list of promising and exemplary programs. This list was generated by an expert panel's review of evidence regarding the effectiveness of various programs. The resulting list contained nine exemplary and thirty-three promising programs—many of which are conflict education programs discussed in this volume (for example, SEL programs, bias awareness programs, and anti-bullying programs).[19]

In March 2000, the Safe and Drug-Free Schools office funded a research symposium of experts in CRE to review existing evidence and to develop a research agenda for the next decade. The results of this symposium were published in the volume *Does It Work? The Case for Conflict Resolution Education in Our Nation's Schools.* As this volume concludes, CRE programs—when conducted well—have many important impacts on students, including increased academic achievement, positive attitudes toward school, assertiveness, cooperation, communication skills, healthy interpersonal and intergroup relations, self-control, and the use of constructive conflict resolution behaviors at home and at school. In addition, CRE has been proven to decrease aggressiveness, discipline referrals, drop-out rates, social withdrawal, suspension rates, victimized behavior, and violence. *Does It Work?* also concludes that there is considerable evidence that CRE has strong positive impacts on school and classroom climate.[20]

## What Are Some Basic Guidelines for Implementing CRE Programs?

For programs to be effective, they need to be implemented well. This section goes over some basic guidelines for implementing CRE; in each of the chapters, the contributing authors will add more specific information about implementing the type of CRE program they are discussing.

Most successful programs follow certain stages of implementation. Some best practices at each stage are included in the list that follows. If you're interested in a more thorough discussion of implementation issues, we've listed several resources for you in the appendixes.

| **Stage** | **Description** |
|---|---|
| Assess needs. | Identify the goals and resources for your school. Assess the degree of interest and potential commitment among students, staff, and community members. |
| Orient staff. | Give detailed information about the nature of CRE and the results of the needs assessment to all members of the staff. Have open discussions about the utility of the program and how it can best fit the school. Also clarify staff expectations for their involvement or how they can support the program. |
| Select the site leadership team (SLT). | Identify staff who are committed to working for the program. This stage should include in-depth discussions of time and resource commitments expected from SLT members. |
| Orient students. | Present the idea to students to stimulate interest and encourage them to be involved. |
| Select students and staff to be involved. | If peer mediation is a component of your CRE program, you will need to select which students are to be trained as peer mediators. You may also be providing additional training to other student groups, such as sports team members or select classes. In any event, you will need to have clear criteria for how students are chosen for involvement. If you are providing staff training, you will also have to determine which staff are to be involved and why. |
| Provide training. | This stage is usually one of the longest and has the most variations depending on the program model being implemented. If you have a peer mediation cadre program, this step involves providing the peer mediation training and additional program implementation training to members of the SLT. If you are using staff training in conflict management, you may need several days of in-service to complete the training. If you are using some form of curriculum infusion, the implementation actually takes the entire semester or academic year in most whole-school models. And if you are using parent and community member training in conjunction with whole-school approaches, you may be providing training in a variety of ways throughout the entire year. |

| | |
|---|---|
| Publicize the program. | Use as much publicity as possible to help students and staff understand the program and how to use it. If you have a peer mediation program, it is essential that you let teachers and students know about it and that you encourage them to use it. If you have a whole-school program, it is equally important that you spread the word about the curriculum infusion or additional student and staff training programs that are ongoing in your school. If you are engaged in a community-linked program, it is essential to publicize the program in an attempt to garner community interest and support. |
| Use the program. | Initiate and sustain the program with regular attention to coordinating, refreshing skills, and maintaining a high profile in the school. |
| Evaluate the program (emphasize student assessment). | On an ongoing basis, but certainly at the end of the semester or year, evaluate how well the program is working, whether things need to be changed, and whether you are interested in and able to expand the program. One very important area of evaluation is to assess the students' learning. Assessment practices should be based on a careful articulation of the skills, abilities, or competencies you want the students to learn. The better you can articulate these at the beginning of the program, the better you should be able to measure them. It is essential to focus on assessing how students have gained emotionally, behaviorally, socially, and academically from their experience with CRE. |

The advice presented in the preceding list can be summarized in terms of some very basic principles that should ground your efforts:

• Always take the time to do a thorough needs assessment, one that includes all parties who may be stakeholders in the program.
• You cannot do too much in terms of orienting school and community members to the nature of the program prior to its implementation.
• Make sure your program is appropriate for your goals.
• Start small and build on that success.
• Carefully select and nurture the SLT.
• Involve a diverse group of students.

- Publicize the program thoroughly and creatively.
- Demand proven qualifications and high standards from training organizations.
- Be patient and plan for reasonable success in a long-term implementation.
- Assess student accomplishment and improvement carefully and in a manner that is consistent with what is being taught.
- Evaluate the overall effectiveness of the program in terms of successful processes and outcomes.

It is clear that CRE programs have a great deal to offer our children. We heartily concur with Sandy and Cochran's conclusion: "Development in CRE and social-emotional learning skills is so critical to the education of our children that we must actively support infusion of this instruction throughout each child's educational experience, both in school and at home."[21]

# CHAPTER THREE

# THE BUILDING BLOCKS OF CONFLICT RESOLUTION EDUCATION
## Direct Instruction, Adult Modeling, and Core Practices

### Carol Miller Lieber

I spent a day in a fourth-grade classroom where a teacher set aside time to teach a lesson in active listening skills from a well-known conflict resolution education (CRE) curriculum. Students played a paraphrasing game and took turns adding new pieces to a story using a talking stick to speak; pairs of students discussed open-ended questions and were required to talk through their ideas and agree on a response they would share with the whole group. The teacher invited students to name the skills they had used during the lesson and give examples of how they had personally practiced good listening. Throughout this series of activities, the students were animated and attentive. Yet when the lesson was over, the teacher buried her class's high spirits and spent the rest of the day barking directions, monitoring seat work, and calling on students to answer assigned questions; there was no dialogue or collaborative learning among students, no reflection about what was learned, no opportunity for self-expression beyond parroting right answers.

Afterwards, I shared my puzzlement with the teacher, and she explained that she couldn't afford to teach "that way" all day. She was evaluated on the amount of time her students spent "on task" and by how closely her lessons matched local learning standards and national achievement tests. I kept thinking about all the "on task" opportunities in which the teacher might have modeled and the students might have practiced the listening and reflection skills they had experienced earlier in the day.

This example illustrates the learning gap that exists when direct skill instruction, adult modeling, and routine practice of these skills in classrooms or the wider school community are not perceived as integrated elements of comprehensive conflict resolution education. If we want young people to become successful at "working it out by themselves," I'd like to suggest three things schools can do to nurture students' development of these vital skills.

## The Power of Adult Modeling

First we need to think about how we model conflict resolution skills in our interactions with students and colleagues. Students get powerful messages from what we adults actually do more than what we say or teach. As Ted and Nancy Sizer remind us in "The Students Are Watching," kids are acutely aware of how we conduct ourselves when conflicts and controversy flare up within the school community. Healthy schools are places where the adult leadership normalizes problems and addresses them with candor and curiosity—where open data and open dialogue form the foundation of collaborative problem solving within school governance. Kids are learning lessons about conflict all the time from how we handle it ourselves.

Another way we show our true conflict colors to students is through our approaches to conflict in the classroom. Even if they've never heard the term, most kids are pretty quick at identifying the dominant "conflict styles" of their teachers. They know who the commander-in-chiefs are for whom "it's my way or the highway." They know the accommodators who develop good relationships with them, but never get around to dealing with real problems constructively. They know the avoiders who ignore unacceptable behaviors out of fear of confrontation or being disliked. And students know what's different about the teachers they love and can count on—the ones who will listen to them, treat them respectfully even when they mess up, and work with them to become more successful learners and more effective people.

For better or worse, our conflict resolution tools (or lack of them) are revealed most tellingly in the ways we manage our classrooms and discipline students. When we become aware of a problem, is our stance threatening, defensive, or inviting? Do we encourage cooperation and self-correction or do we immediately impose a punitive consequence with no opportunity for students to reflect on their choices and try out a new strategy? Recognizing the connection between classroom and conflict management is valuable for several reasons. Our capacities to manage our own emotions, defuse confrontational situations, and communicate positively during a conflict will shape how our students respond when they get into academic and behavioral difficulties. Students take their cues from us. The teacher who snaps, blames, or uses sarcasm when things go wrong, unwittingly encourages students to do the same.

Moreover, when our disciplinary approach includes opportunities for students to develop and strengthen social and emotional competencies, students become more responsible and self-directed. For example, when teachers model how they handle frustration and discuss what students can do when they're upset and angry, students are learning that expressing and regulating feelings effectively is a classroom expectation. Or when classroom management includes the routine use of a "peace place," one-minute conferencing, or other problem-solving protocols, students get direct experience in resolving conflicts that matter most to them.

## The Importance of Direct Skill Instruction and Practice

Second, schools need to identify the best opportunities and entry points to provide direct instruction of key conflict resolution skills and processes. There is common agreement that the capacities to manage oneself effectively, make responsible decisions, establish positive social relationships, handle interpersonal conflict productively, and strengthen group collaboration skills enhance students' personal efficacy, thus enhancing their internal motivation and capacity to learn. Healthy development is contingent upon students' growing and feeling more competent, self-determining, and connected to others at each developmental stage. Students who demonstrate these competencies throughout their schooling are more likely to be academically successful and perform better as independent learners and group participants. Equally important, an individual's mastery of social and emotional competencies will influence success in adulthood and shape her or his relationships for a lifetime—as a worker, a life partner, a parent, a friend, and a citizen. So what options do we have for teaching these skills intentionally throughout a child's school experience?

Over the last twenty years, thousands of schools have instituted curriculum-based direct skill instruction in conflict resolution, social skills, and other prevention and social and emotional learning programs (see Appendix B for a list of curriculum resources). The huge growth of CRE curriculum-based programs is a result, in part, of the federal office of Safe and Drug Free School's promotion of CRE as a vital strategy that increases children's protective factors against risk behaviors. At all grade levels, most curricula provide twenty to thirty-five sequenced, age-appropriate lessons that can be taught throughout the year on a weekly basis or taught daily or several times a week within a more condensed time period.

Research reviews of conflict resolution, prevention, and youth development programming indicate several criteria that successful curriculum-based programs share in common. According to the work of Hawkins and Catalano and key researchers associated with CASEL (Collaborative for Academic, Social, and Emotional Learning), curriculum-based programs that produce positive changes in student behavior include:

- A prescribed sequence of organized, coherent, and developmentally appropriate lessons in which student learning at one level builds upon what has come before and prepares students for what comes later.
- Multiple years of direct skill instruction throughout a child's school experience versus one "dose" for one year only. Prevention research suggests that developing a specific skill competency requires six to eight hits—in other words, a one time experience will not produce a change in behavior.
- A curriculum that incorporates exposure to and instruction of a new skill with suggestions for continued practice in multiple settings and different contexts, tips on teacher coaching and feedback, and opportunities for demonstrations of mastery.
- Adequate training that prepares teachers to implement the curriculum and follow-up support and coaching to increase teachers' skills and sustain quality delivery of the curriculum.

CASEL has suggested several other guidelines that maximize the effectiveness of direct skill instruction:

- Engage students as active partners in creating a classroom atmosphere in which caring, responsibility, trust, and commitment to learning can thrive. Research indicates that encouraging student involvement in classroom decision making strengthens their attachment to school and their interest in learning.
- Integrate social and emotional learning programs into the regular curriculum and life of the classroom and school. Social and emotional learning skills can readily be connected to other thinking skills such as analytical thinking, prediction, synthesis, analogy, and metaphor.
- Use a variety of teaching methods to actively promote multiple domains of intelligence. Howard Gardner's work has made it clear that the various domains of intelligence are interrelated. Activities, such as cooperative learning, artistic expression, group discussion, and self-reflection, that call on a variety of intelligences allow for the strengths and weaknesses of a range of children.
- Teach by example—a powerful instructional technique for emotional and social learning.

- Weave a consistent conceptual thread supporting social and emotional learning throughout the entire school curriculum, rather than introducing a series of fragmented activities focusing on isolated issues.[1]

Even when schools choose a direct skill instruction program that meets many of these criteria, questions about when and where to teach the curriculum present many challenges. With pressures to align all learning to local and national standards, it has become increasingly difficult for schools to find the best fit for CRE skill instruction within their total learning program. Here are a few examples of how elementary, middle, and high schools have met this challenge.

In elementary schools, many educators link CRE skill instruction to specific learning standards and incorporate skill lessons into their language arts, social studies, and life skills curricula. Some teachers go a step further integrating direct skill instruction and the exploration of CRE concepts and processes through an examination of conflict and character in literature and history (see Chapter Nine). Others teach an extended CRE learning unit during the year that meets Health Education learning standards. Some of the most successful and experienced CRE teachers I've met take another direction altogether. They observe their students closely in the beginning of the year, assessing students' social and emotional competencies, and identify and prioritize the competencies they want students to strengthen and practice during the year. Teachers who use this "less is more" approach make a conscious effort to include multiple practices of a particular skill set over several weeks so students begin to see the development of these competencies as an integral part of classroom expectations.

In middle school, the most popular "windows" for direct skill instruction include teaching a set of lessons in advisory period, health courses, and orientation programs for incoming students that extend through the first quarter, or quarterly exploratory classes where all students at a specific grade level rotate through a nine-week conflict resolution class. Some schools establish a schoolwide steering committee that develops social and emotional learning benchmarks and work with the faculty to identify quarterly themes that sixth-, seventh-, and eighth-grade teams implement in a three-year cycle, so that the entire school is focused on the same theme at the same time. Themes such as "Becoming a good problem solver," "Developing self-awareness and self-management," and "Respecting and accepting differences" offer the opportunity to link special schoolwide events and initiatives to team instructional activities. Other middle school faculties take a comprehensive look at learning standards and curricular content at each grade level and determine specific conflict resolution lessons that will be taught in social studies and language arts each year.

In high schools, finding the right place for direct skill instruction becomes even trickier. Most high school teachers find it very difficult to teach a series of sequential CRE lessons as part of their regular academic courses. In addition, there's the added challenge of teaching CRE lessons in ways that don't feel fake to young people. Adolescents are more likely to internalize the value of developing these competencies when they practice them in an authentic context. Youth leadership and peer mediation programs provide compelling evidence that adolescents' social and emotional competencies improve when extended practice of these skills is embedded in activities that students find personally meaningful. Like middle schools, advisory and health courses are the most popular settings for CRE skill instruction. Some high schools have had a measure of success by developing semester electives that combine peer leadership, conflict resolution education, and intergroup relations. Other schools choose to integrate a process curriculum like Program for Young Negotiators or Workable Peace into the required social studies curriculum at various grade levels (see Chapter Five).

Finally, successful implementation of direct skill instruction programs depends on the level of sustained districtwide or schoolwide leadership for the program, financial support, professional development, parent and faculty commitment to the program goals, and the capacity to continue mentoring new "drivers" who will hold the vision.

## Schoolwide and Classroom Practices That Support Conflict Resolution Education

Third, we need to develop a set of core practices that support a problem-solving orientation and students' development and practice of social and emotional competencies within all aspects of schooling: in the classroom, on the playground and the playing field, in codes of conduct and disciplinary policies, in the counseling office, and in the student support center. Developing such a culture takes time, attention, and intention from every constituency—administrators, faculty, guidance and support staff, students, and parents.

How and when adults provide meaningful practice of conflict resolution skills and processes will, in large part, determine how often and how well students actually use these skills in the classroom, in the hallways, or at home—and even how well kids act as models for each other. Teaching students the process of negotiation in a direct skill lesson, for example, has a better chance of sticking when students have opportunities to negotiate what and how they are learning in the classroom.

The rest of this chapter explores how and why a set of core schoolwide and classroom practices can help support a prosocial school climate, healthy peer and student-staff relationships, and students' regular and effective use of conflict resolution skills at every age level. The practices highlighted here are ones that can be universally applied at all levels of schooling. In order to ensure that key practices would encompass K–12 grade levels, I have included some key comments by Chip Wood, program director of The Northeast Foundation for Children and its K–8 program, The Responsive Classroom. Chip's voice adds a critical perspective to this chapter.

The next section highlights four schoolwide practices that support effective conflict resolution education:

- Healthy play
- Student orientation to school
- Service and stewardship within the school community
- Student-faculty initiatives that promote a positive peer culture

The final section highlights six practices that support conflict resolution education in the classroom:

- Developing group guidelines and agreements
- Engaging in negotiated learning
- Holding class meetings
- Cooperative learning strategies
- Monitoring and assessing social skill practice
- Building positive connections through gatherings and closings

## Schoolwide Practices That Promote CRE

When certain practices are modeled and implemented by the entire school community, the resulting environment fosters healthy social and emotional development, conflict resolution education, and a problem-solving orientation. This section explores several activities that support the growth of CRE.

### Healthy Play

We live in a time when recess has been eliminated from many elementary schools, and the closest thing to play in many middle schools is the game of "push, grab, and go," which gets played out in cafeteria lines across America. In high school, outside of organized sports and the drama club, references to play usually spell trouble, as in "You play too much" or "Stop playing around." What happened to the role of healthy play in schooling? David Fernie asserts that when children play, they add to their understanding of themselves and others, increase their knowledge of the physical world, and improve their ability to communicate with peers and adults. We know the value of play for young children, yet we often ignore its importance during later school years.[2]

Healthy play involves invention, rule making, role playing, social organizing, problem solving, physical or intellectual challenges, and the harnessing and release of positive emotions. Chip Wood points out that the spirit of play is as essential for adolescents—who need healthy outlets for physical, sexual, and emotional energy—as it is for younger children, who are developing increasing control over their minds and bodies. In its purest sense, play is child driven: kids are in charge of what happens. Their choices regarding how to play go a long way in shaping both positive and negative social norms in the larger school culture. Play provides countless opportunities to cooperate with others in the planning and doing of an activity. During play, students think strategically, negotiate differences constructively, regulate peer behavior, and fine-tune their abilities to "read" and lead a group.

What can you do to promote play that is fun, fair, safe, and inclusive? First, encourage staff dialogues about the goals, benefits, and types of play that you want to encourage in your school. Discuss how healthy play meets critical developmental needs at different age levels. Invite students to discuss the role of play in their lives and to share what makes play different from other activities they experience. Explore the kinds of school or district policies and structures that support or undermine the importance of play in the learning environment.

Second, think about all the ways that you can make healthy play a core practice of quality education in your school. The Needham Public School District outside Boston sees its recess program as a vital part of the school day and an intentional component of physical wellness and health education in its broadest sense. One of the PE staff's responsibilities is to be out on the playground at recess—working with students to establish norms for cooperative games, encouraging responsible and safe use of equipment, and helping kids choose teams in nontraditional ways. Students know these teachers well, so their authority on the playground and their facilitation of healthy play are natural extensions of their work with children in more formal PE and health education settings. By making recess more than an add-on, faculties are also more likely to think about children's play in a larger learning context. In one school, teachers noticed how difficult it was for students to settle down and refocus in the classroom when recess was scheduled after lunch. Instead of eliminating recess, the school staff decided to stagger lunches so all students could experience a vigorous play time before lunch, thus providing time to shift the energy level before returning to class. Problem solved!

Another vehicle for promoting healthy play is establishing a school Family Fun Night. Through ESR's and Project Adventure's *Adventures in Peacemaking* program, many schools have designed evenings or Saturday mornings filled with high energy games and team challenges for kids, staff, and family members. The gym becomes "play station central" where families rotate from one activity to another, whooping it up as they go.[3] Because this program places equal value on direct experience and reflection, families get to play new games together and then link what they've experienced to their own lives and relationships. Parents always say how differently they feel about themselves and their children after this event, noting that the chance to relieve everyday stress through play while having some fun with their kids just doesn't happen often enough.

At the high school level, one notable exception to "no playing allowed" is the inclusion of adventure-based play in physical education, health, and wellness programs. Columbia High School in South Orange–Maplewood, New Jersey, has built an outdoor challenge course on school property that is the centerpiece of adventure-based PE courses and is also available for use by other student groups. At Lyons Township High School in La Grange, Illinois, staff introduced cooperative games and problem-solving initiatives as a weekly component of regular PE classes. All of these efforts are wonderful examples of how healthy play can be promoted and implemented, by adults and kids alike, to support conflict resolution programs and practices.

## Student Orientation to School

Transitions to new surroundings are never easy, whether a child is entering an elementary classroom for the very first time, enrolling in a new middle school in the middle of the year, or getting lost on the way to first hour on the first day of high school. "Large middle and high schools enroll students from many feeder schools. Students are moving to what is often a larger building and a more complex schedule. They know only their previous classmates, and they may or may not be ready or feel ready for the whole new array of challenges they are about to face. It is no wonder that students cling to classmates who are already familiar."[4] If there is no attempt to help students develop a new school identity and sense of belonging, the cliques and pecking orders already established at previous schools will continue to shape the new school experience.

The general concept of student orientation is absent from most middle and high schools except in the form of cursory "welcome" sessions where hundreds of kids are herded through the building for a quick tour before receiving code of conduct handbooks that are never really explained. Chip notes that even in elementary schools we tend to make many assumptions about how well children are able to navigate a new learning environment without setting aside enough time to explore and discuss the social climate and norms that communicate, "This is how we do school here."

Orientation to school parallels a mediator's efforts to build rapport and develop clear guidelines and protocols or a facilitator's desire to create a positive climate where people trust that they will be respected, heard, and perceived as valued members of the group. The goals of orientation activities, structures, rituals, and routines are the same whether a student is five or fifteen. They include:

- Making new students feel welcomed and important
- Making schoolwide rules, norms, and consequences explicit to new students and families so that everyone knows "what will happen if . . ."
- Clarifying student, parent, and teacher expectations, rights, and responsibilities
- Learning and experiencing core social values (cooperation, caring, respect, and appreciation for diversity) and principles of learning (quality, completion, effort, and reflection) that inform the school culture
- Learning how to navigate the school building, the daily schedule, lunch, and activities
- Learning and practicing problem-solving protocols that students are encouraged to use inside and outside the classroom and learning what students can do when they feel like they need help or find themselves in academic difficulties or interpersonal conflicts
- Learning and practicing classroom procedures that will help all students become successful
- Learning and practicing the kinds of behaviors and attitudes that are essential for establishing positive peer relationships in this environment
- Reducing student anxiety by having a safe place to share thoughts, feelings, and questions about school
- Reducing feelings of isolation and awkwardness by facilitating community-building activities and cross-age group experiences
- Participating in rituals and routines unique to this learning environment that communicate a sense of belonging
- Learning what it means to "take care" of the learning environment and participating in activities that make the concept of stewardship feel real

Obviously, these goals can't be achieved through one morning session before school opens or even a series of activities during the first week of school. Instead, we need to see orientation as an ongoing process that involves old and new students, parents, and staff and affirms the school's vision of itself. Here are a few orientation strategies.

Some schools intentionally rethink the first couple of months of school by integrating orientation activities into all aspects of the school program. For teachers at all grade levels this might include practicing procedures for using essential tools and materials, introducing protocols for collaborative learning, setting personal goals, and instituting weekly reflections about how things are going and what students are learning. Some middle and high schools include a special orientation class for incoming students during the first quarter so students get a chance to "learn the ropes" of being a student in their new school. In elementary schools, orientation to the playground, the hallways, the cafeteria, and even the school bus behavior are all part of a good start.

For younger children, morning meetings or closing circles provide daily opportunities for exploring what's exciting and what's confusing about everything that's new. At the secondary level, Chip suggests that we need to put "home" back into the concept of homeroom, home base, or advisory time. Regular contact and more personalized connections between one teacher and a small group of students make home base an ideal place to clarify and discuss orientation issues as they arise.

Schools that advocate a holistic approach to orientation are also likely to expect teachers to welcome new parents as soon as possible through letters that go home the first week, parent classroom visits, new parent breakfasts, or introductory phone calls to families. At a high school outside of Chicago that enrolls hundreds of recent immigrants every year, the welcome orientation for new families involves simultaneous sessions where students translate the proceedings in their home languages.

Another welcoming strategy at many elementary schools involves pairing up incoming students and outgoing students (i.e., first and second graders) for classroom visits where older students share what they experienced the year before and take their partners on a tour of the building. Other elementary schools arrange for older students to become big sisters and brothers to new kindergarten students and sustain this relationship for two years.

"A number of middle and high schools help smooth the transition by matching veteran students with incoming students during the summer through pen pal (or e-mail pal) relationships and then sponsoring a welcome breakfast where everyone gets to meet and greet. Others have hosted incoming students for a full day the previous spring where new students shadow a freshman or upperclassman. Still other schools have created web pages for incoming students to get information and ask questions" as Poliner and Lieber state.[5] And there is probably nothing worse for a middle schooler than enrolling at a new school in the middle of the year. As part of Roosevelt Middle School's Resolving Conflict Creatively Program in Vista, California, Student Ambassadors not only participate in the school's peer mediation program; they also provide a personalized orientation for students who arrive after the school year begins.

Ideally, new student orientation in middle and high school becomes an important "bonding" event for everyone involved. At Boston's Health Careers Academy, students and faculty developed an orientation program in which pairs of upperclass students are responsible for steering groups of ten new students through a series of activities and reflections to get to know each other and the school during the two-day team-building experience. However your school chooses to develop its orientation program, involve as many people as possible in a variety of activities over an extended period of time.

## Service and Stewardship Within the School Community

Much is already written about the benefits of service and stewardship opportunities within the school community. I'd like to offer three guidelines to consider when constructing an array of service activities for children and young people. First, ensure that every student has opportunities to serve and help in your school every year. A school expectation that "everyone serves" puts forward an altogether different statement than a plea for volunteers. Second, ensure that students are involved in brainstorming initial ideas, choosing what they will do, planning and organizing projects and events, and documenting what they have accomplished. Principles of effective youth development reinforce the importance of student voice and choice in developing meaningful service activities. Third, provide as many ways as possible for students to participate in school governance alongside adults. Whether it's the bathroom committee, a diversity task force, the building and grounds crew, the safe school leadership team, or the student-faculty forum— model and practice civic participation skills (dialogue, perspective taking, prioritizing, consensus building, and collaborative problem solving) with your students. Everybody wins when school governance involves all stakeholders.

## Student-Faculty Initiatives That Promote a Positive Peer Culture

I have never met a teacher who doesn't live for the day when she hears one student say to another, "That might be cool someplace else, but we don't do that here." One goal of all prosocial initiatives to improve school climate is to strengthen positive social norms. A common feature of successful initiatives is student and faculty involvement from start to finish. So what do successful efforts look like?

One Anchorage, Alaska, high school was concerned about the great divide between students who participated in sports, clubs, and other student activities and those students who participated in nothing. A core team of students and teachers that included "nonparticipants" designed a survey to gather data from students that might help the school make changes that would increase student participation. After analyzing the data and meeting with more students and the school leadership team, the school developed a plan that increased participation by 100 percent. Here's what they did. The school instituted a biweekly activity period during the school day because many students said that after-school jobs kept them from participating. During this period students have the option of signing up for an activity, a study hall, or tutoring. Second, the "participation team" solicited activity ideas from everyone in the school, ideas about what kids were interested in and what teachers were willing to sponsor. The result was an amazing set of offerings from tying flies for fishing to fantasy baseball to beading to girl groups who wanted to have a safe place to talk about interpersonal issues. The other notable aspect of the plan was a student campaign to *Participate.* Students were encouraged to bring a friend to an activity; students used posters to announce new activities; and students took care to talk up activities to nonparticipating groups in the school, including special education students and kids who had been suspended. Every quarter new activities were added, and the "participation team" met regularly to assess their progress and make plans for the next year.

On a more somber note, the faculty of a middle school was stressed out by students' constant use of profanity and negative language. The faculty decided they would put the issue to the students, sharing why they felt it was a problem and asking students to explore ways the school could tackle it. The first thing they did was gather data. Math teachers assigned students to graph the frequency of abusive and negative language in five-minute intervals in the classrooms, in the hallways, in the lunchroom, and outside. When the data were collected and presented to all classes, students were astonished at the high numbers and were much more willing to confront their behavior. The next step was setting weekly goals for reducing the frequency of using "bad language." Students and teachers put together a new set of consequences for using inappropriate language that students accepted as fair and teachers were willing to enforce consistently. Consequences ranged from asking students to self-correct using more appropriate language to an in-school suspension for frequent language abusers that involved reading, writing, and reflection on the use of language. Because the whole school was committed to improving the conversational culture, when math students shared their data after a two-month campaign, they were pleased to announce "bad language" had been reduced by 80 percent!

Although this last story is about an antiharassment campaign involving a middle and high school, this initiative could easily be reframed for elementary schools. In a small city district both students and teachers were complaining about a variety of aggressive behaviors from bullying among girls and among boys, sexual harassment toward girls, put-downs about size, looks, and clothes, and the ubiquitous use of the word "gay." The high school's reputation was so bad that middle school students feared moving on to high school. Until faculty and administrators from both schools met to discuss their concerns openly, the problem was buried. With the help of a consultant, the two schools developed a plan to address the harassment issues. Again, the first step was to gather accurate data— Who was being harassed? Who was doing the harassing? Were there any clear patterns to the harassment? Were there underlying tensions between various groups of students that aggravated the aggression? How hidden was the harassment? Did students feel comfortable talking to adults about it? How did kids who were neither targets nor aggressors feel about the harassment?

With a clearer picture of the problem, forty students from the middle and high schools participated in two days of training. From the training activities students and adult advisers created an hourlong workshop that they felt would be the most effective to present to other students. These peer educators practiced facilitating workshop activities. The next step was presenting the workshop to middle and high school teachers with the goal of developing a coherent policy that all teachers were willing to support. Art students participated in a juried poster contest on the theme of countering harassment. Sports teams and school clubs made countering harassment a theme that they addressed throughout the year. Finally, the peer educators visited middle and high school classrooms, conducting their workshops to rave reviews. Harassment hasn't been eliminated, but everyone agrees that they feel more prepared and hopeful about addressing harassment proactively.

These three success stories share many things in common. In each situation, an inspired group of students and faculty addressed the problem collaboratively, beginning the process by defining the problem and gathering data. Second, each initiative had a crystal clear focus that everyone could understand and that the majority of students and faculty were willing to address. Third, each school made their issue a schoolwide campaign involving everyone at some level. Finally, none of these initiatives had a fixed time line. In each case these are ongoing initiatives that are now institutionalized into the school culture. The adults at these schools are aware that with every new group of students, upperclass students and the faculty have an annual responsibility to let all students know, "This is how we do things here." Building a positive peer culture takes years, and these wise educators know it.

## Core Classroom Practices That Promote CRE Education

In addition to initiatives that can be put into place schoolwide, there are several critical classroom practices that promote and support conflict resolution education and social and emotional competencies.

## Developing Group Guidelines and Agreements

Developing group guidelines and agreements can make any learning process more meaningful. When students know how to approach a learning task and know what skills and behaviors will help them complete the task, more kids will be more successful. When students help generate guidelines for a learning experience they are more likely to use their skills effectively.

Shifting the emphasis from "my rules that you follow" to "guidelines we agree to implement together" communicates mutual responsibility for establishing a positive classroom climate where everyone is a stakeholder. When we invoke arbitrary rules in the classroom, we may unintentionally pit the rule breakers against the rule keepers. Furthermore, rules tend to keep the focus on negative behaviors—catching kids doing the wrong thing becomes the goal. In contrast, agreements that describe desirable behaviors that are observable, concrete, and positive invite everyone to recognize and encourage the regular use of these behaviors. In addition, group guidelines become a natural assessment and reflection tool. Teachers and students can engage in an ongoing process of reviewing how well agreements are kept and discussing how to modify agreements so they are more effective.

The practice of making classroom agreements is carried out on two levels: general guidelines for how students work together, learn together, and treat each other; and more concrete guidelines for how to engage in a specific learning experience. In both situations, students engage in authentic practice of conflict resolution skills: defining the problem, sharing perspectives and listening to all points of view, exploring what's negotiable and what's not, identifying mutual interests, brainstorming possible solutions, and reaching a mutually satisfactory agreement.

General group guidelines involve all students in envisioning the kind of classroom in which students will feel safe, respected, cared for, and motivated to learn. One kindergarten teacher I know invites students to share what will help them feel safe in their classroom. Children brainstorm a list of ideas and then draw pictures of their suggestions that become part of their group guidelines.

For older students, I know many teachers who use a learning carousel strategy to generate key data for making their group guidelines. In small groups students rotate from one question to another recording their responses to these kinds of questions:

What things can I do as a student to be successful in this class?

What can the teacher do to support my success in class? What kinds of support from teachers help me to do my best, especially when I'm struggling?

What makes a classroom a safe space where I can be honest and open, where I can say what's on my mind?

What do kids do and say that bugs me the most? What happens in class
   that makes me mad?

In what ways can teachers show respect toward students?

In what ways can students show respect toward teachers?

In what ways can students show respect toward each other?

What can I do to support other students to do their best in class?

What makes learning fun in class?

Teachers and students use this data for developing guidelines that will support
everyone to do their best and be their best.

   More specifically teachers can use this same process for developing group
guidelines for any learning experience. Young children, for example, can help suggest guidelines for using different play areas and learning stations. Older students
can help develop guidelines for making effective presentations or working effectively in team projects. Students can make agreements about how to talk about
controversial issues when students may bring strong feelings and disparate opinions to the dialogue. The common feature in all of these situations is the partnership between teachers and students to construct a learning environment that
supports a shared vision and shared ownership for making that vision a reality.

## Engaging in Negotiated Learning

Negotiated learning is a natural extension of developing group guidelines and
agreements. Negotiated learning is about the "give and take" of classroom life. It
doesn't mean that teachers relinquish their authority or stop teaching the standard
curriculum. It does mean that where and when it's appropriate, teachers and students engage in shared decision making and problem solving around what students
learn and how they learn it. A key aspect of negotiated learning is shifting the
orientation from My Classroom to Our Classroom, and Your or My Problem to
Our Problem. When students are involved in decision making they become more
accountable for their own behavior. Providing more opportunities and support
for making decisions increases the benefits of a productive learning environment.

   Ultimately, a teacher's role is not to decide things for young people, but to help
them see that they have lots of possibilities as they develop the capacity to make
good choices throughout their lives. This is an underlying principle of this book.
Some guidelines for negotiated learning include the following:

• There is rarely just one way to do things in the classroom. Negotiated classrooms offer lots of choices and opportunities for shared decision making. Teach-

ers who negotiate are willing to let go of preconceived blueprints and are committed to exploring alternatives that meet important goals and common interests.

- Most classroom conflicts and disagreements can be handled through problem solving rather than punishment. The disciplinary focus is to support students' self-correction and choose more effective strategies for dealing with behavioral difficulties.

- Teachers and students seem to feel better about themselves and each other when everyone's clear about boundaries—identifying what's negotiable and what's not; and what special needs, constraints, or criteria must be considered as you negotiate together.

- Shared decision making means shared responsibility. Students are expected to take a more active role in their own learning and in the day-to-day functioning of class.

- Negotiated learning works best in a climate where people are reassured that mistakes are part of the process, that nothing will ever be perfect, and where "good enough" is sometimes enough.

- Student and teacher assessments, informal check ins, and discussions about how things are working are essential features of the negotiation process.

In addition, it's helpful to identify goals that satisfy mutual interests. It's important to be willing to seek alternative solutions and to develop criteria for a good solution. Here are a few ideas for establishing negotiated learning.

- Prioritize and negotiate the topics of study in a particular learning unit, knowing that it's impossible to study every topic you'd like to investigate. You can take this a step further by brainstorming the questions and issues students find most compelling about a particular topic and making group decisions about what to investigate in-depth.

- When you teach required material that students find boring and tedious, negotiate how you will all get through learning it. For example, you could explore how the group wants to attack it—a small dose everyday or an intense marathon.

- Make class decisions about the sequence of activities in a self-contained elementary class or the sequence of learning units in a secondary class. In many cases, the arbitrary order of curriculum units is just that.

- Negotiate learning contracts with individual students.

- Negotiate test and project deadline dates as you and students consider other upcoming events and due dates.

- Negotiate how to use limited resources and equipment in class.

- After the first quarter, discuss the learning strategies that students found most and least helpful, interesting, and engaging. Negotiate what you will do more of and less of for the next quarter.

## Holding Class Meetings

Class meetings offer an ideal structure for negotiating group decisions, discussing problems as they arise, and dealing with all things that affect how the group functions. Several features set class meetings apart from other learning structures:

- Students take primary responsibility for generating the agenda and facilitating activities for class meetings.
- Students are expected to practice effective communication and problem solving skills as participants and facilitators.
- Students play a primary role in solving problems and making decisions about issues addressed in class meetings.

Class meetings serve many purposes. One of the most important is creating a special time and space to confront and solve problems that impact the group—whether it's too much noise during work periods, issues around name calling and teasing, or problems with meeting deadlines. Equally important, however, are class meetings that provide opportunities for students to do things that strengthen their desire and capacity to be a high-functioning group. The purpose of class meetings can shift given the specific needs of the group. Some examples include:

1. *Dialogue:* The goal of this meeting is to provide a safe space to air concerns, share feelings and perspectives, and gain deeper understanding of issues raised by students or the teacher.
2. *Planning and Problem Solving:* The goal of these meetings is to use negotiation, planning, and problem-solving strategies to make decisions and resolve issues of concern and interest that affect the group and the learning environment. Meetings might focus on resolving concerns around work habits, cliques, language, and testing or planning special classroom events.
3. *Hypothetical Discussions:* The goal of this meeting is to discuss hypothetical situations or case studies as a way to anticipate and generate solutions to problems before they happen. ("If this happens, then _____.")
4. *Group Reflection, Feedback, and Assessment:* The goal of this meeting is to provide maintenance and support for the group. These activities usually involve group goal setting, check-in's, and assessment of group goals and behaviors.
5. *School Citizenship:* The goal of this meeting is to gather, disseminate, and share

information about schoolwide rules, policies, events, and projects; participate in specific tasks related to official school business and stewardship; participate in specific tasks that promote school spirit and a positive school climate.

6. *Crisis Meetings:* The goal of this meeting is to address situations that require an immediate intervention and attention in a serious, sensitive, and supportive way. Crisis meetings are an important vehicle for reducing tension, restoring order, dealing with a critical concern, or providing care and support for students impacted by a crisis.

You might want to set the stage for a class meeting by developing specific, positive guidelines for facilitating and participating in the class meeting; meeting in a circle or square where everyone can see everyone else; creating an agenda that becomes a routine; reviewing the agenda and identifying the purpose and specific goals of the meeting; soliciting feedback about the meeting when it's over; and inviting students to take various roles as they become more comfortable: class meeting facilitator, summarizer, note taker, time keeper, feedbacker, activity leader, and so on. In addition, group problem solving is more effective when you:

- Encourage active listening by inviting students to paraphrase and summarize each others' ideas.
- Explore different points of view, making sure there is room for respectful disagreement.
- Listen and respond to others empathetically.
- Share the "air time" and ensure that everyone's voice is heard.
- Ask several people to help describe the problem and share perspectives on why it's a problem.
- Identify goals for solving the problem—what do you hope will change as a result of "working it out"?
- Develop several desirable solutions to choose from.
- Ask open-ended questions to gain a deeper understanding of various suggestions.
- Evaluate advantages and disadvantages of various solutions—does this solution work for some people at the expense of others? Does everyone get something they need so it feels like it will work for them?
- Encourage as many students as possible to speak, even if their comments are in agreement with others who have already spoken. This is the way you begin to get a good "read" on the direction the group seems to want to go.
- Summarize the discussion and state what the group seems to think are the most important things to incorporate in the best solution.
- Use straw polls and a consensus process to reach your decision.

- Have the class or a small group plan precisely how the solution will be implemented. The class should also be able to suggest ways to evaluate how effectively the solution achieves the goal of the meeting.

Although you want to communicate your expectation that students will become comfortable facilitating class meetings over time, you will probably want to model the problem-solving process the first few times. You may want to invite three or four volunteers who are interested in facilitating meetings to be part of a class meeting–planning group that plans agendas.

It's important to appreciate that facilitating regular class meetings can feel a bit risky to many teachers. It's an open-ended process. You can't invite students to discuss an issue of concern thoughtfully if you already assume that you have the right solution at hand before you even begin. Yet teachers who have taken this risk have shared with me how their classrooms have been transformed by making class meetings the foundation of classroom management. As one teacher put it, "I was anxious about using class meetings because if I did it right I knew I would not be completely in charge. I was already a good problem solver, and I knew my goal was to help my students become better problem solvers. After using class meetings for a month, I noticed that the climate shifted. The more students felt this was their process, the more attuned they became to working out issues that got in the way of making our classroom a good place to be." Class meetings enable teachers and students to practice their conflict resolution tools and skills authentically.

## Cooperative Learning Strategies

In his book *Nobody Left to Hate,* which was written shortly after the Columbine shootings, Eliot Aronson makes a compelling case for building collaboration and empathy in the classroom through the use of cooperative learning strategies. He urges us to think about the atmosphere created by the process of learning, noting that how we learn in the classroom influences whether we learn and what we learn. Do we encourage excessive competition where winners and losers are predestined? Or do we create a learning environment where everyone is expected to work together, look out for each other, and acknowledge the collective talents and insights that each person brings to the task at hand?[6]

Cooperative learning is an intentional restructuring of the learning process where students share a common purpose to complete tasks in ways that include every group member. Especially when activities are structured for "positive interdependence," one student's success is linked to the success of others.[7] A cornerstone of effective group work is the use of the "jigsaw" process where each student brings information, research, or resources to the group that is necessary for full understanding of the problem and successful completion of the task or final product.

Students who work together are learning how to get along together. When students engage in cooperative activities they are developing lifelong social skills by learning how to communicate in ways that encourage listening and understanding; deal effectively with people's differences in work styles, skills, interests, and points of view; acknowledge the contributions of others as they help each other and ensure that everyone is included; share leadership roles and responsibilities, and accountability; and practice the kind of "give and take" necessary to make decisions and plans that everyone agrees to implement.

The skills cited above reflect the same skill set necessary for effective conflict resolution. In classrooms, we often assume that students know what collaboration is and we assume that they know how to cooperate. Neither of these assumptions is necessarily valid. Cooperative learning provides the opportunity for teaching and practicing these skills intentionally. At the same time, we are also communicating the message that every student's voice matters and every student has something important to contribute.

## Monitoring and Assessing Social Skill Practice

It's not enough to teach and practice skills that promote group cooperation and interpersonal effectiveness. Logical next steps include observing how students practice these social skills and providing feedback that can help students use these skills more regularly and more effectively. At the same time we want to help students build their internal capacities to monitor their own behavior, assess themselves, and set goals for improvement.

One of the biggest benefits of integrating conflict resolution into daily classroom practice is the opportunity for students to strengthen their metacognitive skills. Conflict resolution education strategies help us slow down and think about what we're doing, why we're doing it, and how we might do it better. Teachers who take time to monitor, observe, and assess students' social skills create a learning culture that supports reflection and invites self-correction. Here are three suggestions that can make monitoring and assessing social skills a core classroom practice.

First, develop a list of specific behaviors and attitudes that indicate active participation and effective use of social skills by taking cues from agreements, procedures, and expectations that you have established. A group of middle school teachers generated the following list of active participation indicators:

- Raises thoughtful questions that help the class gain a deeper understanding of an issue or topic of discussion
- Takes a leadership role in carrying out an activity
- Gives helpful feedback about class activities and experiences
- Takes on various roles and responsibilities in small-group learning activities
- Shares resources and materials fairly
- Gives words of encouragement to other students
- Shows appreciation for other students' contributions
- Participates in problem solving when issues and concerns arise that affect the group and the class
- Volunteers when help is needed
- Takes a risk to try things that are new and challenging
- Shows friendliness toward other class members
- Puts out positive energy when the group needs it
- Shows ability to work effectively with different students
- Listens to others without interrupting
- Respects other people's personal space and comfort zones
- Disagrees with others in ways that are respectful

Second, use your list as a starting point to achieve a number of important functions, such as:

- Document students' participation grades, checking the behaviors you notice and jotting down observations that give you a snapshot of each student's skills.
- Provide personal feedback to students.
- Help students set goals for themselves and then assess how they're meeting their chosen goals.
- Identify specific social goals that you will be observing during a learning activity.
- Invite student groups to identify three skills they want to be observed using during a cooperative learning activity.
- Engage individuals and groups in written and verbal reflections that enable them to assess their strengths as well as skills they find challenging.

Third, cultivate the habit of noticing and recognizing students' use of social skills. Provide daily opportunities for you and students to give concrete, immediate feedback about what you and they are learning and experiencing in the classroom. This process can be as simple as a "thumbs up, thumb down, thumbs in the middle" assessment about the practice of a particular social skill or a more deliberate assessment of group process that might include these kinds of questions:

- What are some of the ways each person in your group participated and/or contributed?
- What skills, tools, and attitudes helped your group to complete your task successfully?
- What situations, actions, or statements made it more difficult for the group to work together effectively and how did the group handle these challenges?
- How could you have worked together to be more effective?
- What positive leadership, communication, and conflict resolution skills could you practice to improve the way you work together in the future?

## Building Positive Connections Through Gatherings and Closings

When students and teachers know each other well, they are more likely to trust that their classroom will be a safe and supportive place for them to grow and learn. Gatherings, closings, sharing circles, or morning meetings all provide a structure for listening and speaking in ways that communicate respect, understanding, and empathy—core principles of conflict resolution education.

Chip suggests that taking the time to share stories, responses to interesting questions, appreciations, or reflections about what's going on in children's lives creates a powerful opportunity to know and be known. Through expressing one's own thoughts and feelings and hearing from their peers, students strengthen the feeling that we are all important and we all have something important to say.

Gathering activities set the stage for learning by inviting everyone to participate in a brief common experience, where everyone is acknowledged and everyone is invited to share. An important guideline for gatherings is respecting the "right to pass"—the choice to only listen is as powerful as the choice to speak. Gatherings usually take about ten or fifteen minutes and might begin with a question or sentence stem to which everyone is invited to respond. Topics should be ones that all students can comment on without feeling embarrassed or defensive. Invite students to generate topics and questions that they'd like to include. Here are a few sample starters:

What's something new and good in your life right now?

What's something you'd like to learn about or learn how to do that's currently not offered here at school?

What is the best present you've ever received? Why was it special?

What's one schoolwide rule that you would change to make school a better place for everyone?

What do you think are the qualities of a good friend?

What's something you're good at that ends with "ing"?

Name something you hate to spend time doing and something you love to spend free time doing.

Name one word that describes how you feel today and why.

Gatherings are a great Monday morning starter and serve as a good transition activity during the school day in a self-contained classroom. In secondary classes they can provide a needed change of pace during the week's activities. Because gatherings open up a lot of personal information, teachers get a fuller picture of who their kids are. The informal data gleaned from gatherings can provide direction for future interactions and instructional approaches with individual students.

Closing activities provide a way to wrap up the time the group has spent together and send off the group at the end of class or the end of the week. Like gatherings, closings create opportunities for every student to be heard. Where gatherings focus mostly on sharing personal stories and reflections, closings provide an excellent vehicle for students to give feedback on what they've experienced in class, communicate what they've learned, and assess their progress and personal development. The quick "read" you get from the group can help shape what you do the next day or guide changes you make to your instructional plan. A few examples include:

- Tell us in five words or less, what's the most important thing you learned today about yourself, about the group, about the topic?
- What's a banner headline of five words or less that would best summarize what we did, learned, and discussed in class?
- When you feel discouraged, what do you say to yourself to keep going?
- What's the best thing that happened to you this week?
- What's one thing you're looking forward to this weekend?
- What's something you've accomplished this week that you're proud of?

One of my favorite sayings sums up the goal of gatherings and closings: "I don't care to know what you know unless I know that you care about me." Making time for personal sharing offers the opportunity to connect. It lets students know that you want to know who they are.

◆ ◆ ◆

In conclusion, effective conflict resolution education programs are built on a foundation of positive adult modeling, developmentally appropriate direct skill instruction for students, and prosocial schoolwide and classroom practices. These core elements of CRE can be implemented in any school by all teachers regardless of grade level or academic discipline. When kids and adults have opportunities to learn and practice their conflict resolution tools and skills throughout the day with each other and their peers, schools can become places where caring and conflict resolution is the norm rather than the exception and kids can become powerful contributors in healthy, civic communities—at school and beyond.

# PART TWO

# WHAT WORKS
## Success Stories in Conflict Resolution Education

# CHAPTER FOUR

# THE HEART OF THE MATTER
## Social and Emotional Learning as a Foundation for Conflict Resolution Education

Rachael Kessler

Anger, frustration, yearning, hurt, and sadness—all these emotions can arise when our needs, beliefs, or desires come into conflict with those of another person in our world. Peace, joy, relief, excitement, tenderness, and surprise—all these can attend the reconciliation between people or groups who have overcome great differences to resolve a conflict. Conflict is resonant with feeling. Teaching and learning about conflict takes us directly or indirectly into these feelings. How we manage our own feelings (intrapersonal intelligence) and how we respond to the feelings of others (interpersonal intelligence) are crucial to our ability to engage in the constructive problem-solving behavior that is a primary goal of conflict resolution education (CRE).

In this chapter, I briefly introduce the framework of emotional intelligence and explore its implications for CRE. Finally, I suggest some strategies from the field of social and emotional learning (SEL) that can help lay the foundation for effectively introducing students to conflict resolution.

## Emotional Intelligence: A Brief Introduction

The capacity to resolve conflict is one of several social skills essential to a broader competency that Daniel Goleman has called emotional literacy.[1] Emotional literacy includes being aware of emotions, managing emotions, being motivated to overcome setbacks, being empathetic, and developing social skills (including communication and conflict resolution). [2]

*Self-awareness* is the foundation without which the other capacities cannot develop. First, we must help our students know themselves—know what they feel, need, believe. Only when they know what they are feeling can they begin to *manage* those feelings—that is, to express or contain or transform those feelings in constructive ways.

*Motivation* as an emotional intelligence is, according to Goleman, the capacity to keep going despite setbacks. When the going gets tough, what sustains us? What allows us to persist despite frustration, fear, or even failure? This kind of motivation bears a strong resemblance to what others have called resilience.

*Empathy* is the bridge from the emotional to the social capacities. When we are self-aware—knowing what something feels like inside ourselves—we can begin to recognize and know what it feels like in another. And, in many instances, empathy requires not only self-awareness but also the second emotional intelligence: we need to *manage* our own feelings and beliefs well enough to turn the volume down so that we can see and hear the feelings and beliefs of others.

Finally we come to *social skills,* which include the ability to communicate, to build healthy relationships, and to resolve conflicts. Each of the previous building blocks is essential to helping people learn the skills for dealing constructively with conflict.

## Emotional Intelligence and Conflict Resolution: An Essential Partnership

The relationship between emotional intelligence and CRE can be seen most easily by taking a closer look at the six-step model that appears in many CRE programs.

1. Calm down; agree to solve the problem.
2. No name-calling or put-downs.
3. Use "I messages" to express your feelings and needs.
4. Listen to the other person carefully.
5. Look for solutions that are best for both.
6. Choose the best solution.

Let's examine this sequence, looking at the social and emotional skills that are preconditions for the success of each step.

## Calm Down

Telling someone to calm down is rarely effective. Even telling ourselves to calm down may not be enough. How do we help children learn how to calm down—or "self-soothe."

We have to know that we're getting angry or afraid before we can calm that anger or soothe that fear. This may sound simple, but recall how easy it is to find yourself escalating an argument that can become quite destructive before you even realize that you are angry. Once our anger or fear is triggered, we have only a momentary opportunity to soothe ourselves before the "old brain," the reptilian brain, takes over and we are in fight-or-flight mode. "The hijacking occurs in an instant, triggering this reaction crucial moments before the neocortex, the thinking brain, has had a chance to glimpse fully what is happening."[3] Once we are "emotionally hijacked" we are no longer on the pathway of constructive problem solving. Creativity and critical thinking—the higher-order thinking skills needed to propose and evaluate new solutions—are frozen when the brain has been hijacked by fear. So learning how first to recognize what we feel (self-awareness) and then quickly to identify a strategy for self-soothing (handling emotions) is essential to keeping our minds and hearts open to resolving the conflict that triggered our emotions.

## No Name-Calling or Put-Downs

If a child has succeeded in calming down, he may indeed be able to resist calling names. In Goleman's schema, this ability too would be considered part of *managing emotions,* the category that includes the ability to delay and control impulses. In my own work in SEL, the Passages approach, I have found a different method. I discovered that obedience to a rule-based respect is not very dependable in any circumstance and is particularly risky in the heat of conflict. "To believe that one can teach respect through coercion," say Brendtro and Long, "is to confuse respect with obedience."[4] Authentic respect arises from meaningful connection. When students feel connected to themselves, they can respect themselves—a precondition for respecting others. When students experience a genuine connection to others, they begin to feel empathy, respect, and sometimes even compassion. This experience of respect based in empathy is far more likely to preempt a student's impulse to hurl names or put-downs than the restraint that comes from following a rule.

## Use "I Messages" to Express Your Feelings and Needs

In this step we are focusing on the skill set of effective communication: speaking authentically and with acknowledgment of personal responsibility and, in step four, listening deeply to understand. Students are often prepared for speaking authentically by practicing I messages, which often go like this:

I feel _____ when _____
because _____.
And I need _____.

    But it is not enough to learn the formula, no matter how creative or experiential the training. When it comes time for resolving a real conflict in the classroom, students cannot use I messages unless they can identify what they are feeling, have the vocabulary to express what they are feeling, and feel safe enough in the classroom to express a genuine feeling.

    Classroom safety is critical to the student's ability not only to say the I message out loud but also to identify his feelings. A student's capacity for self-awareness can be dependent on the safety of the classroom. In an atmosphere of disrespect or threat, a student may not even be able to know what he is feeling.

    Later in this chapter, we will look at how strategies from the field of SEL can support the growth of safety in the classroom and can help students learn how to identify and express their feelings.

## Listen to the Other Person Carefully

There are many forms of listening. There is *not listening,* when a conflict has so aroused the fight-or-flight chemistry that the brain keeps running an angry and defensive patter in the mind while the other person speaks. There is *listening to find fault* in the other person's statement so we can pounce on her argument when we next get the floor. Then there is *listening carefully*—with a care that begins with genuine attention, moves into the respectfulness of an open mind and heart, and culminates in understanding and empathy. Our students can engage in *empathic* listening when they have developed the ability to take the perspective of others. This capacity to take multiple perspectives is an important building block for the creativity and critical thinking that leads to the constructive problem solving described in the final two steps.

## Look for Solutions That Are Best for Both, and Choose the Best Solution

Once again, self-awareness is crucial as a student looks inside to see the deeper need that underlies conflict. Negotiators have taught us that a creative solution often arises when we attend to the genuine needs of the two people and not to the positions that appear to provoke intractable conflict. Empathy is crucial to listening to and respecting the needs of the other. Safety in the classroom is important here because inquiring into our needs and expressing our needs can cause us to feel very vulnerable. Safety is also a key to encouraging creative and critical thinking. In an interview for *Educational Leadership,* Renate Caine explains the basis for this principle in terms of brain function: "When we feel threatened, we down-shift our thinking. Downshifted people feel helpless; they don't look at possibilities; they don't feel safe to take risks or challenge old ideas. . . . Real thinking —making connections, higher-order thinking, and creativity—is incompatible with that kind of environment."[5]

Finding a solution that works for two people in conflict also requires the participants to manage their feelings of frustration, impatience, disappointment, and fear that may come up along the way. The motivation that makes it possible to find a solution involves the ability to maintain hope and optimism despite set-backs.[6] The social skills of effective communication, problem solving, and sensitivity to others also contribute to the discovery of a fair and enduring solution.

◆ ◆ ◆

Of course, CRE is far broader and deeper than this six-step model. CRE develops awareness about attitudes toward conflict and toward dealing with differences and prejudice. It develops an appreciation for different learning styles, beliefs, attitudes, and talents that can lead to enrichment when we learn how to effectively manage and resolve conflict. The effectiveness of dialogues, role plays, paired-shares, and personal storytelling that go into developing awareness and responsibility in these areas is also dependent on a foundation of social and emotional skills.

## Laying the Foundation: The Caring Learning Community

What follows is a brief description of strategies that can lay the foundation to support a successful CRE program. For over fifteen years, I have worked with teams of educators around the country in both private and public school settings to create curriculum, methodology, and teacher development that can nurture the inner life of young people as part of school life. I call this approach the Passages Program—a set of principles and practices for working with adolescents that integrates heart, spirit, and community with strong academics. This curriculum of the heart is a response to the "mysteries" of teenagers, and their usually unspoken questions and concerns are at its center.

I first discovered this approach at the Crossroads School in Santa Monica, California, where I worked for seven years as chair of its department of human development, building the team that created the Mysteries program. In the 1990s, I began to take the gifts of Mysteries into schools around the country—

adapting, refining, and expanding the curriculum to include what I learned from colleagues in the new and growing field of SEL.

In some schools, Passages is a course or advisory period focused on learning the life skills of self-awareness, meaningful communication, building healthy relationships, learning readiness, and personal and social responsibility. In other schools, teachers have been trained to integrate the principles and practices of Passages into teaching an academic subject. What follows is a brief summary of the activities of the Passages Program, during my time there as program coordinator.

## Creating Classroom Agreements

To achieve the safety and openness required for meaningful exploration and resolution of conflict and diversity, students and teachers worked together carefully for weeks. We collaboratively created agreements—conditions that students named as essential for speaking about what matters most to them. Together we made a list (and these lists look remarkably similar from class to class, age to age, and year to year). The list included the following "ground rules":

No interruptions

No put-downs or "bagging"

No judging

Respect

Honesty

Fairness

I added certain "nonnegotiables" after the students came to the end of their brainstorm. First was "the right to pass." Students become accustomed to having their participation measured by speaking, and I wanted to ensure that in this realm of personal feelings, they could make choices that honored their own rhythms and boundaries. I also added "the willingness to forgive" because, as human beings, we are bound to make mistakes sometimes. We may violate one of these agreements, but that doesn't have to be the end of our trust. If we are willing to work on forgiveness, we can heal and even strengthen our classroom community. (Some CRE programs take this even further, offering the skills and strategies needed for forgiveness and reconciliation through programs in restorative justice.)

I found that students were most active in generating agreements to handle their conflicts. The students experienced a sense of ownership of the ground rules for the classroom; in the months that followed, they were much more willing to honor them than they would have been had the rules been imposed from "outside."

## Building a Vocabulary of Emotions

Developing a vocabulary of the emotions is another important step in fostering the communication needed to resolve conflict. This vocabulary can be taught in ways that are playful and creative, using the arts to illustrate ideas through color, metaphor, movement, and gesture as well as direct verbal explanation. In working to develop this vocabulary, students also cultivate self-awareness through the use of these words in reflection and writing about their own lives; they also develop empathy by sharing this reflection with others.

Using the Passages approach, we found that *symbols* are a powerful way to help students move quickly and deeply into their feelings. "Take some time this week to think about what is really important to you in your life right now," we ask the high school seniors in a course designed to be a rite of passage from adolescence to adulthood. "Then find an object that can symbolize what you realize is so important to you now." The following are some student responses that show the depth of their thinking:

> "This raggedy old doll belonged to my mother. I have been cut off from my mother during most of high school. We just couldn't get along. But now that we know I'm going to leave soon, we have suddenly discovered each other again. I love her so much. My relationship to my mother is what is really important to me now."

> "I wear this ring around my neck. It belongs to my father, but he has lent it to me. It's his wedding ring, and my parents are divorced. My father travels a lot and I worry about him. It feels good to have his ring close to my heart. And it reminds me of how precious relationships are. And how fragile."

A principal in Canada told me the story of a first- and second-grade class she taught in which she worked with symbols:

> I talked with my students about life being like a journey. As little as they were, they seemed to understand. They drew pictures about their journey. We talked about their journeys. Then I asked them to look for an object in nature that reminded them of themselves and of their journey. A first-grade girl brought in a tiny pine cone. She said, "This pine cone is at the beginning of its life as a tree. It reminds me of me because I'm at the beginning of my journey as a person." A second-grade boy brought in two jars filled with shells. "I call these brain shells," he said pointing to the first jar. "They remind me of me because I'm very smart." Then he held up the jar in which the same shells were crushed. "These crushed shells remind me of me too. They remind me of how hard I am on myself when I don't do things just right."

Symbols are particularly important for adolescents because they allow unique expression at a time when young people need to create a separate sense of self. We can see that even for young children, symbols lead to powerful self-awareness and meaningful communication, and can be used effectively in the classroom.

Symbols can be used as a private exercise in self-awareness: "Draw or sculpt a symbol of what you are feeling right now. You don't need to show it to anyone else. It's just for you." "Write a metaphor about what friendship means to you. You can share it with the group or keep it for yourself, putting it in your folder to look at when the semester ends."

Whether students communicate their feelings and thoughts to each other or just for themselves, expression is also important for developing the ability to manage emotions. If a person has no opportunities for appropriate expression, the effort to manage his or her emotions can be misdirected into the suppression of feelings, which often leads to ill health and unexpected outbursts when the pressure builds up. In addition to encouraging appropriate expression, SEL programs (and many CRE programs as well) take students through lessons in anger management. Students learn to recognize the signs of anger rising in themselves or others, develop strategies for calming that anger in themselves before it leads to "emotional hijacking," and prevent the eruption of anger by understanding patterns of how their anger is triggered and what they do that triggers the anger of others. In addition, students can learn the dynamics of fear and even shame and discover the resources that people can use to manage fear and shame.

## Listening and Speaking

Deep listening and authentic speaking are two other practices that ensure safety in the classroom. Students learn to listen without interruption, questions, or immediate response, practicing first in pairs and later in sharing circles. Deep listening is a gift in its own right and can also be an important precondition to the skill of *active listening,* which is important in the negotiation process. Authentic speaking is encouraged by deep listening because students can look inside for what they want to say only if no one is prompting them with questions or reassuring and guiding them with encouraging comments. This kind of speaking helps students cultivate self-awareness and clarify their identity.

Practicing deep listening in a circle has a powerful impact on building classroom community. In Passages, we call this the practice of Council—a highly structured way of sharing words and silence. In Council, each person is given an opportunity to speak without interruption or immediate response. Usually the students are responding to a theme raised by the teacher. Often we go around the circle, and anyone is free to pass. In some settings, teachers add a ritual dimension to Council, such as using a talking stone or stick or other objects from nature. Students may also add a meaningful centerpiece for their circle, such as something from nature or a special symbol. In the Passages approach to Council, we often choose a student to be timekeeper who gently enforces a time limit so that no one is left out because others have gone on too long. We invite a round of "connections" after each student who wants to has spoken. Connections are a time to let someone know that she has moved you or that her story has reminded you of something similar or very different in your own experience.

Over time, the practice of Council encourages the quiet students to begin to speak because they do not have to fight for their turn. Their once-hidden thoughtfulness and wisdom begin to captivate the students who have previously dominated the conversation. All the students learn to listen deeply and discover what it feels like to be truly heard. Feeling seen and known by their peers and teachers, students begin to feel a sense of belonging that increases their resilience and their willingness to speak vulnerably about feelings and needs.

Respect is essential to the Council process. Respect for the speaker is conveyed when we do not interrupt with probing questions, advice, or anecdotes. Respect for the listeners is conveyed by speakers who learn to speak briefly and to the essence of their story rather than rambling on. Respect for the personal timing and solitude of young people is expressed when we encourage students to choose when they want to speak, at what level they want to share, and whether they want to speak at all.

Let me illustrate with a story from a Council held years ago, during which students grappled with the deeper issues of conflict in the world and in their hearts and minds.

The outbreak of the Gulf War was a deeply troubling moment for our school. Parents of high school seniors were worried about their boys being taken. Students, teachers, and parents alike were struggling with the moral and political dilemmas of going to war. I was teaching at an extremely progressive school, and many of the faculty were veterans of the teach-ins of the 1960s. We decided to hold a teach-in that week to examine the issues in Kuwait. The whole school, close to a thousand of us out on the basketball court, listened to speakers representing different points of view. The last speaker, a young man from Kuwait, spoke of the suffering of his people and expressed his gratitude for U.S. support. From a large contingent of antiwar students came the muffled but discernible sound of hissing and booing when he asserted the need for the United States to send troops.

At eight the next morning, when I met with my tenth-grade human development class, I thought to myself, *What better time, what better place to discuss all the feelings that were roiling about the war than this class in which we had worked so carefully to create the safety for authentic communication?* I knew it was essential to suspend the topic I had planned for that week (we were in the midst of a series on human sexuality). The students looked both relieved and apprehensive when I said we would use our Council to talk about the war. The first few comments were brief and matter-of-fact. Then Mikaela spoke.

"I feel so confused," she began. "I'm definitely against war. So I don't think we should be getting involved. I think it's a big mistake. I think it's immoral." Then her voice began to quaver. "But yesterday . . . at the teach-in . . . when that young student spoke . . . the one from Kuwait." She looked around the circle and took in the attentive eyes, the heads nodding in recognition. "He was so sad . . . so scared. His family is in such danger! Such terrible things are happening to his people. And when he told us what was true, what was real for him and for his people, our students jeered and booed him!" She began to cry. "Can you believe they did that?" she looked earnestly around the circle again. "Can you believe they would do that? How could they? He's a human being, with real feelings and beliefs. I don't happen to agree with his beliefs either. But how can we do that to each other? Just because we don't agree, how can we treat each other that way?"

She passed the smooth stone to her left. Many of us were in tears. The room was silent for a while.

Mikaela had challenged us to see how easily our humanity is eroded when politics became more important than people. The students who followed spoke passionately about their own feelings for or against the war. Their views were often polarized, yet each was listened to with great interest and compassion. I had never before seen such a hot political issue explored with such mutual respect among adversaries—not among teenagers and not among adults.

The principles and practices we've looked at in this section allowed this group the power to hold conflict in ways that did not splinter the group but increased its strength and maturity. The safety of our classroom community, the profound respect that emerged from weeks of deep listening, the practices that helped students clarify their own identity and speak authentically about their feelings and views—this constellation of experiences allowed these young teenagers to be courageous and articulate in expressing feelings and ideas that were certain to provoke disagreement among their peers.

## Tailoring Programs for Different Settings and Ages

Passages has been successful in private as well as public schools. The methodology has been used in a separate course in human development or in an advisory-like structure. In other schools, it has been infused into academic classrooms. The methods for building community and facilitating meaningful communication are very effective in helping students deal with others who seem very different from themselves in their beliefs, culture, gender, and race.

Although my own experience with the Passages approach has been with middle school and high school students, I have worked with many teachers who adapt these teaching strategies to the elementary classroom. Also, many teachers, like the Canadian principal cited earlier, have intuitively created similar strategies to promote the social and emotional learning of their students. With younger children, shorter time frames are usually more effective—for example, holding a minute of silence rather than the five minutes that middle students can build to effectively. When younger children practice Council, they may each speak to a theme for less than a minute, whereas adolescents have the patience to listen for two or three minutes per person and often have much to say once they feel safe. Playfulness and movement are often most comfortable for elementary school children and for older adolescents. During early and middle adolescence, many students become inhibited and threatened by improvisation games or dance, although they seem to immensely enjoy watching others who are still comfortable with these activities.

## Engaging Parents

Parents play a vital role in the Passages approach. First, we engage in dialogue with parents about our objectives and methods in a way that is responsive and respectful to their deeply held beliefs and values. Ideally, parents will not only hear about these teaching strategies but also experience them for themselves. On back-to-school night for middle school parents, we briefly introduce the course and then lead the parents in several activities. First, a game allows them to loosen up and connect at a playful level. Then we invite them to experience a Council in which each parent may talk about what is difficult for her about raising an early adolescent and what she is discovering is really working for her and her family. Parents appreciate not only being informed of what their children will experience in the class but also having the opportunity to learn from the wisdom of other parents and to share their own.

In classes designed to support critical transitions in the life cycle, such as the high school "senior passage" or the eighth-grade transition out of middle school and into high school, we also create a ceremony toward the end of the course that includes parents. Practicing a "witness council," parents create a circle of support around an inner circle of the young people, who talk about how they are feeling at this moment of endings and leavings and big decisions. Asked to bear witness to what they have just seen and heard, parents often express immense gratitude for the thoughtfulness, eloquence, and maturity they see in the students. Then the parents go into the center, and the students form the witness circle. Students get to hear how other people's parents, as well as their own, are feeling as the students make this critical transition. They listen to the fears, nostalgia, excitement, pride, and regrets. Then we ask parents to look back in memory to when their child was very small. They picture a very precious moment with their child as a toddler. Then they look at their child now as an adolescent or young adult child. And we ask each parent to speak directly to his son or daughter, letting the child know how he sees and feels the child's growth.

## Cultivating the Teaching Presence

There is one final dimension to creating a caring learning community in which CRE can flourish—what I have called the *teaching presence*. Because "we teach who we are," teachers who invite personal sharing into the classroom also find it essential to nurture their own capacities to safely and appropriately give and receive vulnerable testimony about feelings, needs, and challenging issues.[7] Teachers may engage in personal practices to cultivate awareness and compassion as well as in collaborative efforts with other teachers to create mutual support for the challenges and joys of entering this terrain with their students.

The capacity of the teacher to *care* deeply for students is the foundation of "the teaching presence" and fosters the capacity of students to care deeply for one another. When students don't trust adults—a common phenomenon in today's society—they are not motivated to learn from us. "The bonds that transmit basic human values from elders to the young are unraveling," write Brendtro, Van Bockern, and Clementson in an article about why so many youth are wary of adults.[8] Particularly in a discipline like CRE, which requires students to talk about feelings, needs, and social issues, students need to know their teachers care. If a CRE curriculum is implemented in a mechanical or halfhearted way—if teachers are not genuinely caring about either their students or the subject and if teachers are not modeling the principles and practices in the relationships their students witness—young people become cynical about conflict resolution and shut down their interest in learning about it.

◆ ◆ ◆

Most educators in SEL programs consider conflict resolution to be a set of skills that are essential to integrate into a comprehensive program. Many conflict resolution educators similarly consider the practices and principles of the field of SEL critical to the implementation of a comprehensive approach to their discipline. Some programs have been conceived as an integrated blend of the two. Each field has much to gain by looking deeply into the connections between CRE and SEL. We can learn from each other's more specialized gifts and offer our students a set of experiences, skills, and attitudes that will bring greater harmony, authenticity, and peace to their own lives and to the life of our planet. Our students are hungry for meaningful connection, and these skills and practices are essential tools for youth as they learn how to work out their own problems and build their own respectful relationships.

# In Their Own Words

## "I Know That I Have Grown a Lot Emotionally"

*Lincoln Junior High School has been working in CRE for over five years. The school is located in a suburb of Fort Collins, Colorado, and has lower test scores than other schools in the district. It works with the most diverse and most needy population in the area. With a grant from the district back in 1996, a team of teachers took a five-day class from a local training organization and came back ready to implement a peer mediation and conflict resolution program. One of those teachers, Colleen Conrad, was transformed by the process, and over the last five years has become one of the leading figures in her district for implementing SEL strategies in the classroom. Randy, one of the editors of this book, spoke with ten ninth graders who are taking honors English with Colleen Conrad. The students are Carmin Jones, Ashley Manzaneres, Megan Charles, Daniel Workman, Ethan Mapes, Cameron Rosen, Wilson Cecil, Kelley Burke, Jamie Anderson, and Ian Ebersole. Listening to the voices of these students, one hears about a classroom that has a different way of being, of learning, and of expressing itself.*

What stands out most with the ninth graders in this English class is the difference that open, honest class discussions had made in creating a sense of community. "I think that chemistry in a class is really important. If you don't like the people you are in a class with, then normally you are not going to like the subject at all until you get a better class. I consider everybody in the class my friend and so I feel honest and open when I talk to them in discussions. I think that the discussions bring us closer together as a class," says Carmin.

"The discussions break down a lot of judgments about a lot of people. You go in and you think 'So and so does this so I don't want to be with them.' There are so many stereotypes. You see the people and see that they are just like me—they may not act exactly like me but they are like me. We have come to still respect each other even though we may have completely different perspectives. Even though we have different opinions, we still like hearing each other's opinions. You learn things from other people and you can apply them to your life too."

One of the boys in the group, Jamie, says this about the class: "We are all pretty much one big happy family. We have classroom meetings all the time. We all share our own point of views and nobody yells at you for saying 'You're wrong, this is the way it is.'" Ian's favorite part of the class is "everybody having a sense of friendship. Everybody connects." He says, "Basically everybody is a friend in that class."

Having a sense of community where everyone treats each other with respect and camaraderie also leads to a more relaxed atmosphere for interacting academically, according to Ethan. "It makes presentations easier. . . . It is nice having a class where there isn't anybody trying to act cool." Cameron agrees: "I don't get as nervous [when I talk or present]. There are no kids trying to be like big and bad or anything. We all respect each other. It just makes everything easier because we know that whatever we are going to do, other people aren't going to make fun of what other people think." Wilson also likes the feeling that has developed in the class. "It is kind of a closer environment, like camaraderie or something. It develops a relaxed atmosphere. It is definitely closer than any other class." The ease of sharing openly without fear of ridicule is a powerful force for learning and growth for these students.

Ashley confides that other classes aren't meaningful enough to her life. "A lot of other classes are kind of boring. You feel comfortable in this class because you can talk about anything you want. You can get questions answered. Right now, I'm so frustrated with my math class and I have talked to my teacher about it because I am learning stuff I know that I am never going to use. It is so hard to learn it. In this class, our teacher makes you think. I am a totally different person than when I started this class in eighth grade, and a lot of it is because of the emotional stuff, the internal thinking that we have done."

Learning about the emotional side of life is appealing to these youth. Says Daniel, "[Our teacher] mostly asks us more of what we feel more than factual information. It's kind of nice . . . to write about what we feel." It is also providing not only academic growth but deep personal growth as well. Says Megan, "It helps me understand people better, even adults. We are doing the kind of emotional discoveries that my mom says people don't make until they are in their forties. [Our teacher] is forcing us to move outside the box and think for ourselves. I know it is going to help me in the long run and help everything make sense. I feel like I am gearing myself up for college." Says Jamie, "You grow emotionally because you have to think about your assignments and you have to reach deep inside yourself and try to find out the answer to the essential question. I know that I have grown a lot emotionally." Ian adds, "It is not like math where you question the significance of the stuff you are doing. In this class we use the values that we brought out of ourselves that we didn't really know we had."

In addition to class discussions, students develop emotional intelligence through various curricular issues that naturally highlight this competency. According to Megan, "We are working a lot on prejudice. You hear this all throughout your life, 'Don't judge anybody, treat everybody equal,' but something about the way [the teacher] does it really makes you promise to yourself that you won't [be prejudiced]. You really understand what they are saying about prejudice—it's not the same clichés all the time." Jamie echoes this thought: "We do a lot of stuff dealing with racism and letting us know what other people—who aren't white or don't live in the United States or aren't wealthy—go through, like with the Japanese and the Civil War and World War II. We learn what they went through emotionally and we just build from that and learn how to talk socially from that." And, says Ian, they learn "what a single person can do."

"I think that most of the assignments . . . make you think a lot deeper than most of my other classes because in those classes it is basically 'Do the work, get it done, get a good grade.' Some of her assignments make you think more about yourself," says Kelley. All of the teacher's books and class projects seek to "help you understand what the author was writing about and see if you can relate that with your life," says Jamie. Ian says, "In this class we learn the emotional histories of people, like what people were thinking during the civil rights movements and the women's rights movements . . . not just the facts about everything. We learn how their lives were being treated."

For some of the students, however, the class can get repetitious. Says Cameron, "It can be bad sometimes because it ends up coming down to the same thing, what the values are. I don't have a problem with that but a lot of the time it just ends up being the same after awhile." Wilson agrees, "[Our teacher] has a lot of good ideas . . . but sometimes she lets that turn into what she expects us to think, like what we should be thinking. After a time that gets useless because after a time my writing turns from what I feel into what I know she wants me to feel." We talked more about this powerful concern, but the students didn't have too many answers about how to avoid this "group-think." Some felt that the class should learn from books that don't have such a strong moral or social justice perspective. Perhaps there can be too much of a good thing.

Whether this is true or not, a teacher's grading assistant for the class who happened to be present during this interview felt that a main purpose of the class was to eschew group-think and encourage individual thinking. She was surprised that a student would "feel pressure to say what the teacher wanted him to say, especially in that class." From her point of view, the teacher "treats their opinions with such respect that she would take the issue seriously. She would probably want to make that the topic for a class discussion. Some teachers would think it was really out of line, but she would say, 'OK, let's talk about that. Why do you feel this way?'" Nonetheless, the opinion expressed was an important one that we should sincerely seek to understand.

In the process of learning about others less advantaged than themselves, the students were learning a lot about who they are, what they believe, and how to stand up for themselves. Says Megan, "Being a teenager, you are really focused on yourself and your own little world. She is teaching us to focus on things besides ourselves while still working on our own personalities and finding out who we are. We are still helping other people and getting outside our own little world, and it's really good." Ashley says, "When I first came into this class, I didn't want to join in the discussions because I was too shy or afraid that [the others] might think

I am stupid or something. But now after being in this class, I am not afraid to stand up for what I believe in and do what is right, or what I think is right. Even if I don't agree with somebody in the class, I know that I can get my perspective across to the class to tell them what I think."

Carmin continues, "When I came into eighth grade I kind of wanted to be like everybody else, but I never will so I've got to find myself. This class has helped me find who I am so I haven't had to pursue who others are to be like them. It has made me stronger in myself. I am also not afraid to do things anymore. I have strength in myself and I trust myself more. Parents are always talking about midlife crisis. I don't think that anybody in this class will have a midlife crisis because we are going through the types of evaluation that everybody talks about when they go through their whole midlife crisis stuff. So I think that it is really good and it has just helped a lot." Ian says it directly: "This class makes you want to stand up for yourself."

As teenagers, students can sometimes feel discriminated against because of their age. They often don't feel respected by adults. Kelley feels differently in this class and sums it up this way: "I feel a lot of people are discriminated against because of their age. This class makes you feel more important because you can express your opinion and find out what you do believe in. We are not treated like two-year-olds like we are in a lot of other places, because we get respect from each other and from the teacher—and that makes you feel important."

The way the class is structured has enabled students to be more reflective not only about themselves but also about what they have learned. It has made them more critical thinkers. Says Kelley, "After being in this class you kind of rethink some of the things that you learned because you are getting a wider view of the world and the things that are possible." But they fear that this type of class might not be for everybody. Says Ian, "Some people just don't want to think that deeply." But with this teacher, says Carmen, "you want to think at a higher level."

Some might question whether the class is rigorous enough or intellectually challenging enough. According to these students, the class is easily both. Says Carmen, "This class doesn't mean that we don't have that much homework. We sure have our fair share of homework. We do all the academic stuff. It is just that intertwined among all the academic stuff is the values. Honestly I think that a lot of the time people put too much emphasis on tests, because tests are not what are going to get you through life. Testing of yourself will get you through life, not testing whether or not you know all the characteristics of writing. Testing is not going to help you be a good person and be successful. Maybe it will help you with your career, but to have good strong values, that is going to get you farther in life."

"It's just different in this class," says Megan. "In the rest of them, it seems like they are just reading out of a book. [Our teacher] teaches from experience and always lets us know how we are going to use this in our life. Recently, she had us take a survey about what we think is important so we are not doing stuff that we don't want to do or we don't think is necessary, and that makes it a lot easier and a lot more meaningful."

As a part of listening to her students and fostering authentic dialogue on topics dear to the hearts of adolescents, their teacher started a new project with her students. Says Ashley, "[Our teacher] is starting this thing called Mystery Questions. Whatever question you have in your mind, just whatever you are thinking about at this time at this age, you can put it in a basket and she won't tell anybody about your question. Then she will pick it up and read it in front of the whole class and have a whole class discussion on it and what you are thinking about in life. It just helps to express your feelings about things in the world and yourself today. It helps you relate to yourself." Megan agrees: "There are a lot of questions that I want to ask that have been really bugging me but I feel kind of stupid asking somebody. But if I got the whole group around, then I would get all these different perspectives besides my own."

At least for these girls, they bring home what they have learned and talk it over with their parents. Says Ashley, "I find myself going home and telling my mom what happened in English class. As a family we sometimes have the same discussion and I get my family's perspective. We discuss together what we think is right." Kelley adds, "My parents really like my being in this class."

In concluding, this is what these students said about a class that includes and emphasizes the social and emotional side to learning: "I wish a lot more classes were like this"; "This class has taught me patience"; "This is the one high point of my day"; "This is the class that I want to stay in. I don't want to leave it"; "Now that I think about it, all these assignments that we have done and everything that we have learned makes sense. At first, you really don't know why you are learning this stuff or why you are reading this book. But after you get finished with the project and you look at where you were before now, it makes total sense because it made you grow not only physically, but mentally and spiritually."

*This is Colleen's story about how she began implementing SEL and CRE into her classroom.*

"I went to school thirty years ago where the teacher was in control, where your job was to teach the kids and there was not a whole lot said about learning but a lot said about teaching. Basically kids had few capabilities to govern themselves and [people said] that 'they really shouldn't be given a lot of say in the classroom because then what they are going to ask for is things that you don't want, things that will get out of control or get out of hand.'"

But Colleen found a way to give kids more "voice and choice" in her classroom, with amazing results. "I started working with [two local training organizations in conflict resolution and SEL], and this big door opened, and it all fell into place, and it all made sense. What's worked for me is to change the climate of my classroom—to start by believing that my students are capable young adults. In our culture, by the time they are thirteen, they are making some independent, fairly serious decisions. A lot of those decisions they are making incorrectly because they haven't been taught how to make decisions; they haven't been taught how to work with other people; they haven't been taught how to share their feelings. They have the basic happy, mad, sad emotions and they are surrounded by the idea that the only way you solve conflicts is violently, either with verbal violence or physical violence. In my school a lot of my students come from an environment where violence is an everyday part of life. But they were really bright and curious and open to someone caring about them.

"The first year I did this it was really scary because I said, 'We are going to try something different here. Please don't sabotage this.' I sat down and talked with them about it and said, 'I have never done this before and we are going to start slowly and I am going to try some new things and let's try to make this work, and if it doesn't work let me know.' I went to my principal and he said, 'I don't care what you do as long as your kids do well on tests'—that was the bottom line, and it is still the bottom line. So I decided to quit worrying about the tests because when I started looking at the kids, what I saw missing was their ability to function like human beings—not so much their academic ability, for they could learn rote facts. They didn't know how to be human beings in any settings, even with their best friends."

Colleen shares how she found a way to infuse this work into her academic day. "To me the easiest place in the world to start is with literature, which is all about relationships and emotion and how we get along and how we express ourselves. So I built a curriculum around literature that dovetails with human adventure, emotions, ordeals, and experiences, and I tried to make sure that with every piece of literature I taught, we talked about the social and emotional aspects *and* we talked about how to resolve conflict—because that is what literature is all about.

"The first year I just started with the literature and I added a few things and it went pretty well and the kids seemed to like it and they seemed to respond well, and what I discovered is that I liked them a whole lot better too. I have always liked going to work, but suddenly I really liked going to work. But I realized that there was something missing, and that piece was building a community.

"So the second and third year, I started really working on that piece first. My principal was not pleased about that because what I did was I committed my first three weeks of school to nothing but community building. I didn't touch literature or writing or grammar or anything for the first three weeks and he was very suspicious about that. I had some parents who were calling in and saying,

'I thought this was an English class. So when are you going to start teaching English?' But at the end of the first semester, I was able to document that I was exactly at the same point that year that I was at the year before when day one I started teaching English. Then my principal said, 'That's OK, you can go ahead and do this.' What happened is that by building that community first—and I have learned since then . . . how to integrate literature into the community-building piece—I sort of satisfy everybody. I actually do start teaching literature right away. But it is literature with a focus on building community."

As a result of this new way of teaching, she found a renewed interest in education and a reinvigoration of her vocation. "Suddenly what is happening in my classroom is that I love being there. It has become a really safe, respectful place. I have absolutely no discipline problems—they don't exist. And it is not because I am this marvelous, wonderful person. It is because the kids have built a community where they feel safe, where they respect each other, where it is OK to have different ideas, where we listen and explore together. And every year I learn as much as they learn. I have students who are turning into real human beings right before my eyes, which is the most gratifying and wonderful experience. It has made my teaching open up into a whole new realm of reward and fulfillment. My students are saying things to me—verbally, in my evaluations, in their papers—that let me know that this is a place where they feel good about being.

"So, for me, I can't understand why a teacher would not want to do this. It changes your students' willingness to learn. It changes your relationship with them. It changes how you feel about your own job. It changes the safety in your own room. It changes the dynamics as far as discipline. It changes how much they learn. I feel like I don't teach so much as they learn. It is so much self-directed. I started to redefine what *teacher* means. It is not that I share all of my great knowledge, because my knowledge is limited. It is that they learn to dig for the knowledge. They learn to ask the questions and start exploring and start coming back with the answers and they share it together and they learn.

"I feel safe enough with that now that I can [even do this with my substitute teachers] and it happens without any discipline problems. I have people who will 'sub' only for me because they have said to me, 'It is so obvious when we are in your room the students have such great respect for each other and for you.' They would never do anything that would bring pain to a guest. It is because I started building a community and the kids are getting something they don't get in a lot of places. They are getting a place that is safe, a place where I don't criticize them or I say 'you can't think that.' And that is not to say that I agree with everything they think. I disagree with a lot of things that they think. You see, I come from a very, very conservative background. I come from a home that was very racist. My father is an extreme racist. My brother is a racist. I came from a background that was not open or accepting. Part of building [my classroom] community is that I respect [my students] as much as I want them to respect me. The kids and I together have managed together to build this community."

Colleen talks about the connection between academic performance and building strong student relationships. "We go into schools and we want to change the ways kids behave. We want to help kids move up in the economic, social-emotional ladder, yet we are not willing to build a relationship with them. That's never going to happen then. When they leave our classrooms, they are going to be exactly the same as when they came in. No matter what great stuff we teach; no matter how well they do on their test scores. I have been given classes that have been labeled 'gifted and talented' and I have been given classes that have been labeled 'high risk.' It doesn't matter. It works equally well at both ends of the spectrum. I just believe in this work so much that I can't understand teachers' being unwilling to make it a part of their work."

Many teachers might balk at the time it would seem to take from their already packed day, but Colleen found it wasn't as hard as others might think. "It was not hard. I did not create completely new lesson plans. I did not have to satisfy any chunks of time where I did nothing but this. I took what I was already teaching and I changed the discussion here a little bit. I added a conflict piece here. I did an anger management piece here. It was like ten minutes here, thirty minutes here, one day here. But I did not change my curriculum at all. I still teach all of the district-wide curriculum. I meet all the state standards. Nothing changed except adding those little pieces that a teacher should do on a regular basis anyway in order to keep growing."

She found that seventh- and eighth-grade boys don't like touchy-feely activities at first, so she started slowly with this group. "I am very careful that the first month we do nothing at all that involves physical touch. We spend the first month mostly getting to know each others' names, doing really neutral things like 'What's your favorite color?' and 'Everybody give three facts about yourself.' We do a lot of cooperative learning groups. We start with a book called *Seedfolks* [which is about a group of strangers who come together to turn a vacant, garbarge-filled lot into a community garden] and I read it out loud to the kids the first week of school and then we start talking about where they all come from and how we can build that kind of a garden in the classroom. I do really nonthreatening things to begin with where kids can talk not about their personal feelings but about their family heritage, about things we have in common, and just getting to know each other. We sit down and do 'wheel within a wheel' where for thirty seconds we talk about your favorite movie, your pet that you had, what you did this summer, and then rotate so they get to know each other that way. That kind of gets past the initial 'euwwh' feeling.

"The next thing I do [and although eighth graders don't want to touch each other, they do want to be physical] is that I start to do physical games. We play the sock toss where they learn each other's names some more. They love the game where they have to get into a pretzel and get untwisted. I had them do the game where they had to create a machine and act out the machine without any words. By the end of October, they are pretty much used to what I am doing. When I have them count off by fours, or by colors, or any other way I divide them, they pretty much do it readily. If I say, 'Desks to the back of the room, we are going to be in a circle, you have thirteen-and-a-half seconds' (they love counting in odd numbers) they are on the floor and do it really well. It just takes a couple of months for it to happen. Some days when things aren't going well, we just play together.

"I also do a lot with solos and silence. I teach them from the very beginning that silence is a good thing. It is not a threatening thing that we need to be uncomfortable with. I start with thirty seconds and build up to a minute, then build up to two minutes with the eighth graders. Now my ninth graders do ten minutes a day. It is so much a habit that if I forget, they remind me. I [even] go to the back of the room and sit down. I have ten minutes solo too, which I love."

Colleen also has her students writing in journals constantly. "They journal every single day. They do journals that I grade that are related to what we are studying. They do journals that I read but I do not grade that are related to their reflections, what they are thinking, what they are feeling, what is going on. I read everything they write and they know that from the beginning. I write back to them in their journals and that seems to fill the bridge for us. What I tell my students is that if there is something that is private and they don't want me to read it, they should fold the page over and I won't read it. They expect me to respond and sometimes they ask me questions in the journal."

Still, she says, "there are still some kids that are not comfortable with this even after all the work you do and you just have to honor it. Those are the kids who always pass in the sharing circles; those are the kids if it is a game where you ask them to hold hands, they will ask to step out; those are the kids who sometimes try to sabotage things. And, what I have seen happen there is that if a student is trying to sabotage things, frequently the other students will say 'Jeremy, you are not helping things work today; why don't you just observe.' And they ask him to leave the circle. So, they kind of self-monitor each other. I don't have to do that. There are some kids, because of abuse, who don't want to be touched or who because of childhood experience can't trust an adult. Some kids will never learn to trust a female. I just keep treating those kids respectfully. My expectation is that everyone in the room will treat those kids respectfully even if they don't respond. And I had to learn that I wasn't going to save 100 percent of the children."

As these activities aren't the normal way things are done at school, Colleen has faced some resistance and fear from parents. "I do have some resistance from parents, who think I am doing touchy-feely things instead of teaching; who think

I am stepping over the boundaries of what should be taught by parents. With things like visualizations, I am very careful. I never ever ask students to visualize something that I have put in their minds. I sometimes ask them to close their eyes and think about whatever they want to think about and picture whatever they want to picture but I never tell them what is going to be there. I try to be really respectful of each person's spiritual leanings. So with solo I say 'You can use this time to pray, to meditate, to remember, to completely clear your mind and do nothing—no one is going to ask you what went on in your mind during this time.'

"I would say that we have three reactions from parents. We have the parents who are violent themselves; who are aggressive and who are unwilling to change and learn. Because we do not have a parent education piece [teaching them conflict resolution skills] at our school, which I think is a real weakness, those parents do not learn how to change their way of relating to their children. I have had kids who have come back to me and say 'I tried that "I statement" stuff with my dad and he beat me up.' So one of the things we teach our kids is to be smart and to know when to get out of an unsafe situation. I wish we lived in a world where that weren't true, but it is."

The second reaction comes "interestingly enough from some of my most highly educated and well off parents who don't want me playing with their kids' minds. Their kids have grown up in a fairly polite environment, and they have been successful in the business world because they have learned how to be polite. Then they say to me, 'My kids don't need this.' What I have noticed about these kids is that many times they are devoid of any kind of emotional foundation. They may know manners, but they don't know how to relate to other people —and some of those kids are the most bereft of self-esteem. What I have to say to those parents is 'Trust me with your child's education; I am teaching your child skills that will work in the workforce.' They want to know their kids will be successful in their jobs. So when I say, 'I am teaching them to learn how to work with each other; I am teaching them interpersonal skills that they need in the workforce;' they say 'Oh, so you are getting them ready to go to work . . . that's OK.'"

The third reaction is from "the middle-of-the-road parents. They care about their kids. They want their kids to be safe. They want their kids to learn, but they are not real comfortable with this whole touchy-feely thing. What tends to happen is that as the kids go home and say 'No, it's OK; we're having fun there and we are learning things there,' then the parents are OK. Those are parents who are sometimes willing to be in my room, or go on a field trip with the kids. These are the kinds of parents who do start seeing some changes. I get every year wonderful notes and messages from parents that say 'This really made a difference for my kid.'

"One of the fears that parents and teachers and administrators have is that I have a classroom without boundaries, which is the furthest thing from the truth.

It is just that I have a classroom where the students have helped establish the boundaries that make them feel safe, and it becomes an environment where I don't have to use verbal or physical force to keep those boundaries in place. There are quite a few boundaries in my room. One of my boundaries is that I will never raise my voice. The first thing I say to them on the first day is 'I will never raise my voice. You have heard how loudly I am going to speak. So we have to figure out a way for this room to work, because this is it.' And at the end of the year, kids say to me, 'Thanks for keeping that promise that you would not raise your voice.' It is not a room without boundaries. It is not a room without ground rules. It is just a room where we respect each other. It is like a family."

Colleen talks about how she deals with the fears and resistance of parents and her administrator. "I invite parents into my room to observe what is going on. Usually by the end of the year my relationship with the kids is strong enough that most parents have come over to think that it is OK. My administrator says, 'Whatever you are doing is working, so I am not going to question it.' He has been in my room and has done sharing circles and councils with us."

One of the unique aspects of Colleen's efforts in SEL is how she has managed to tie it into the academic day. Recently, the whole school adopted an International Baccalaureate program, which has a heavy emphasis on integrated learning and essential questions. Colleen talks about how these essential questions have helped support her educational goals. "All of our lessons have to be built around essential questions. The question has to have more than one answer, it has to require new information for the students to be able to answer, and it has to be something that is applicable in fifteen to twenty years. We have created six, building-wide essential questions which every teacher has to address, so for the first six weeks, our first question is 'What makes a community?' In order to answer that essential question, they are going to have to build community in their classrooms. We are spending one whole day at the beginning of the school year talking about how in each person's class that essential question can be answered. So in math, what are you going to do to build a community and answer that question? In PE, where they really need to be a community and so seldom are, how are you going to build that community? [What about] in Tech Ed? I really think it's going to start happening without teachers being able to put a label to it because they are going to have to answer that essential question.

"The last week of school we dedicate to affirmation circles, where we spend a whole week affirming each other. I have them draw names out of hats and affirm the person whose name they drew. I have them pair up and do some affirmations. This last year they said, 'We want a circle where we do nothing but an affirmation circle for you.' It was just amazing. I was crying by the time it was done. On the first day of the last week of school, I give them a big piece of construction paper and tell them to fold it over and design something on the front that depicts how they feel about the class, with the idea that it would go to someone else in the class, they didn't know who, but it would be a gift they gave to someone in the class. Then I took them home and put a wonderful poem on each and wrote something that I learned from each student. At the last day of school I read each one aloud and gave it to the student and it was powerful.

"Students are under pressure to perform and to meet all these expectations—society's expectations, their family's expectations, their own expectations—I hope they have some emotional tools to do that with that they maybe didn't have two years ago. The biggest obstacle has been teachers saying, 'I don't want one more thing to do.' The secret I think is to somehow convince teachers that it is not one more thing to do. It is doing what you do with a little different twist so it becomes a way of life. All the research seems to say that if we meet our students' social and emotional needs they will be better learners. They can't remember if they are not socially and emotionally healthy.

"For the first two years, I felt like a renegade. It was tough. There was no one else in the building doing this. Fortunately, I had [the trainer] who kept saying, 'What you are doing is OK' and kept advising me, and I kept coming to workshops. You really need a support system, even if it is just two or three people to help you out—that makes a big difference."

As a result of all this innovative work in the classroom, Colleen is seeing change—not only in her students but also in other teachers who have become interested in learning more about what she does. She puts it this way: "What I am seeing is that students have little light bulb moments, like 'We could use this in the hallways.' Or, sometimes in our sharing circles when they get to pick the topic, they get to talk about issues that they are having a hard time resolving. We ask 'How could you do that differently, what skills can you take with you?' So I would say it is happening, but it is happening slowly. Other teachers say to me, 'You know, your kids mentioned that you did this in your class and it worked,' or 'Your kids are talking about this thing they call a solo, tell me about that,' or 'Why do you let the kids ask the questions and lead the discussions?' [This] shows me that the kids are requesting it.

"If I could say anything about this work at all, it is that it makes people whole people in all parts of their life. And it doesn't just make students whole people, it makes me a whole person and it feeds that part of me that is spiritual and emotional and intellectual. It would be such a gift to teachers as well as students if we could get schools to understand that it is creating these whole, healthy people."

I asked Colleen to share a story about a time when she saw the benefits of this learning come to life. She described a situation when two of her more challenging students got into a big fight in the back of her classroom. "All of a sudden in the back corner of my room, there was this eruption of really violent threats, filthy language. A boy and a girl were hurling these threats and insults at each other and I thought 'Any minute they are going to kill each other.' So I just said, 'Tony and Jasmine, in the hall immediately,' which they did, thank goodness. Then I said, 'Tony in that corner, Jasmine in that corner. Don't go near each other.' I told them, 'This is not working; what is happening here?' And Tony said, 'We need to step back and talk about this in a different way. I am sorry I was calling you names.' And she said, 'I am sorry I stabbed you with my pencil.' So they both apologized and I asked them, 'Can I trust you out here for three minutes to work this out? Because I need to go back into the room and explain that everything is OK.' And they said, 'Yeah, you can trust us.' And I thought to myself, I could lose my job over this. So I said 'OK, don't make me look bad here.' Then I went back into my room and shut the door. We talked about what happened with the rest of the class, and how things got out of hand. I told the class to 'go back to working in your groups; I am going to see how they have resolved things out there.' I went out and they were talking calmly. They said, 'This is what started it; we both know what triggered it for each one of us; this is how we think it needs to be resolved. Would you please put us in a different group, because we are still feeling uncomfortable about being together, but it's OK.' And I said, 'All right, I will do that.'

"First of all I could not believe that in the middle of something that was really emotional and intense they listened to me, but they did. And then, they said, 'Yes, it is OK for you to go back into the room; we are going to be able to work through this.' And they did. To me, that's why we should do this. With kids who are the very highest risk, the most likely to become violent, five years ago what would have happened in this situation is that those kids would have had a physical fight. They would have been suspended from school. And what would that teach them? Everything that has always been reinforced in their life—that you solve things physically, then the authority system, the system that is always against you anyway, kicks you out of school for a while, but what do you expect, that is what always happens and then you come back and you do what you have always done anyway. It just was amazing to me. I absolutely believe that it is making a difference. It's probably making little differences in little places. I don't want to say that it is working everywhere, but I do want to say that it is making a difference. And I see my kids using it in a lot of different ways."

CHAPTER FIVE

# "WE CAN HANDLE THIS OURSELVES"
## Learning to Negotiate Conflicts

Jennifer K. Druliner and Heather E. Prichard

Conflict resolution education (CRE) programs teach a variety of processes and skills, one of which is negotiation. Negotiation-based programs are different from other kinds of classroom CRE programs in that they focus primarily on teaching the process steps of negotiation to all students, often in a series of classroom lessons that build on one another. The goal is to provide students with practical problem-solving skills, ones that empower them to work through their conflicts themselves instead of relying on an adult to intervene and "fix" the situation.

Johnson and Johnson highlight five strategies for managing conflict: (1) *problem-solving negotiation,* in which both parties identify both the issue at hand and the relationship as very important, and therefore negotiate to help achieve what they want and resolve tensions in the relationship; (2) *smoothing,* in which one party believes the relationship is more important than the issue, and gives up his or her goal in order to maintain the relationship; (3) *win-lose negotiation,* in which one party tries to push the other to a solution that meets his or her goals, because the relationship is not as important as the issue; (4) *compromise,* where the goal and the relationship are moderately important and neither party can get what he or she wants entirely, so one or both parties give up part of what they want; and (5) *withdrawal,* in which neither goal nor relationship are viewed as important enough to bring one or both parties to negotiation.[1] In this chapter, we focus on problem-solving negotiation and the programs that teach those skills.

## What Is Negotiation?

In order to make sense of what students will be learning in a negotiation-based program, it is important to come to a general understanding about the definition of the term *negotiation*. Fisher and Ury, whose best-selling book *Getting to Yes* helped popularize the process, define negotiation as "a basic means of getting what you want from others. It is back and forth communication designed to reach an agreement when you and the other side have some interests that are shared and others that are opposed."[2]

A successful negotiator does several things: distinguishes the parties involved in a conflict from the issue itself; focuses on parties' *interests*—their underlying needs—rather than their stated demands or *positions;* and works with the other party to create options that will satisfy both. According to Bodine, Crawford, and Schrumpf, "The skillful negotiator strives to be an empathetic listener, suspends judgment, is respectful, and has a cooperative spirit."[3]

The goal of collaborative negotiation is a win-win outcome, one in which both parties are satisfied. Although there is some variation, the basic negotiation process involves a series of steps: (1) parties identify the problem and agree to negotiate; (2) each party relates his or her side of the conflict and listens to the other party, and the listener then restates what she or he heard to make certain the understanding is accurate; (3) parties brainstorm possible solutions; (4) parties agree on a solution that satisfies both of their needs; and (5) parties implement the agreement. These steps are common to a variety of conflict resolution processes, including mediation, but negotiation is the only one involving two or more parties directly engaged in problem solving on their own behalf, without the assistance of a third party.

It is important for both parties in a negotiation to be willing to work together to resolve their dispute. "The first choice for resolving conflict is negotiation, because when it is engaged in correctly by skillful negotiators, it allows the parties in a dispute complete freedom to solve their problem together. If the negotiation doesn't work out, the next logical step is to seek assistance from a third party, a mediator."[4]

## Negotiation-Based Programs in Schools

Classroom-based negotiation programs empower students to act as their own mediators, by teaching effective communication skills (such as active listening) and familiarizing them with the negotiation process. The basic steps are similar to those used in mediation, but without the third party. These steps generally include the following: having each party explain his or her side of the story while the other party listens, identifying underlying needs, brainstorming solutions, and identifying and implementing a solution that works for both parties. To help students remain engaged and understand the concepts, these programs typically are interactive, and they use activities and role plays that teach the skills and process steps. Rather than integrating the negotiation material into students' regular coursework, many classroom-based negotiation programs are designed as a stand-alone series of lessons in which students are taught the negotiation concepts. Although the topic is beyond the scope of this chapter, it is important to note that the skills of negotiation may also be taught as one component of a comprehensive, schoolwide CRE program.

There are many programs that teach the skills of negotiation. In the following sections, we highlight the Program for Young Negotiators, Talk It Out, and Teaching Students to be Peacemakers as examples of classroom-based programs that differ in scope and methodology. Although not all three define themselves as negotiation programs, they all teach students the basic process steps and skills of negotiation. The Program for Young Negotiators is a set of ten lessons designed for middle and high school students; Talk It Out is a process aimed at elementary school students; and Teaching Students to be Peacemakers is a comprehensive program for K–12 students that teaches negotiation along with other conflict resolution processes.

## Program for Young Negotiators (PYN)

PYN is a negotiation curriculum that teaches students the skills they need in order to solve everyday problems. Designed for use with middle school and high school students (ages eleven through sixteen), PYN is "not about confrontation or violence" but rather about "working together to accomplish your goals" so that students can "win without making others lose."[5] Based on negotiation theory developed at the Harvard Negotiation Project and on Fisher and Ury's groundbreaking book *Getting to Yes,* the PYN curriculum was field-tested in public schools for three years before being published in 1998. Pre- and postcourse evaluations have shown that PYN helped decrease disciplinary problems in the school.[6]

The PYN curriculum is a set of ten interactive sessions that use role plays, games, group discussion, and reflection exercises to teach skills. Each session is about ninety minutes long, so the program takes about fifteen classroom hours to facilitate from start to finish. Although it was designed as a stand-alone program, PYN lessons can be incorporated into regular coursework to help reinforce the skills that students are learning.

The initial session offers students an overview of negotiation and its goals. Subsequent lessons focus on competition versus collaboration, understanding different perceptions and attitudes, distinguishing between needs and demands, dealing with anger, creating and evaluating options, developing effective communication skills, and advocating for oneself. The lessons as a whole introduce students to a variety of negotiation concepts, including the distinction between interests and positions, option generation, collaboration, fair standards for creating and choosing options, and the concept of a *best alternative to a negotiated agreement,* or BATNA.[7] The BATNA is what each party is willing to walk away with if she cannot achieve what she originally set out to get through negotiation.

Educators who have previous experience facilitating interactive programs or who are familiar with facilitating conflict resolution skills and concepts may choose to teach the curriculum without training from SERA Learning, the organization that now produces PYN. (SERA is the acronym for Skills to Empower, Reach and Achieve.) However, SERA recommends that facilitators receive training from the organization prior to instructing students. Whether one teaches the curriculum with or without prior training, an effective teaching or facilitation style is one that is encouraging and enthusiastic and that creates a safe and positive environment for participating youth. Allowing adequate time for preparation and implementation is also important.

## Talk It Out

As a peaceful alternative to the "fight it out" approach, Barbara Porro created Talk It Out to teach elementary school students to handle their conflicts positively and without adult intervention, using a six-step process. These six steps are similar to the process steps of mediation but are implemented without the assistance of a third party: (1) stop; cool off; (2) talk and listen to each other; (3) find out what you both need; (4) brainstorm solutions; (5) choose the idea you both like; and (6) make a plan; go for it! Porro notes that the Talk It Out approach is best suited to the "'garden variety' conflicts that occur in most classrooms—teasing, putdowns, who's first, who's the boss, not sharing, taking things, telling secrets, cutting, bugging, hitting, pushing, cheating, rumors, gossip—to name a few."[8]

Porro encourages teaching the Talk It Out process steps throughout the school year, rather than in a concentrated set of lessons over a short period of time. Teaching the steps over a longer period of time helps students better integrate the skills of Talk It Out into their daily interactions and efforts to resolve conflicts. Porro designed the curriculum to be flexible, and she encourages teachers to make it their own by adapting the lessons to their students' needs and learning styles.

For some students, a designated "cool off" space in the classroom may be the most effective way to reinforce step one; a suggestion box and colored markers may encourage other students to engage in the brainstorming process.

### Teaching Students to be Peacemakers (TSP)

A program for K–12 students that teaches negotiation along with other conflict resolution processes, TSP is the most comprehensive of the three models described in this chapter. As program developers David and Roger Johnson point out, when we are in conflict, we must take into consideration dual concerns: (1) reaching an agreement that satisfies our needs and meets our goals and (2) maintaining an appropriate relationship with the other person.[9] The equal emphasis on reaching a satisfactory resolution and valuing the relationship demonstrates the far-reaching scope of the program.

By starting with lessons that kindergarten students can understand and building on those lessons each subsequent school year, TSP provides students with twelve years of negotiation and other conflict resolution training. The TSP program helps students develop the skills to manage conflicts effectively.

The implementation phases of TSP start with creating a cooperative climate and teaching students that conflicts can be useful and that a conflict-free life is not realistic. Once students have learned these basic tenets, the program teaches students the purposes and skills related to negotiation and mediation procedures, increasing the level of sophistication every year from kindergarten through twelfth grade.

Recent research studies of the TSP program demonstrate that, over time, students who master TSP negotiation and mediation procedures tend to use them in actual conflict situations in the classroom, in other school settings, and at home. The research also suggests that negotiation and mediation training—when integrated into other coursework—also positively impacted students' academic achievement. This research is encouraging for those schools that wish not only to teach students effective negotiation skills but also to integrate conflict resolution into their academic curriculum.[10]

## Challenges of Negotiation-Based Programs

Negotiation programs are valuable and provide a variety of benefits. However, they are not able to meet the needs of all students, and there are challenges to implementing them effectively.

## Not Everything Is Negotiable

Although negotiation-based programs teach important life skills and help students handle many of the everyday conflicts that arise in a student's life, it is vital to remember that negotiation is not always the appropriate process to use in resolving conflict. Johnson and Johnson point out that "students must always have the option of saying 'no' to negotiations. There are clear reasons for doing so, such as the issue [at the heart of the conflict] being illegal, inappropriate, it will hurt other people, or they do not think they can keep their word. There are also unclear reasons, such as intuition, being unsure, not seeing the right option, and having changed their mind."[11]

In addition, many classroom negotiation programs either do not thoroughly address the role that power plays in negotiation or assume that effective negotiation can compensate for a power imbalance, which is not always the case. In fact, as in the case of bullying, expecting students to negotiate conflicts that involve a serious power imbalance can actually increase the imbalance and the plight of the party with less power.

If the parties have an unequal commitment to working out a problem, one disputant may have a stronger negotiating position than the other. Or if one student is an ESL student who is new to the school and the other is on the debate team, the new student may feel at a disadvantage due to a potential language barrier and pressured to agree to a resolution that is not ideal.

It is important for program facilitators to help students understand the limitations of negotiation; otherwise, students may overrely on their new skills and hold the false assumption that negotiation can solve any problem. As Porro points out, prejudice, discrimination, bias, racism, and scapegoating are issues beyond the scope of classroom negotiation.[12]

## Diversity, Power, and Negotiation-Based Programs

For students to become effective citizens of a multicultural, pluralistic society, it is crucial that they learn to respect and honor differences in class, gender, ethnicity, religion, belief system, ability, and sexual orientation. Schools committed to supporting the needs of diverse populations should offer broad-based CRE programs that support efforts to improve intergroup relations and address assumptions about differences, in addition to teaching conflict resolution skills and concepts such as active listening, perspective taking, and empathy. It also is important for programs to underscore when negotiation is and is not an appropriate resolution process. To ensure equal treatment of all students, effective negotiation programs in schools should explicitly include lessons that help students understand the relationship between diversity and power in the negotiation process.

Negotiation is said to be the most empowering conflict resolution process because it involves parties directly working together to solve their problems, without the assistance of a third party. However, negotiation processes actually may be *dis*empowering for students, particularly if the conflict at hand is rooted in or involves unequal distribution of power, resources, or voice. To illustrate this point, we offer the following example.

Two high school student groups apply for funding for a special project during the fall semester. One group includes members of the football team, debate club, and lacrosse team. The other group serves as an empowerment program for young women and maintains its effectiveness by limiting the number of participants. Due to a budget shortfall, there is only enough money to fund one group project, unless a creative solution can be reached.

The two student groups agree to negotiate how the funds should be distributed. During the course of the negotiation, it becomes apparent that the smaller group simply has less leverage and voice. The larger group, representing a broader, more popular constituency, has more clout and is better positioned to achieve its goals. In this case, negotiation would be ill advised and might do harm.

As Hocker and Wilmot point out, "If one party in a negotiation has more power than the other (or is perceived to have more), the conflict is unbalanced. Balancing the participants' power through the use of restraint, empowerment, or transcendence, is often a significant factor in successfully negotiating an agreement. If power imbalances cannot be successfully addressed, a third party may be necessary."[13] Power imbalances may play out in a school setting in the following way. Whereas two equally popular students may be able to negotiate a dispute successfully, there may be serious power imbalance issues if the same conflict occurs between students of unequal social standing. In this case, the involvement of a third party may be helpful. Because negotiation programs may not directly address such issues as differences in power and perceptions about race, class, gender, culture, and ability that may impact students' ability to negotiate successfully with one another, it is important for teachers to help students examine issues of power and diversity in meaningful ways, paying particular attention to "in-out" group dynamics in their school.

## Ensuring the Longevity of Negotiation Programs

Although they may be used at any grade level, negotiation-based programs are often aimed at middle and high school students because they teach communication skills that empower young people and enable them to resolve conflicts themselves. However, it is important to remember that no single program can eradicate conflict in the classroom or school, and that is not their purpose. In addition, programs based on a specific set of lessons are not typically designed with longevity in mind. Negotiation programs are intended as skill development for individual students rather than as an institutional component to affect school climate or deal with ongoing structural and disciplinary issues. Hence, negotiation programs are not implemented and do not need to be sustained in the same way as other CRE efforts, such as peer mediation. Making these programs sustainable requires commitment from teachers and administrators. Such a goal may be more effectively met if educators are able to come together as a unit, to share success stories, challenges, and creative ways to integrate CRE, and specifically negotiation, into the core curriculum.

Ideally, a school will offer a variety of conflict resolution programs and teaching tools, so that each student will have the opportunity to learn conflict resolution life skills in the classroom and to take advantage of schoolwide conflict resolution programs. Some teachers may choose to teach a stand-alone, negotiation-based process curriculum over a period of ten or more weeks. In addition, a school may offer peer mediation for all students who seek a neutral third party to help them resolve specific conflicts. Those interested in a "peaceable classroom" approach may opt to infuse negotiation and other conflict resolution skills and concepts into their teaching subject throughout the semester or school year. "Peaceable schools" serve as learning institutions where negotiation, mediation, classroom-based conflict resolution, and schoolwide programs are cultivated and fully supported. It is important for each school to assess its own organizational climate, needs, and curricular goals in order to determine the most fitting and realistic combination of negotiation, mediation, and classroom-based CRE programs in light of its budget and level of commitment.

## Maximizing Parent and Community Involvement

Schools seeking to gain support from families and the local community might offer weekend skill-building trainings for parents and caregivers, siblings, and interested community members. By doing so, the school expands and increases support for and understanding of these important problem-solving skills, while advocating a commitment to nonviolence. Once they have received training, parents and caregivers may volunteer their time to serve as classroom cofacilitators or aides when negotiation lessons are offered. In addition, schools may encourage parents and caregivers to talk with their children about the skills they are learning and how they may be applied at home or in the community. All of these approaches demonstrate the utility of negotiation and conflict resolution skills in all areas of life.

To offset the cost of making training available to members of the surrounding community and to increase the number of stakeholders in such programs, schools may seek donations of time and money from local businesses, religious houses of worship, and individuals. These resources will not only support negotiation and conflict resolution training at the school but also strengthen the ties between school, home, and community.

◆ ◆ ◆

Negotiation-based programs teach students ways to identify their needs and the needs of others. They also teach young people how to work together to resolve day-to-day conflicts that arise. The skills taught in negotiation programs help students communicate effectively so that they are able to work through basic misunderstandings, identify underlying needs, empathize with others, and brainstorm solutions to shared problems. These life skills, when used by young people who also understand the interplay of power and conflict resolution, can empower students to become healthy, effective citizens.

# In Their Own Words

## "I've Changed After the PYN Training"

*Brentwood School District serves a very diverse student population in Brentwood on Long Island, New York. Bobbe Frankel, a guidance counselor, and Gail Alexander, a principal, were instrumental in bringing the Program for Young Negotiators (PYN) to the district several years ago. With many other teachers and administrators, they have helped make PYN a real success. It is now mandated in forty-three sixth-grade classes throughout the four middle schools in Brentwood.*

*On a sunny winter day, several of the students from Brentwood East Middle School and Brentwood North Middle School agreed to share their insights about their PYN experience with Tricia, one of the editors of this book. At Brentwood East, Tricia spoke with Brittany Pagan, sixth grade; Alyssa Rizzuto and Veronica Dixon, seventh grade; Micah Brown, Jeannette Mendez (also a peer mediator), Raul Tatis (also a peer mediator), and Edgardo Aponte, eighth grade.*

The students describe what they did in the PYN training. Micah explains, "In the class we acted out role plays to look for outcomes. We'd do it the wrong way and then do it the right way." Raul says, "Yeah. It taught you wrong and right and what to do in these situations." They all chime in: "We sang a song about how peer negotiation is good and other things. We learned about empathy, negotiation, collaboration, I–you statements. We had to do a role play about who got the orange, negotiate and collaborate to get to a win-win outcome." Alyssa adds, "We had the workbook and we did little activities. How to break it down, brainstorming options, interests and positions, and we had to pick the best thing."

But it wasn't always easy. As Veronica says, "It took a while for us to get it. In the beginning most of us did not get it as fast as others so we were struggling." But she notes that it got easier and more and more beneficial: "When we started playing role plays we got it automatically. The light switched. Then we could express ourselves in the PYN and tell each other how we feel. Most of us became friends because of the PYN and the fights stopped because of the PYN. We are able to negotiate with other people."

At first, there was a little attitude problem with some students. According to Jeannette, "In the beginning people didn't want to accept it. Everyone was saying this is going to be a waste of my time. You judged it, 'What is this going to do to help me?' You think, 'This isn't going to help me at all.' But then you get into the training and you see that it is going to help you solve your problems, work together, notice people's body language." Raul seconds her: "And at first you see it's a lot of work and you think 'Oh my God, not something else.' But the program really helps you with life, helps you set your goals and set your standards for life."

What kinds of things had they learned from PYN and how had they changed as a result? For Micah, "It was tough to start role playing. Some of the first words were tough. And most of us were just shouting 'cause we didn't know each other very well. Then everybody got to know each other through PYN and we started to get more open about ourselves and the people around us." Raul notes that "it also changed our attitudes, it made us more outgoing. It makes your attitude a positive thing, it helps you stop thinking about the negative things in life."

Being in PYN was fun, especially at "graduation" time. Jeannette explains, "At the end of PYN you have a graduation. It's fun. You get up and tell them what you learned. We had a play and you would see how teachers and counselors were teaching the other kids. We got T-shirts, diplomas, and pizza. And all the schools came together. Two more schools joined us." Micah explains, "We got these shirts that said 'East, West, North, South—we got your back.'" He reveals the importance of this in his next comments: "Back a long time ago the schools didn't like each other. If you went on that side you'd get beat up. If you went on this side you'd get beat up. You couldn't go to the other school's territory 'cause you'd get beat up. When PYN started, a lot of kids started to know each other, so a new generation started to come cool with each other and not have a lot of beef."

The PYN experience has been very helpful in breaking down barriers based on students' racial, ethnic, and age differences. As Raul says, "The PYN program made it clear that what's important is how you are on the inside, how you act toward the world." Starting early is very helpful, as Jeannette indicates: "I think it's good they started PYN in sixth grade 'cause sixth grade is where you join different groups, that's when you have to realize you can't only hang out with a certain group of people because they come from the area you come from. It helps you realize there are other people who are the same as you, they're just people."

Age and grade differences are very important to many students in middle and high school. Transitioning from one level to the next poses challenges that PYN can reduce. According to Raul, "The fifth grade is like the eighth grade. You're going to be going to a new school. You'll be meeting a lot of new people at that school. You can't worry about what they're going to think of you. You just have to be yourself, act the way you are, don't change yourself to be better than somebody else or make somebody like you." And Jeannette notes, "It's the same thing with grades. Just because you're an eighth grader doesn't mean you can't be chill with a sixth grader."

Each of the students talked about the aspects of PYN they particularly liked. Brittany tells us, "I like that it helps us think of ideas, and then we can help other people think of ideas, they can brainstorm too. The thing that I also like is cooperation. We're telling our ideas." Veronica adds, "I like that it helped us get along better as a class. We learn it as a class, which means we work better together." And Edgardo likes "the role playing because it actually showed us how to solve problems, it showed us how we could use it every day." The vocabulary of PYN attracted Micah: "I like to expand my vocabulary sometimes because it helps me. I like the words and I like to study the words and use them in everyday life."

Some of the students felt they had really changed through PYN and that their parents, teachers, and friends had noticed. Jeannette shares, "I like that after the PYN people actually noticed a change, that I've changed after the PYN. Like my parents noticed that I'm breaking things down, not stomping my feet on the floor. It helps you see the world different." Raul adds, "You become a more outgoing person and also I know it really helped us on the conflict breakdown [looking at the elements of conflict and how it can be managed]. I know that if the world had it, the conflict rate, the killing rate would be a lot lower. Like with drunk drivers, if they had PYN they'd think more about the consequences of driving drunk." Alyssa says, "I used to have a really bad temper, but then I had PYN. I used to say, 'You did this to me,' 'You did this,' but now I use a lot more I statements where I tell them how I feel."

Through their PYN experience, the students were able to build friendships. As Veronica says, "PYN changed a lot of us. Without PYN there would be fights breaking out all the time, nonstop. Like before, I didn't like Alyssa, but now I know her a lot better, and now we're friends. I know what she's going through. PYN helps a whole lot with the fighting, but it also helps with the family and friends. It helps you solve your problems with your parents so you don't have to be a runaway or something like that. If I had a problem, like I'm mostly doing the chores and my little sisters aren't doing anything, I can say, 'Mom, can they do something and I'll do something tomorrow?' and then we'll alternate or switch. We'll negotiate on how to do that."

For some of the students who are peer mediators, they see a strong link between what they learned from PYN and how well they are able to mediate. Jeannette explains, "I'm a peer mediator. Without the PYN training it would have been a lot harder to mediate those kids. Without the eye contact, without the listening skills, without knowing how to break down the problems easier." Raul, who is also a peer mediator, comments, "Also, it helps you have a lot of empathy. Knowing that people do things because of what happens in their home."

Before the interview, guidance counselor Bobbe Frankel had asked the students to think about a word or term from PYN that was really important to them. Their reflections reveal how much they have internalized the lessons of PYN.

Micah's favorite word is "Backup plans. 'Cause in life if you don't have a backup plan then you're done, you're not going to get anywhere. Say you want to be a lawyer but you don't get that; you need a backup plan to, say, own a company. Or if you can't own a company you need a backup to be an accountant.

Without a backup plan you can't be what you want to be. It helps a lot in your life. If you want to do something but can't or don't have the time, you need a backup plan. PYN really helped me learn how to look for backup plans."

For Brittany it is "body language. If I have a problem they'll see how I feel because of my body language, see that I have an attitude because of my body. One of my teachers always thought I was having an attitude with him even though I wasn't, so he'd give me attitude and I'd give it right back to him. So then I moved to another teacher and I didn't have to use my body language anymore unless it was positive."

Choosing one term is tough for Alyssa. "Attitudes, empathy, body language and perceptions." But then she shares a story that emphasized how crucial all of these terms are in being safe and strong. "I was approached this year. I was at a bus stop and this guy just pulled over and asked me to get in the car. I didn't do anything, I just tensed up and walked away. If I did my body language wrong or said something wrong to him anything could have happened. When I got to school I needed empathy." Alyssa has also learned ways to express her natural tendencies toward leadership. "I like to take charge, I'm a leader. After PYN I realized I can't always be the leader at everything. Somebody else has to be the leader. And I have to collaborate with them."

Jeannette likes "collaboration, because working together is important. You can get work done easier. If you do things alone it takes you a longer time. But if you break things down and give half the job to someone else it makes it lots easier. Like in mediation, if you break things down to help them get at the point of the problem, they can take it from there."

For Raul, it's "win-win outcome and goals. I try to have me win and have you win too. Both parties get something out of it. Say my girlfriend wants to go to the movies and see a movie I don't want to see, so I wait it out for her to see her movie and then later on she'll be willing to see my movie. Me and Micah collaborate a lot 'cause we have the same goals to be musicians. We're lyricists. That really helps with our friendship. We collaborate a lot. Also the peer mediation work, the goal is to solve the problems, to become friends."

Edgardo resonates with "I statements. Right now I have a problem with one teacher. She always thinks I'm trying to catch an attitude with her, but I'm not. So I have to use I statements with her to show her that I don't want to argue with her. I don't want to get in trouble. The I statements work. When you say, 'You this, and you that' it's like you're blaming. But I statements show how you feel. When I use I statements people take me more seriously and listen more because they don't feel like they're getting attacked. Like my mom, when I don't want to argue with her it works."

*The students at Brentwood North Middle School also had PYN in the sixth grade. Steven Posada, Stephanie Correa, and Jasmine Smith, all seventh graders, talked with Tricia, Bobbe, and a teacher, Cheryl Thomson.*

We start by talking about what they had done in their PYN training. Steven begins, "We were taught different ways to avoid fighting, ways to talk through things. For example, we did a role play where we were fighting over an orange, and we learned that if you stopped fighting and listened to the other person you saw that you both could share the orange and get what you want." Stephanie learned "who we could come to if we had a problem. You know how some kids are afraid to come to teachers sometimes, they might think they'll get in trouble, but we were taught that we could come to teachers too. We also learned how to bring problems to our parents and close friends. If someone wants to fight you, some teachers may get you in trouble, and if you go to your parents they tell you just not to do it." How you approach the other is important. As Jasmine states, "We also learned how to control yourself and go up to your teachers and get help. Never go against the person."

How would they use these skills if confronted with someone who wanted to fight them? Stephanie thinks, "You would stand up to him and tell him, 'What's the problem? Let's talk about it, if you hate something about me just tell me and I'll try to change the way I act or something.'" Steven's approach would be to try and understand the other: "Say you're going to get in a fight and you don't want to tell the teachers 'cause all your friends are going to start making fun of you, so you can learn how to negotiate out of it. I'd first ask him, 'What's wrong with you, why did you push me?' And if he says, 'You were in my way,' I'd say, 'Oh, I'm sorry' and try to be nice to him, try to give him different things to do other than hitting me."

All of them have seen a use for their PYN skills at home. It is clear that they don't stop using PYN at the school door. Jasmine shares, "Because of having PYN I think I got more mature, I think I found an easier way to solve my problems with my friends and my family. Eye contact is very important when you are using it with your friends 'cause that way you can show them you are listening and that you really feel what you are saying. If you're not making eye contact they don't think you're paying attention. You could be listening but they don't think you hear what they're saying. If my parents told me I can't do something, I ask them, 'Why won't you let me?' And they explain and I'll go OK. But I know now that's why they didn't want me to do it so I understand them better."

Steven says, "I use it with my cousin a lot 'cause he's always at my house and he always wants to play Nintendo, but I like to watch TV and movies. So we made a schedule so one hour he can play Nintendo and the next hour I can watch TV. And we didn't have to go to our parents to work it out." Steven also uses it with his parents. "I'm really close with my mom. She gets home from work, she has a lot of problems with her back, so if I ask if she can drive me over to soccer practice or to my friends she'll get really mad and say, 'I just got home from work and I'm tired.' So I'll ask her if I can go on my bike. I'll try and find different ways to do it so she doesn't have to get tired." But every technique has its limitations. Steven notes, "But my brother yells at me no matter what. If I step into his room I'm dead."

Stephanie lives with her mom, "so I kind of use it a lot with my mom. Like, sometimes she comes home from work and she's in a bad mood so if I ask her for something she'll be yelling. And so I'll calm her down and tell her what's wrong and talk things out. It's made our relationship better. I try to understand what she's feeling and she tries to understand what I feel."

What about their academic achievement? Have they seen any improvement in their grades or learning because of what they learned in PYN? Steven says, "Yes, because people who are in trouble a lot get in a lot of fights, and usually they don't succeed. But if you stay out of trouble and try your hardest you do a lot better in school." Stephanie says, "It really helped me. Last year I wasn't doing very well in a subject so I tried to get better this year with my skills and I got better with the subject."

It's also helped them negotiate with teachers about what happens in class. "In English we were reading this book and nobody liked it and it was very, very long," Steven explains. "So I tried to tell her to make it a little more fun, to do some role playing like we did in the Young Negotiators. Instead of doing it every single day, some days we could do something else. She changed, and for a week we did not read the book." Jasmine adds, "That's what I did in science class. All we were doing was writing notes and notes and notes. Everyone was complaining. We were just answering questions. So we thought about doing it like *Jeopardy* and he said OK. People started liking class a little more. My teacher was like, 'We can try this.'" Stephanie used it in math "because you know some teachers get really boring in math. I told my teacher, when we're doing really hard problems try to use flash cards 'cause that will help us more in understanding."

But Steven reminds us that a support system is critical for a student to learn and apply conflict resolution skills. "We are all good with this because we have people at home who care. But there are kids that if they get in trouble and the principal calls home they just don't care. You need a different way to approach different people. This helped us a lot because we talked about this to our parents. Like I tell everything to my mom. But these people that really haven't talked to their parents—it's hard."

*Cheryl Thomson, a sixth-grade teacher at Brentwood North Middle School, has been teaching PYN.* "Every Friday first period we do PYN. We have the time available, and that once a week is definitely devoted, maybe one or two periods. It will take all year to cover the PYN curriculum. At the first of the year we'll put a poster down at the end of our hallway and on it we'll put PYN, and then each week as we're learning a new concept or a new vocabulary term I'll have some of the kids go out and draw a picture, write a poem, do a scenario, so it's a work in progress.

"As the program goes on, some of them will actually get a lot from it. One girl last year was not one of the most popular students, kids used to pick on her, and she'd come out with the words and use the PYN terms to get them to treat her better. I've had several experiences where the kids will tell me how they are using this at home. One student told me, 'I was at home and I was having a fight with my brother and I told him let's sit down, what do you want, what do I want, how can we compromise.' I thought that was great, at least I know I'm reaching these kids. I may not be seeing it in the classroom every day, but I know they're using it at home."

It has really helped her discipline in the classroom, too. "Now if there is a fight I don't even need to get into the fight; I'll just say, 'What's your side, what's your side,' they kind of take it over themselves; whereas before I was kind of the whole facilitator to it. They're doing it themselves now without me having to be the judge, jury and all that. That's a big thing."

But Cheryl is realistic that kids aren't always motivated by a desire for world peace. "Sometimes they make fun of it. I don't know whether they're doing it for the brownie points or just being facetious. Then they'll be trying to negotiate with me over detentions or something. They say, 'Well you've got to understand that this is what happened' and they'll come up with this whole big scenario and try to negotiate with me. Will they win? Probably not, but I think it's great they're using those skills with an adult to try and get something that's more beneficial to them."

But she sees it really take hold when they use it in real life. "We always put it in our program: 'Well if you want to stay out late on a Friday night are you going to whine or are you going to use your negotiation skills?' You'd be surprised how many of them come back and say, 'I won it because I didn't scream, I didn't yell, I didn't throw a temper tantrum, I just laid out my plan.' And that's what we teach them, to lay out a plan, follow up on that plan. I'm not going to say it always works; there are always kids who are fighters. But even with them you see a glimmer, they hold back, are less likely to fight. If at home they're fighters and swingers, telling them it's not win-win is not likely to break that pattern."

*In many schools, teachers and administrators make the assumption that PYN is not appropriate for special needs students. The Brentwood experience denies this assumption. The sixth-*

*grade special education teachers at Brentwood East, Arnette Barnes and Felicia Bruce, have used PYN for several years and talked with Tricia about their success.* Arnette Barnes has "been using PYN for several years and you can see the change in the students. We do the program over a period of ten weeks with a lesson every day, so they get a continuous exposure. I don't really have to make any changes to the curriculum for the special education students. The things that change are how they talk to one another. I see them stop and think, 'What can I say in terms of the PYN that will make the situation better?' It makes teaching much easier."

*Felicia Bruce, Bobbe Frankel, and Tricia met with some students from the sixth-grade self-contained special education classrooms who had just started PYN this year—Nicole Rogers, Richard Calliste, and Randy Morris.* "I learned how to get along with others, how to cooperate, how to make a problem go away without violence," Nicole states. Bobbe comments that Nicole has changed a lot since PYN. Tricia asks Nicole how she had changed. "I don't give attitude as much [demonstrates attitude]. I learned that you can solve problems instead of being disrespectful and giving attitude as much. Attitude causes more problems than it solves. It took me a long time to learn this. I learned that there's other ways you can handle a situation instead of the ways we used to handle it. You can solve problems differently."

PYN has also helped Nicole think about her goals and what she wants to become. "I want to be a poet. The work I do in PYN helps my poetry. Once PYN started if I would have something hard to say, or when I said it, it would come out with attitude, I could put it in a poem." Bobbe agrees: "Yes, Nicole wrote a beautiful poem about her perception of gangs."

Nicole is trying to find a different path. "I have two brothers and two sisters and one of my brothers went the wrong way and ended up in lots of trouble. The other one is in Maryland with my aunt. My sister also started going the wrong way. She's better now but she's in a different school. My other sister's still real bad. I'm learning these new skills so I won't end up like them."

Apparently she is being successful. As Bobbe notes, "I've seen the most drastic change in Nicole's personality. Like night and day. Nicole has really, really changed." Felicia concurs: "When Bobbe said that Nicole is probably the student she's seen the greatest change in, that's probably an understatement. Nicole was very angry before and she's taken some of that anger and used it as positive energy, to redirect it and do some really positive things. I don't want to go into too many specifics, but I saw a person she used to have a very bad relationship with, someone she was very hurtful to, and now she's kind of taken that child under her wing, offers her help, and does things on the computer with her."

Richard has also benefited from PYN. "I'm learning to control my anger. I did a role play rap about Brooklyn."

One day I was walking down the streets

When I saw Bloods and Crips trying to shoot each other

I was afraid they would try to shoot me,

But I jumped in the store and then I locked up the door

I looked through the window and then I went back to my house

"Before PYN if someone made me angry, I'd beat them up. I hurt one boy. Now if the same thing happens I just walk away. I just look down and walk away." He even taught himself a technique to help him calm down when he starts to get angry: "When I catch myself in anger I put my hand over my heart and breathe deeply three times." Randy says, "I learned long-term goals from PYN. I want to go to college and get a college education. I want to get a diploma."

It is striking how much they are using expressive arts with the PYN program, especially for the special education students. Bobbe explains, "[Felicia] does great work with the special education students and PYN. She teaches them to use all of their senses, letting them use a lot of expression in ways with poetry, art, and drama. These kids can really use their expressive personality! They get so much closer to their emotions."

Felicia also stresses the notion of community and building community through PYN. "We incorporate a lot of techniques to keep peace in the classroom and to build support and collaboration so that they help one another. I write a play that gives a role to each and every student in my class. Last year we called it 'These Hands Won't Hurt.' And we coordinated the banner which had everybody's handprint on it with their first and last names under the handprint and a statement of commitment that they would make. And it incorporated a PYN vocabulary word and told about how they were going to resist the temptation to hurt another person. Then they acted it out, lots of different scenarios. This year my star rapper will be Richard and one of my narrators will be Nicole. You try and take what was a negative for the kids, like in the beginning of the year Nicole might have said she had a big mouth, but now she's using her big mouth for really positive things, to be a role model."

As Felicia notes, "One of my favorite words is community." Nicole adds, "When we're all in the class and one person is not doing what the rest are doing, the teacher says, 'We're all a community and we all have to work together.'"

Overall, Felicia has no doubt that PYN is helpful for these students and others like them. "The PYN process helps them accelerate the maturation process. It helps them develop tolerance. And accepting the difference between 'us' and whoever 'them' is. It's a level of maturity, education, and understanding. It's hard enough at twelve. Even regular education kids struggle with those issues at twelve and thirteen. PYN just helps them. We create real-life situations from their lives. A lot of my kids have witnessed serious violence. Bringing it to their level, making it real, and teaching it throughout the year really makes the difference."

She concludes, "You see changes. Some of them are dramatic, some of them are subtle. But they're evident. Because it gives them tools to draw from, skills they didn't have before."

*Maureen Keeney, a reading specialist and educational diagnostician at the New Castle County Detention Center (NCCDC) in Delaware, shares Felicia Bruce's enthusiasm for using PYN with special needs and at-risk kids.* Maureen explains about the kids at NCCDC, "The kids are sent here usually by a court, or sometimes the police bring them here until they can go to court. They're committed here for so many days or are waiting for a program opening. They have a regular education program, a principal, and six teachers covering science, social studies, language arts, career training, exploration, and life skills. The kids are here at least thirty days—sometimes ninety—sometimes they're here a long time if they did more serious crimes."

She just finished her first use of PYN. "I started out with thirteen boys but by the time I was done I only graduated three because I was only able to do the lessons twice a week and the boys leave here so soon. The boys really liked it. They liked the PYN book, they liked the whole program. I won't say I watered it down but I was very flexible and I changed the program a bit. I didn't treat it as rigid as it says in the book. I kind of felt the need of the group at the time; we talked to the kids first and then adjusted. The boys volunteered to be in the program. I met the students after school and told them they had to sign a paper committing to it and they did. I only lost one boy. I told them there would be a graduation and there would be shirts. They love shirts here. That was incentive for them.

"They enjoyed it. Every day after every lesson they had a journal writing that they really liked doing. They were really honest, and they told me they thought it would help them. A lot of our kids when they leave here are not going to return to school. Hopefully they'll get the GED, but they need to understand what it's going to be like going back to the workforce. They did a really nice job in this program of giving real-life skills in real-life contexts.

"The book was really simple. Anyone could follow the book. If you were in a regular school you may be able to handle it differently. But we discussed a lot, they were very willing to discuss. I was very pleased with it. It was a very positive experience.

"I had one chance to see one of the boys negotiate with a teacher outside in the hall and he was using the skills. He did a fine job. He got back in the classroom. The teacher was kicking him out of class and if they get kicked out of class they can get a red violation. They don't want that because if they get too many they can be locked down for a day and they don't want that. Evidently he didn't really talk back to her but he was voicing his opinion and she took it as talking back. He got really upset and he didn't understand it. So then he asked if he could talk to her and he pulled her aside. I don't know exactly what he said but they talked very nicely and then she let him back in. Later I said to him, 'I noticed you were using your negotiation skills' and he said, 'Yes and they worked in this case.'

"A lot of these kids have anger control and impulse control difficulties. That would be a good program as well. But I still think the PYN helps with this, it has a couple segments on that.

"If someone is going to use this in a discipline school or a detention center or a prison environment they have to be flexible. They have to know what works in that situation. The first couple of classes we had, the boys were like 'Mrs. Keeney, we can't take this and do it out in the street.' I said, 'No, you're going to have to, the only way you are going to change things in your neighborhoods and your schools is by bringing this to them and showing them how to do it. Your mission is to do that, to bring all this positive learning to the street and use it.' But it didn't discourage them from doing the program; they still did the program."

*One student, Karl Benson, a sixteen-year-old, had recently completed the PYN program at NCCDC.* Karl explains how he uses his PYN skills at the Center: "Sometimes we argue and sometimes they try to fight and I just tell them to sit back and talk to each other, listen to each other, have people work each other's problems out. I'm trying to train them with the skills I've learned since they haven't had the PYN training yet. It's going pretty well. I would sit on the far side and see them, first they'd start arguing and then they'd stop and then they'd start talking with each other and trying to come to agreement." But, as he accepts, "A couple guys aren't interested in it, but I just let them alone."

The PYN materials were realistic to Karl. "I liked the role plays and the videos where they were working their problems out. They were situations I could see myself in. Everybody here should be asked to go through PYN. It would help things out a lot. If it weren't for Ms. Keeney, she taught me you don't have to argue with people, you can talk it out. I like it and it helped me a lot."

# CHAPTER SIX

# STUDENTS HELPING STUDENTS
## Peer Mediation

### Richard Cohen

*During soccer practice, Shaji overheard one of his teammates, Adrian, saying that all In-dians eat is "goat food." Some of the other kids laughed. Shaji likes the food his mom gives him for lunch, and he is proud of his heritage. Although Shaji has never had a problem with Adrian, Adrian's "joking" is starting to get on his nerves.*

School-based peer mediation is one of the most popular and effective ap-proaches to integrating the practice of conflict resolution into schools. From the start of the modern conflict resolution education (CRE) movement in the early 1980s, peer mediation has been one of its centerpieces.[1] Many thousands of schools in the United States and in dozens of other countries have implemented peer mediation programs, and these efforts serve almost every conceivable student population.

The convergence of a number of factors helps explain the status of peer mediation:

- Increasingly, educators—in rural and suburban as well as in city schools—were troubled by an increase in the amount and the tenor of student conflict. There consequently was a burgeoning interest among educators to explore this issue.
- When students become involved in conflicts, especially when students take actions that are disruptive or that contravene school rules, educators have a

clear mandate to intervene. The question is not whether to act but rather how to intervene in the most effective manner.

- The mission of most schools includes helping young people develop the knowledge, skills, and attitudes that will enable them to succeed as adults. One of the most essential sets of skills is the ability to resolve conflicts effectively.
- Peer mediation encourages students to apply conflict resolution skills when it matters most—when they are in dispute. This characteristic sets it apart from other conflict resolution models that do not include a formal effort to encourage students to use their skills when they are actually involved in a conflict.

Peer mediation elegantly marries educators' mandate to intervene with their mission to educate and empower young people. Additional features have led to the widespread implementation of the peer mediation concept. For one, it is very effective. Upwards of 80 percent of the time that students attend a peer mediation session, they are able to create a satisfactory solution to their conflict that lasts over the long term. And, very important, student mediators love doing this work. Mediating is an eminently rewarding way for students to improve their schools. Consider these typical remarks from peer mediators:

*Being a mediator makes me feel good. It makes me feel that the more I help people, the more I appreciate myself as a person and as a mediator. I have more respect for myself and others now. I try my best to achieve more things in life.*
MIDDLE SCHOOL STUDENT

*Mediating has helped me to be more open to other people's problems. When the disputants lay their problem on the table they're saying, "We trust you." It's a great feeling when they come [after the session] and tell you what became of it.*
HIGH SCHOOL STUDENT

Educators see significant benefits from peer mediation. They cite the following as their goals for implementing peer mediation programs:

- To make their schools safer and more productive places to work and learn
- To resolve student conflicts effectively
- To teach students conflict resolution skills
- To encourage students to take responsibility for their school life

## Peer Mediation's Roots in Conflict Resolution

Before we look at the basics of peer mediation, it is first necessary to understand the conflict resolution principles from which it arose. The most fundamental of these is that conflict is a *normal* and unavoidable part of life. No matter what we do, how much money we have, or how spiritually enlightened we are, conflicts will nevertheless persist.

The second principle is that conflict often carries within it a *positive* potential for learning and growth. Such growth might include discovering more about oneself, creating an effective solution to a difficult problem, appreciating the perspective of others, or even improving one's relationship with a rival; in any case, conflict usually contains the seeds of constructive changes as well as the potential for destruction and suffering.

A final principle of conflict resolution, and one at the heart of the mediation process, is that it is often in one's self-interest to *work together* with one's adversaries. Competition, although fine on athletic fields, is an inefficient and usually ineffective way to resolve disputes. People are usually much better served by approaches that emphasize collaborative problem solving—that is, struggling together to craft solutions that meet all parties' needs (so-called win-win solutions). When warranted, collaborative approaches use resources efficiently, minimize suffering, and provide the maximum benefit to all parties.

Taken together, these axioms of conflict resolution argue for schools to create a systemic approach to resolving disputes. Peer mediation is just such an approach.

## What Is Mediation?

Mediation is a structured method of conflict resolution in which trained individuals (the mediators) assist people in dispute (the parties) by listening to their concerns and helping them negotiate. There are four essential elements of mediation:

*1. Voluntariness.* Parties choose to participate in mediation, and once the process begins, they choose whether and how to resolve their dispute. Parties are free to conclude the mediation process at any time and pursue other means of resolving their conflict.

*2. Impartiality.* Mediators refrain from demonstrating judgment about right and wrong and strive to be unbiased at all times. They also have no power or interest in forcing parties to take any particular action. When agreements are created, they are fashioned according to the wishes of the parties.

*3. Confidentiality.* Information that is shared during mediation is held in the strictest confidence by mediators and coordinators. Parties are informed of any exceptions to confidentiality—typically information related to dangerous or illegal activity—before they begin the process.

*4. Self-Determination.* During mediation, parties are encouraged to take responsibility for their actions in the past and for their behavior in the future. Regardless of their role in the conflict, all parties participate in creating a resolution to the dispute.

Typically, mediation sessions begin with an opening statement in which the mediator explains the process, clarifies expectations, and attempts to put the parties at ease. This is followed by an opportunity for each party to explain his or her thoughts and feelings to the mediator without interruption. The mediator often asks questions and summarizes parties' concerns after each has finished speaking.

Next, parties are encouraged to talk directly to one another. The mediator asks questions that bring unspoken issues to the surface, and strives to create opportunities for the parties to understand each other's perspectives (if they so choose). When this facilitated dialogue has run its course, and parties have understood each other as much as they are willing, the mediator encourages parties to discuss what it is they need in order to feel that their conflict is resolved. This often results in the creation of a written agreement that is signed by the parties. (Elementary school mediators create verbal agreements.)

## How Peer Mediation Programs Operate

After a school makes the commitment to implement a peer mediation program, a diverse group of students representing a cross section of the student body receives intensive training in the mediation of disputes.[2] Upon completing their training, these students, working in teams, offer their services to their peers. Interpersonal conflicts that are appropriate for mediation—usually all disputes except those that involve weapons, drugs, or serious harassment or violence—are referred to the adult in charge of the program, called the peer mediation coordinator. Referrals can come from any member of the school community: students, teachers, administrators, support staff, and parents.

After receiving a referral, the coordinator conducts a brief intake interview with the students in conflict to explain the process and to determine whether their conflict is appropriate for mediation. If it is, and if they choose to participate, the coordinator selects appropriate mediators, schedules the session, and is available to supervise during the session. Mediation sessions must be conducted in an area in the school that affords both auditory and visual privacy.

Peer mediation sessions usually last less than one hour—fifteen minutes in elementary schools, thirty-five minutes in middle school, and fifty-five minutes in high schools on average—and the overwhelming majority result in agreements that are acceptable to the parties. When sessions are complete, parties might return to class or be escorted back to the counselors or disciplinarians who initially made the referral.

Educators who have implemented peer mediation programs attribute many benefits to them. Although many of these benefits are based on anecdotal evidence, quantitative research is beginning to substantiate educators' claims. The benefits mentioned most frequently in association with peer mediation are that it

- Resolves student conflict effectively
- Teaches students essential life skills
- Motivates students to resolve conflicts proactively and collaboratively
- Improves school climate
- Engages all students, even those who are considered "at-risk"
- Prevents conflicts from escalating

## Discipline Is Not Conflict Resolution

It is important to note that schools traditionally have not had a systematic approach to managing student conflict. Instead they have had *disciplinary* systems that by default were used for conflict management. As we will see, this is not an effective approach to helping students reconcile interpersonal differences.

The first reason is that disciplinary systems do not distinguish between disciplinary offenses and interpersonal conflict. Most interpersonal conflicts between students are just that—*between students*. They do not involve the violation of a school rule. Two students in conflict over a boyfriend, for instance, might never take action that constitutes a disciplinary offense. As a result, their conflict—like the majority of student interpersonal conflicts—would never come to the attention of the system. In effect, students must wait for their conflict to escalate, leading one or both of them to break a school rule, before the system pays attention. The potential for students to refer themselves or their peers for conflict resolution assistance is also lost.

In addition, school disciplinary systems rely almost exclusively on sanctions and negative reinforcement. Theoretically, such "negative feedback" steers young people away from destructive behaviors and toward proper conduct. Unfortunately, however, sanctions alone do not help young people understand, take responsibility for, or control their actions. Even more to our point, sanctions are often experienced by students as unrelated to the content of their interpersonal conflicts. Sure, one ninth grader might have pushed another angrily, but the pushing itself was only the ultimate action in a drama that might have more to do with a friendship turned sour or a lack of respect or a misunderstanding than with "violence."

Of course, disciplinary consequences serve an essential function in schools, and conflict resolution principles and skills can inform and improve school disciplinary processes. But applying sanctions alone usually does little to help students truly resolve interpersonal conflicts.

## Students as Mediators

Peer mediation programs not only emphasize the efficacy of the mediation process for resolving interpersonal conflicts but also enable *students themselves* to do the mediating. The peer mediation concept recognizes that students bring unique strengths to this work. Young people understand their peers and know the pressures, the attitude, and the language of their times. They know what their peers think is important and why. This gives them a natural advantage as mediators.

Student mediators also have no power *over* their peers, and this implicitly empowers them. Young people often experience adults as "trying to get us to do something," but in peer mediation, with no authority figure to resist, parties are forced to confront themselves and each other.

Students also command a tacit and unique sort of respect from their peers. When mediation sessions are conducted with poise and professionalism by students perceived to be "cool," their peers naturally listen. For this reason, coordinators carefully select teams of student mediators to suit the needs of each group of parties. Young people are distinctly suited to mediate the conflicts of their fellow students, and this accounts in part for peer mediation's effectiveness.

## Peer Mediation in Elementary Schools

Important differences exist between peer mediation programs implemented at the elementary level (ages six to eleven) as opposed to those at the middle and high school levels. These differences arise in response to the developmental abilities of elementary students as well as to the structure typically employed to educate them.

### Developmental Considerations

Elementary peer mediation programs generally operate in grades four through six. Only by fourth grade can students consistently demonstrate, in an age-appropriate way, basic aptitudes of mediation—for example, summarizing what another has said, understanding the importance of perspective in human relations, and appreciating the subtleties of confidentiality. Sometimes fourth- through sixth-grade students will serve as mediators for their younger schoolmates, but in general only upper elementary students are trained as mediators.[3]

In addition, the process taught to elementary students is simple and delineated. Student mediators are supplied with a mediation note page on which a series of steps ("Summarize what the first party has said. Ask the first party how she feels. Thank the first party for speaking") is outlined. Ten-year-old mediators follow these steps closely; they find it more difficult to "go off the page" and create spontaneous interventions than their counterparts in middle and especially high schools. It is important to mention here that as this is a young field, conflict resolution educators still have a great deal to learn about how to tailor their efforts to address young people at differing developmental stages.

### Structural Considerations

Elementary students are usually educated in so-called self-contained classrooms in which they remain with the same teacher (and group of peers) for most of the school day. As a result, it is much easier for these teachers to *deliver* and, equally important, to *reinforce* conflict resolution curricula in their classrooms. Curricular approaches to teaching conflict resolution are therefore more popular and effective in elementary schools than in middle and high schools.

When elementary students do mediate, they usually do so during the unstructured recess typical of elementary education. Teams of peer mediators are assigned to each recess, and they wander the playground, wearing special T-shirts, carrying their mediation clipboards, ready to offer their services should their classmates require assistance. Some elementary teachers also create so-called conflict corners or peace places in the classrooms, where students go to negotiate mutual solutions to problems. When the students in conflict need help, their peers are asked to serve as informal mediators.

## Promising Developments in Peer Mediation

Considering that tens of thousands of educators and students across the globe are applying the peer mediation concept, it is no surprise that interesting innovations are reported each year. The following are a few that deserve greater attention:

***Mediating an Increasing Range of School-Based Disputes.*** When peer mediation was first introduced, most sessions involved relatively simple disputes about rumors or teasing. Now student mediators, with assistance from adults whenever appropriate, regularly handle such challenging disputes as those involving large groups, racism, parents and their children, gangs, teachers and their students, and coworkers.

***Growing Sensitivity to Issues of Culture and Diversity.*** Mediation is fundamentally concerned with being sensitive to the parties' needs. Still, assumptions at the core of the mediation process—the importance of talking directly to those with whom one conflicts, of making eye contact, and of openly expressing feelings, to name but a few—can appear offensive to people rooted in many non-Western cultures. School-based mediators are continually modifying their work to make it effective and acceptable to the populations they serve.

***Including Parents.*** Although relying solely on parents to oversee a mediation program is risky, schools have discovered a variety of ways to involve them. Parents help supervise sessions (especially in elementary schools), are trained in conflict resolution skills for use at home, and are encouraged to use mediation services when they cannot resolve disputes with their own children. (These disputes are mediated by students along with parent volunteers who are trained as mediators.)

## The Challenge of Implementing Peer Mediation Programs

As is true of any school change effort, it is quite difficult to implement peer mediation programs that live up to their potential. Many efforts falter from the start, and many more disappear after only a few years. Three initial ingredients are absolutely essential for a program's success:

1.   *Enough interpersonal conflict to warrant initiating the program.* If mediators do not have the opportunity to mediate cases, few of the benefits associated with peer mediation programs will be realized. Each school must determine what constitutes "enough conflict." Some programs handle only twenty cases a year, others mediate over five hundred. As a general rule, if your program won't mediate at least one case per week, then peer mediation might not be the best fit for your school.

2.   *Administrative support.* For peer mediation to succeed, administrators must work aggressively to overcome attitudinal and structural resistance within their schools. In particular, administrators in charge of discipline must be willing to

make referrals and support student mediators' efforts. Even when students' behavior warrants disciplinary consequences, administrators can encourage them to resolve their underlying interpersonal conflict through peer mediation.

3. *A peer mediation coordinator.* Like the coach of the basketball team or the conductor of the orchestra, the peer mediation coordinator oversees all aspects of a peer mediation program. The more resources this school-based adult has in terms of skill, commitment, and time during the school day, the more successful the program is likely to be. Coordinators should be compensated either with time during the school day that can be devoted to peer mediation or with a stipend.[4]

Additional actions schools can take to increase the likelihood of success include the following:

• *Developing a comprehensive school philosophy or pedagogy that encourages students to take responsibility for their own education and work cooperatively with their peers.* Students who grow accustomed to making significant decisions will be more comfortable accessing mediation services when they can't resolve a conflict on their own.

• *Integrating conflict resolution into the school through other avenues, including administrative practice, teacher training, and the general curriculum.* A valid criticism of some peer mediation programs is that a handful of students receive intensive training while most students receive very little. Although few schools are interested in implementing what has come to be called the whole-school approach to CRE, it is worth striving for. Ideally, students should find collaborative conflict resolution processes modeled for them at every turn.

If these fundamentals are present in a school, chances are high that a strong mediation program will result.

## Getting Started

Implementing peer mediation programs requires careful planning, and many issues need to be addressed for the program to work. Consider the needs of your program for the first three years of operation if possible. The following are ten of the most important questions to consider:

1. Who will coordinate the program?
2. How will the mediation program be funded?
3. Which students and staff will be trained to mediate?
4. Who will conduct the peer mediation training?

5. When will the training be scheduled?
6. Which issues will be mediated?
7. Where and when will mediation sessions be held?
8. What is the program's confidentiality policy?
9. How will the school at large be informed about mediation?
10. What kind of follow-up training and support will be provided for mediators?

Once your program is operating, a number of indicators can help you determine whether it is reaching its potential. Although each school must arrive at its own definition of success, the more your program shares the following characteristics, the more "mature" your peer mediation program is:

When the call is put out for volunteers, at least 10 percent of the student body applies to be a mediator.

The program directly serves at least 10 percent of the school population each academic year (for example, in a school of eight hundred, a minimum of eighty students use mediation services during the year).

Students themselves refer one-third of the conflicts that are mediated.

Administrators perceive the program to be an integral part of the school and strongly resist any attempt to do away with it.

Two significant cautions are in order. First, having a peer mediation program in school should not imply that educators abdicate responsibility for fairly and consistently enforcing rules and norms. Some behavior is unacceptable, intolerable, and an occasion for administrative action first and peer mediation in addition (and only if it is appropriate). Adults should make this clear to students in no uncertain terms.

Second, not all conflicts are appropriate for mediation. Those that involve persistent harassment or bullying and a marked imbalance of power between victim and harasser, for instance, are often not suited to mediation. Student mediators can and have successfully managed a wide range of challenging conflicts, but coordinators must screen every case to determine its suitability for mediation.[5]

◆ ◆ ◆

At the beginning of this chapter, I laid out one typical scenario that could be handled by peer mediation. In the case of Shaji and Adrian, the soccer coach would have referred them to the peer mediation program. Both students would then have a chance to discuss the issue of the "goat food put-down" and find a way to repair the relationship and get to the root of the problem. In many cases involving put-downs and discrimination, peer mediators help disputants express their feelings directly to the other person and find ways to address perceived and actual racial discrimination in a safe and productive process. In overwhelming numbers, students like Shaji and Adrian leave mediation feeling good after having worked out the problem themselves.

When implemented effectively, peer mediation is one application of CRE that can become a vital part of school life. Student mediators are excited to offer their services, student parties are grateful for the help, and educators wonder how they got along without the program. This is a win-win all around.

# In Their Own Words

## "Peer Mediation Makes the World Better"

*Horace Mann Middle School is in only the second year of its peer mediation program, but in those two years the program has become a central part of the way conflicts and discipline issues are handled. Founded in 1931, Horace Mann is an old, inner-city school serving approximately 650 students; 90 percent of its student body is of Hispanic ethnicity. The students and staff who tell us their stories here see the program as a critical factor in providing alternatives to fighting and other types of violence. Here is what they say about the program.*

"Al Rodriguez" and Amber Quintana are two seventh-grade mediators. Al has been a peer mediator for two years and is quite experienced by now. The peer mediation coordinator asks him to mediate many of the more difficult cases, and he seems to truly understand its potential for good at school. "I think mediation is good because everybody can talk to each other and tell each other's sides. Most of the time there is confusion about what happened about rumors or something, and once they can confront each other they can talk then, and they really don't have a problem. I think mediations are good because it can stop a lot of fighting. Once they get it off their shoulders, why they were fighting, they start talking to each other and they stop." Amber, who is also in her second year, agrees: "I think peer mediation is good because most of the time kids need someone to talk to. . . . It's better to talk to someone your own age."

Changing the fighting culture is something the program seeks to accomplish, and the peer mediators have found that having an alternative helps bring about this culture change. "I think that fighting should not be your first choice. . . . The mediation I was just in was where two girls were friends and another friend asked [one of the girls] if she wanted to fight and she said no, that she didn't want to, but her friend told the other girl that she did. So it was mostly her friend instigating just to get them to fight and to be entertained." The mediation helped these two stay friends, avoid a fight, and make a plan for talking with their other friend about spreading rumors and starting fights. Amber goes on to say, "My first choice would be to talk to the person I am having a conflict with; ask why I am having problems with them and why they are having problems with me and then maybe go to peer mediation if it got any worse than that. But fighting would not be the first choice."

Both Al and Amber like being peer mediators. Al says, "I enjoy being a peer mediator in order to help other people. . . . We have made a lot of friends as peer mediators and we have made a lot of friends with people we have had mediations with." Amber agrees: "Sometimes we see people in the halls that we have helped and they stop us and say, 'Hi, thank you for how you have helped us.'"

When asked whether mediation could help others besides schoolkids, Al says this: "If we had something like peer mediation where all the leaders of the countries could come talk to each other, then I guess it would solve a lot more problems than war. Most of the war is just misunderstanding; just like fights here at school." For Al, the program has been a real success at the school. "When I was here in sixth grade there were a lot of fights and a lot of bad stuff happening here. Since we started peer mediation last year I haven't seen that many fights." Amber agrees: "I think that it has helped our school a lot and I think it would help other ones too. Most of the kids we do mediations with are all friends now." Al says modestly, "I guess the teachers like it. There are some teachers here who refer kids to mediation." Actually, there are a lot.

*Claudia Rodriguez, Lisa Chavez, and Melodie Gonzales are all eighth graders who have been in fights at Horace Mann Middle School and have used peer mediation to help solve their problems.* When they first went to peer mediation, it was hard. "At first you are nervous because it's your enemy that you are having a peer mediation with. But at the end, it comes down to an agreement that you are friends," says Melodie. According to them, it not only feels good but also works. Still, they say, "When you come down you just want to fight them." Claudia agrees: "At first I was just scared that [the other disputant] would just tell her friends and all that and kick my ass but when we talked we became friends and it helped." All agreed that coming to peer mediation after that was easier because they knew what to expect.

From their point of view, the peer mediation program has truly helped the school. Claudia says, "I think that it is good for the school to have it because when I was in sixth grade we didn't have it and there were more fights and rumors in the school. Since they started it last year there aren't as many fights and there aren't as many problems because you can solve it yourself—you can solve it verbally not physically. This peer mediation helped us learn that it's not really worth fighting; it makes it worse and you should just talk about it with your friend using your peers."

Lisa goes onto say, "I think it has really changed the school because before this program came, there was a bunch of fights every day and since this program came there haven't been any fights." Melodie agrees: "Since they started peer mediation, it is cool because people won't fight, they just need to talk it over." Each of them knows personally because they have all been in fights before and weren't afraid of fighting. Now they use peer mediation a lot to solve their conflicts. They say that kids should do this more because it makes such a difference—and, according to Claudia, "Kids could learn more things about why they are fighting."

However, there are limits to the kinds of situations in which peer mediation works. Says Melodie, "It depends on the person. If they are bullies, then they think it is stupid. But if you are the average kid, then it's cool because you don't want to start a fight and you want to be friends with everybody. Bullies think it's dumb because they think you are going to snitch on them. If it's a bully, they would rather fight about it than use words." Clearly, these students believe that peer mediation works with students who want to participate in a fair, give-and-take process and that most bullies want to get their way even if it isn't fair. The chapter on bullying will also address this dynamic at the elementary school level.

Even when a person is dealing with someone who isn't a bully, choosing to talk it out rather than fight it out is hard. "When you are alone it is hard to talk to your enemy," says Melodie. But the girls also talked about the alternative and the intense peer pressure to fight. "If you were just to go up to them in the hallway [and try to talk it out] then people will crowd around you and think you are going to fight. It's like peer pressure. But if you are alone in a room with a mediator, you just talk about it and it's better than having the whole school around you and peer pressure you to fight."

So how do they get from the hallway, where students are eager to be entertained, to the peer mediation room? You have to make a decision, they say. "You either just walk away to your class or you fight—it's your decision. It's either you talk about it or you get suspended." Although avoiding a suspension may seem an easy choice to make, for them it's not. Says Lisa, "It's very hard walking away because when you walk away they start saying 'chicken' and calling you names and it gets worse. . . . You want to walk back there and fight them, but then you just have to think about it."

Melodie has learned from peer mediation to catch the first signs of a fight and prevent it before it escalates. "You come [to the peer mediation room] at the first sign of a fight. And you talk about it before anything occurs in the hallway." And, Claudia says, "Students should just go to their class and leave them alone because it's not their problem." All agreed that friends and teachers should encourage the two people to use peer mediation rather than fight.

Using peer mediation rather than fighting also has the advantage of helping with schoolwork, they say. "When somebody wants to fight you it's just on your mind. You can't concentrate on your schoolwork," says Melodie. For Lisa this is what happens: "You are nervous and worried about it and can't even do your work. You are shaking too much. You can't write." Claudia agrees and says, "You are angry at everybody around you, and [when you know you are going to peer mediation] it relieves you."

In closing, these three girls who used to fight a lot say this about the program: "I think it's pretty cool that we have it. I am happy that it came to our school." "Peer mediation really does help. Some people say it doesn't, but mostly about 95 percent of the kids think that peer mediation helps. I do and a lot of my friends do too, because if you want to be cool with somebody but they don't like you because of rumors, then it really solves the problem. There used to be more people in the detention hall or fighting. Now there are more people solving their problems than in the past. It has really helped out me and my friends to talk it out."

*Hallie Bradley is a school counselor and the school's peer mediation program coordinator.* Though only in their second year of the program, she feels it is well established. "It's pretty well publicized in our school. A lot of our kids know if they are having problems they can come for mediation. The first year we advertised for it, but this year we haven't even needed to advertise for it because it is so well known throughout the school." Mediations are growing in popularity at this school because "in our newsletters we mention that the mediations are going on in English or Spanish. . . . I don't need to go rally up kids for peer mediation—they come here. [It works because] kids don't like to go to adults for help and . . . [because] they can request help from a peer. They are just really receptive and open to it. They don't want to get suspended regardless of what their parents are telling them, because they have school rules to follow. A lot of our kids love our school and it's a very culturally supportive school . . . so [peer mediation] is a way to keep them here, and they know that if they go and try to solve it they are better off."

Although the school has created a comprehensive educational program with a wide variety of activities for kids to engage in, it does have a fighting culture to deal with. "There is a lot of fighting that goes on. We have a lot of kids [for whom] it's a trained behavior, and their parents aren't necessarily opposed to fighting. I often have kids in my office that say, 'My mom said if she pushed I should push back'—not walk away, not involve the police, but push back. So it's a coping mechanism that a lot of our kids are taught through their family. We are just giving them another choice or option to solve their problems."

And the peer mediation program has begun to make real changes in this culture. "There is less violence at the school, now. There's not as much fighting. And kids know where to go if they are having problems. It's not looked down upon to go for mediation—it's kind of like the norm. It's part of the school climate. It's a great way to let kids use their voice rather than violence, and they are doing that." However, she says, "I think that there are some kids that have [violence] so deeply ingrained that they use [fighting] to be suspended. But I think a lot of kids aren't fighters. They will see it as a great way not to have to fight. Although some of the kids have violence deeply ingrained in them . . . they are seeing the alternatives."

Hallie has seen the program tackle a wide variety of issues. "I have had some mediations about lice and rumors about lice. . . . I have had some about flirting or bad flirting. I find it helpful to use their language. I have had parents that

have been heavily involved; the parents of the kids that are disputing are disputing themselves on our school property. When it gets to that level it goes to administration. I have had family battles . . . where one student's mom doesn't like
her friend's mom. 'My mom told me to jump her,' a kid will say. It's like the Judds
and the Clampetts." Was it successful? "I haven't seem them back so I guess it was.
. . . We have even done mediations about racism or perceived racism, and those
have been helpful to get things out in the air and get the kids to honestly talk about
it. I have had success. You need a really special kid [as a mediator] who knows
he isn't going to be biased."

Although mediation and bullying don't always mix, in certain circumstances
where the power is not too imbalanced, it can work—and Hallie points this out.
"It helps a lot with the bullying. It deters bullying, and when kids are feeling bullied they come in and we do mediations; we get an agreement about what behaviors are going to go on between those kids." She does, however, put clear limits
on cases suitable for mediation. "I don't allow mediations where there has been
any physical contact until they have served their suspension. I will, however, do
mediation after a suspension. The more severe mediations I recommend that an
adult should do because of the liability. For example, two girls ended up getting
into a pushing fight after basketball in the bathroom and then their parents got
involved and started screaming in the street at each other—and then the parents
came in to the principal. This was a case for the administration to handle."

The peer mediation program works hand in hand with the school administration and disciplinarians—and Hallie tries to do so in a manner that respects the
need for classroom instructional time. "We work closely with the student adviser.
If she has kids that have a conflict and are getting suspended and they have fought,
then upon their return they get a mediation. The less time we can keep them
out of class, the better. I do a preliminary sort of gauge, like 'Are you scared?' 'Do
you feel you are going to be hurt today?' to make sure they are going to be OK
and to gauge how soon the mediation is to happen according to if there is violence or if violence is about to happen. It is hard because we only try to pull kids
out of electives [so their test scores don't go down]. But [teachers] don't want those
problems in their classroom either, and they request [peer mediation]. It's just a
delicate balance. . . . But if it is going to end up in violence, I have to pull them
no matter what even if it is out of a core class. If somebody's going to get jumped
after school, the mediation is going to have to happen.

"It is the coolest thing to see a kid be trained as a mediator and become pro-
ficient and capable of doing mediations and seeing that grow and seeing how it
helps mediators develop. Our counseling office is a lot more effective because of
student mediators. It's wonderful to see them grow."

*Lyons and Hygiene Elementary Schools are small schools separated by ten miles in a distinctly rural area of Colorado. Because the schools are so small, both programs are run by the same school counselor. Is peer mediation different at an elementary school? Are there many differences between a rural school program and an inner-city program? Here's what students and teachers say about peer mediation at their school.*

"I like being a mediator because I like helping students solve their problems. I think it makes the world better," says Liz Vitale, a fifth grader who started mediating this year. "You have to try to understand their problems and have to try and think that if you were in their shoes how you would feel." Her friend Amber Nelson, who also started mediating this year, agrees but shares some of the frustrations with it too. "At times it can be frustrating when people are going back and forth with the blame game, but other times it's OK or cool." Both girls have learned how to deal with the blame game when it comes up. "We use some of the probing questions that we were trained to use to get them out of the blame game," says Amber. "I try to keep asking them questions so they don't have time to keep talking to each other and keep the blame game going," adds Liz.

In addition to handling the blame game, mediators also need to be able to handle unruly or unfocused disputants by setting clear limits with them. "There were three people in here and two mediators. [At one point] we had to refocus them by saying, 'You gotta stop it and we have to solve this because we are not just here to be monkeying around. We are here to solve your problems and go. If you are just going to be goofing off we are going to have to send you back to class.'" After that, the disputants did settle down and resolved their problem.

Whether it is through probing questions or through establishing an atmosphere of seriousness, it seems that these and other strategies work. "Sometimes kids come in and they are really mad at each other, and the mediators talk to them and help them get to an agreement and they go out in a more peaceful state than when they came in. That's pretty much our purpose," states Liz. According to Amber, "I think it has made a definite difference in our school because before we started doing the Peace PALS [PALS stands for Peace, Acceptance, Love, and Social Responsibility] and mediation I thought there was a lot more fights going on and the kids didn't respect each other that much."

Both of the elementary schools use mediation and negotiation to solve their problems. The steps are similar and can be used with or without a neutral third party. Says Liz, "Usually what we save mediation for is when someone has a big problem. Like if someone just pushed you and got the soccer ball to their side. The peace place [which uses a four-step negotiation process] is a shorter way to solve the problem. The first graders find you [easily because the peer mediators have orange vests on]." The shorter way is a series of footprints painted on the ground depicting the steps to negotiation. Amber puts it this way: "When you are outside on duty, we can take them over to the peace tree and there are steps on the stone, which shows them how to do it." Each process has its benefits, and the mediators can use both depending on the seriousness of the issue.

Amber and Liz have both seen "trouble" turned into "peace" through the mediation process. "We did this one mediation and there were these two kids and they were sort of acting like bullies to each other and they were cussing at each other and they were fighting. And now they are friends again." Randy asked them how they did it. Their answer was simple—they just took them through the mediation steps and it was that easy. But they do recognize that getting to the mediation "table" may not be that easy. It may be threatening, anxiety producing, or just plain scary. "A lot of the times when people come into mediation they don't want to do it and then they get here and they don't mind as much because they feel like it is a more comfortable area and there are no teachers and they can make it work better and it is from a kid's perspective," says Liz.

The Peace PALS mediators take turns working lunch duty with the younger kids—and they love it. This is an opportunity for the older kids to help the younger students solve problems on the playground. "When we are outside, I can really see the difference with the younger kids because usually they are arguing back and forth about stuff that they can resolve peacefully as opposed to just hitting and punching each other, so really I think it has made a difference because now that we have Peace PALS they know that someone else is there that knows what they are going through to solve their problems," says Liz. "I think that if there were adults as mediators, for the little kids I think that they would think that the adults were trying to overpower them. If I was a little kid and I had to do a mediation with an adult I would be a lot more nervous because I would feel that the adult would tell on me. I am even reluctant to tell my parents stuff, so I think it is better to have older kids as mediators."

Amber agrees: "A lot of younger kids don't really listen to adults because they get enough of their parents at home and they think that adults are just the same. But when an older kid talks to them we are sort of setting the rules for them and maybe when they get older maybe they will do Peace PALS." And, says Amber, "they are kind of used to seeing me out there. It's a cool feeling."

Both mediators are clear about why this is important for kids and for the world. "Kids sooner or later become adults and if the kids learn how to do this now, learn how to get along with their friends and people they don't get along with, it will definitely make a difference when they are older because they will know how to resolve their conflict," says Liz. Amber continues, "I think it will definitely make the world a better place because when we grow up we can teach it to our children and they can teach it to their children and it can be passed down from generation to generation and if we can pass it from generation to generation, it can spread."

Peer mediation is also about being of service to people other than yourself. Liz says that "after I went into Peace PALS, my life changed. It can really change people's life. I love being with younger kids because I feel responsible for helping others to talk it out." Amber agrees: "It is really cool to watch because you see how you are helping someone else's life as opposed to just yourself. . . . A few months ago, I babysat two girls. They were really wild and I sort of tried to use mediation steps to help them solve it and I got it solved. I felt really good about it because they live right next door to me and they said that when I am old enough to start babysitting for a longer time they want me to come back. It is a way of impacting others' lives in a way outside of school. You don't have to be a Peace PAL to construct peace, you can be a regular person. You feel just the same way."

*Karen Benge-Rosson is the principal at Lyons Elementary School, which according to her is "a very, very small school" with 175 kids. She loves the benefits of the mediation program and finds ways to use it with her daily discipline needs.* "Having a peer mediation program has been really enriching for me both professionally and personally. . . . To have a backup of a mediation program, particularly with our Peace PALS, is critical. I use them regularly as a part of our disciplinary approach. When kids come into my office in the middle of a conflict, they aren't always ready to mediate right then. I will go through my administrative thing, like tell them about the rules and why we can't have this kind of behavior and . . . then 90 percent of the time I will refer them to mediation as a principal referral. After they cool down a little bit I will call down a student mediator. I had Alicia do our mediation that day and she was incredibly skilled. I just kind of sat and kept quiet. In fifteen minutes she followed all the rules of mediation, was very businesslike and a very good listener and got them to agree to a set of written kinds of agreements about how they are going to treat each other in the next couple of weeks. I was so impressed. Truly in fifteen minutes she accomplished what would have taken me twenty-five to thirty minutes, and I probably would have been far less effective at getting these two boys to agree. It was very, very impressive to watch this ten-year-old little girl take a hold of the situation and get these two boys to shake hands, look into each other's eyes and agree not to harass each other. So I consider mediation an absolutely essential part of our program here at the school. It is truly changing the culture of the school."

As a principal, she knows that conflicts are inevitable in the classroom. However, she also knows that the program must, and can, work in collaboration with teachers' intent on maximizing instructional time. "The reality is that if you have kids that are not getting along and wanting to hit each other in the classroom, it is going to disrupt the learning to the point that everybody is going to be disrupted.

Teachers recognize that [mediation] is a good alternative to losing instructional time through emotional angst. I think that the other thing that kids look forward to is that somebody is going to solve it, and rather than being totally dominated by the feeling of hurt for the next two-and-a-half hours, they are less obsessed with the slight or the hurt knowing that at 1 P.M. they are going to have a mediation and an opportunity to solve this. I see it as buying a whole lot of instructional time."

*Michele Bourgeois is the school counselor who coordinates the peer mediation and Peace PALS program, which is in its third year.* "It takes at least that long for the whole student body to recognize that they have an alternative. Now kids know that there is a good chance that they will be referred to mediation if they have any sort of conflicts or complaints. It is just a part of their life now. They seem to have a little more respect or responsibility for it." Karen agrees: "They have more ownership of it when they have to go face-to-face with their opponent and talk it through. It is certainly not as a punishment but as an alternative to continuing their behaviors that are not productive."

Michele knows that talking directly to one another is key. "When they hear they have to mediate the problem among themselves instead of having me resolve it, the whole dynamic changes. It's like they are not there to get somebody in trouble and to blame them, because it doesn't do any good anymore to just blame, so they automatically take that responsibility and ownership."

Students have even used mediation not only to solve their own disputes but also to help model for their parents how to resolve their conflicts. Says Michele, "We had two parents who very much got involved in their kid's disputes and were basically telling their kids, 'You can't talk to that other person,' to the point where it was having an impact on school. These kids mediated . . . and resolved their problem, and part of their agreement was 'We want to show our parents that we can get along, and we are going to keep our conflicts between us and not involve our parents.'"

In conclusion, the principal had this to say about the peer mediation program: "I don't see this as a program that is just a shot in the dark. This is a program that will build."

# CHAPTER SEVEN

# "WE CAN DO IT TOO!"
## Peer Mediation for Special Education Students

Paul I. Kaplan

*Ralph requests student mediation with Allan because Allan is always joining in with other students on the bus in "making rude comments" about him. Ralph is a seventeen-year-old eleventh grader diagnosed with emotional disabilities who has great difficulty making friends in school. Allan is a new ninth-grade student this year with a history of depression and a number of hospitalizations following suicide gestures. Allan tends to be a follower and joins in the negative peer behavior around him.*

*Their mediators are Tiffany, a senior with a history of bipolar disorder, and Ken, a tenth grader. Ken's challenges have included difficulties with reading and the resulting behavior problems that have been expressions of his frustration and embarrassment.*

*During the mediation session, Ralph admits that he wants to be friends with Allan and that he sometimes invites teasing by being socially awkward and inappropriate with other students. Allan admits that as a new student, he joins in negative behavior, but denies ever instigating it.*

*The mediators help these disputants work out the following agreement: Allan agrees to help Ralph "get into those groups" of other students, to "try to be friendlier," and to "explain to peers that Ralph wants to be in the group." Ralph agrees simply "to get along with Allan"—that is, to begin practicing better social skills with this sympathetic peer who has, after mediation, a better appreciation of the challenges Ralph faces.*

*Tiffany and Ken sign the agreement, ask Ralph and Allan to sign it, and invite the disputants, successfully, to shake hands.*

This example illustrates the value student mediation can have in a special education setting. The learning that takes place for both the disputants and the mediators can go a long way toward helping special needs students develop confidence and self-esteem. The disputants see they are capable of solving problems with the help of peers, that their problems are indeed solvable, and that they have the resources to come to helpful agreements. The mediators find that they can transcend their disabilities and the labels they've carried with them. They see that they can be of great service to their school community.

Student mediation programs and conflict resolution education (CRE) are rare in the schools that serve special needs students. Student mediation programs such as the one that has run successfully at Hannah More School and other special education schools prove that an ideal setting for these programs does indeed exist in the special education arena.

## History of Special Education

For most of our nation's history, schools were allowed to exclude, and often did exclude, children with disabilities. According to the U.S. Department of Education, prior to 1975 "One million children with disabilities were shut out of schools and hundreds of thousands more were denied appropriate services. Since then, the legislation changed the lives of these children. Many are learning and achieving at levels previously thought impossible. As a result, they are graduating from high school, going to college and entering the workforce as productive citizens in unprecedented numbers."[1]

IDEA, the Individuals with Disabilities Education Act, mandates that eligible children with disabilities have available to them special education and related services designed to address their unique educational needs. IDEA, and most especially the provision of special education, has its roots in the past. Public Law 94-142 mandated a free appropriate public education for all children with disabilities, ensured due process rights, and mandated Individual Educational Plans (IEPs) and least restrictive environments for all children with disabilities. This law was passed in 1975 and went into effect in October 1977.

Examples of the disabilities that fall under the IDEA mandate include but are not limited to autism, hearing and visual impairment, emotional disturbance, mental retardation, specific learning disability, orthopedic impairment, attention deficit disorder, attention deficit hyperactivity disorder, asthma, and diabetes. Examples of services mandated by IDEA, where necessary to assist a student with a disability to benefit from special education, include but are not limited to consultation and evaluation, counseling and social work services, assistive technology, parent counseling and training, speech and language therapy, and extended-year services.

## Special Education and Peer Mediation

Special education and peer mediation appear to be products of the same climate of serving and empowering children. Within ten years of the passage of P.L. 94-142, peer mediation programs began to emerge in public school systems in Massachusetts, Florida, Hawaii, and California. Creative educators began to see the tremendous value in empowering young people to help their peers resolve conflicts and develop lasting agreements. Currently there are peer mediation programs in public school systems throughout the United States, as well as in Canada and other countries abroad.

Despite the growth of peer mediation programs for "regular ed" students in public schools, there are few programs available for students in public or private special education. In an informal survey conducted in 2001 of school members of the National Association of Private Schools for Exceptional Children, only one school reported having an active peer mediation program.[2] The Maryland Association of Non-Public Special Education Facilities reports only four such schools with active peer mediation programs, including Hannah More School, where I am director of clinical services and coordinator of the peer mediation program. Some schools report that there is some form of CRE for this population, but the curriculum that exists takes the form of social skills training and behavior management, rather than conflict resolution as a specific skill.

The five private special education facilities that have successful peer mediation programs share some attributes in common. All five schools place a high value on academics leading toward graduation, individual and group therapy, and parental involvement. They each serve a population that is predominantly classified as emotionally disturbed, with a number of learning disabled and autistic students being served as well. According to IDEA, students who are classified as emotionally disturbed have long-standing problems that adversely affect their school performance. Typically their inability to learn is not related to intellectual or health factors. Rather, they have difficulty building or maintaining relationships, they show inappropriate types of behavior or feelings under normal circumstances, and they often feel unhappy or depressed. Students diagnosed with schizophrenia are also considered emotionally disturbed.

Goals of peer mediation programs in these special education settings are similar to, and are adapted from, peer mediation programs for regular education students. The goals include the following:

- Learning to help their peers who are in conflict find their own solutions
- Engaging their peers in active problem solving
- Learning and practicing the art of compromise, active listening, and focusing on common interests and areas of agreements to solve conflict

For special education students, the practice of peer mediation is especially relevant. Many of these students are very familiar with conflict in their lives, in their families, in their communities, and in former schools. For some of them, their disabilities have been the cause of family strife—for example, disagreement between their parents over child management. Frequently they have "normal," successful siblings who represent a standard for success they are unable to reach. As young children, these special needs children become the butt of teasing by peers, and often are the unwitting victims of insensitive teachers and school staff who, unaware of the children's limitations, often assume they are merely lazy and treat them as such.

Their special frustrations often erupt in physical acting out, typically when they reach middle school if not before. The onset of puberty and hormonal changes further confuses and disrupts their self-image. It is not uncommon for special needs students to be attracted to antisocial peer groups who offer a sense of belonging in exchange for both loyalty and delinquent behavior. These students, as a result, often sense an inability or unwillingness of parents and school personnel to truly listen to their issues and concerns.

Special education students usually respond quite readily to their peers' offer to mediate a conflict. It is remarkable how quickly special education students, both as disputants and as mediators, grasp the significance of, and use the opportunity for, this kind of empowerment.

Program goals for peer mediation typically are a decrease in school truancy, a decrease in aggressive behavior between students, and improved school climate and teacher morale. Peer mediation programs in special education share the same goals.

## Hannah More School's Peer Mediation Program

Hannah More School opened its doors as a private, nonprofit, residential treatment center and therapeutic day school in September 1978. Since September 1982, the school has been solely a therapeutic day school. We provide individualized academic, vocational, and therapeutic programs to middle and high school students who have been identified as emotionally disabled, autistic, or learning disabled, or whose behaviors have interfered with their ability to be successful in public school. Students are referred to our school following a meeting with their public school administrators, special educators, and parents. At this meeting, a determination is made regarding the student's disability and the level of service required to meet the student's special education needs. If it is decided that the special education resources within the students' public school jurisdiction are insufficient to meet their special education needs, a referral is then made to a school like Hannah More School.

It was during my own training in divorce and family mediation at the University of Maryland that I first learned of peer mediation. Peer mediation was relatively new, but when I thought about training special education students to resolve their own conflicts, special education seemed like an ideal setting to train mediators. Students with educational disabilities had all "been there" and knew about conflict firsthand; many were more than turned off to adult intervention.

## Introducing Peer Mediation

I had the sense that our students would be natural mediators. I believed that they would have an interest in making a contribution and helping peers and that they would be good at it. Because I was proposing a new program for our school, one that to some degree represented a considerable paradigm shift, I had the sense that I would need a "marketing" strategy for my fellow administrators, staff, and students. Similar to staffs at many schools, especially special education schools, our staff typically relied on a token economy of rewards and consequences to "manage behavior." Indeed, the reward program has been called our *behavior management system.* The model is a typical authority-based model whereby staff give or take away rewards and privileges.

Integrating a student mediation program within a system of rewards and privileges is challenging. Faculty and staff need to be encouraged to empower students to help each other find solutions to their conflicts. This does require a shift in thinking about the ability of young people to solve their problems without creating new ones. Some schools, such as Hannah More School, have found a way to conduct both programs concurrently. For example, after one student assaulted another one getting off the bus, the student was given the proper disciplinary response. He was also told that he would be expected to participate in peer mediation with his victim.

We are very clear that mediation is voluntary, so it becomes necessary to cajole and encourage students to make the decision to agree to mediate. We have built in some "amnesty" for students who elect to mediate—their consequence, such as time in in-school suspension, will be reduced. An additional challenge is asking faculty and staff who have not been trained in peaceful conflict resolution to constantly model the arts of positive communication, problem solving, and compromise when dealing with student misbehavior.

I first introduced the concept of peer mediation at a summer administrative staff meeting. I explained that many schools throughout the country were looking at ways to train students to resolve problems among their peers and that I believed our students would be excellent mediators. Staff concerns about this suggestion included issues with confidentiality, fights breaking out during mediation sessions, too much time being taken from class to conduct mediations, and the amount of time necessary for preparation.

To calm those concerns, I told them that the mediations always begin with ground rules and a pledge of confidentiality by all parties, mediators as well as disputants. I also explained that in many peer mediation programs, there is a nonparticipating staff member present in the mediation room, and that this would be our model. I committed to arranging the mediation sessions such that as much as possible they would be held during students' lunch periods to reduce their time out of class. Finally, I agreed that we would spend the first half of the coming school year laying the foundation to conduct our first mediators' training in February.

A very important factor in getting administrative support was and has continued to be the strong support of the head administrator of the school, the president of Hannah More School. It would appear almost impossible to begin and maintain such a program without the top administrator's mandate. Indeed, the very first day of orientation week of the 1991–1992 school year, our school president announced, "We will be creating a peer mediation program this year." Our director of education followed with the same endorsement.

The theory and practice of peer mediation were explained during staff meetings in fall semester. There were obvious doubts among some staff that students could be trusted with this responsibility or that peer-mediated conflicts would make a difference in the life of our school. At times it seemed surprising, and even discouraging, that professionals dedicated to teaching young people had so little faith in their potential!

It cannot be overstated that it is absolutely critical to take the time to educate administrators and staff regarding the purpose of student mediation and the great value it can have in a special education setting. Indeed, some schools with the resources and the time spend a large block of time training all the staff in mediation and CRE before introducing the idea to students. Faculty familiar with the purposes, vocabulary, and methodology of the program are likely to believe in and endorse it. Similarly, investing time to train parents creates a continuity between the positive conflict resolution that will be happening at school and the constructive conflict language students hear at home.

Our next step after educating the staff was to introduce peer mediation to our student body in three back-to-back weekly assemblies. During the first, a staged conflict arose in the audience between staff actors, dressed as students and wearing signs with "disputant" around their necks. They were invited on stage, where their colleagues, wearing "mediator" signs, sat prepared to assist in a mediation. At the second assembly, students were invited to play the role of disputants, and staff remained in the role of mediators. At the third assembly, students played the disputants' and mediators' roles. Following this last demonstration, students were told that these assemblies were our way of introducing peer mediation to them.

The purposes were explained to them: that we wanted to help the students help each other resolve conflicts and help all of us have a safe, peaceful school. (Additional program goals—namely, helping students build individual conflict resolution skills and develop increased competency with peer relationships—have surfaced that we did not stress at first but that have clearly become very positive outcomes of the training and of the students' experiences as mediators. A number of our mediators over the years have also been active as student council members, senior class leaders, and participants on sports teams and in service activities.)

We discussed the types of conflicts appropriate for mediation: "He said, she said" conflicts, arguments, fights, rumors, threats, and friendships gone bad. We also explained the qualifications necessary to be considered for training as a mediator: having passing grades, the respect of peers, and Level II status (our level just above entry level for new students, and the easiest to achieve). We explained that we would be recruiting students to train as mediators and would be asking for recommendations from students and staff. (Over the years, our committee has actively recruited students who may not be recommended because they have behavior problems. We have found some excellent mediators this way.) As we learned later, a number of our students thought that all mediations were done publicly on the stage in assemblies wearing signs!

We began recruiting mediators for our first two-day training in 1992. Students responded positively to the offer to train mediators to serve the school. My colleagues and I have trained a new group of mediators every fall since then. Since the beginning of the program, Hannah More's mediators have completed over three hundred successful mediations. Very few have ended without a signed agreement and a handshake. There has never been a physical confrontation between disputants during a mediation session.

## Training Peer Mediators

Training is conducted in rented space in a nearby church. The training lasts for two days. The trainers make an attempt to treat the students as very special. Snacks and lunch are provided, and an attempt is made to keep the training active and stimulating. The training is conducted in the fall after students have had a chance to settle into the school program. Training is limited to twelve students because students with emotional disabilities benefit from smaller groups and as much personal attention as possible. Alternate spaces are provided at the training site for breaks, and physical activity, such as Frisbee or soccer, is available after lunch. The attention span of some of our mediation trainees is short; frequent breaks are built in. Having three or four trainers breaks up the rhythm and tone of the training to keep it interesting and fresh for the trainees. Humor is used throughout the training. Students are treated like the young professionals they will eventually become.

For special education students, the ground rules for the training are made very clear at the outset and, when necessary, are reiterated. Behavior problems during mediation training are very rare. The experienced mediators at the school are invited to join the new trainees for lunch on the second day of training and to spend the afternoon session in activities designed to integrate old and new mediators. Periodically, students and trainers sit in a circle for debriefings to make sure the students are "getting it." The natural ambivalence that some of our trainees feel about becoming mediators is addressed in the debriefings; some are unsure about whether it is "cool" to be a mediator. (In the early years of the program, mediators did not want a fuss to be made about their being chosen. More recently, students clamor to be trained and recognized. Being a mediator has indeed become cool.) During these debriefings, stress is placed on the importance of their making up schoolwork missed during training and during mediations.

Typically both middle school and high school students are selected to be trained at the same time. There has never been a problem mixing the two groups in the training. Indeed, there have been some middle school trainees (and mediators) who have demonstrated maturity and skill more typical of older students. We have also had middle school students mediate conflicts between high school students, and because they receive excellent training and their mediation outline is right in front of them on their clipboards, there has never been a problem with this.

## Implementation

Several days after the training is completed, the new mediators are given a "test," which is a simulated mediation session in which staff trainers play the role of student disputants. Not all trainees "pass" the first time. Some use the test as additional training. All trainees do eventually pass. For the first live mediation, new and experienced mediators are paired as co-mediators.

In our school, Request for Mediation forms are a bright pink color and are visible and available in a tray in our resource room. All teachers also have a folder of request forms to make available to students if conflicts arise during class. As mentioned earlier, conflicts for which students request mediation in our school are those typical of regular education programs: "He said, she said" disputes, rumors, threats, or friendships gone awry.

For each mediation session, the mediators have the completed request form, the outline of the mediation steps, and a blank agreement form. The questions the mediators use to evaluate the disputants' agreements are right on the agreement form. Mediators are given a few minutes before the session to strategize the way they will take turns in the session. Mediations are set up by the staff mediation coordinator. We avoid having mediations right before lunch because mediators and disputants may have a hard time concentrating with empty stomachs. All our mediation sessions are observed by one of the staff trainers, and, after the session, the trainer discusses with the mediators what they liked about the session and what they think they could have done differently.

Hannah More mediators have participated in peer mediation conferences with regular education students. They have also presented at conferences. At one presentation with an audience of four hundred school psychologists, a question arose about confidentiality. The students explained that they are particularly sensitive to the need for confidentiality and that it has been a rarely violated rule.

Ongoing cheerleading for the mediation program is necessary. Although the program has gained increasing acceptance over the years, administration and faculty occasionally call on traditional ways of handling student conflicts when things are busy. Staff are sometimes called on to do the resolution rather than peer mediators. In such situations, staff typically spend much more time resolving the conflict than peer mediators do.

## CRE at Hannah More School

Over the past three years, a simple conflict resolution curriculum has also been developed and implemented at Hannah More School. The teachers of the curriculum make six weekly visits to the same class each quarter to teach students some of the language and skills that the mediators learn in their training. Topics addressed are the definition of conflict, responses to conflict, active listening, bias awareness, brainstorming, and peacemaking and peace-breaking behaviors.

The classes have been taught by the director of education and the director of clinical services. To have the top academic administrator team teaching this course has given it additional credibility for the class teachers who participate (and who in the process are also being "trained"). The plan, as suggested in the interviews in the "In Their Own Words" section of this chapter, is to continue to build in the curriculum design area so that this course and others like it are offered as curriculum presence throughout the school.

◆ ◆ ◆

Like many schools with student mediation programs, students at Hannah More School are eager to learn and to practice helping others. Their emotional and learning difficulties do not prevent them from enjoying success as mediators. Indeed, for students in special education, peer mediation represents one of the most genuine ways they can transcend the challenges they have faced and be of service to the school community.

# In Their Own Words

## "Every School Should Have It"

*Hannah More School has had a peer mediation program for ten years, a very long time to sustain a program in any educational environment, but especially noteworthy given the special education students at Hannah More. What has contributed to the program's success? How has the experience of being a mediator or using mediation helped the students? Several members of the school share their thoughts with us to answer these questions.*

*Nina Brown is a new peer mediator, just trained this past fall. She's an eleventh grader who's been at Hannah More since the eighth grade. Her goal is to major in creative writing in college, and she hopes to continue writing poetry and prose as a profession.* Before this year, she used peer mediation as a disputant, and that experience led her to want to be trained as a mediator herself. She explains why she was drawn to mediation: "I enjoy helping people. It's a good thing to do; there are lots of conflicts out there. If students feel they can relate more to their peers, they'll open up a little more and take things more seriously."

Every case she's mediated has ended successfully. When asked what she does well as a mediator, she says, "Having a positive attitude, remembering the rules of mediation, keeping a straight face—even when you're nervous—but they realize that and they don't take any offense to it." Sometimes though, it's hard to have the disputants take you seriously. "When they sit down there's a possibility they might start acting up. There was one kid who just kept playing around; I don't feel he took it very seriously, but after a while he started to pay more attention because he saw that we took it seriously. . . .

"Mediation makes me feel very happy and fulfilled—like I have made a difference. I wanted to be a mediator so I could gain the trust of my peers. I'm also the vice president of the student body; if they can trust me in mediation maybe they can trust me enough to come up and give me ideas to make the school better. I really enjoy being a positive influence on people."

*"Brittany" Bosshard, a graduating senior, is also a new peer mediator trained this past fall.* Although she's only just become a mediator, Brittany has known about peer mediation since elementary school. She recalls, "They wouldn't let me be a peer mediator in elementary school. I wanted to be one then but I got in trouble so they wouldn't let me. I thought I could help people. We all thought peer mediation was a really cool idea. People were really positive about it and a lot of people joined, the popular kids joined, so it was a popular thing to do."

After years of watching others serve as mediators, she has now done three mediations. As she notes, "The kinds of conflicts that end up in mediation are lots of boyfriend-girlfriend and a lot of stuff that happens on the bus. A lot of it is about respect—respecting space, not talking trash."

When she reflects on what makes mediation a success, she says, "When they actually talk to each other, when they put their feelings out there, when they're in there and they work it out for themselves."

But she is also quite sensitive to how difficult it is to do mediation well. "I've known everyone I've mediated. I haven't had to mediate anyone I'm really close with. It's really hard to remain neutral. I wouldn't want this to come out afterwards like 'You didn't take my side.' I've never had that. The closest I've had was this kid who doesn't have very many friends and he adores me, so it was really hard to be in there with him talking about respect and how nobody gives him any respect and not try and take his side because he's so alone. . . . I try to keep it real, I want them to feel comfortable. Most of the kids who come in are pretty comfortable with me. I'll try a little joke or something to lighten things up."

For Brittany, peer mediation is a valuable program. "It's been a really positive thing. It's one of the best ways to solve conflicts if people are serious about it and willing to work through it. It makes you think about it and it makes you think about your actions toward others. Every school should have it."

*"Susan," like Brittany and Nina, is a high school student recently trained as a peer mediator.* Susan also experienced peer mediation from the other side of the table at her old middle school, but it wasn't as positive an experience as she had hoped. "When I was in middle school they had peer mediation, but when I went it seemed like everybody was on the other person's side, so I thought I'd try to mediate and do it right. I like to help solve problems."

An aspiring chef, Susan has found opportunities to use her mediation skills at work. "On weekends I work at a restaurant. I have used my mediation skills there. One of my employers was having a conflict with a coworker. The coworker got mad because he thought the other was trying to get him fired. He had asked somebody to work for him but that person didn't. He was really angry. They were both talking back and forth to me so I talked with him and helped him understand some of the things he was doing wrong and I got them both to talk it out."

She has a deep sense of the importance of helping teens like her learn more constructive ways of dealing with life's challenges. "I've been through so much in my life. I'd like to be able to talk to teens, tell them how to handle it. Talk to students about mediation and my past—I'd tell them it's hard, you have to learn how to deal with things . . . that you can even use it with yourself to try and get over things."

*"Carey," a graduating senior, is the most senior mediator in the Hannah More program.* Carey has been mediating at HM since he was in the seventh grade. Six years as a mediator is a real achievement for any student. But he's honest that initially he

wasn't completely sold on the idea of peer mediation. "At first I wasn't interested in being a peer mediator because it was my first year and I was a little seventh grader and I was intimidated by the other kids. But my teachers thought it would be a way to open me up, so they suggested I try mediating. So I said OK. I was pretty scared. My first mediation was with two high schoolers. At first I took it a little lightly 'cause I was arrogant and a little immature and I had a pretty big temper. But over the years I progressively got better and got more mature and let it go into my personality."

Looking back on his mediating throughout middle and high school, he acknowledges that mediation has made a big difference in his life. "I've changed, my reasoning skills, my talking ability, all around. It's really helped me in the outside world, dealing with people." It's also helped him as an auto mechanic who works on race cars and vintage cars. He even uses his mediation skills in his neighborhood. "I've had to learn to talk my way through things. I've grown up in a pretty bad neighborhood down in East Baltimore, and learning to talk your way out of situations is a very important skill. I've used it more than once—unfortunately."

Over the past six years Carey has mediated more than fifty cases—a mediation record that many adult mediators would find impressive. "I've dealt with cases dealing with all kinds of things—sex, violence, things you wouldn't think a child would be able to handle. Some were pretty serious, some with my own friends. But I needed to learn over the years to be neutral, to leave the outside me outside and have the mediator me in here." Convincing the parties that he will be neutral is sometimes difficult, especially when the parties are his friends. "They always come in like, 'My man, yo Carey what's up?' The whole way I talk to them changes. I keep eye contact, talk to them directly; the way I talk to them they start realizing they can't do this, they start calming down. They might get a little more respect for me."

Carey sees mediation helping the kids who use it. "Most of the time when you have a bully they are bullies because they don't talk, can't talk, and are used to settling things with their fists, but in mediation they learn to talk, they can say what's on their mind without being called for it [getting in trouble for it]. They start taking to it, they start liking it. This one disputant started messing with this boy just to be messing with him. The boy did kinda geekish things to get on his nerves. When we went to the mediation the boy was pestering him because the boy knew he was smarter than him. After we talked it out the bully started acting real nice, his grades picked up a bit, he started getting along. If I see the feelings start to come out, a person's getting real emotional, I say, 'Talk to him, tell him how you feel.' 'What do you have to say about that, knowing that they feel like that?' Usually it doesn't matter how tough they try to be, they start to loosen up, feel a little humility."

The student-to-student help is the core advantage of peer mediation. "It might have something to do with it coming from another peer rather than an authority figure. Letting the peer, for this one time, become the authority figure but be on neutral terms and everybody can speak freely. 'Cause you don't get that in the outside environment; conversations are usually one-sided, you get judged for what you say. But in here, everybody's neutral, everything stays between us so people can say what they feel in a nonthreatening manner."

Given his stature in the program, Carey knows that the other mediators look up to him. "I feel like a father walking around. You have to have a certain stature to you, you can't be a mediator and go off the wall, do things you know you're not supposed to do. At the same time, we're not perfect; we mess up just like everybody else. I've been a mediator for six years, I've been preaching peace for six years, but even I get into a fight every once in a while. It's unavoidable in high school. Sometimes things happen."

He also remembers that when he came into the program there was a mentor he really looked up to. "She was the best. I try to get up to her standards but I don't think I can cause she was really, really, really good. She just ad-libbed off the paper but she kept on script, but she put it in slang words—you know, straightforward ways that everybody can relate to. It worked really well with her and I've tried to pick up her style."

He thinks more mediation between students and staff would be a good thing. "I'd like to see more staff and student mediation. Some of the kids rebel against the staff and some of the staff have attitudes about the kids and that's not a very good working relationship when that starts happening. Sometimes staff-student mediations can open up a relationship. The staff resists mediation; they're the teacher, they think, 'I'm the grown-up, nobody's going to tell me what to do, I'm not going to sit here in a meeting with a little kid saying what I did wrong or what I could do to solve the problem.' They look at themselves as staff who do nothing wrong and the kids messed up somehow. But that's not the case sometimes. Sometimes staff come in and have a bad day and say something insensitive and the student could be legitimately hurt. Sometimes I try to bring that up. Sometimes I go off script a little on purpose 'cause sometimes you have to be a little more human, get down to that emotional level and try to open them up and have a look at what's going on here."

What does he think about involving parents in the program? "It might be a big step in pushing the program along to get parents to support the program, maybe even get them to use it in their own households. Teach parents the basis of mediation, it might help them in their relationship with their own kids, that's a very good idea. A lot of times when kids come in here with problems, real messed up, it's because of something that happened at home."

*Thus far we've heard from mediators whose testimony is undeniably positive. But one of the criticisms sometimes leveled at peer mediation programs is that they help only the mediators. James and Sam would beg to differ. As disputants who have used peer mediation but have not been mediators themselves, they see great advantages for the disputants as well.*

*James Magill is a seventh grader and has been a disputant in three mediations.* "It just seemed like the right thing to do. I knew they wouldn't take sides. It worked. There was a boy that was always talking about my mother and we went to mediation and now we're friends. Another time I went with my best friend because I snapped at her and she requested it. We worked it out in mediation. With my best friend it was really hard 'cause I didn't want to lose our friendship, I had known her since fourth or fifth grade. The mediators made us talk about our problems, then I felt better.

"I can really solve my problems now. I just ignore people some times. There's this other boy, Charles, in my class. We're always getting on each other's nerves. We're not allowed to talk to each other in A.M. or P.M. home room. I try to ignore him. When he says something about me or to me I do get upset. But I'm better at blowing him off now. I've learned how to trust people because I've learned I can trust the mediators not to take sides, so it helps me trust other people."

*Sam Wirtz has also been a disputant in several mediations. Sam is very articulate about his experience with mediation and what he has gained.* "I'm very good at solving things, sometimes not with myself but with other people." He uses mediation as a disputant because it gives him "a chance to make up with the person I was angry with, so I don't have to walk around with that feeling that I hurt someone and didn't do anything to make it better." In mediation it's easier to deal with his conflicts because "with the mediators there it's easier for me to say what happened without getting angry at the other person, without wanting to hurt them in some way. 'Cause when I get angry I yell and scream and hit things, try to hurt people or do something bad." It's easier for him to be calm with the mediators, so it's easier to hear them as well. "If I get angry I don't hear what they are trying to say to me—I wouldn't be hearing what you were saying—I'd be hearing but I wouldn't be able to understand."

He feels he has learned a great deal about anger management. "If you ask any of the people that have me in class they'd be able to tell you when I first came here I was really angry. I'd walk out of the building and start yelling and cursing. Now if something bothers me I'm able to go up to someone and talk with them. I've noticed that about myself, I'm able to have better relationships with people. At my old school with my anger I'd get so depressed I'd just walk out of class. Since I've been here I just keep getting better and better. Today one of the people I was having trouble with earlier was kind of getting on a lot of people's nerves, and he started getting on my nerves, but I just moved away from him. . . . It was something I told the mediator I would do. I just moved to sit with other people and then he stopped. Instead of walking out of class, now I request a time out, go to the resource room and calm down instead of getting so angry I can't function. I've gotten better at talking with the teacher or the person about what's going on. I used to make threats to people, but I don't do that as much now.

"I try to do this at home. When I get more tired, I get more irritable. I've gotten irritable here and at home because I've been having pain in my wrist, which was previously injured. When it hurts I get more sensitive to even the smallest insult. My parents have told me that they see a difference in how I act and how I behave when I've been angry and then go to my room to cool down. If I'm having a conflict with my parents I tell them how I'm feeling—even if it has to do with them—sometimes if I don't feel like dealing with it I'll walk away and then after ten or twenty minutes I'll come back to talk about it. It makes me feel better because I'm able to use my skills to handle my anger. And they're starting to get better by recognizing what angers me and what doesn't. All this depression started when I was eleven or twelve and now I'm fifteen. They've made a lot of progress. Each of us has made progress in anger control."

*The students clearly support the peer mediation program and have benefited from it. School administrators support the program too, but also struggle with such challenges as gaining teacher buy-in.*

*Mark Waldman, president of Hannah More School, has been a strong supporter of the peer mediation program throughout its ten-year run.* As the lead administrator at the school, he remembers that "Paul [Kaplan, the head of the peer mediation program] was really clear and focused from the beginning, and like with any program, if you don't have buy-in from the administrators first it's not going to work in a school setting. He worked really hard to get myself as lead administrator and the other school administrators bought in to why this was a good thing. He was successful in doing that."

For Mark, the motivation for implementing the peer mediation program initially had more to do with developing individual mediators' skills than finding a way to handle discipline cases. "I know for me personally, early on in the program, I became convinced that regardless of whether the disputants found it successful—and I think certainly many, many of them have—simply the experience that the mediators themselves gained going through the training and going through the practice, the skills that they acquired, made it worthwhile even if there was never a dispute mediated. We're working with a very specific portion of the population. Kids who are here are already identified as kids who, by and large, have problems getting along with other people. So for them to learn some skills that they could then use in their own lives—that made the whole thing worthwhile, even if the disputants didn't find it so. And we've had kids say, 'I've used this at home' or 'I've used this in the neighborhood.' That's tremendously rewarding."

Still, convincing people that kids with these problems can handle peer mediation is not always easy. "The trickiest part for us as adults is being willing to step back and let the kids do it. Particularly being in the helping profession you want to jump in and help instead of reminding ourselves to at least ask the question, 'Can we let the mediators handle this?' We've had staff say, 'These kids can't handle that'—it's easy sometimes to forget that 25 percent of the staff has turned over since you last explained the program, so you need to constantly be selling it and reselling it. Our staff is the same as any staff; there's always going to be a certain percentage who don't buy in to it."

Overall, his advice on the "best practices" for this kind of program are "getting staff bought in, involving the kids in the planning of it, giving enough time to make it work, gauging the commitment of key people to make sure it has a real chance to succeed. It's not a tremendously expensive program; it's making the commitment of time and human resources to make it happen."

*Ruth Norwood, staff person in the resource room, does intake for the mediation program.* Before the mediation program began, most of the student conflicts and discipline situations were handled by staff resolutions, whereby staff like Ruth would gather information about a conflict or a disruptive incident and then decide what needed to be done with the student. Since the peer mediation program, staff resolutions are not as frequent.

Ruth explains, "Students will come in and talk about a conflict and ask for mediation. Sometimes if we see a conflict we'll set [mediation] up. Perhaps a fight breaks out and more times than not, if they've made an agreement in writing, if there's another problem they'll come back to the resource room and say, 'So and so agreed to this' and then we can do one of two things. We can take it back to mediation or we handle it as staff resolution. We try to use mediation. . . .

"The beauty of the mediation program is it is teaching them to handle it themselves. The biggest use of it is for 'he said, she said' or provoking situations—to try and keep those kinds of conflicts from escalating. Because once it gets rolling they don't know how to stop it. With these kids things escalate very quickly. We want to teach the skills so things don't get to the point of a fight.

"Mediators become role models—I've seen them encouraging students to take things in a more positive direction. In most cases the mediators mediate for more than one year. Every fall we train a new group and give a refresher training to the returning mediators.

"I've been here fifteen years, and before we had this program we'd constantly be in the resource room doing staff resolutions. We still do handle a lot, but we do far fewer because the mediation program handles them. Students are more willing to listen to peers. Both programs get a resolution, but peer mediation empowers students."

*Dr. James Smith, psychologist, mediator, and cotrainer with Paul I. Kaplan, is one of the members of the teacher-staff committee that oversees the program. He has been involved from the beginning and has been able to lend his expertise in training and learning design to the mediator training and program publicity.* "It took a year or so to get staff behind the program. There are some people who are holdouts who feel that students shouldn't be mediating, but they're in the minority. We're pretty much at full-school buy-in; maybe one or two don't agree but they are not vocal about it. . . .

"For some students, being mediators brings about changes in their behavior. I'm not going to tell you that they all have perfect attendance, always get one hundred points on their behavior sheet, never get into another argument—because they are kids with special needs too. But it opens up a whole new way of communicating with people, of negotiating, of listening to people. When you gain the skills, you don't lose them—once a mediator always a mediator.

"They identify with the mediation program, they get a lot of positive reinforcement from their peers and from us when they're in that mediator role. So it does enhance their self-esteem."

# CHAPTER EIGHT

# EXPRESS YOURSELF!
## Expressive Arts and Conflict Discovery

### Sarah Pirtle

When third graders at Westminster West School in Vermont were creating verses to a song about anger, one girl became visibly excited about her writing. She wrote, "I feel like a volcano. I feel ready to pop." The expression on her face said, "I've never had words for this before, but now I do." In finding within her these two short sentences, she had crossed a threshold. Discovering words that expressed the texture of her upset feelings, she moved from a position of being embedded in anger to having more consciousness and more choice. She asked, "Can I bring this home to show my mom?"

Arts are a vital complement to building conflict resolution skills. When we couple arts activities with discussions that build conflict resolution skills, the skills can be more tangible and reflection can deepen. These third graders explored anger when upset feelings weren't actually erupting; they used writing to befriend anger. Students tried out new ideas: that anger sends a message we can pay attention to and that we can learn to express anger's message constructively. By interlacing the lesson with songs and creative writing, the skills themselves were anchored in a multifaceted way.

Expressive arts include a panoply of activities: drama, dance, musical theater, graphic art, visual art, performance art, music, and creative writing, to name the most common forms. All of these artistic endeavors offer opportunities for *con flict discovery*, a process of reflection and increasing awareness about one's orientations to and reactions to conflict.

Art has the power to connect people and build community. In addition to developing an affirmative classroom climate, activities with music, storytelling, creative movement, poetry, and dramatics can help students gain deeper understanding of social situations, reinforce important social messages, and provide direct opportunities to practice skills relating to conflict resolution. Assignments in drawing, painting, and sculpting, as well, can be structured to explore the dynamics of relationships. Over the past two decades in particular, songwriters, poets, and conflict resolution trainers have been devising new material to explore peace building through creativity. For example, even conflict scholars and practitioners respond when a reknown artist like Peter Yarrow from Peter, Paul, and Mary helps them think about conflict in new and dynamic ways, as he did in his presentation to the Association for Conflict Resolution in October 2001. Songs can be a powerful tool for teaching about conflict. Carol Johnson's song, "In the Very Middle," is a nugget of bias awareness:

> In the very middle you're a lot like me
> A shining personality.
> The clothes and the skin
> Are just the covering.
> In the very middle you're a lot like me.
>                         WORDS AND MUSIC BY CAROL JOHNSON © 1982, NOELDNER MUSIC

Here is another song used in conflict resolution training in elementary school classrooms. It helps bring emotions to the surface and spark conversation among students about conflicts with friends.

> I'm so angry I can't see straight.
> I'm mad as a bull breaking down a gate.
> You and I are in this fight.
> Gotta find a way to set things right.
> Talk it out. I don't want to do it.
> Talk it out. Do I have to go through it?
> Talk it out. There is no doubt.
> Gotta jump back, come back, talk it out.

By acknowledging the difficulty of addressing conflicts and handling anger, the song invites students to discuss the feelings that arise for them and the choices they have when they are in a conflict. The song provides distance from the situation, making it easier to discuss it and gain new awareness.

When songs enter a classroom, they introduce a topic in an engrossing way. A family counselor from North Parish School in Greenfield, Massachusetts, says, "Students need a nonthreatening way to talk about feelings and basic values. Music is an ideal vehicle for working on personal and family issues. It appeals to a love of fantasy and can also speak to real-life skills. Songs can zoom in on important themes." Songs bring in an empathic voice and allow us to talk about things that are hard to talk about. Songs can let us know we are not alone in what we feel and what we face.

When I use "Talk It Out" as a jumping-off point for discussion, I say, "What are the reasons we'd rather not talk out a conflict? Let's discuss with each other why it's hard." Students answer, "It's a risk. Things could get worse. You might get rejected. You could lose the friendship. You could make a fool of yourself. You're taking a chance." The song helps them feel that turning point in a conflict where we can make a new choice. Here are the rest of the lyrics:

I went up to talk to you.

But you turned your head. What can I do?

I try to talk and you run away.

Gotta jump back, hear me out today.

Talk it out. You don't wanna do it.

Talk it out. But I wanna go through it.

Talk it out. There is no doubt.

Gotta jump back, come back, talk it out.

How can we be friends again?

How can we be friends again?

I really want this fight to end.

Gotta jump back, come back, try it again.

I didn't give up. I said, "Come on,

This fight's going on too long."

"I know," you said, and you nearly cried.

Jump back, come back, we both tried.

Talk it out. I'm gonna burst.

Talk it out. Do I have to go first?

Talk it out. We can mend.

Jump back, come back, try it again.

Talk it out. What did you say?

Talk it out. I see it your way.

Talk it out. You're my friend.

Jump back, come back, friends again.

WORDS AND MUSIC BY SARAH PIRTLE © 1993,
FROM "MAGICAL EARTH," A GENTLE WIND RECORDING

This song was recorded with a cajun band, and the fast beat helps convey the anxiety, the quickening heartbeat, as well as the excitement that comes with taking a risk. Students discuss what happens in the song: "Why do you think the friends didn't want to talk out the problem? Why did they change their minds? What situations in your own life does the song remind you of?" The song is also used for a role play in which partners face each other in two lines, each line representing one of the two characters in the song.

Music is but one of the vehicles of the expressive arts. As I detail in the book *Discovery Time for Cooperation and Conflict Resolution,* a number of activities using many different forms of art are being used by educators across the country. Students in art classes have drawn cartoons of real-life conflicts and have designed "children's peace statues." In gym class they have created dances of Yes and No. In classrooms they have cooperated with partners to create peace flowers, researched heritage quilt squares to honor their family backgrounds, and participated in making a bulletin board display of people in history who stood up against racism, sexism, and other forms of bias.

The following seven concepts help explain why the expressive arts are powerful resources for teaching creative conflict resolution skills and respect for diversity:

1. Expressive arts make learning about social skills concrete rather than abstract because students interact with people, materials, and concepts in a tangible way.
2. Arts build community, warmth, and enjoyment, and that increases learning.
3. Expressive arts introduce new ideas and messages.

4. Expressive arts help students become aware of their feelings and help them express their own insights and emotions. Arts open our hearts, and that's essential for character building.

5. The arts are a pathway for contacting our inner resources. They allow us to bring to the surface and address what is intangible.

6. Expressive arts provide an avenue for practicing constructive and nourishing human interactions.

7. Expressive arts allow students to make their own discoveries about peacemaking.

Each conflict is a new discovery process. When people are in a conflict, they are in an improvisational process; no one script or recipe gives the right words to say. Disputants rely on what they have internalized, the mental map of skills they've acquired, and the intention in their hearts. Art can help them recognize their skills. Interpersonal and intrapersonal development involves making our own meaning, making our own personal investigation. For teachers and trainers leading expressive arts activities, these activities will be different each time they are offered. The activity gets adapted to the specific classroom situation; the leader brings his or her own skills, gifts, and insights; and the unique insights and contributions of the students get incorporated. The activity is expanded and transformed as students discover together afresh.

# Arts for All

Leading arts activities to develop conflict resolution skills is not just the province of professionals associated with the arts. Conflict discovery activities can be led by a wide variety of people: classroom teachers, reading specialists, school counselors, gym teachers, parents, other community resource people, art or music specialists, peace educators, artists in the schools, storytellers, and musicians and other performers who provide concerts and residencies. Here are guidelines for teachers to use in choosing and leading activities and for schools to use in selecting resource people to come into the classroom:

• Look for activities that engage the thinking and the creativity of students. Avoid didactic songs or presentations. Focus on activities in which students can be directly involved.

• Make sure to create and maintain a safe classroom atmosphere. The arts are a place of vulnerability. Set clear agreements so that sharing takes place in an affirmative context, and make sharing optional. A dance reveals our body in motion. A song reveals the sound of our voice. A poem reveals what matters to us. The arts expose who we are. Create an environment respectful of the risk involved.

• Foster independent thinking. Use questions and activities that have room for multiple answers rather than only one recommended answer.

• Create a setting where students can feel that they are an artist in their own way. This means it is particularly important not to set an artistic standard that others must attain or to let artistic competition, ranking, and judgment hold sway.

• Approach the activity without grading. The value in the classroom of using the expressive arts can't be measured in the same way we can measure attainment of vocabulary words. We see the value in the warmth traveling around the room, the increased compassion toward a classmate whose story is now better understood, the engagement of students working as partners together.

## Examples of Students in Expressive Arts

Rachael Kessler emphasizes in Chapter Four the importance of helping students know themselves better as a step toward managing their feelings. When Hannah Hoose, from Portland, Maine, faced the taunts of a classroom bully, her parents encouraged her to handle her feelings by writing a song. She created this song when she was in fourth grade:

> I don't care about, I don't care about,
>
> I don't care what you say about me.
>
> I am strong and smart and I'm lots of fun.
>
> I'm myself and I know what's true.
>
> I don't care what you say about my clothes.
>
> I know I am as good as you.

Later Hannah recorded the song with her father, Phil Hoose. Teachers and school counselors play Hannah's song and use it to encourage discussion.

Hannah and her father also wrote a song together about bullying, and the lyrics have been turned into a picture book called *Hey, Little Ant*. It shows a dialogue between a child about to squish an ant and the ant itself. In the book, the child has a chance to see things through the ant's point of view. At the book's website, www.heylittleant.com, teachers can learn a variety of lesson plans that derive from this engaging book. The story is particularly valuable for schools because the reader is invited to decide the ending to the conflict. The last lines of the book say,

"We'll leave that kid with the raised up shoe. What do you think that kid should do?"

A poignant and effective way to engage students is for them to hear the creations of other young people. At Mohawk Junior High School in Buckland, Massachusetts, seventh-grade students worked on songwriting and then shared their work with another class that met during the same time period. Songwriting was launched by presenting such simple sentence starters as "I wish that . . ." or questions like, "If you could talk to the world, what would you say?" One girl wrote about a close friend who died in a car accident after being hit by a drunk driver. In their song "Talking to the World," Nick Soviecke and two of his classmates wrote:

> Talking to the world.
>
> Listen to me.
>
> I feel like a slowly dying band.
>
> I feel like a person passing through time.
>
> I feel like a bomb about to go off.
>
> I'm angry there is war.
>
> I've had enough.

When they shared their writing, the songs were met by applause from students. Hidden thoughts had a chance to be heard.

Middle school students from the Greenfield Center School in Massachusetts developed a "Hate Crimes" play in fall 2001. Seventh and eighth graders researched the origins of hate crimes and discovered that there had been nine thousand hate crimes against people of Middle Eastern descent since September 11, 2001. Students chose specific anecdotes and wove these into their play. As characters, they read the actual words of a person who was a victim or initiator of a hate crime. They also included scenes about exclusion among classmates as well as examples of books and movies that promote bias.

## Promoting Awareness Through Expressive Arts

The use of drama, songwriting, stories, or any form of the expressive arts to teach positive social skills is a part of an awareness model of learning. This is the opposite of a punishment model, in which it is assumed that students will act in prosocial ways if they understand the negative consequences they will incur if they don't. Disassociation and denial can increase when students are seeking to avoid punishment. Awareness encourages students to take responsibility for their behavior and to engage in decision making.

An awareness model is based on these beliefs:

- Students develop prosocial behaviors as they see them modeled. Students need guidance, and they need opportunities to practice these behaviors.
- Students change when they are given clear standards of what is acceptable and valued and are provided with a place for growth.
- Students change as they move out of being embedded in behavior that feels automatic and are able to become aware of themselves as authorities of their own behavior. For instance, they no longer "are anger" but "have anger" and are able to listen to anger as a signal and make decisions about how to work with its message.
- Students change through compassion, and they are held accountable for their actions. Social mistakes become times of learning.

In *Linking Up!: Using Music, Movement, and Language Arts to Promote Caring, Cooperation, and Communication,* I share many songs I've used in early childhood and elementary school classrooms over the past thirty years.[1] One of these songs is called "Sing About Us," and it was created to increase awareness of diversity. The chorus says, "You don't have to be just like me to be my friend."

In a language arts activity based on songwriting, children choose a dimension of diversity—such as eye color, favorite activities, ethnicity, or learning styles—and explore the differences of people in the class within that dimension as they create new verses to the song.

Some of my friends are Puerto Rican.
Some of my friends are French Canadian.
Some of my friends are Navaho.
You don't have to be just like me to be my friend.

Some of my friends learn songs by hearing them.
Some of my friends like to look at the words.
Some of my friends share songs with sign language.
You don't have to learn the way I learn to be my friend.

Another song is a finger play for young children. The tune is a traditional song that begins, "There were two in the bed, and the little one said—roll over," and the words were created with second graders in Bellows Falls, Vermont. As we sing the song, we use index fingers to portray two friends talking out a conflict. Teachers have reported that after introducing the song to four- and five-year-olds, some children will use the finger movements from the song as a signal to ask each other to talk out a real conflict.

### *Two in the Fight*

There were two in the fight

and the little one said, "I'm angry, I'm angry."

But the other one started to run away.

"Come back and hear what I have to say.

"Come on back, come on back. We can figure this out.

"Come on back, come on back. We can figure this out."

There were two in the fight

and the other one said, "I'm angry, I'm angry."

But the little one did not run away.

"Tell me what you have to say.

"Keep talking. Keep talking.

"Talk it out. Talk it out. We can figure this out.

"Talk it out. Talk it out. We can figure this out."

MUSIC, TRADITIONAL; WORDS BY SARAH PIRTLE
AND SECOND GRADERS OF CENTRAL ELEMENTARY SCHOOL,
BELLOWS FALLS, VERMONT

The arts can give us a new perspective by giving us ideas to digest in calm moments and by building awareness that we can use when we face real conflicts.

## Using Conflict Discovery Activities Within the Curriculum

Arts can be embedded effectively within units of study. For instance, classroom teachers take works of literature that are already part of the curriculum and use the expressive arts to focus on the social skills and conflicts embedded in the stories. For example, *Angel Child, Dragon Child*, by Michelle Maria Surat, is a sensitive story for first through fourth graders that can foster awareness. The tale focuses on a new student, Nguyen Hoa, who has recently arrived from Vietnam. It shows how a principal facilitates reconciliation between Hoa and Raymond when Raymond teases her and expresses prejudice and misunderstanding. Doing activities related to the book can make these concepts more real to students.

The story can be read aloud, or students might take turns reading sections of it. While they listen to the story, they can draw and then share their drawing with a partner. Next, students might use creative dramatics to act out three scenes they select from the story. Third, they could complete sentence starters using the phrase, "I don't understand why . . ." from the viewpoint of each of the main characters in the story. Finally, they can think about something from their own lives that is sparked by the story and create their own expression using a sentence starter.

Science units can be enhanced by creative movement and dramatization that help elementary school children get inside their subject matter and explore the concepts kinesthetically. During units on sound, for instance, students act out how sound progresses through the parts of the ear. Astronomy units and biology units have a wealth of concepts to explore, such as planets moving in orbits or the actions within cells. Weather units can be enhanced by acting out the water cycle and the movements of clouds. What is significant is that as they work together, students will get practice in their negotiation and communication skills.

Karen Schweitzer, an elementary school teacher at the Anne T. Dunphy school in Williamsburg, Massachusetts, has worked with these ideas in her kindergarten, first-, and second-grade classes:

> We do a lot of group-building skills apart from conflict. We're trying using rhythm and movement to teach that. Some years ago an artist was here and did some music and conflict work with the kids. We did some songwriting with her. It was just great. And then a couple of years ago, when I went to kindergarten, we had a whole school celebration of solstice. We used rhythms and counterpoint rhythms together. It struck me that in using this there were things the kids really had to pay attention to in being in a group. And so last year we studied musical instruments. The kids experimented with the musical instruments first, making their own sounds and their own music. Then we had them moving to the rhythms and starting to get into groups, and afterwards we came back to the classroom and had a discussion [about] "What did you have to do to make that work?" They realized that they needed to be listening to other people; they needed to be working together to make the sounds. When [the artist] was here, one of the things she did really well was to stop after doing something and ask the kids, "Now what was hard about that?" It's really important to give kids a chance to think about and talk about what makes something hard and what they

can do about it. So now I try and do the same thing when we do group games. Those are questions that kids need to learn how to answer. They don't just know how to answer them. It comes from having those kinds of conversations.

It is common during an expressive arts exercise for a conflict to occur. These conflicts can be welcomed as an opportunity for teachers to give specific guidance. Very often a chronic problem surfaces—one student dominates the decision making, or another pushes rather than speaks to be heard. At these times you can help the group talk about what is occurring and show them how they can make new choices.

For instance, first graders at New Hingham School in Chesterfield, Massachusetts, were studying the behavior of animals. They used creative dramatics to focus on ways that animals cooperate together. Students divided into small groups and imitated animal behavior by becoming beavers building a home, elephants assisting a calf stuck in mud, or birds leading a baby bird back to a nest. As arguments developed, the class created a procedure for negotiating how to work together. Small groups followed these steps: (1) sit down together in a circle; go around the circle and allow each person to say what part of the action or sequence she would like to be; (2) the person across the circle from her repeats what she said to make sure she is understood correctly; (3) everyone gets her choice of what she wants to do; it's fine for more than one person to do the same thing; (4) find a way to blend together the ideas of each person.

When conflicts erupt during an expressive arts activity, it is a teachable moment. What's valuable is that the teacher can give direct guidance and coaching. The conflict isn't hidden away on the playground of an elementary school or in a lunchroom of a secondary school. The activity stops while agreements are reinforced, and students get help talking together. A group of middle school students developing a skit, for example, will spend as much time working on listening to each other and negotiating differences of opinion as they spend on writing lines and developing stage blocking. Teachers are encouraged to take the time to help with communication and not let the artistic product take priority over the process of getting assistance with social skills.

## Three Models for a Schoolwide Focus on Social Skills Through the Arts

We have been looking at individual lessons and activities in expressive arts and conflict discovery. Schoolwide sharing with the whole community is an effective way to focus on conflict resolution and respect for diversity through the expressive arts. These models require an investment of time from the principal, school counselor, English department team, or PTO member who coordinates the program, as well as additional planning on the part of teachers. But it pays off in the powerful message conveyed to students.

## Model One: Schoolwide Language Arts Theme

Every class in the school or every class in one grade level explores social skills during the same week or month, but each engages in different activities. Teachers select a skill and use various expressive arts to help students develop that skill. It's helpful to select a name for the schoolwide social skills unit, such as Talk It Out, Unity and Diversity, or Building Bridges. Within that theme, teachers choose whichever expressive forms will be most effective for themselves and for their class—poetry, music, storytelling, creative dramatics, movement, artwork.

Teachers will often be amazed at the understanding of complex ideas that students exhibit in these exercises. When Trudy Teutsch's fifth-grade class at Buckland-Shelburne School in Massachusetts was developing skits about making decisions, Polly Anderson, the art teacher, engaged the students in creating ink drawings about what it feels like to make a decision. Student Wade Bassett drew a giant "No" that was being opened up by a cloud of tiny words saying "Yes." He said, "Yes is persistent and begins to dissolve No."

At all age levels, hallway displays of art are effective. For example, in the Anne T. Dunphy Elementary School, student art projects were displayed in the hall. One visitor to the school noted the following:

> I was standing outside an art display where kids were asked to design their dream world, to describe what their dream was. One project was called Welcome to the World of Kindness and Justice. The writing on the project said, "My dream is that people won't make fun of other people, my dream is also that people will stand up for the people who are being made fun of." The display had a number of stick figures made out of pipe cleaners. The explanation said, "This scene is in the World of Kindness and Justice. This scene is about a girl who is being made fun of, her hair is messy and is colored differently. The short kid is standing up for her. Another kid is handing her a brush. The bully is picking on the short kid and a taller kid is standing up for the short kid." This is just one of several projects that decorate the halls and help students think about social issues.

In an elementary school or middle school, sharing can also take place in a schoolwide assembly. In larger schools or secondary schools where one huge assembly would not be possible, clusters of four to six classrooms might come together to do an exchange and present their work to each other. In a secondary school or for any grade level where a more abbreviated exchange is preferred, two classrooms can pair up and share their work with each other.

For instance, eleventh-grade English classes coordinate the literature they are studying with contemporary poetry and songs about feelings. The strong emotions in Shakespeare's plays might be studied at the same time as art classes are encouraged to consider how artists have depicted strong emotions of sadness through the centuries. Music classes might study the different use of instruments in symphonic arrangements to communicate various emotions.

Schoolwide language arts themes can also integrate special needs and regular education students in their efforts. At the Brentwood East Middle School in Long Island, Bobbe Frankel and Felicia Bruce have used such efforts in conjunction with their work teaching negotiation skills. As the regular education and special needs students learn the negotiation skills material, they are encouraged to create rap lyrics, poems, and pictures to illustrate their understanding and application of the concepts in constructive negotiation.

There are limitless ways that schools can create schoolwide themes for conflict resolution education. Of course, it is always important to make sure that the activities are age appropriate. There are many activities appropriate for grades one through eight that can be used in a schoolwide assembly program. The following are some examples:

- First graders dance to this poem:

  A wall will shut out a friend.

  Build a bridge and let the sunshine in.

  Children illustrate the meaning by moving with a partner.
- Second graders recite the words of *Hey Little Ant* by Phil and Hannah Hoose and then show three different endings to the conflict between the ant and the child.
- Third graders make illustrations depicting recess conflicts using a cartoon panel format, and show productive ways the conflict can be solved.
- Fourth graders sing "Walk a Mile" by Jan Nigro of Vitamin L and choreograph movements to the lively song about empathy. The refrain is, "I want to walk a mile in your shoes. I want to know what you think and what you feel, so I really want to walk a mile in your shoes."
- Fifth graders use the theme Don't Leave Anybody Out, and present original poems with multiple ways of interpreting inclusiveness.
- Sixth graders dramatize the conflict in the short story "The Zax" by Dr. Seuss and create a new ending showing productive negotiation between the protagonists.
- Seventh graders develop skits showing mediation of a common conflict at school.

- Eighth graders select a relevant contemporary song and lip-synch to a recording.

Let's look in more detail at a weeklong unit in an elementary school that has chosen to focus on anger management. During the first day, students discuss how they know they are angry, and they brainstorm the range of ways a person can work with their anger. They notice that some people like to be by themselves when they are angry, others seek a friend, and others seek an adult. Some want to be in motion and get more active, whereas others want to curl up. As they look at all the options a person has to help him calm down or hear himself better, each student conveys in a drawing which of these methods he feels will help him the most. Later in the week, they share their drawings and discuss what they have discovered about themselves. As a next step, they interview other people in the school building to generate more discussion and learn what adults in various roles—the principal, the cook, the guidance counselor, the custodian, the librarian—do to help themselves when they are angry. This culminates in a skit that students develop for the assembly. Their dramatization could show one student asking for a hug, another grabbing a stuffed toy and sitting in a bean bag chair, another scribbling angrily on paper. They create a chant to use in the skit: "Everyone gets angry. But there are different things we do. What helps you slow down and figure out what's bugging you?"

## Model Two: Assembly of Songs and Poems for Students and Parents

In this model, most appropriate for elementary and middle schools, a team including the school librarian, guidance counselor, music specialist, and participating teachers locates songs and poetry that will potentially be relevant. They look for material related to conflict resolution, respect for diversity, multicultural education, gender partnership, and bias awareness. Parents also can be encouraged to search for poetry, stories in books and magazines, and songs relating to friendships and relationships.

Five to seven classrooms learn a song or poem to share in an assembly. Ideally, students have a hand in choosing what they want to perform. At the assembly, a member of each participating class announces why their class chose that selection to present, what they liked about the song or poem, and how it relates to building their school community.

In the evening the program is repeated for parents so that they can learn more about the conflict resolution work of the school. Schools have found that one of the most effective ways to bring parents out to learn about social skills is to have a performance that includes their children.

## Model Three: Partnership Assembly

In this approach, a staff person—school counselor, music specialist, or art specialist—takes responsibility for facilitating and coordinating the assembly. The event could be called School Celebration or Social Responsibility Assembly. Several classrooms or individuals share music, art, skits, or dances that celebrate values of communication, cooperation, and mutual respect. At the assembly, students are the announcers. Sing-along songs, presentations of work from art classes, and celebrations of those who have birthdays that month help bind the school together.[2]

What makes the difference in ensuring that such programs will last is to set them up as regular events. If a school decides that November is always the month that they'll do an activity on social skills and that the assembly will always occur on the third Friday in November, teachers can plan ahead, save potential ideas in a folder, and be ready to gear up for the program.

◆ ◆ ◆

The arts give us a chance to explore our fundamental relationships to each other. Humans grow and change; we are like plants in a garden, not like cogs in a machine. Just as plants require care, watering, weeding, and patience, young people's social selves grow gradually, drawing on many sources of nourishment. A single conversation, poem, or group activity contributes to a gradual accumulation of positive experiences.

When young people are taught that violence, aggression, and domination are important for success and survival, they are drinking in and breathing in messages that are essentially toxic. Yet they learn them well because of their thirst to participate in the human community as they see it defined. The adults in young people's lives can act as guides and elders to help reorient them.

When we engage in CRE, we are part of the effort to correct those behaviors and values that are incoherent, chaotic, and essentially unproductive so they become coherent, coordinated, and life enhancing. It is the work of generations, and each part we contribute has value. A song by Ruth Pelham puts it simply and beautifully: "We're all a family under one sky." Within this family, even the smallest actions help build a more caring community.

In our work we are not imposing or adding on prescriptions for behavior. We are going with the grain of the universe. We are endeavoring to organize our schools and classroom in the same way that the earth is organized to perpetuate healthy life. The arts help us make dynamic discoveries of how to be at once an individual and a member of many interlocking communities. The arts help young people express themselves, explore themselves, and receive themselves.

# In Their Own Words

## "A Powerful Healing Tool and a Powerful Communication Tool"

*As described in the chapter, elementary students can benefit a great deal from expressive arts programs. One of Sarah Pirtle's students, Torrey Byrd, talked with us. A sixth-grade student, Torrey has been writing poetry and prose since the third grade. Now twelve, she has been attending Sarah Pirtle's Journey summer camp since second grade.* "At camp, you go to the woods, you can play, be very spontaneous. We have workshops like clay making, dance, or writing workshops. I would pick writing workshops and songwriting workshops. Mostly it just lets you express yourself."

She remembers that when she was in second grade, "Sarah came to my school and taught us songs. Sometimes I write poetry and the songs will just come along with it. Sometimes I make up tunes to words I already have."

Some of her words are found in the poems she writes, such as the following poem.

### Connection

I feel like

I share my soul

I am another

I am still me

I am connected—how can I be

Another, and still me?

I look like

I am just me

I am really two

I am really one

I am really me

How can I be

Two, one, and still me?

Two one and still me.

TORREY BYRD, FIFTH GRADE

Torrey says she goes through stages during which she writes a lot if she has free time. She wants to be a writer when she grows up. "Poetry and prose and that stuff. Songs are a nice hobby. Sarah says there are lots of songs floating around and melodies and you just grab one. Anybody who has seen a lot of it and has encouragement can learn." But it is clear her first love is poetry. "You have to listen to what's happening in your head; what's hard is sharing it with other people. I like poetry because part of it is you don't want other people to understand. Only you can understand the meaning of that poem."

In addition to her arts achievements, she has learned about conflict through the expressive arts programs. "At camp, kids would have a fight and would try to tell on one another. They would come to Sarah and she would let them solve conflicts. If you were having a problem she would help you know what was going on." Torrey was a peer mediator at her last school. About that experience, she summarizes, "You have to listen to the people and let them work it out for themselves."

*Drama is a natural outlet for CRE. One of the longest-running dramatic arts–CRE efforts is the Peace Theater program developed by the Good Shepherd Mediation Program (GSMP) in Philadelphia. To learn more about this program, we talked with Cheryl Cutrona, the executive director of GSMP, and with several of the high school students who worked as actors in Peace Theater.*

*Cheryl developed the idea for Peace Theater. For the past twelve years she has nurtured this program and has seen the benefits for the students on the stage and the students in the audience.* "Last summer Peace Theater performed for 4,410 campers, ages five to twelve, at seventy-seven camps in the Philadelphia area—a typical summer for this impressive troupe. Peace Theater, developed by the Mediation Program in 1991, is an interactive theater experience designed to 'increase the peace' by encouraging children and youth to use communication and problem-solving skills to address interpersonal conflicts as an alternative to physical fighting. Peace Theater began as a summer camp special event designed to encourage children and youth to resolve conflicts peacefully without resorting to shouting and fighting. . . .

"The kids who are performers think it's wonderful. One boy, a middle school student, joined in 1996. At first we could barely hear him—couldn't hear a word he was saying. He turned out to be one of the best performers and is getting his degree in theater and has performed in several professional shows. Some kids from CAPA [Creative and Performing Arts High School] have come year after year because it is such a good experience. Some kids stay for three or four years."

And, Cheryl notes, the performers gain much more than performing skills. They also learn a great deal about conflict through the presentation of these ideas to an audience. "Because they have to be able to teach the conflict concepts, they learn it better. Each show is different. Even though they've learned it at the beginning of the summer they have to be able to really know it to apply it in any situation. The improvisational theater requires them to be very good active listeners, and they need to collaborate to work smoothly as a company."

Because many of the skits in Peace Theater are developed by the performers from their own experience, the dramatic portrayal can help them work through some of their own issues—and go on to great success. "One girl had abuse in her history. A skit she developed told kids what to do if they were abused. Since her Peace Theater work she has graduated from law school. One kid has his own performance theater, got his degree in psychology, and does psychodrama."

Although it's sometimes difficult to know how much impact the Peace Theater show has on audiences, Cheryl reflects that "the younger they are, the more they get out of it. They are more engaged. For each conflict that is encountered by the performer, the audience helps them apply a four-step conflict resolution process to get out of the difficult situation. Playing through several conflict scenarios helps the audience memorize the four steps. The teachers say the students really like it and really learn. There was a camp in Northeast Philly with low-income minority kids that had a Peace Theater performance. The kids wanted them to come back again and again. One of the performers, Burgandy, recalled she had done some circle time with these kids and asked them if they could name a person who had influenced them. One child said 'Peace Theater.' That young person's response made Burgandy appreciate the performers' responsibility as role models."

One factor in Peace Theater's success is that the actors are teens and young adults, so the audience members identify with them. "The closer in age they are to the students, the more the students engage with them. We do shows for age groups 5–8 and 9–12. We design age-appropriate performance material. Typically, the 5–8 performance involves less improvisation and more group participation. The 9–12 performance involves more improvisation, and audience members are invited on stage to perform with Peace Theater. One skit is a game show—audience members are selected to be contestants. The performers stage a conflict, then the contestants are asked to select the ending from several choices that demonstrate various conflict management styles. For example, one ending might be confrontational, another accommodating, and a third is collaborative. After the contestant chooses the ending, the performers act them out demonstrating the value of using conflict resolution skills."

Peace Theater works well for audiences of all ages. For example, Peace Theater performs a free annual show called "Home for the Holidays." "It spotlights intergenerational, family disputes that might occur over the holidays. Family members and community members of all ages can see themselves in these situations and see different ways to handle their own situations."

*Devin Oliver, "Kevina Summers," and "Sharona Kressel" are Peace Theater actors.* Devin, seventeen, is student body president at Franklin Learning Center High School. "I started Peace Theater this summer. In the first two weeks you have mediation training from nine o'clock to three o'clock. It made me start thinking whether I should take this to my school, start mediation at my school. After the training we started working on the skits for Peace Theater. The skits focused on four steps. Stop and Think. Talk and Listen. Share Ideas. Try It Out. For each step we made up little hand movements to help the kids learn.

"I worked with the three- to five-year-olds, so the skits were more like Disney or Candyland. We took ideas from popular shows like *RugRats,* changed the characters around. Like, we did a little treasure hunt, and during this journey we'd approach a problem, and the kids knew they'd need to be able to use their conflict skills to help us work it out. Sometimes we did improvisation, responding to the audience. We did a thing called Game Show. It was a wonderful experience, especially if you love kids.

"The main thing was to make sure the kids learned the steps. Most of the camps Peace Theater performed at took charge of this. The camp posted the steps inside the camp to help kids remember and encouraged them to use them."

Devin notes that his experience with Peace Theater has started to influence his home life. "I live with my niece and nephew and they're both seven now. By me being out there every day with other kids, I brought a different side of me home. I'd come and try some of this with them. It made me look into my own family members more. I brought them to the show a couple of times. They even saw a difference in me. . . . I haven't really tried to use it in other situations. I know I should have, but I'm going to look into it. It's a lot easier to use it to help somebody else than to use it in your own situation."

*Kevina and Sharona have been best friends throughout high school. They've also been colleagues for the past four years in Peace Theater, both starting when they were in ninth grade.* As Kevina recalls, "I liked it because we had a chance to act and work with kids and come up with our own shows. We learned a lot about conflict resolution. We learned how conflict has different outcomes: win-win, win-lose, lose-lose. We learned about how to address kids and about the four steps . . . and how we could teach them how to use this in everyday life.

"The interaction really helped them learn the ideas. It's not like putting a piece of paper in front of them. And we're giving them situations that we know they have been through. Sometimes we have to ask the children in our lives about the kinds of conflicts they go through. Then we bring it back to Peace Theater and develop various skits. We tried to not deal with parental or teacher conflicts cause they were too in-depth or too sensitive. We concentrated on peer conflicts. Lots of it was about sharing or not having any friends. Sometimes it was about being different and being hurt by it."

And working in the troop was sometimes tough. "Each had four people in it. It's like any other situation. People you are with every day, for the most part people got along, but people are people, some had a bad day and some had tempers. We had our days where we had our little petty arguments. We had to remind ourselves to use these for our own conflicts. In my third year I became a facilitator. You have to be a good leader, deal with everybody's mood swings, deal with camp directors, etc. Sometimes it can be overwhelming."

But it's definitely worth it. "A lot of the camps we go to every year, and kids say they remember the four steps from the last year. After the show we ask kids whether they are going to use the four steps and most do. For most of these kids this is new for them. They're not used to seeing theater. We also inspire kids to be actors and actresses.

"I have always been a positive person even before Peace Theater. But for me to teach it to somebody else—Peace Theater has made it easier for me to explain how to handle conflict to others, to my peers and family, how to handle a situation in a more humane manner."

Sharona was a theater major in the Creative and Performing Arts High School and was excited by "the opportunity to work with kids, to help them in some way. That was really important." She knows that Peace Theater made an impact on kids who saw it. "Even today when I go to the grocery store in different neighborhoods kids come up and speak to me. 'Don't you remember me? We saw your show.' 'Do you remember what you told me about this?' They ask if I remember skits and discussion. They always ask for us to come back."

There are challenges working with the older kids, Sharona says. "If you get through to the nine- to twelve-year-olds you're really doing something. They already have in their mind that the show is stupid and they aren't going to like it. If you go in and don't act, it works better. They're more willing to hear what you have to say once you expose your real self to them. Then they let you be someone else. But the five- to eight-year-olds are more open minded and ready to get into it."

In her four years with Peace Theater, Sharona "learned a lot about conflict, being so I've been there so long it was kind of put on my back to try and solve problems. You couldn't just argue with people, you had to fix it. I worked with *a lot* of different people in a *lot* of different situations. In my first year I had to mediate a situation between leaders who were knocking heads the whole time. I had to be the bigger person in the situation and let them know that they had to be bigger too."

She also applied her conflict skills outside the Peace Theater context. "In high school, with some of my best friends we really had to use the four steps a couple of times. They may seem babyish but they actually do work and did work in a lot of situations with my friends."

Her work with Peace Theater has made a lasting impact on her. As Sharona says, "I'm in mediation for life." And her experience supports the importance of expressive arts efforts in CRE: "Literally when they say the children are our future, I agree with that statement. If we don't better them as people we're going to have a big problem, we're going to have a heck of a world."

*The fascinating synergy between expressive arts and conflict resolution education is shared by program directors, artists and trainers, and students who have had the opportunity to work in these innovative programs. We begin with a broad discussion about national level initiatives to link CRE and the arts with Zephryn Conte and Russell Brunson who helped develop and implement the Arts in Peacemaking project of the National Endowment for the Arts (NEA), the National Center for Conflict Resolution Education (NCCRE), and the Office of Juvenile Justice and Delinquency Prevention (OJJDP) of the Department of Justice.*

*Zephryn Conte—author, creative arts and conflict resolution educator—brings a wealth of experience to this dialogue. Her consulting organization, Environarts, Inc., is inspired by her thirty-year background as an artist, classroom educator, and therapist and her many observations about the nature of effective learning and teaching.* "Environarts programs and practices are based on the philosophy that most life learning is driven by people's inner needs and perceptions of reality. Effective life learning occurs in nonacademic settings because our internal needs usually connect organically with our object of learning. Environarts mission is to offer learning experiences that reinforce the connection between people's internal and external environments."

Because Conflict Resolution Education (CRE), and Emotional Intelligence (EQ) provide necessary frameworks and curricula for developing pro-social ideologies and skills, these combined with the arts become a powerfully holistic technology for building leadership and community.

Zephryn's own early educational journey began with learning through dance, music, theatrical and visual arts. "I began dance lessons and began performing at five. I had a wonderful teacher who recognized my own leadership qualities and so I began apprentice teaching at sixteen. Through movement I learned kinesthetically how to break down information so students could grasp it and experience success. I would observe students feeling the power of their spirits coming through their bodies. In this active, learning experience there was tremendous affirmation. I came to realize that active, experiential learning environments enhanced memory retention because the stress of any poor self-esteem was released through the active involvement—so with decreased stress, came increased learning.

"I've appreciated my opportunity to learn firsthand what neuro-scientific research is now confirming. Kinesthetic learning, as well as using many kinds of diverse teaching modalities, is critical for attention and memory."

As a New York City Board of Education arts education specialist, Zephryn was trained in CRE. For several years she taught CRE and EQ classes to high school and middle school students. She then began training adults, while developing her expertise at integrating CRE skills and practices into creative arts and other subject area classes. Over time it became second nature to fuse CRE and EQ ideologies with creative arts activities. Time and again it proved a powerful combination of practices for students to learn about themselves, develop life skills, and build community. "As I worked with educators, I observed that they were not teaching skills or using facilitative strategies that promoted interaction or enhanced social and emotional learning. They were teaching 'subjects.'

"As an Arts and CRE specialist my work was to support administrators and classroom teachers to consider the importance of relationship building. I helped them to integrate the skills that would enable them to do that successfully within their various professional settings or school and classroom communities. As a consultant and trainer, I came to appreciate the difficulty for people in making the paradigm shift needed to move from punitive to collaborative practices. I began to see how necessary it was to integrate exercises in creativity as a way of expanding perceptions and building the mental and emotional resilience that would allow that shift to occur.

"Whether working with young people or adults, I have seen that in order to create a more effective group learning environment it is necessary to start with what is coming from inside of people, otherwise you won't have their participation and they won't authentically connect with what they are learning."

For the last four years, Zephryn has consulted with the NCCRE in the NEA/OJJDP–sponsored *Partnership for Conflict Resolution Education in the Arts.* They developed a training that she facilitated at close to thirty sites across the country, which was specifically designed to address artists working in the community with at-risk youth. "While artistic people tend to be more creative in handling groups, very often they lack the peaceable group dynamic skills and facilitative strategies that are informed by the practices of CRE and EQ. In addition, many of their students were at very high risk, with some incarcerated in detention centers. I have repeatedly seen how wounded children act out later, and how those most troubled are usually the ones who have been most silenced. That's why these young people respond so well to arts and CRE programs. Artistic expression combined with CRE and EQ training is a powerful healer because it gives them a voice and an opportunity to create something positive from their pain.

"I strongly feel that the adults facilitating these youth have a responsibility to help them cultivate a more positive social consciousness by first helping them to care about themselves, and then care about others.

"This kind of healing education is moving the field into the realm of the human spirit because it is more about the unseen aspects of life and learning. Artistic mediums play an important role in making those aspects visible. In a simple yet powerful way, making art offers the maker a psychological safety valve, because the art object can be detached from its creator. While there is some vulnerability in making a work of art, distance from the creation allows objective analysis to occur. This type of analysis can provide a powerful tool for healing and communication. In this type of environment, if learners are also introduced to a palette of effective communication and problem-solving skills (the curriculum of CRE and EQ), I have seen amazing transformative education occur."

*Russell Brunson is a conflict resolution specialist who has been involved with a variety of projects in expressive arts and CRE.* As a staff member for the National Center for Conflict Resolution Education, Russell helped "facilitate a dialogue with NEA, OJJDP, and NCCRE on how they can integrate CRE with the arts, with drama, poetry, clay work, multimedia, dance, and music.

"The goal of the partnership was to give kids more background, have students exposed to CRE in different ways. I would go in and work with art teachers, teach them general CR skills, and then let them develop ideas on how they might integrate this in their arts discovery."

Some of the projects that stand out in his memory give a strong sense of the eclectic nature of the work. "University Eastside Community Collaborative Multicultural Art Center—one of their artists is going to teach teenagers CRE through comic books. They're going to make various trips around the community to visit CRE school programs and mediators in community mediation, and how people in the community are involved in violence prevention. Then they are going to develop a comic book as a resource for kids to teach them conflict resolution skills. Her idea was that kids you work with pick up CRE information and information in general more with this approach. And it's part of a partnership with University of California-Riverside. Students also have to research conflict resolution resources. So it has a research/library component too."

When he does the training he covers "conflict in their community and conflict in their world. We have kids share their stories so it's real for them—so they can identify. We talk about how conflict is a natural thing, getting them to talk about what choices they have made and what choices they would make. This brings out that CR doesn't always work. And we talk about basic needs—talk about how kids meet their needs. It's easier for them to grasp if they understand what needs motivate them, how needs cause conflict, and how needs can affect resolving it. It's great to watch the artists teach basic needs like belonging through dance or drumming, etc. And there's a strong emphasis on communication skills—I try to get the artists to talk about communication through their arts. Toward the end of the training we cover the basic negotiation process and group problem solving."

Having come from a background in community mediation, Russell also earned his law degree, but was drawn to a role as an educator and practitioner.

His work with artists has touched on CRE and many kinds of expressive arts. "Baltimore Clayworks [which sends artists out to work with kids in after-school programs] were the best at understanding and making conflict resolution alive for the kids. They were able to make their stuff very accessible to kids." Sometimes the artists used the information for their own conflicts. "The Brooklyn Children's Museum had a staff conflict that was going on that came to a head in the workshop. I helped facilitate that dialogue; they learned the skills through this experience." And he was very impressed with a group of dancers in Denver. "I asked them to teach some CRE skills through dance. Communication skills and responses to conflict and how conflict resolution looks as a dance—they were able to make it come alive. In the Los Angeles Center they had dancers who took over the floor. They were able to make the negotiation skills really come alive in dance."

One of the striking aspects of this work was the artists' attitudes toward the kids. As Russell recalls, "The artists never had the issue that 'kids can't do this.' They were very open about the abilities kids have. They worked in after-school arts program, lockup facilities, music schools, Police Athletic League (PAL), etc. Some might have even had some probation work. The artists who did go into schools—their biggest problem were teachers and administrators who thought the artists didn't know what they were doing and thought the artists were getting in the way. The teachers would take it as a free period instead of really learning from and working with the artists. Lots of artists wanted to leave the schools because of this resistance. There were some arts teachers working in the schools. They really appreciated classroom management skills and were taking baby steps toward that and getting this to work within the structure of the schools."

After seeing the difficulties of integrating this into regular arts curricula, Russell concludes, "It can work both ways, but probably better and more flexible in after-school programs. If there is a conflict resolution education program already going on, having artists come in and work through that is good."

He sees these programs as particularly effective for at-risk kids. "There was one young man who was having issues in school with conflict because he just wanted to draw; he didn't want to do regular work. When they were teaching conflict skills in group he wasn't that receptive. But when I sat down one-on-one and talked to him about conflicts he was having, he was able to really focus. It gives you a chance to reach kids who haven't performed well in regular schools. One program working with at-risk kids is In the Heart of the Beast [Puppet and Mask Theater in Minneapolis]. They allow at-risk teens to come and work for the company and create a touring show for the community. They wanted to integrate conflict resolution into their team work (setup and teardown of sets, etc.) but also to get them to be able to apply their insights about conflict in their shows. . . .

"My ideal would be having kids be able to share their stories through the arts—share more positive ends of their stories—how well they dealt with things. Giving them ways to learn the skills and be able to show them to kids in a different setting. Kids on kids. Then linking them with the schools and the conflict resolution in the schools. So you can teach the same skills through different means. I would love to see us bring conflict resolution into technology and Web design and making games. Software stuff that integrates conflict resolution to the twenty-first century. More graphic arts stuff. So kids can learn this on their own and pick up these skills as well." Russell has been active in making some of this ideal a reality. He recently completed the website "Out on a Limb" (www.urbanext .uiuc.edu/conflict) for elementary school kids.

# CHAPTER NINE

# MAKING MEANINGFUL CONNECTIONS:
## Curriculum Infusion

Rachel A. Poliner

One of the most frequent questions I hear from teachers regarding conflict resolution education (CRE) is, "When am I supposed to fit *that* in?" Because teachers feel enormous pressure to teach within prescribed curriculum frameworks and to ensure their students perform well on standardized tests, this question is not surprising and not to be dismissed. Another frequent question is, "I taught a lesson on that skill. Why don't the kids know how to use it yet?" Considering our society's expectation of quick fixes, we can't find that question a surprise either. Given this context it is important for teachers to have options for CRE that minimize the addition of new programs while deepening learning.

One of these options is for teachers to infuse CRE concepts into core curricula—that is, to seek out the natural links between CRE and the regular curriculum. Brian Knox, principal of Roy Elementary School in Northlake, Illinois, says, "Standardized testing compels us to teach to the skill. CRE infusion allows us to teach to academic and social skills simultaneously." For example, history is full of conflicts that offer students case studies for observing escalation, identifying leaders' choices and styles, considering varying perspectives, and searching for alternative courses of action. Relevant case studies are by no means limited to international conflicts and wars. They can also be found in the history of the civil rights movement, industrialization, women's rights, immigration, and any other unit of study. Literature, likewise, is an infinite source of infusion opportunities. The climax of a story is the peak of its central conflict, whether that conflict is internal to a character, between characters, or between groups of characters. Even mathematics and science offer infusion opportunities. Mathematicians and scientists have different points of view and face personal challenges (internal conflicts) in their research. Any current social or environmental issue will include conflicting applications of math and science.

Infusion is implemented by identifying where conflict resolution and social-emotional skills and concepts are related to core curriculum content. The aforementioned examples demonstrate this strategy. Alternatively, infusion can be organized by themes—for example, using a theme of heroes and courage and connecting that to multiple content areas while observing and practicing the skills that would support heroism and courage. Students identify actions in any arena where a character (fictional or real) is taking a stand; managing his or her anger; making careful choices; becoming an ally; promoting understanding; or being inclusive, respectful, resilient, or perseverant. Teachers offer skill lessons to deepen understanding and offer practice with those skills.

Teachers have used themes to frame the positive behaviors that promote effective conflict resolution and social-emotional development—for example, friendship versus bullying, community versus isolation, tolerance versus prejudice. Other themes that teachers have organized include justice, peace and security, honesty, and responsibility.

There are many benefits for students and teachers of a curriculum infusion approach in CRE. Students of all ages, especially early adolescents, often find it safer to describe a fictional character's emotions before reflecting on their own. Students can analyze contributing factors to a conflict, identify problem-solving options, and map out possible consequences of those actions, watching how the whole process played out in history or in a piece of literature. In so doing, they build skills for connecting the dots of their own actions and choices. Teachers find it easier to motivate students when they connect academic materials to students' lives. And, because teachers build their infusion approach by exploring their own curriculum rather than teaching a prepackaged curriculum, infusion encourages a true sense of ownership and an unusual professional development process.

This chapter offers a framework for enhancing CRE through layered learning. The layers include the classroom environment that supports infusion, direct skill instruction, and infusion itself. The chapter identifies professional development helpful for teachers, highlights important decisions for administrators, and gives examples of curriculum infusion.

## The Framework: Layered Learning

Educators know that for students to learn something well enough to remember it and apply it, they need to work through several stages and receive consistent reinforcement in multiple layers of classroom life—in lessons and learning strategies, in teachers' behavior, and in classroom routines. This is especially true for subtle skills and more so when we live in a society that often models behavior counter to those skills. We need to be introduced to a concept or skill; we need to apply it to something we already understand; we need to see it modeled; we need to practice it, engage in self-reflection, hear feedback, practice some more, and improve. Finally the skill might be something we internalize. Layering CRE by infusing it into classroom practices and curricula gives opportunities for many of these stages that an isolated program might not be able to elicit.

A teacher recalled a lesson she had used with her students about stereotypes and prejudice. She thought it was well constructed, and the students seemed engaged. The day after the lesson, she was horrified to find that one of her students had written an ethnic slur on the bathroom wall. Her first thought was that the lesson must have failed. She described her experience to a developmental psychologist who gave her a new insight. Children need multiple experiences to learn a new behavior. On first exposure, some will need to try out the negative side of the skill as much as the positive side. It is to be expected. Kids test boundaries as part of their learning process. Teachers and administrators implementing a CRE program should not expect one lesson to "fix" their students. Instead of judging such a behavior negatively, this teacher realized she needed to understand it as part of the process—which can be ongoing when she infuses CRE concepts throughout her curriculum.

Educators often wonder how they can assess progress in CRE. Curriculum infusion can help with this concern, as it involves many opportunities for self-assessment, peer feedback, and teacher coaching and assessment. For example, student participation in historical role plays or in writing alternative endings of stories can show teachers the extent to which students understand the concepts. As students write journal entries reflecting on their actions and statements, they are monitoring their own progress. Teachers and students can create and use behavior rubrics for marking improvement through observation and self-reflection.

## The Classroom Environment That Supports Infusion

Infusion is most powerful when it offers insight not only into the behavior and motivations of characters in literature and history but also into the behaviors and motivations of students. Infusing conflict concepts and interpersonal skills into the core curriculum will include kids' making connections to their lives, writing in journals, and sharing reflections with classmates. This happens best in certain environments.

Students need to be in classroom environments that are safe—physically, emotionally, intellectually, and socially. That does not mean the environments are easy or unchallenging, but rather that they are safe enough so that children can take risks. A student who believes she will be ridiculed for asking a question is not in an intellectually safe classroom. That classroom is thus not intellectually challenging, as this student is learning to take no risks. Chapter Three of this book discusses how to create a safe environment through establishing classroom agreements, implementing community-building and problem-solving processes, and modeling respectful and caring leadership. Those steps benefit not only students' social competence but also their academic achievement. Infusing CRE into curricula does not replace the establishment of a learning community; it reinforces it, expands on it, and helps students internalize it more deeply. In such a classroom, students can learn more about their academic subjects as well as about themselves.

Sadly, some teachers and schools have avoided, or even banned, certain novels or topics in history and science because of the controversy and strong emotions that can be raised when kids learn about compelling human experience. Students can perceive that controversy isn't allowed, that adults won't guide them, that polarization is inevitable, and that common ground doesn't exist. These are harmful messages. Students need practice to live in a diverse democracy. When teachers infuse CRE into the classroom environment, students learn to participate respectfully in discussions, to be sensitive to others' emotions, and to be conscious of others' points of view.

Further, research and logic tell us that establishing a safe and respectful classroom community will prevent disruptions, leaving more time for learning. Even though this belief makes sense to me and every teacher with whom I've ever worked, it requires a leap of faith—for teachers, administrators, students, and parents. Spending time (and yes, it does take time) to create a caring and respectful classroom means that teachers are investing time early that will pay off later.

In addition to giving examples of infusion, the narratives later in this chapter describe the classroom environment that supports infusion. When done well, CRE in classroom practice and curricula is a seamless whole.

## Creating Successful Curriculum Infusion

So often we think we have to implement a Special New Program in schools to attain certain learning objectives, and we assume that once it has been implemented, the program will be sufficient to attain and sustain the goals. True, implementing a specific program may bring a skill area into focus for faculty; they will participate in professional development days and get new materials. These are important benefits. Moreover, students need to have direct instruction in CRE skills. CRE programs implemented in health education or lessons taught during class meetings or advisory groups, for instance, are a crucial foundation.

However, any program is likely to have a limited life span. It takes intentional effort to connect the crucial concepts and skills of the program to the enduring curriculum and classroom practices. This is where an infusion approach to CRE can be successful. It provides an opportunity to identify and expand on the natural connections between CRE and core subject areas so that CRE concepts and skills will become embedded permanently, even if they become less obvious than they would be when in a special program.

## Professional Development That Supports Infusion

There are two important professional development components necessary for infusion to be done well. The first is a strong grounding in CRE and social and emotional learning (SEL). This is not a training to use a set curriculum or do a specific intervention. That kind of training is not sufficient for infusing CRE into curricula. Teachers need and deserve professional development in the skills and concepts of the field; they need to participate in multiple experiences of those skills and concepts. They will be introduced to CRE, practice it, see it modeled, and apply it to material with which they are already familiar. The facilitator can offer sample lessons, establish a supportive process, and encourage creative collegial work.

Second, teachers will need ongoing time with colleagues to identify infusion opportunities in their curricula. A CRE consultant or coach will likely be helpful. Establishing a means of documenting and sharing lessons will enhance infusion over time. This process may not look like the entertaining kind of professional development that some faculties are accustomed to, but most will come to appreciate it as their own learning community. A process I have used with faculties in several districts has included these two components. We focused on infusion into the literature and language arts curriculum. Professional development started with a few days on emotional intelligence, various problem-solving processes, communication skills, and establishing a sense of community among diverse learners. We did exercises to improve our own skills and understandings of these areas, experienced activities for classroom use, and reviewed important information from research and practice. We applied each skill or concept to a piece of literature, a writing exercise, or both, providing many models for those connections. We identified links to the district's frameworks as we went, giving teachers reassurance that their work was on target with the district's goals and bringing those frameworks to life. Many states' curriculum frameworks include standards on workplace and life skills, such as problem solving, collaboration, communication, decision making, and responsible self-management. Making the links between CRE and distinct frameworks has been easy to do in districts across the country.

We also went through a process for establishing safety as a collegial writing group. Because the prospect of writing together was scary for many of the participants, it was an important moment for empathizing with how children might feel in class and for modeling how to establish effective learning communities. With this foundation, the teachers spent numerous hours crafting original and insightful questions related to the literature of their choice, and outlining an implementation plan for embedding that piece of literature in a sequence of lessons. The sequence provided a thorough and developmental exploration of the CRE concept or skill. Ann Swies, who teaches kindergarten in the Mannheim 83 District near Chicago, spoke for many primary grade teachers when she reflected, "This approach is so different from our typical comprehension questions. I'm holding higher expectations of my students and learning how they can develop higher thinking and self-management skills." A fifth-grade teacher, upon hearing a similar remark from a first-grade teacher in her workshop, let out a sigh of relief that all the teachers in her school were realizing their shared responsibility to help children build skills for reflecting and for answering open-ended questions.

This professional development process had the additional benefits of building teachers' leadership abilities, deepening the intellectual conversation among teachers, and modeling a process they could apply to other curriculum areas. Carolann Wais, assistant superintendent of the School Administrative Unit #63 in New Hampshire, commented after an infusion workshop, "The teachers have a whole new sense of ownership and confidence. Now they are able and willing to share skills with their colleagues." Helene Mellon, assistant superintendent of the Bennington Regional School District in Vermont said, "The kind of open-ended integrative questions that teachers are learning to ask in this program is exactly what we want them to learn to do in all curriculum areas."

Such a collegial process can be formalized into mentoring relationships with teachers new to the school or to CRE. In another district, we took advantage of the middle school team structure in which teachers had common planning time and shared students. The common planning time allowed for informal mentoring.

## Administrative Challenges and Opportunities

Much of CRE has been implemented through programs; an outside specialist provides material and a specific approach for delivering the material. Some teachers take to it well; others put it on a shelf with the rest of their rarely used binders. One of the benefits of implementing a program is that everyone is engaged in the same effort—at least that is what's hoped. Of course, no one program fits every teacher's style, and too many programs leave teachers knowing how to teach the lessons specifically involved without knowing the underlying principles that they could have found their own way to teach.

In some ways an infusion approach to CRE is harder to "manage." There will not be particular lessons all prepared in a sequence. Infusion will not be designated for a special time each week, and it may not feel like an ever-present focus. The lessons through which kids are getting direct CRE skill instruction will be more predictable, whether those lessons be in a health class, experiential education class, morning meeting, or advisory group.

As teachers integrate CRE and SEL skills and concepts into their own understanding of their fields, support of the effort, not management, will be what they need; most useful are the sharing of best practices at faculty meetings and support for the vehicle used for documenting and sharing lessons, whether it is in files or binders or on a district's website. Administrators can also encourage connections between CRE and schoolwide efforts, including holiday celebrations, service projects, drama performances, or art displays. The challenge for administrators is to provide just enough leadership to keep the skills and concepts of conflict resolution in focus.

One of the beauties of an infusion approach is that CRE will happen even if the main thrust of curriculum improvement and professional development is elsewhere. The danger of the approach is that it can be forgotten among other pressing efforts. CRE curriculum infusion, like any serious intellectual endeavor, will benefit from the time adults have to learn together, and will be challenged if teachers rarely have time to share collegial practice. The most effective infusion learning groups have included teachers who share responsibility for a content area (for example, language arts), a theme (for example, democracy), or a skill (for example, problem solving). Infusion can help teachers see the connections between what are otherwise structured as isolated subject areas. Some districts have held summer workshops or arranged for graduate credit to support the effort.

An important way for administrators to support infusion of conflict resolution into the academic curriculum is to infuse the same concepts and skills into school culture, including the adult culture. In several districts, a separate institute has been conducted for administrators. One of the goals of a curriculum infusion approach is to help students understand that good conflict skills are not limited to a particular time of day or to the counselor's office, nor are they used only by mediation team members. Principals can greatly enhance teachers' parallel understanding by modeling effective communication, problem-solving practices, and negotiated management with their faculties. One principal used the negotiation terms of *positions* and *interests* as the faculty was reworking the discipline code to sort out the behavioral outcomes (interests) that faculty hoped students would internalize by obeying school rules (positions). Another principal chose to promote a sense of community among teachers by starting faculty meetings with gatherings—sometimes a poem, sometimes a sharing moment, other times an exercise related to emotional intelligence.

## Examples of Infusion

So what does infusion look like? The following sections provide examples of infusion in core curricula.

### English, Language Arts, and Drama

After attending workshops on the concepts and skills, many literature and language arts teachers quite easily see the connections between CRE, SEL, and learning to read and write. They see that studying the plot of a story is a matter of observing the escalation and deescalation of the conflict. They see that students can deepen their study of characters by identifying characters' emotions, understanding their points of view, and observing their choices and communication styles. Students can rewrite dialogue to demonstrate the effect of communication choices on relationships and plot. They can write in journals about their own experiences in similar situations. These connections help students internalize CRE skills and concepts *and* help students improve their ability to read and write. The options really are infinite. Following are several examples, starting in at the kindergarten level.

Ann Swies, a kindergarten teacher, chose to focus on emotions, believing that her students were developmentally ready for a wider array of vocabulary for describing how they felt. She chose a picture book each week in which one or more emotions was evident. I observed her class during their lesson on the word *afraid*. She used *Sheila Rae, the Brave*,[1] by Kevin Henkes. In the beginning of the story, Sheila Rae is never afraid; she is so brave that she is cavalier. Sheila Rae rides her bicycle with no hands and growls at stray dogs. Ann asked her students if they do these things. They said no, they would be afraid to do them. Ann discussed with her students that sometimes feeling afraid can help you know what is and isn't safe.

The story continues. Sheila Rae's younger sister, Louise, is frequently afraid. One day, when Sheila Rae in her bravado wanders off only to become lost and desperate, Louise has followed her, stayed vigilant the whole time, and knows the way home. Louise was afraid, but that didn't stop her. She overcame her fear.

Ann engaged students in a discussion of times when they had been afraid and helped them identify what they did to overcome the fear. The students drew their stories and finished the sentence, "I felt afraid when _____, so I _____." Over the course of the year each child had created a booklet of his or her own stories about many different emotions.

Ann's lessons introduced children to "feeling words" and related those words to the children's own experiences. Through weekly exploration, she helped them know that emotions change and that people can make choices even when they feel strong emotions. She further reinforced their development of emotional vocabulary with art projects, feelings check-ins, and many other practices.

A third-grade teacher can use *The Summer My Father Was Ten*,[2] by Pat Brisson, to engage students in a discussion about taking responsibility for one's actions, dealing with feelings of guilt, and befriending someone from a different generation and culture. She could follow that with *Mrs. Katz and Tush*,[3] by Patricia Polacco, which also highlights a friendship across generations and cultures, in this case between an elderly Jewish widow and a young African American boy. While the reader learns about their differences, he also watches their friendship grow through their sharing care of a cat and noticing similarities in Jewish American and African American experiences.

Fiction is especially helpful in CRE because it touches the mind and the heart. When students read *Marianthe's Story*,[4] by Aliki, they cannot help but *understand* more about emigrating to the United States and attending school before being able to speak English, while they *feel* more empathy for a child in that circumstance. The same is true for *Thank You, Mr. Falker*,[5] by Patricia Polacco, the story of Patricia's own struggle with dyslexia as a child. Students expand their perspective-taking skills both cognitively (whether they can take the point of view of the other) and emotionally (how well they empathize with the other). Effective conflict resolution requires both. Each of these stories is also useful for helping students learn to identify bullying behavior, consider the motivation of bullies, and imagine possible interventions.

It is important to note that an infusion approach in language arts is not merely about choosing and reading books with a social message or a conflict nicely resolved. Simply reading the book aloud and moving on to other classroom tasks does not necessarily encourage CRE. Teachers who want to infuse CRE into their literature lessons have crafted careful questions for whole-class discussions, small guided reading groups, and individual journal reflections that encourage students to connect the story to using CRE concepts or skills in their own lives. They are also embedding those stories and discussions in an ongoing exploration that includes direct instruction of skills, and reinforcing CRE through such classroom practices as peer editing (which builds feedback skills) and respectful discussions (listening for understanding and disagreement without put-downs).

The infusion lessons become increasingly sophisticated as children move into reading chapter books. Students in grade five or six who read *The Cay*,[6] by

Theodore Taylor, see the main character, a white boy named Phillip, change his images of war and people. In this World War II story, Phillip thinks of war as exciting until he witnesses a ship's destruction. His image of war is changed, as is what he believes counts as bravery. Students can observe closely what interactions lead Phillip to shed his stereotypes of Timothy, a West Indian man. *The Cay* also offers memorable scenes in which Phillip has every reason to feel desperate and to give up his struggle, yet instead he overcomes setbacks. There are crucial lessons for young readers about finding one's own motivation, facing enormous obstacles, and building resiliency.

All of the concepts and skills mentioned so far can be applied to Mildred Taylor's novel *Roll of Thunder, Hear My Cry*,[7] often read in middle school. Students can observe characters' escalating behaviors, their decisions, and the consequences of both; they can identify characters' emotions and management of emotions; they can learn about power and prejudice. Many other CRE skills can be infused into a study of *Roll of Thunder* as well. If students are asked to identify the emotions of one or more of the villainous characters, they can build empathy precisely when empathy feels like a stretch. They can learn about perspective taking when they analyze various characters' points of view, and they can see how different perspectives affect conflict. Further, they can see that sometimes the most courageous action is not a loud escalating behavior that uses power over people; sometimes it is an act of sacrifice that restores peace. All the while, students are improving their comprehension skills.

A ninth-grade teacher reported to me how her students had outlined the escalating conflict in Shakespeare's *Romeo and Juliet* in an enormous graph on the chalkboard. Another high school English teacher used *Of Mice and Men*,[8] by John Steinbeck, to expand their vocabulary of emotions (important at any age level) by inferring what characters are feeling, as feeling words are rarely mentioned in the text. Students can explore characterization by analyzing the conflict styles of the characters when they argue over whether or not the dog should be killed.

High school students who read the mystery *Sacred Clowns*,[9] by Tony Hillerman, will learn about Navajo culture and different forms of justice. In the book, Officer Chee feels caught in the tension of upholding the law and its system of punishment and upholding another form of justice that restores balance and makes amends. This and other novels in which characters are sorting out how to make a situation "right" are opportunities to consider restorative justice.

Drama courses can contribute uniquely to CRE, as the following example demonstrates. Students need practice to internalize a new behavior, especially one that is supposed to be useful at stressful moments. Drama performances, by definition, offer that kind of practice. A middle school teacher engaged his students in writing scripts of typical early adolescent conflicts, using those scripts to practice writing and saying I messages in particular. This teacher then videotaped the performances so that other classes could use them as discussion starters.

There is an infinite array of infusion opportunities in literature and language arts. This tiny sampling barely scratches the surface. Several published guides and series are now available connecting CRE to specific stories, and these materials can be helpful models, but teachers who learn the foundation concepts of CRE and SEL can infuse those concepts into the study of any piece of literature they choose.

Some districts have involved parents in their approaches to literature infusion. For example, the South Coast districts in Massachusetts (New Bedford, Fall River, and surrounding towns) give families carefully selected books and questions crafted to encourage summer reading and child-parent dialogue about conflict and character. Other schools offer workshops for parents or hold book fairs with demonstration discussions. When parents are involved, the concepts can be reinforced at home, and parents can improve their own conflict resolution skills. Books can be chosen for a parents' workshop in which characters who are parents deal effectively and creatively with conflicts. For example, introducing the terms *positions* and *interests* and then applying those to *First Pink Light*,[10] by Eloise Greenfield, can open a discussion about dealing with power issues with children.

## History

It is fairly obvious that studying national and international conflicts and social movements is, in and of itself, part of CRE. Students learn about factors that contribute to conflict and change, actions that have and can be taken, and the consequences of those actions. Teachers consistently report that when CRE skills are infused into their regular curriculum, students learn more about the historical figures, events, and movements than they had before, because students see clearly that the topics are connected to their lives.

But social studies is not just the study of major events, dates, places, and actions. It is also preparation for living in a democracy. Many of the creative techniques that teachers employ in social studies education are or can be CRE related, whether or not the teachers already identify them as such. Explicitly linking CRE skills offers understanding of escalation, motivation, decision making, and a study of alternative courses of action. Moreover, CRE infused into social studies classes encourages attitudes (such as respect for different views) and processes (such as dialogue) that promote conflict resolution, and provides experiences in community problem solving and real-life examples of restorative justice.

For example, fourth-grade students studied a local problem in which different groups wanted different things. Students interviewed family members and neighbors to learn about their points of view, then brainstormed options. Third graders in another classroom did role plays of people invested in and affected by Christopher Columbus's voyages. (A good literature connection would then be to read *Morning Girl*,[11] by Michael Dorris.)

Oral history interviews, used by many teachers, make history personal for students, help build listening and questioning skills, and deepen students' understanding of their place in history. Whether the interviews relate to immigration, civil rights, women's rights, the labor movement, or any other aspect of modern history, students from upper elementary through high school can appreciate individual choices about how to act on an issue, how to be patient through long-term change processes, and how contexts and choices change over time.

In a high school world history course, which included the study of world religions, one teacher chose to make her comparison charts come alive by inviting four people to class, each representing a different religion. In a "rotation station structure," small groups of students interviewed the guests. Working in that structure, rather than listening to a panel of speakers, students had more active and intimate interactions and more practice questioning and listening.

Infusion of specific CRE concepts can highlight certain dynamics of history. For example, in their unit on the Russian Revolution, a middle school teacher's students analyzed the positions and interests of the peasants and of the bureaucrats, giving them a deeper understanding of the motivation of individuals and groups. Infusing positions, interests, and brainstorming into the study of the American Revolution is also useful.[12]

A high school teacher had her advanced placement European history students identify the conflict styles used by leaders at the Treaty of Versailles. She reported that applying the concepts of conflict styles to this study gave her students much more insight into why some promises were kept and others were not.

There are also dedicated materials that connect CRE to social studies. *Talking Peace: A Vision for the Next Generation*,[13] by former president Jimmy Carter, offers primary source material at a middle school reading level. Students read about peacemaking skills that have failed and others that have succeeded, and the application of those skills to international conflicts and to interpersonal conflicts. Former president Carter's thoughts about historical conflicts, his comparison of global perspectives on human rights, and his personal stories about negotiations allow students to connect skills they have been practicing to the larger world.

*Conflict in Context: Understanding Local to Global Security*[14] offers an in-depth study of the dynamics of conflict and significant skill-building lessons that can be applied to many regions, periods, and issues. Activities on security in students' immediate environment build up to case studies of real international human rights issues, such as land mines, free trade, debt relief, and child soldiers. Students can see connections between local and global security issues and problems.

Another curriculum, *Dialogue: Turning Controversy into Community*,[15] highlights that the very way in which we conduct public discourse on controversial issues connects CRE to curriculum and classroom practice. A middle or high school social studies course with a unit on debate can offer an alternative unit on dialogue. Through debate, students gain skills in critical thinking and advocacy, but the goal of debate is winning. The goals of a dialogue are learning rather than winning, building relationships rather than creating enemy images, and deepening understanding rather than polarizing an issue. Dialogue as a structured form of discourse on controversial, complex issues also promotes critical thinking, but of a different nature. Students learn to listen in order to understand instead of listening in order to rebut. They learn to ask questions that uncover assumptions and respect varying interests, instead of asking questions that attack. They are engaged in identifying their own assumptions and encouraged to stretch their thinking to embrace multiple points of view.

## Mathematics and Science

It is often a surprise to teachers that even mathematics offers opportunities to infuse conflict resolution concepts and skills. Particularly within an interdisciplinary unit or course, there are many connections to be made. Such activities have the added advantage of helping students see that math skills really do relate to their lives. For example, after each major census count of U.S. population, representatives in the U.S. House of Representatives are reapportioned. Math and social studies students may find the often dry civics lesson on reapportionment to be much more interesting when it is a math puzzle that involves controversy related to political parties, urban and poor communities, states with large or small populations, and regions that are growing versus declining.[16] Students can understand the alternatives and the choices made.

A fifth-grade teacher organizes his math curriculum to build on students' interests, such as connecting math to issues of equality and fairness, using math to uncover stereotypes and to understand history.[17] Students can conduct polls, or classroom or community censuses. They can collect evidence of data being used to support opposing viewpoints. All these activities encourage students to see that math is part of the language people use if they are to participate in solving complex problems.

One middle school teacher reported his frustration at how many times he had tried to teach the skills of calculating mean, median, and mode, and wondered why his students couldn't seem to remember the techniques. When he grouped his students in teams to conduct their own data collection projects on topics of real concern to them, everything changed. His students learned the skills quickly, applied them, and did so while practicing their interpersonal and cooperation skills.

Like math, interdisciplinary science units offer innumerable opportunities to identify different points of view, look at questions of fairness and justice, and consider how communities act to solve problems. Any environmental issue can involve research, interviews, role plays, dialogues, and problem solving. Some of the same kinds of projects mentioned earlier can be useful in science, such as oral history interviews. For example, in a study of systems for dealing with garbage, students can interview relatives or neighbors who are older or from another country and find out how long they kept things, how much they threw out, where their trash went, and so on.[18]

Students are likely to find the news more interesting when they notice that science usually involves conflicting viewpoints. Certainly, current topics related to genetics, energy use, nutrition, or other complex issues will offer practice and application of CRE skills.

Changes in technology throughout history offer another approach to case studies. The story of how longitude was finally determined, for instance, is an epic story—one combining history and science—of individuals fighting institutions and persevering despite setbacks.[19]

## Infusion's Many Benefits

Infusing conflict resolution skills and concepts into core subject areas supports students' development of conflict resolution competencies. It deepens their understanding of academic material. It encourages a sense of community. And it offers teachers a focus for interdisciplinary learning.

A story from a first-grade bilingual classroom serves as a summary example. After experiencing an activity on stereotypes at a professional development workshop, a teacher chose to adapt the activity for her first graders, connect it to the picture book *Oliver Button Is a Sissy*,[20] by Tomie dePaola, and use math to explore students' similarities and differences.

All of this started with a potato. The teacher asked students for words that would describe potatoes, and listed them on easel paper. Students were then put in pairs; each pair was given a potato to study. They were to get to know their potato so well that they could pick it out of a crowd of potatoes. The teacher collected the potatoes in a bin, mixed them up and asked the students to pick out their potato from the bin. All pairs were able to do so. An interesting discussion ensued about how all of the potatoes could be described by the words offered earlier, yet each potato was also different once you got to know it well. The teacher summed up this portion of the lesson by emphasizing that even people who are grouped together in some ways are different in others.

She then held up the book *Oliver Button Is a Sissy,* mentioning that the main character, Oliver, likes to do some activities and does not like to do others. Around the room she placed easel paper with questions for students, "Do you like to dance and sing?" "Do you like to play ball?" and other questions related to the story. Students traveled to the easel sheets in their pairs, each pair including a boy and a girl. Each student wrote his or her response on the easel paper, the boys in one color of marker, the girls in another. The teacher collected all the easel sheets and, with students, made bar graphs comparing girls' responses with boys' responses. For each question, there was a tendency for or against that activity by gender, and for no question was there a unanimous answer. Many of the boys liked some activities, but one or more boys disliked each activity. The same was true for the girls. The teacher reinforced her earlier message, that even people who are grouped together in some ways are different in others.

She then read aloud the story, in which Oliver likes to draw and dance, does not like to play sports, and is called a sissy until students see how talented he is. The students identified Oliver's feelings, empathized with his situation, and compared it to their own experiences. They read the story in Spanish before lunch and in English after lunch, each time reinforcing academic skills and social competencies.

◆ ◆ ◆

Connecting academic content with children's lives in a variety of ways is a powerful learning experience. Through these kinds of activities, children are able to learn prescribed content, such as language arts and mathematics, as well as see important links to how people can and should manage themselves and relate to each other. They learn and practice CRE skills, apply them to multiple contexts, and assess themselves and are assessed by others. They experience CRE skills in the reinforcing layers of a classroom community, direct skill instruction, and curriculum infusion. These are the same natural links we hope they bring to their lives outside of and after schooling.

# In Their Own Words

## "Infusion Lets You Do Lots More with Less Time"

*Pierce Middle School in Milton, Massachusetts, and Lincoln Junior High School in Fort Collins, Colorado, participated in the National Curriculum Integration Project (NCIP), a nationwide project to study models for infusing CRE into curriculum content areas in middle schools. Started by the Colorado School Mediation Project, NCIP has yielded considerable insights and resource materials that can be found on its website (www.ncip.org). As part of the project, schools participated in teacher and student interviews. The following are excerpts from some of those interviews done in the last year of the project.*

*Pierce Middle School is a part of the Milton School System. We spoke with "Ally," vice principal and a critical force behind the school's involvement with NCIP.* As Ally explains, "We worked with teachers in the sixth grade who were committed to using the curriculum in their classrooms. Our sixth-grade teachers were in teams and that allowed them to have common times for meeting and planning, which is absolutely necessary [for successful infusion]. It also gave time for common coaching, etc. We found the first year when it was open to everyone and we only had meetings after school [that] it didn't work nearly as well. It's really important to consider administratively how the school structure will impact the ability of teachers to participate in this kind of innovation."

There were several reasons for focusing on CRE. "We chose to use CRE curriculum infusion as a way to deal with diversity and conflict issues in the classes. I thought it was very successful. Even without some of the funding, some of the teachers are still continuing [the CRE] because it worked so well. The students want to feel empowered, and the teachers want to retain control. The [CRE curriculum infusion] gave both the opportunity to get what they wanted."

Ally feels strongly that the CRE infusion has benefited teachers and students, but she also feels that it had an impact on her as an administrator. "This experience has even helped me as an assistant principal. If I could let go of 'I'm the boss' and let the students have some say with how we dealt with problems, then the teachers probably could. Some of these real traditional things we were holding on to we let go of. We still have concerns, but on the whole it's a much better attitude. You have to understand that academia is not the only thing we're here for."

But she is also very realistic about what it takes to make this kind of program work. "Unless every staff person becomes involved in some fashion, you lose ground. The standardized tests are here to stay. The teachers never get to forget they are expected to prepare students for that."

*Several of the teachers from Pierce talked with us about their experiences. "Lauren," "Carlo," and "Dottie" all taught sixth-grade language arts. "Bran" is the drama teacher. They were attracted to CRE infusion for different reasons.* As Carlo explains, "My primary interest in getting involved with this was learning how to deescalate conflict. Like sitting down with a student who doesn't like me and telling him it's OK to say why you don't like me. I learned not to get mad at his mad." Lauren notes, "We learned how to deal with and recognize conflict between us and colleagues as well. It made teaching it so much more important. And we share some of these stories with the kids, and they see that we're human and we need to work these kinds of things out as well."

Yet Lauren notes that for her, CRE infusion was a lot easier last year when she taught language arts. This year she's teaching mathematics, and the shift is not easy. "Now that I'm teaching math it is harder to keep the CRE infusion going. It's not as natural for me to see where to fit it in."

But she wants to be able to find a way. In her experience, the CRE helps with classroom management and helps students learn conflict content: "What makes it easier is integrating it into the curriculum. You never have enough time, but the infusion lets you do lots more with less time." Bran agrees: "It works on lots of levels, so the learning is happening in fairly subtle as well as very obvious ways."

"It is a huge commitment," Lauren states—a sentiment shared by all. Yet, as Bran says, "It's definitely worth it. But we need planning time, meeting times, more teachers on board so you don't feel so isolated. You can feel like you're in a vacuum and wonder, for the hour and a half I'm going to see these kids, will it really matter." These teachers are constantly faced with the realization that the way schools are structured is often antithetical to what is needed for a curriculum infusion program to work.

Each teacher has success stories about specific infusion projects that have worked well for him or her. Bran, the drama teacher, shares one of his successes: "I give kids a mini training on conflict skills and have them write their own skits about conflict and have them come up with their own resolutions to it. My acting workshop went into the different seventh-grade classes to teach about the conflict process and escalation and then field questions from the classes. We did this for three days in a row, and at first I was jumping in a lot to answer the students' questions, but by the third day they were answering all of the questions themselves and using the language and they weren't even trying and weren't aware. So that showed true integration to me. . . . They really got it and it was great."

Lauren has been honing her skills for three years, having been one of the first teachers to work with NCIP. She's the first to acknowledge that the learning curve really takes time. "Technically, it's year three, but honestly this is the first year that I've really worked on integrating the material. We do peer editing for writing assignments; they work together as peers and help each other out with whatever they need assistance with."

Dottie sees a "better relationship among the kids" due to CRE infusion. "We talked about the issue of safety . . . making circle safe for everyone to express themselves no matter how silly an idea or issue sounds . . . and so even the different kids can talk and the rest of the group is very tolerant and respectful. And I try to have them 'solve' the problems, although I do interject occasionally." In terms of integrated lessons, Dottie really liked the "point-of-view glasses for the *Roll of Thunder* book, which is having the students take on a different role of one the characters, and they have to write down what experience they think that character is having and what result they think that character wanted to happen."

Dottie definitely sees a difference: "They're learning how to walk away from conflict and not let it escalate. And I think the NCIP material is about making the kids feel more cared about because it's more than just academics. I've gotten ideas about how kids can feel more like equals. These are really good activities that give the kids a sense of being taken seriously and learning that what they think matters and counts for something."

One of the techniques she uses to help them develop emotional awareness is "journaling, because that's a way for them to bring their own experience with the subject to the paper, and it gives us an opportunity to talk about these things together, at another time. It allows us to deal with the issues."

*"Johan" is the guidance counselor for the sixth grade. Johan has been involved in NCIP because he's always dealing with conflict, and it gives him the opportunity to help the teachers before conflict arises.* Johan sees "some of the kids come in here and apply stuff to other kids. I see them taking on my role with each other and try to facilitate conflict interaction between their peers. Sometimes they'll even come to me and explain the situation and ask for advice about how best to advise their peers, which is really good. But then when they are in conflict, they don't apply these things so well. This is a hard thing for the sixth graders. A lot of them just shut down in conflict."

*We also had an opportunity to talk with several students in the CRE infusion classes at Pierce. The interviews were anonymous, so fictitious names have been used here.* When asked what is different about the NCIP classes, Dan says, "It makes you think. It makes you learn how to respect each other. Sometimes when someone says something you don't like, you have to hold your mouth." Mike notes, "You also think about how you can help. You think more about what's going on, like something you never noticed before which is really big. . . . It just comes to you."

Jake feels "like there's more liberty in the classroom; the teacher still enforces that we do our work and do it well . . . but she understands how we feel and makes it more comfortable." Alyisha adds, "She treats us more like adults. And she lets us speak our minds; she believes in freedom of speech, like if you have a strong opinion she let's us express it." Of course, as Alex reminds the others, "She does have ground rules for how you express your opinions. One person at a time. She likes that you can disagree with someone, but she expects you to respect them and talk in that way."

Julie likes "when we have open discussions. . . . Everyone can talk. Usually, we talk about a chapter in a book we're reading and we can discuss how we feel about it." Fran likes "when we do essays. . . . The teacher calls them narratives, and lets us write on anything we want . . . whatever subject we like . . . but it has to be written and like a story."

Trish tells of one of her favorite assignments: "We read this book called *Roll of Thunder,* about slaves, and then we did an analysis of commercials. . . . And we looked at how commercials carry on stereotypes we have. I like when we do book reports. . . . We get into groups and get a partner and then read a book and then we do a project—like we did a newspaper last time, or we do artwork projects or skits about whatever book we read."

Stan "liked the wax museums too. Where we dressed up as the person we picked and enacted those characters for back-to-school night. . . . And you can't talk but have to try to show as much about the character you can through your dress and the props and the background. When you have to act out the person you get to know them better; you know what it's like to be popular, or hated . . . how it feels to be them."

One of the most important lessons from this work was expressed by Bran: "We have to do a lot of group work together, and sometimes, even often, you find yourself working with someone you don't really like that much. But you know that you don't have to be best friends in order to learn to work well together. By the end of the year we feel we can work with anyone on anything."

*Students from Lincoln Junior High School in Fort Collins, Colorado, also had very strong opinions about the value of CRE infused into their curricula. Once again, fictitious names have been used.* One group of students was in a ninth-grade honors English class. When asked to explain the difference between this class and other "conventionally taught classes," Dawn said, "She really challenges us. She gives us lots of homework and projects that will help us in our everyday lives and not just stupid assignments. There's a lot of new things to do in her class; it's not just like the same old things. Lots of things that ask us to think about larger issues like community. She cares about what we learn and how much we learn and what we learn to do with it. The big projects we work on ask us to think about a lot of areas in our lives. Like an autobiography project we did where we had to learn about our family history and gather information on our family and background and put it all together in this major presentation."

Jerome added, "The peace notebook was another one. She gave us a list of quotes and then we had to find images or draw pictures that further explained or illustrated the quote. It was valuable because it helped us see that even in war there could be peace. Like I found a picture of the Vietnam War where there was a picture of a soldier holding and sheltering a little baby." Lots of students said their favorite project was the Holocaust project. As Susan said, "We learned a lot of information about the Holocaust, watched movies about it. Then we put our feelings about it in reflective journals and put it all together in a notebook. Now we're doing rites of passage, where she asks us how much we've grown and changed throughout this year. This year I've changed a lot mostly because of what we're doing in this class. Now I know a lot more about the world. I have a lot more confidence in myself because I see connections I didn't see before. She's asked us to do work I didn't think I could do, and now that I've done it I feel much better about myself as a student." Perhaps David sums up the benefits as well as anyone: "Sometimes it's exhausting. But I feel like I'm ready to go to high school from her class, but I don't feel that way in my other classes."

The students are very aware that a critical component of the success of this class is the time the teacher takes to build community in the classroom. As Raul says, "Other teachers think about teaching the class as a whole, but [this teacher] takes the time to understand each of us as individual people. Her class is a lot more focused too. Things are really on task but we also feel like she's connecting with us as kids." Maria explains, "We really know each other better in this class than in other classes. In lots of the big projects we have to share something from it, and that gives us insight into each other. We have lots of class discussions and you get to know what other kids are thinking and what they like or don't like."

"Everyone is willing to work in her class. We know we're getting a lot out of it and having fun," Harry feels. "You learn that if you needed to talk with her she'll actually listen to you when other teachers don't and won't."

*Developing a school structure and providing staff development that enables this kind of work is very difficult. It requires a dedicated and visionary administration. Carolann Wais, assistant superintendent of the School Administrative Unit #63 in New Hampshire, has been working to support these initiatives.* "The work in conflict resolution was the first time I consciously made an effort to do something that was infused into the curriculum." Carolann's background as a teacher helped her see the value of curriculum infusion for teachers: "I was an elementary school teacher for six years, a middle school teacher for six years, and a high school teacher for six years. I became a director of special education for grades six through age twenty-one. That's where I picked up a lot about conflict resolution and infusion. I worked a lot with the teachers. Everything they did was deescalating, dealing with emotion. Because I come from a special education background I already thought in terms of teaching to the whole child. And coming from the mind-set of knowing how affective development relates to learning is key."

Carolann sees clearly the dangers of teaching only to the test and the benefits of CRE infusion for meeting broader educational standards. "You need to pay attention to the emotional health of the student. Special education has always understood that. If you look at the state standards for each of the major curriculum areas, they have problem solving and decision making throughout. We did an analysis of the results of New Hampshire state testing, and realized that weaknesses in problem solving and multistep thinking were affecting scores. We're looking at how to infuse the problem solving into every single area. We're just now getting the awareness that we need to be working on this."

Carolann feels that for teachers to be successful in these programs, "There has to be a belief that it's necessary. And then you need to embark on a process of education in terms of giving people   principals, staff members, teachers—enough information so they can come to the conclusion that CRE programs are necessary too. Once they do that, they're home. . . .

"In order for administrators and school boards to value CRE they have to see results. Because the boards (at least here in New Hampshire) decide what goes into the budget, we need to collect data that links CRE to student achievement. It will take data, and we're learning how to collect that data."

*The philosophy of curriculum infusion is congruent with a whole-school model whereby CRE is infused throughout the school in all grades and in a variety of ways. One elementary school in Williamsburg, Massachusetts, is an excellent example of what a school can become. The Anne T. Dunphy Elementary School is a small school in a rural part of the state. David Sprague, school counselor, has been working at Dunphy for nine years and coordinates the SEL and CRE programs.* As he explains, the school has a very thorough program. "For example, our third grade has a yearlong program with weekly group problem solving, group challenge, cooperative learning, cooperative games. We end up with an adventure day where we go away from the school and do rockwall climbing. In the fall we do a six-week team-building session to bring classes together and help teachers build community in the classes and throughout the school."

The decision to develop a CRE philosophy rather than simply adopt preprepared programs was intentional. "The shift we made was to focus on the whole school. I did some peer mediation programs a while ago and evolved away from that for a couple of reasons. We really want everybody to be learning this stuff. We're really trying to integrate it, to really make it such a part of the life of the school that it's not a program, it's a way of life at the school. I've worked hard to individualize what I do with a classroom based on the uniqueness of that classroom that year. We do have universal themes that we want to accomplish. But how we do that is going to look a little different every year based on the kids. My impression is that [in most places] they buy into programs and almost feed it into schools, and administrators make the decisions because that's their way of using the money from the 'safe and drug-free schools' area. So it's driven by where the money is, and it's tailored just enough to meet the mandates of the grant, but it may not really meet the needs of the classroom or the teacher. Lisa [Peloquin], the sixth-grade teacher said it nicely: 'We don't teach it, we live it.'"

The teachers feel very strongly about their commitment to CRE in all curricular areas and at all grade levels. *Susan Smith, third-grade teacher,* says, "The whole idea around conflict resolution is a way I want kids to be able to think about everything. I value the kids' thinking and it's not just limited to an area. Part of the culture in the classroom is that we problem solve all the time. But it also applies when they're thinking in any subject area. It's not about me telling them how to behave, but setting up opportunities for them to have to think about how you can get along with people. Just like you set up opportunities for how they learn about addition or some other content."

Susan acknowledges that "There's lots of common messages across classes. We wouldn't have different grades playing well together if they weren't getting those same messages. We've been working on including kids this year. David sets up opportunities in our class meeting for our kids to do something that allows them to think about inclusion and talk about it [without using the term *inclusion*]. There's the potential for having 'cliquey' groups, something that often happens in third grade. I often will have children who might be intentionally excluded by their classmates. In the morning we sing a song and five students can suggest a song. I'm noticing that the children who are initially excluded eventually begin to be chosen to give a suggestion. There's no high stakes in this activity, but in the past with many kids with their hands up, these children would not have been picked. As the year goes on they are often chosen. There's something that's happening. I really think that it's working. I think that's pretty cool."

In this school the structure is used to help the CRE process. The first- and second-grade classes loop—the same teachers have the same students for two years in a row. *Johanna Korpita and M.J. Long teach the first and second grades.* Johanna reinforces the importance of the looping: "I only have fifteen students and I get to keep them for first and second grade, so we're really a family. We're together for two whole years and that's a lot of time for six- and seven-year-olds. A lot of what we do here is what you want to do at home. It's so important because we're such a little school. Every teacher knows every child's name, their dog's name, etc. You really get to know the students and they get to know you. The size makes a big difference. We take a lot of time to talk about their feelings. We have a very kind school, giving, caring, and it is a family. That's a tremendous part of what we try to do here." As M.J. explains, "Parents have remarked to us that they couldn't imagine anyone saying anything hateful or mean within our classrooms. It's just not the atmosphere. It's a zero tolerance for anything other than kindness and respect. We treat children with respect. We model respect. One of the things we do is empower them to speak up for themselves."

Says M.J., "The key to success is just giving it the time that it deserves. At the beginning of the school year we spend the first month on social curriculum. In first grade, it's about how you treat the person you haven't been in school with before. Knowing them as a person is a very important part. They meet our children. They know our lives. They know we're real. The parents come in. Everybody comes in. We're an extension of their family."

*Karen Schweitzer has been teaching kindergarten, first, and second grade for eighteen years, twelve of those years at Williamsburg. She has used puppetry to help children learn about conflict.* "I have two puppets whose names are Celeste and Myron. Children get introduced to them at the beginning of the year. We start out by showing that if someone is doing something you don't like, you need to be able to tell them. The puppets come out to help us talk about things that have happened in the classroom or to talk about things that haven't happened but we need to bring up. What I find over the years is the kids will take out Myron and Celeste and kind of play act, snuggle with them, use them to talk through problems they have or make up. Most of what I do has a philosophy that is consistent through the years, but the actual implementation changes with the kids."

*Jen Black, sixth-grade teacher, has been at Dunphy Elementary for four years.* "We have class meetings, and if anything is going on that they are unhappy with, they write it on a piece of paper and put it in the agenda box and then we talk about it. There was an issue with who gets to use the computers. They came up with really creative solutions. What I tend to find is that when we do these group problem-solving strategies the kids almost always come up with something that all of them can agree on. Another example is the locker issue, top lockers and bottom lockers. Kids don't like the bottom locker cause somebody's over them, they have to bend down, etc. They agreed that instead of having locker assignments the same all year, on the ninetieth day of school they'd switch. They're able to identify the problems. I hear them reminding each other to put their problems in the agenda box. . . .

"In this school, kids are typically involved in solving conflicts. One student felt like an area on the rug was becoming cliquey; the same kids were always using the same space. So they came up with a rotating space thing. One of the things that works is doing a lot of small-group and partner stuff. Throughout the year I tell them they are going to be working with others, and they need to be able to get along with anyone."

*Lisa Peloquin, the other sixth-grade teacher, has been at Williamsburg for eight years.* "The kind of conflict programs we've been talking about really started full force about six years ago. So I've really seen a change over the years. When I took the job here there were twenty-eight students in the class. They were wonderful but rambunctious. Until then there had been no social curriculum. At first, I got flack and others got flack for trying to help the students take care of their own conflict. The next year we turned our attention to changing this, so we started a lot of conflict resolution work. . . .

"You just acknowledge that even though they're children they're human beings, and they can work things through if you provide the structure. There was a new boy who joined class. He was disrupting, throwing his folder on the floor, etc. If someone acts up they'll get a reminder. The other kids were wondering why he wasn't getting a reminder. He kept slamming his folders. At morning meeting the kids decided to have a little huddle and see what could be done. They had made a list of rules at the beginning of the year and they took the rules to the boy and said, 'This is how we do things.' No judgments, no nastiness. They asked him if he would sign it. He did and they said, 'Great, now you're one of us.' And that was that. Then they told him about reminders and examples of those. Just in the course of the past week since this incident he's changed so much. He's been a charm all week long. And I can't take credit for it; all the credit goes to the kids."

*Several of the students at Anne T. Dunphy Elementary School also realize how special the environment is. Mariah Sylvain and Katie Riel are sixth graders who appreciate the efforts at CRE.* "Last year there were a lot of problems. This year there have been fewer," Mariah says. Katie adds, "It really helps to sit down and talk about stuff when you have a conflict. If you don't it just gets bigger. Then it gets to the point that you try to get other people involved, you try to turn people against them."

*"Frederick," a sixth grader, came to this school in the fourth grade.* "Here they talk to you about it and explain how you are to handle things. They make you see that you could do things better rather than just telling you, 'You were wrong.' At my old school they'd just tell you to sit somewhere. Here they talk with you and help you work it out with someone." This approach has made a real difference in the way Frederick deals with his peers. "I rarely have conflicts with friends. I have four or five things I can do to make sure a conflict doesn't get worse. I have a bad temper problem. If you came in and got me really upset off the bat, I probably wouldn't be a very nice person. I'd totally disregard you. To calm myself down I just tell that person to leave me alone and try and get away from them. Sometimes I write songs about how I feel. It helps me work through the feelings because I get distracted by it."

*Jon Long, a sixth grader, has come to this school only this year.* But, as he says, "I like it here better. It's a smaller school; everyone in our class can second-guess what anyone's going to say because we know each other so well. We do a lot of name games in the beginning of the year. We have team-building activities. Friendship-building activities. Some of it was outside on ropes. Like there was this one beam you walk across. Everybody came together that day and supported everybody else even if they hadn't been friends before. Every once and a while somebody says or does something. But we're together a lot."

But Jon admits that the kids at Dunphy aren't perfect. "Sometimes people are different and they get called a name. When it happens sometimes other kids stand up for them. Sometimes they have to go to the teacher. There are kids who are more respected but they don't act like it." But overall, Jon feels a real camaraderie with his Dunphy classmates: "At my old school the kids who were looked up to were stuck up about it, thought they were better than you. But not here."

# CHAPTER TEN

# MAKING THINGS RIGHT
## Restorative Justice for School Communities

Alice Ierley and David Claassen-Wilson

*Sarah and Abby have been best friends since elementary school. At the start of their eighth-grade year, three male classmates, former friends of theirs, began making fun of the girls. Although the teasing started off in a playful way, by December it had gotten out of hand. Under pressure from their peers, the three boys made a series of rude and threatening comments to the girls during recess in front of a crowd of students. Sarah and Abby were crushed; they ran inside crying. Although they had been close friends with the three boys for years, the incident made them so ashamed that they didn't want to return to school the next day.*

Every day in schools across America, this type of scenario is played out, with the usual results. Schools focus on punishment for the offenders by removing them from the school temporarily and perhaps employing police charges. But what about Sarah and Abby? How will their fears and concerns and those of their friends and family be addressed? What will be done to prevent a reoccurrence? In this chapter, we describe a new philosophy being used by schools to address these questions; at the end we revisit Sarah and Abby and the outcome of this incident.

## The Punitive Approach to Discipline

The central approach to school discipline in our society might be described as punitive discipline. Despite its widespread use, this approach is largely ineffective at addressing the concerns of students who have been harmed and developing empathy in those who have caused the harm. Punitive discipline measures are those that use the strategies of *external controls* (that is, rewards and punishments imposed by authority figures) and *taking away* from the wrongdoer (for example, the right to attend school or participate in community life). Although these strategies may address the pressures of time, due process, and temporary safety concerns, they may inadvertently legitimize authoritarian behaviors and attitudes, or reward negative behavior by continuing that which is not wanted to begin with (for example, a truant child being "punished" with further time away from school).

## The Restorative Justice Alternative

A growing number of school communities across the United States have begun to explore the use of restorative justice processes as a means of addressing the limitations of punitive discipline measures. In such states as Colorado and Minnesota, educators are implementing a variety of restorative discipline alternatives to traditional measures such as detention, suspension, expulsion, and police charges.

Many school districts have found restorative justice to be a more effective means of addressing school and victim safety and transforming discipline into a learning opportunity. In schools using restorative justice practices, an offending student is given the opportunity to participate in a restorative discipline process as a means of repairing the harm done to those affected by the wrongdoing. These processes are voluntary for the parties and may be offered in lieu of punitive discipline measures, as a reentry process following traditional discipline, or in combination with reduced sanctions.

## Restorative Justice: An Overview

Since the mid-1970s, a growing movement of criminal justice practitioners, law enforcement agencies, and a variety of community-based organizations has been attempting to reform the way our society deals with crime and wrongdoing. This movement, known as restorative justice, represents a set of principles and practices for dealing with crime and wrongdoing. Rather than focusing exclusively on the punishment of offenders and their removal from society, the chief concern of restorative justice is to identify and repair, to the greatest extent possible, the harm done by crime and wrongdoing. This is achieved by holding offenders directly accountable to those they have harmed, giving victims a direct voice in the process of repair, restoring the safety and trust within communities, and providing more meaningful outcomes for everyone affected.

Currently there are over one thousand programs in operation in dozens of countries worldwide, each representing an ever-expanding variety of restorative justice services to victims, offenders, and communities affected by crime. A wide variety of restorative practices are being used around the world, such as victim-offender mediation, community accountability boards, family (or community) group conferencing, victim impact panels, sentencing circles, reparative boards, and peacemaking circles. Many of these models are based on the wisdom of "tribal courts" and the peacemaking processes that indigenous cultures have used for thousands of years.

Howard Zehr, an early pioneer of this movement, coined three "restorative questions" that have guided these restorative practices around the world.[1] The questions are contrasted here with the "retributive questions" that have characterized the dominant response to crime in Western culture:

| *Restorative Justice* | *Retributive Justice* |
| --- | --- |
| What is the harm that was done? | What is the law that was broken? |
| How can that harm be repaired? | Who broke that law? |
| Who is responsible for this repair? | How should they be punished? |

These "restorative questions" are not to be understood as negating the importance of laws and rules in civil society, but rather as allowing concern for the human side into our thinking about justice. By integrating Zehr's questions into the traditional justice paradigm, restorative justice rests on the following assumptions about crime and justice:

- Crime is defined not simply as a violation of law but, more important, as a violation of people.
- Offenders are to be held accountable not only to authorities but also directly to those they have harmed.
- Victims and communities are to be given a direct role in the process of seeking justice.
- Justice should balance the needs of victims, offenders, communities, and authorities where no single set of needs dominates the others.
- Partnerships and common objectives among all stakeholders in a crime (justice agencies, communities, and so on) are essential for optimal effectiveness.

There is a growing body of evidence to support the use of restorative justice principles and processes as a more effective response to crime. The following is a basic synopsis of the research findings:

- Victims and affected community members are more satisfied with restorative processes and outcomes than with the traditional system.
- Offenders who meet directly with those they have harmed are more likely to complete restitution agreements than offenders whose restitution is court ordered.
- Victims and affected community members experience a greater sense of safety as a result of participation in restorative processes.
- Offenders who meet directly with those they have harmed are less likely to reoffend than those who do not participate.[2]

## Restorative Justice in Schools

Many of the different methods of restorative justice mentioned earlier, such as victim-offender mediation, community group conferencing, and peacemaking circles, have been found to be useful in school settings. Here we briefly describe several restorative justice practices and give examples of their application in school communities.

### Victim-Offender Mediation

Although new teachers frequently voice a need for training in classroom management, very little time is spent in helping educators learn how to handle behavior problems. Most educators are left to develop their own methods based on a crude system of rewards and punishment that varies widely from class to class.

In an effort to provide consistency to these day-to-day discipline matters and to make discipline a learning opportunity, some schools have elected to practice a form of victim-offender mediation—one of the early models of restorative justice. The entire staff is trained to facilitate these brief meetings between offending students and those affected. Rather than focusing on the rules violated, who broke the rules, and the punishment to be incurred, students are taught to focus on the harm done, repair that harm, and determine who should take responsibility. Offenders accept responsibility for their behavior and voluntarily agree to meet with the victim to discuss the incident. Victim-offender mediations can be held as on-the-spot interventions that take a few minutes, or can be more involved meetings after school in a neutral setting.

*A third-grade student accidentally bumps into a second-grade boy while running through the hallway, causing the second grader to drop his books. A teacher who witnesses or hears of the incident sits down with both students. The teacher questions, rather than instructs, the students about what happened, how the incident made the younger boy feel, what the older student was thinking about when this happened, what the younger boy needs now to "make it right," and whether the offending student is willing to take responsibility.*

*If one student ruins another child's art project, the teacher might choose to sit down with the students at a later time to help them "make things right." If the offender takes responsibility for what happened, and both students agree to participate, the teacher would help them come up with an agreement to repair the harm done.*

## Community Group Conferencing

For serious offenses, a process known as community group conferencing is frequently employed. This model was developed in New Zealand and Australia and is based on the tribal justice model of the Maori people. Building on the basic process of victim-offender mediation, community group conferencing adds a third dynamic of "affected community." This includes community members who were indirectly affected by the offense and wish to participate.

In a community group conference, the parents of victims and offenders are encouraged to come together with staff, affected students, victim, offender, and occasionally law enforcement personnel, to discuss the offense. Trained facilitators then guide a structured process for identifying the harm done to each person and determining what it will take to hold the offender accountable while making things right for the victim and community. At the conclusion of each conference, a formal agreement is generated, one that may involve restitution, community service, letters of apology, or any other ideas created during the conference. One or more participants are then assigned to help monitor the agreement to completion and mentor the offender as needed. If the offender does not successfully fulfil the agreement, then the case is referred to the traditional process.

*Following the theft of a bicycle by a middle school student, school administrators brought together the offenders, victim, parents, and school resource officers to address the harm done. After the offender agreed to replace the stolen property and volunteered his bike repair skills in the community, the victim expressed relief to the offender that she was not personally targeted by the crime. The victim was also pleased that the group was responsive to her suggestion for community service involving bike repair.*

## Circle Processes

"Circles" have recently emerged as an additional way to address a wider variety of justice and discipline issues in schools. Circles generally involve the creation of a "ritual space" where a talking piece may be passed among participants as a way to guide the process. Although the practice of circles takes many different forms, it is acknowledged as an ancient way of resolving issues and conducting dialogue that can be found in various cultures throughout the world. Those who advocate the use of circles speak of getting to a depth that is difficult to achieve in any other way. There are many examples of circle processes and traditions, such as the council process and peacemaking circles, and circles used in classroom meetings.

Schools using peacemaking circles might bring together a group of students to address specific incidents of wrongdoing or a pattern of misbehavior that has created an ongoing problem. Rather than actively facilitating a structured process, the teacher acts as "keeper" of the circle by asking a carefully crafted set of questions to help guide the dialogue. Participants then work toward consensus about what is needed to respond to the offense. In addition to dealing with specific incidents of wrongdoing, talking circles or dialogue circles might be used as a basic problem-solving tool for communication and decision making on a wider variety of issues, such as in the council process. A teacher might elect to hold a classroom meeting each week to discuss various issues students are dealing with in their home lives or at school. Circle processes are unique in their flexibility of form and application.

*When the put-downs had finally gotten far too common in a seventh-grade homeroom, the teacher decided to put the issue on the agenda for the next scheduled classroom meeting. Initially, the circle participants were split—some minimized the issue, and others thought it was a significant problem. But when the keeper of the circle, the teacher, kept bringing the questions back to harm instead of blame, the group finally was able to reach some common agreements. It turned out that the class wanted to keep the issue on the agenda for three weeks running while they explored the issue, talked about how to make change in their classroom, and discussed how to begin changing the broader school community.*

## Challenges and Drawbacks to Restorative Justice in Schools

Restorative justice is not a panacea for all discipline issues in schools. It is, however, a set of principles that provides an important perspective and set of opportunities. The use of restorative justice in schools does not replace, but rather supports, other systems and structures in schools. For instance, remedial and therapeutic approaches to student behavior can be integrated into a restorative process or addressed in separate but complementary processes.

Restorative justice works primarily through intervention, though it also can prevent future conflicts by addressing the important feelings and needs of community members following an incident of harm. Thus it prevents future problems from those who feel victimized, those who feel unfairly punished, or those who never learn accountability. Prevention also results from comprehensive training that helps teachers work with minor incidents as they arise while also creating a norm of valuing support *and* accountability.

Instituting restorative justice practices in a school will not eliminate all student suspensions. But the practices can be combined by attending to the victim's needs and following up with suspended students as they reenter the school community.

There are two areas of misconduct that may be inappropriate for restorative processes: persistent or severe bullying and cases of serious sexual harassment or assault. In situations of severe power imbalances, or where the potential for re-victimization is high, bringing offenders and victims together may do more harm than good. Although a growing number of practitioners are using restorative processes for these types of serious crimes in the adult world, this application should only be attempted by those who are well trained and experienced in the field, and only in close collaboration with the appropriate mental health professionals. Being restorative in other ways, however, such as by attending directly to the needs of victims and soliciting their input into disciplinary decisions, is appropriate. Even when the specific processes themselves are not used and no meeting takes place between victims and offenders, there can always be a restorative *response* to wrongdoing, based on restorative justice principles.

## Essentials to a Successful Restorative Justice Program

There are several things that are essential or very helpful in guaranteeing the success of a school's restorative justice program. Offender accountability is a must. Parental and community involvement is a great addition to a school's efforts. In addition, the intense emotions attached to these practices need to be embraced.

### Offender Accountability

One challenge is that community group conferencing and victim-offender mediation rely on the willingness of the identified student to take responsibility for the harm he or she has caused. Therefore, when a student denies any wrongdoing or any intent to be held accountable, he or she will not be able to successfully participate in either of these processes, and schools must seek the best alternative way. School communities that persist in being restorative will find that students' willingness to be held accountable increases over time, as the need to defend against blame and recrimination diminishes.

## Parental Involvement

The more severe the matter being addressed through any restorative process, the more imperative parental involvement becomes. Because parents frequently have strong feelings and perspectives regarding discipline matters in which their own children are involved, schools have historically been wary of actively seeking their involvement. Parents who have not had a voice in previous discipline matters may harbor a great deal of distrust for administrators and law enforcement agents. By creating a venue where parental voices can be heard and validated, schools can quickly turn an adversarial parent into a tremendous asset to the school. The strong desire to do what is best for the students involved can easily become the common ground where school, parents, and law enforcement can meet.

## The Importance of Emotions

Restorative justice processes frequently involve intense expression of emotions from participants. Feelings ranging from anger to sadness to joy may be expressed through crying, raised voices, or laughter. Although it is a common instinct to avoid intense emotional situations, the expression of these emotions may be key to achieving a sense of healing between those involved.

In his book *Crime, Shame and Reintegration,* John Braithwaite uses the term *reintegrative shaming* to describe the key emotional dynamic at work in restorative justice.[3] This is not the exclusionary form of shaming that says, "You are a bad person," but rather a collective condemnation of those behaviors that violate social mores, combined with a clear message of support and opportunity for reintegration of the wrongdoer back into the community.

## Mirroring the Community and Embracing Diversity

Restorative justice is most effective as a tool for students when it is fashioned to reflect the diversity of the community it seeks to serve. As in most conflict resolution processes, balance becomes an increasingly important concept as the diversity of the participants increases. Participants in a restorative justice process can bridge cross-cultural misunderstandings related to age, gender, race, or class if they are given opportunities to directly understand the intentions of offenders and the needs of the victim. By inviting the participation of support persons for victims, offenders, and the greater community, and by training a broad cross section of facilitators in restorative processes, the school's restorative justice coordinator can develop greater understanding and support for restorative justice.

Additional ways of ensuring that the restorative justice process is culturally appropriate might include sharing food before or after the process, using a talking piece that is familiar to the participants in a peacemaking circle, and using the first language of the participants.

The most culturally "biased" aspect of restorative justice, however, is the presumption that underlies conflict resolution in general—that the best results are reached by having people talk directly to one another, with support from others. When this presumption is a poor fit for a group of people, or where face-to-face contact is found to be inappropriate, restorative justice may offer other important principles on which to rely. Victims can be empowered to give input about their needs and wishes, whether they communicate these directly or through an intermediary; and discipline systems can encourage outcomes that repair harm rather than take away from students, by using well-crafted community service options.

Some of the toughest diversity issues that affect discipline in schools today, however, are the variety of beliefs held by adults about youth, their worthiness, what influences their behavior, and when is it worthwhile to take time for repairing relationships involving children. When schools are able to embrace commonly held values on those issues, they can more easily draw together as a diverse community with a unified vision.

## Utilizing the Assets of Each Age Group

Restorative justice can be made developmentally appropriate for each school-age group by keying in to the unique qualities of different school levels and age groups. Elementary teachers who are with a group of students most or all day throughout the school year have an excellent opportunity to create everyday justice right in the classroom. Class meetings can be a place for sharing values, establishing common norms, and processing wrongdoing in a restorative manner. Mini victim-offender mediations may occur daily. When young children don't have to think they are in trouble and will be punished, but instead are asked to attend to harm they have caused, their defensiveness tends to fall away.

At the middle school level, where peer relationships rule, community group conferences may begin to incorporate more student participation by including young people as members of the community. This also helps build peer expectation of accountability and support. Class meetings can still be an effective tool, although the shift to multiple classes in a day presents a scheduling challenge.

At the high school level, with near-adult competencies beginning to emerge at the same time that more severe misconduct is showing up, it makes sense to partner with students wherever possible in building a restorative capacity within a school. In a community group conference, students can serve as members of the affected community, act as cofacilitators, and even be lead facilitators in mediations and community group conferences.

## Where to Begin

Restorative justice has been introduced to schools through educators, juvenile justice systems, and nonprofit organizations interested in improving schools. Interested parents, educators, and students can look for groups in their area that may already be involved or interested in this movement. Reading available materials and looking for contacts through the Web is a good way to begin. Restorative justice, school discipline, and zero-tolerance policies are all useful topics to review. Reviewing a particular school district's discipline policies is also helpful.

Schools that have already begun to incorporate conflict resolution programs are often the quickest to respond to the concepts of restorative justice because both approaches engage in distributive decision making (decisions made by those involved in a situation), creative problem solving, and making consensual agreements.

Depending on available resources, schools can begin with help from direct service providers outside the school or by seeking training and technical assistance to integrate restorative justice practices internally. Schools that integrate the practices internally can involve students (particularly at the high school level), parents, law enforcement personnel, and other community members to help manage the time challenges of integrating these processes.

◆ ◆ ◆

At the beginning of the chapter we described the harassment of two middle school students, Sarah and Abby. We return to them now to show how restorative justice practices work for them.

Fortunately, administrators at their school, along with a number of community volunteers, had just received training in restorative justice. After meeting with the three boys who were responsible for this harassment, the assistant principal gave them a choice: a five-day suspension with police charges for harassment, or a three-day suspension with participation in a restorative justice conference upon their return. After hearing how they had affected Sarah and Abby, they agreed to participate in the new program to help make things right with the girls.

After the two facilitators described the program to Sarah and Abby, they agreed to participate. Three days later, the boys sat face-to-face with Sarah and Abby, numerous parents, school administrators, and the school resource officer assigned to the case. The beginning of the meeting was tense with anger and fear. As the facilitators guided the conference, each of the boys told the group what they had done. Sarah and Abby cried openly as they recounted their feelings to the boys.

"We were great friends with you guys until you started listening to what other people told you to do. You just hurt us in a deep way." After hearing from the girls and a room of concerned adults, each of the boys apologized individually for what he had done. "We should never have taken things this far, and we'll do what it takes to make up for what happened."

At the conclusion of the conference, the anger and fear had given way to discussions between the students on how they could repair their relationship. Once the formal process was complete and the agreement was being signed, the parents of the two girls went over to thank the three boys directly.

"We know it wasn't easy to come in and own up to what you did. We have faith that you can learn to treat our girls with respect from now on." The three boys were soon reintegrated back into the school, and a relationship of trust was ultimately restored with their friends Sarah and Abby.

# In Their Own Words

## "People Actually Learn to Be Better People"

*Crested Butte Community School is a K–12 public school located in a resort community at the north end of Colorado's Gunnison Valley. Serving only 360 kids, it stands as one of the district's most innovative schools and is willing to take on new projects to "pilot" them for the rest of the district. At the beginning of this year, the school started one of its state's first school-based restorative justice programs.*

*"Travis" and "Rickie" are high school students who participated in a community conference because of their involvement in a sports-related incident that caused harm to others. Each of them expressed his feelings about going through the restorative justice circle in an interview with Randy, one of the editors.*

"The meeting kind of cleared up a lot of things because we talked about a lot of things and we felt better. It gave us a sigh of relief," says Travis. His friend Rickie agrees: "It left us with a good impression. We weren't as scared about what would happen." Travis continues, "We had to talk to all the classes in the beginning, and we just told them what happened and what not to do and how to resolve it. And then we talked to some elementary kids, maybe first through fifth grades about bullying, about what you should do if you are getting bullied, and how to resolve your problems. Then we also took a period each week during gym class and watched the little kids during recess and played games and refereed them."

When Randy asked them if the process was easier or harder than just being suspended, they readily admitted that it was harder. They were both suspended for five days. It hurt their grades being out of class, and it was also hard facing their victims and hearing how others felt about their actions, especially their parents. Says Travis, "It's not fun. It's hard work. But I thought the restorative justice process was really good. It really worked out and kind of helped everyone." Rickie adds, "Our parents were kind of shocked, but they really liked that circle meeting."

*"Jared" and "Derrick" are both sixth graders at Crested Butte Community School. Both of them have participated in a restorative justice circle dealing with a situation in which they each had been bullied.*

As a preface to their remarks, it is worth noting that using a restorative justice circle to deal with cases of bullying represents one of the most difficult, if not controversial, uses of the process. However, the school administration wanted to do something more than just suspend students without any chance for a clarification of the feelings and needs involved and a chance at achieving a more meaningful resolution for the harm done. The first case involved two bullies that harassed Jared, slammed him against the lockers, and then shoved him inside an open locker.

Jared was willing to participate in a restorative justice circle to face his offenders, seek some healing, and help craft an agreement for a meaningful consequence.

Says Jared, "I think it's a good idea to tell them how you feel about it instead of just suspending them and it's over and then they come back to school. I think it helps them knowing how I felt and how much it hurt me for them to do that to me. I think they kind of clued in and said, 'Wow, look at what we did to him.'" It also helped, he said, because they had to go to other classes and talk about bullying, which wasn't easy for them.

His mother and father also participated in the circle process. At first they were quite angry about the situation because these kids had been bullying their son for years. But, Jared says, "They thought this communication thing really helped out and it was good to talk to the families."

As with many cases of restorative justice, one has to be clear about how one defines success. It may be deemed successful if the victim gets a chance to confront his offender and ask why he or she did it; it may be successful for the community to jointly agree on a meaningful consequence; it may be successful for the offender to have to listen to many others' points of view. But success may not change the bully. The impact on the bully of talking it through depends to a large degree on the severity of the bullying behavior and the willingness or ability of the bully to change.

During the conference, Jared did have some concerns about the sincerity of the comments being made. "I didn't really think that they were sincere about it. Two weeks ago Rickie [one of the bullies] came up to me and he was like, 'Jared, I didn't really mean all that stuff I said [that hurt your feelings].' I didn't really think he was sincere. The first day that I came back to school, I was nervous to see them." Since then one of the kids hasn't bullied him. But the other still is a bully.

In Derrick's case, he was out at lunch when some horseplay turned serious. Some older, "super-intimidating" kids punched Derrick, and he had to escape through a back door of the school. "They were mad at me," Derrick says, "because they were flicking peas at the back of my head during lunch and I asked them to stop. I told [an adult] . . . and she made them clean up the mess after lunch and so they got mad at me." This is a perfect example of how traditional punishments can fail to address the underlying issues and only serve to cause situations to escalate into further violence.

Derrick was willing to participate in a restorative justice circle, though he did have a few of his friends come with him to provide support and add other voices in the process. "I thought it was good because now we talk, and they sat with me at lunch." Usually, "when you come back the next day you are all scared that they might get more mad at you and hurt you even worse." With one of the kids, "I thought he changed. He is really nice to me now. His Dad was really hard on him and I think that really helped." That kid, incidentally, used to be the victim of a lot of bullying and sort of fell in with this other group of bullies.

Despite the inherent risks in this type of dialogue, both Jared and Derrick would use the restorative justice process again, because it was better than suspension without dialogue and it gave them a voice in a safe setting in which some healing could take place.

*Jordan O'Neill is the counselor for the middle and high school students at the school, and with the principal, Stephanie Niemi, she coordinates the restorative justice program at the school.*

Jordan explains, "We are using [restorative justice] as part of our prevention efforts. When there is an issue that has happened between two kids we'll say, 'Listen, you have a choice: you can either get suspended and not deal with this at all or you can come and be involved in a conference or circle and get out of the punishment of a suspension,' unless the offense requires legal intervention by an authority." Jordan continues, "Whenever there is a kid who comes to me in private and has a complaint involving another student, we are doing conferencing between him and the other student along with any other kids that have been affected."

Using the restorative justice processes of community conferences, victim-offender mediation, or peacemaking circles has, within one year, become the norm for how moderate to serious discipline issues are handled. "In our discipline realm, we haven't had any incidents that have involved more than two students that have not gone the restorative route. Three to four suspensions this year were resolved the morning of the day they were allowed to come back to school. A restorative conference or circle occurred and a plan was put into place for coming back to school and repairing the harm—and it has been really, really powerful."

Stephanie says, "We had a situation where two freshman boys literally assaulted a younger student; they walloped him pretty good. There was a lot of history between the families. There was a suspension, but to repair all the harm that had been done there was a huge restorative justice circle—three sets of parents and all of the boys that were involved. All the cards were out on the table and things were essentially repaired." Jordan continues, "The history is the real focus of the story because the parents held grudges against each other from years' worth of teasing between their children. Each family had their incidents, where in the parking lot one kid had been snippy to another kid. The circle gave us the venue to not just deal with the incident between the two boys against the younger boys but the parents to face each other and problem solve together, and they ended up [leaving] the circle with smiles and handshaking, and then on the street the parents reported later [that they started to talk to each other and see each other at social events]." Not only that, but the kids were able to see their parents repair the harm through a positive process. As Jordan puts it, "It has far-reaching impact not just between us with our discipline issues but within our community."

Because restorative justice is based on the strength, support, and supervision of a caring community, it seems to work well in those places that have a well-established sense of community. In this vein, Stephanie notes, "In a small town you see a high shame factor, and it goes from the students all the way to their parents. I think that approaching discipline in this manner allows everyone to keep their integrity intact and do the right thing."

We all know how sporting rivalries between high schools can lead to pranks gone awry and inappropriate competitive behavior. Most schools openly disdain this practice, but in a recent episode between Crested Butte Community School and a neighboring school, the administration showed another way of dealing with the problem. A team from another district "came to play our school and a kid, on a dare by some older kids, said some pretty inappropriate things to one of the girl team players at our school. The other school district was having a fit and [sought a] pound of flesh from their student because of his inappropriate comment. Those people didn't want to know this kid and care how he felt—and he was mortified. Even though [the other school] chose not to participate in a restorative process, we gave him (and his friends who dared him to do it) the opportunity to talk with us, the people that he harmed here and our image as a school. [Even though his school had also been insulted by inappropriate comments,] he came up with his own restorative plan of writing an apology letter and then teaching sportsmanship to younger kids so they don't repeat the same thing."

One of the other key reasons for using restorative justice in their discipline process is to help avoid the negative impact of labeling, often inherent in a traditional punitive process. Says Jordan, "These kids can get labeled as mean kids, bullies, whatever, when in their hearts they are not." In addition, restorative justice helps students take more ownership and creativity for "making things right." Says Stephanie, "There are creative solutions that the students themselves arrive at in terms of how they can repair the harm."

Students can also spread the word about the effectiveness of the restorative processes. In the example in which the boys from another school had hurt a girl at their school, the boys "have spoken to other classes about the incident," says Stephanie. Jordan adds, "One of the solutions from this circle was that the boys would take leadership positions in teaching respect and kindness within the school, and they have been going down to the elementary playground during their lunch and refereeing games and teaching sportsmanship." Says Stephanie, "We love that you have to trickle down the wisdom that you have learned from your experience. We are using that a lot."

Many schools are seeking to reduce their suspension rates, and Crested Butte Community School is no different. However, they see dealing with the problem not merely in terms of reducing unwanted statistics but also in terms of promoting growth and learning among students, staff, and community. "We are trying to steer clear of suspensions because it has been real problematic in the past to send a kid out and then to have no reintegration into the school community. It is a huge bone of contention for me. [As a result of our new restorative justice program] we are probably down half the number of suspensions from last year, and for a school of 350 that's pretty good."

Both Stephanie and Jordan agree that discipline is handled differently than before. "We used to have a dean of students who . . . had a military background. If you were in trouble it was very, very, very punitive. It was not restorative at all. There were no options to make up or make amends for your mistake. You just sort of took the punishment, which was usually detention or suspension, and it put us all out. Then it was kind of done until the next time, and there usually was another time soon after. Sometimes he would just drop it and say, 'Boys will be boys.' And he would let them go, and we would all wonder why it would happen again a week later." Having a new way to handle serious discipline issues "has totally changed our discipline for the school," says Stephanie. "I would say that it is a little bit more labor-intensive in terms of dealing with things, but it resolves a lot of stuff, and we are not seeing the repeat performances that we have in the past, at all."

With serious issues, such as physical or sexual harassment and assault, schools have to take into consideration certain board policies regarding these issues and the consequences that are meted out. Says Stephanie, "When you look at board policy, sometimes you are stuck and there's not a whole lot you can do, but you try to be as flexible as possible. When a kid gets a suspension, which I am not thrilled about, at least when they come back we try to do some kind of reintegration through a restorative justice circle."

As this process is more time-intensive, they have faced the issue of taking more time from teachers who have less and less time each year. Says Jordan, "We have some teachers who would love to be involved, but the issue is time. We do have something called common planning time in the morning five days a week, and that is one of the areas where we have been able to facilitate the conferences without impacting instructional time. More teachers would like to be trained in terms of classroom management, but it is very hard to stretch them beyond that."

Because the process is based on the value of community participation, it is not surprising that their program has also begun to affect the community. Says Jordan, "It has spread to the community a little bit. We had a kid who got in a lot of trouble this year selling drugs to another student, and through a restorative process he has come to the [parent-community restorative justice group that supports restorative justice initiatives in the school and community] to speak to the police officers about why he has been doing some of the things he has done.

It is really eye opening. There was a high degree of shame for him, and for him to speak to these people openly and honestly about situations he is facing is a huge step in the right direction." Stephanie agrees: "The whole goal of this group is to come up with answers to what else can we offer kids so they don't feel bored enough to go out and get drugs and where can they get their belief systems and moral systems together. And he is participating in those conversations as part of his restorative work."

Says Jordan, "In some of the circles that I have held in the classroom, some of the parents have shown up just to be a circle member." Stephanie adds, "With the less formal ones we have very much had parents' involvement. They think it's great. The parents who are at the conferences love it, even the ones I thought would be really hard parents. It offers their kid an out to be something other than the bad kid. A lot of these parents have repeat-offender types of kids, and they are sick of that role."

Thanks to the success of the program, the principal is eager to incorporate restorative justice language into the school's discipline policy handbook and its parent handbook. "I want restorative justice measures to be used whenever possible. I don't care for our discipline handbook. It is very negative, and I want to change that."

Both the principal and the counselor are undeniably positive about this new program. Stephanie states, "It has changed the dynamics of the school. It has broken down some traditional walls that we have had with discipline before." Jordan agrees: "I just can't say enough good things about it."

*This next story takes place at an elementary school in Louisville, Colorado, and shows how students can be the driving force for positive change, especially when supported and encouraged by wise adults willing to listen and believe. T.R. Burman is a fifth grader at Coal Creek Elementary. After sitting through a presentation with his mom on restorative justice, he knew that his school should start something like that. His school already had peer mediation and a conflict resolution program, but he felt that they didn't address the more serious problems that occurred at the school. With a group of friends, he took the idea to the principal, and they are now thinking about starting a program.*

Says T.R., "It started out with tetherballs because they were being destroyed. People would hang on them and drag their heels while the tetherball swung them, and one of the tetherballs had broken off, and I said, 'There's something we need to take care of.' I started talking about [starting a restorative justice program] with my friends. It is sort of like conflict mediation because of the way it resolves things with the people who saw it happen, people who were affected by what happened, and then people who have ideas about what could be done next time to avoid it happening. And that is what restorative justice is."

One of the other girls involved in the project says that it's about making a wrong right. "They can do something wrong, like they could break a tetherball, and they could come and apologize and stuff and help put in a new one, and that would be like making a wrong right. . . . Last year in our class there were a couple of boys who were sticking crayons in the pencil sharpener, and I think that they should help pay for it. Say you get $3 a week as allowance, then you would give $3 for a couple of weeks until you had $11 to give to [the teacher], and you would be responsible for paying [to fix it]."

The principal was intrigued by the students' plan because it was a way to help students feel safe about taking responsibility for what went wrong and then taking some action to make it right. "That's exactly what we mean," says T.R. "Because one thing that somebody does can affect everybody else at the school. Somebody can ruin [the teacher's pencil] sharpener and then that affects everybody that goes to art that week until he can get another one. So we need to have some way to have them take responsibility for what happened. That's the key thing."

*Our final story takes place at Fairview High School, where once again it was the students who came to a staff member with an idea to create a restorative justice program. It is now in its third year. Up to fifteen students make up the Student Conflict Hearing Board, which is a student-driven restorative justice program that accepts cases from the administration and uses a restorative justice circle to repair the harm. Here is what Laurel Kalish (twelfth grade), Abbey Radis (twelfth grade), Julie Frankel (eleventh grade), Quekan Ibidiunni (eleventh grade), Renee Jakaitis (twelfth grade), and Michelle Jakaitis (ninth grade) had to say about how it works and what benefits it offers.*

"When we get a case, we preconference with everyone," says Renee. "We talk to them and see if it will work. Then we all go into a room and go around and talk about what happened and then talk about what can be done to repair the harm that has been done to the community. We have had three cases so far this year. They came out pretty well. The strangest one we had was with these two guys on the football team where this one guy jumped this other guy. Both parents of both kids involved wanted to be there. The parents really gave a lot when going around the circle. By hearing the offender take responsibility for it, they were really impacted by it—and hearing everyone's side. I think everyone felt really good about it afterwards because they just had this sense of understanding."

Julie agrees: "I just think that the most important part of it is that we are repairing the harm that is done and not just sentencing their punishment, because more times than not [punishment] doesn't really do anything, and it makes the person more aggravated and they want to come back and do more damage. I think that repairing the harm and making sure that the affected community as well [as the "victim" and "offender"] are treated well and taken care of [are important].

I think most of the time in society you are usually not given a chance to explain why. It doesn't seem that people really care about the reason why this happened; they are just ready to punish and accuse someone."

Abbey goes on to say, "Something else that I think is important about the whole restorative justice process is that the needs of the victim are really met. Normally, there is just a punishment and it is taken care of by the administrators, so the victim doesn't really get to have a say and they don't really get to express why this hurt them. It is not only that the offender gets to explain but it is that the victim really gets to be a part of the process and really feel a sense of closure and completion." Says Laurel, "That was sort of how it started, because the administration was handing down sentences and they weren't allowed to tell other people what happened and so the victims had no idea [how it got resolved]."

The students agree that parents who have gone through the process have really liked it as well. "They were really, really happy with both of [the cases]," says Renee. "They were really glad to hear everyone else's opinions. It helped them a lot. This one mother was just really distraught after her son got beat up, and she didn't like sending him back to school [because of] how dangerous it was. It really helped her to hear from the other mother and father about how they were raising their child. It was good for them."

All the students think that it is a program that should spread. "I think absolutely having programs like this around the nation would be good because people need options and need to know more than just zero-tolerance policy, and that is pretty much across the board with how our nation's schools are run at the moment and it doesn't work, I don't think," says Laurel. "The offenders keep on offending. They don't ever learn why it was really wrong. They are punished. A lot of the times they are suspended and just stay at home and just watch Jerry Springer. They are affected by it because they can't come to school and see their friends. But they don't have to do homework, they don't get credit for homework, and they don't actually learn anything from it. But sitting down with us and actually learning what they did that was wrong and actually apologizing. I mean, apologizing is such a big thing, especially if it is meaningful. I think people actually learn to be better people through this because they realize they can't just get away with it."

Julie agrees: "I think the best thing the offender can learn is how they have affected the victim and how the victim was hurt, and if they see how the victim was hurt then they are going to learn a lot more than just being punished and having to go out of school. I think it is a lot more meaningful."

"What I have noticed as a result of the Student Conflict Hearing Board," says Quekan, "is more . . . people being aware of consequences and of what they are doing. It's not like, 'Oh, this is going to get me in trouble' but it's like, 'That is really going to hurt the person I'm affecting.' It has been brought to their attention because they realize what we are trying to do."

As a student-run program, it still has yet to be fully supported and used to its full potential by the administration. The students would like more cases, and they offer these suggestions for others in their situation: "Get the word out. Make sure everyone knows about you." "Make sure the administrators are on your side and understand that they can work in collaboration with you and that it can go hand in hand with their usual policies." "I think it's definitely a good thing to work with them rather than against them."

*Rose Lupinacci is the school counselor who facilitates the school's restorative justice program.* "I got into it because students had asked me and I could really see the need. Once I got the training, I felt really confident that it would work really well with schools. I think the things that have worked have been working with the administration closely and reminding them [about this option]. For them they get so many cases and it's so much quicker to deal with them right away and give them a suspension, or say, 'This is what you have to do, here is your work detail,' case closed. Whereas we are asking them to do a few more steps when they consider the Student Conflict Hearing Board. We are asking them to back up and slow down and get all the people involved, call parents and do a little bit more work. And we will do that work for them. They just have to think of that option . . . and [we have to remind] them that the students are completely capable of doing this."

She continues, "[You have] to be creative getting your name out there. There is really no other way of us getting cases because policy and district rules dictate that we have to go through the administration, and they decide what happens. But I am very hopeful. The first year we didn't get any cases. The second year we got about nine or ten. This year we have had only three so far, but they were really hard. They weren't the regular 'he said, she said' conflicts. They were suspendable cases, much more intense situations. They are trusting us with a little bit more intensity. . . .

"I think the whole process just makes so much sense to me. And what makes most sense for me is to have students take over the process. In a middle school or elementary you may not be able to do that, but [at the high school level] having them be involved in the process is so huge. They know what goes on in the school—often more than we do—and they can ask the questions in a way that makes so much more sense to the students than I can. I am always there in the 'hearing' . . . but I try to keep my mouth shut in the process because . . . they know it much better . . . and it is their culture."

One example of a success story occurred in a "theft situation where a couple of girls broke into another girl's locker and stole a bunch of stuff. It was a successful conference because afterwards I saw them in the hallways hanging out together and they were friends again; they had welcomed the person back into their group. It was a pretty serious situation because there was a lot of money involved. They didn't have to go through the legal channels; [if she had] she would have potentially been arrested for that. But they were able to go through us and it worked out much better."

After three years with the program, Rose is excited about the results. "I think with the kids that have gone through our process it has been phenomenal. With the football team, it made them look at a lot of different policies they had within their own group and it created a situation where it was more of a team issue. The coach started initiating [discussions about the way things were done after the 'hearing' process]. It is easier to just go sit in a room with an administrator and get your suspension versus having to deal with us. We are a lot more of a force. They have to really kind of own up. . . .

"Maybe after five years, we may be a regular staple with the administration. I do think other schools should do this with kids. We underestimate their ability to do this."

# CHAPTER ELEVEN

# SCHOOL BULLYING
## Prevention and Intervention

Beverly B. Title

Everybody has a story about a time when he or someone close to him was a target of bullying. Some even remember bullying others in ways that Dr. Larry Brendtro calls "recreational ridicule."[1] Lunch money may have been taken, and, in the worst cases, maybe a few teeth were lost in a fistfight. Many adults seem to feel that bullying is just a part of growing up; they got through it, and so will their kids. Some ask why it seems to be such a big deal today.

The answer is quite simple. What used to involve fists now often involves gunfire. The tragedy at Columbine High School shocked us into acknowledging that youth violence is different today; it has become far more lethal. Eric Harris and Dylan Klebold were not bullies; on the contrary, they were targets of persistent bullying. Columbine forced us to see that often the most dangerous people in our schools are not the bullies but the chronically victimized. As we read newspaper accounts of school shootings that have occurred over the past several years, the word *bully* continues to appear. One thing most of the young shooters have in common is a history of being bullied. We need to rethink bullying and pay closer attention to those who are being victimized.

Rethinking the deeper impacts that bullying has on our school culture is important for existing conflict resolution programs. Many such programs have a long history of creating safe and caring youth cultures and providing students and staff with specific skills to confront injustice, but the recent attention to bullying has expanded the importance of this work and has been the impetus for providing language and additional strategies for surfacing and handling this more serious form of conflict and violence. Likewise, bullying prevention programs can benefit from the comprehensive experience that conflict resolution programs offer, as shown throughout this book.

Over the last twenty years, a body of research on bullying has emerged, conducted largely by Dan Olweus of the University of Bergen in Norway. In 1993 he published the seminal work in the field, *Bullying at School: What We Know and What We Can Do.*[2] Olweus's work pointed the way for schools to take responsibility for safety in a new way. It set the stage for the current attention to bullying, calling for schools to be accountable.

## How Do We Define Bullying?

In response to safety mandates, schools should begin with a definition of bullying informed by research. The No-Bullying Program, developed for grades K–8, is one of several bullying prevention programs built on Olweus's research. It defines bullying as "whenever someone uses his or her power unfairly and repeatedly to hurt someone."[3] The program describes three types of bullying behavior:

1. Physical bullying: harm to another's body or property
2. Emotional bullying: harm to another's self-worth
3. Social bullying: harm to another's group acceptance[4]

Bullying may be carried out by an individual toward another individual. It more frequently occurs, however, as a group process, in which a group engages in bullying an individual or several individuals of another group. This is particularly common between certain social groups, for example, "jocks" bullying "geeks." The group phenomenon often starts about fourth grade, when girls, who generally mature socially before boys, start to target other girls. This early harassment tends to be social bullying. Group bullying peaks at the middle school level, as do all forms of bullying, but it may be carried over into high school.

Some group bullying is intended to be more playful than mean-spirited. The "recreational ridicule" that Larry Brendtro talks about is conducted more for the amusement of those who are bullying than for the actual damage it does to the individuals who are targeted. In other cases, such as bullying that targets gay youth, the bullying activity is more intent on doing actual harm to those who are targeted.

# Misconceptions About Bullying

Olweus's research revealed that many of us hold false beliefs about bullying. These misconceptions have led us to inadvertently exacerbate the problem and give students bad, sometimes even dangerous, advice. Acting on these distorted beliefs has diminished students' confidence in the capacity of school personnel to create safe environments. Students don't believe that reporting bullying to adults at school will make a difference; in fact, they believe that telling an adult will make matters worse.[5] Bullying always involves unequal power, and adults have the capacity to equalize the power imbalance. Thus it is important for adults to be well informed about the research findings about bullying and to intervene when they encounter bullying or when it is reported to them.

## Children Need to Solve Their Own Problems

One popularly held conception that interferes with adults' willingness to intervene in bullying conflicts is the belief that children need to learn to solve their own problems. Although this is true, solving the problem is often not possible in a bully conflict due to the significant power imbalance. For the same reason, it is usually not appropriate to refer bully conflicts to peer mediation. Bullies don't believe they have to play by the rules; they will agree to a mediation process and then manipulate it to their advantage. Even when adults intervene, they need to expect that bullies will try to use manipulation techniques on them as well.

## Victims Should Stand Up to Bullies

Another belief that leads to dangerous advice is that a victim should just stand up to his or her bully and that that will solve the problem. Although it is true that bullying can be stopped by standing up to the bully, this strategy is successful only if the victim can match the bully's power. In truth, most people who are victimized have been specifically targeted because of their inability to fight back successfully. Bullies are excited when their victims try to fight back. Telling a victim to stand up to a bully is likely to lead to another victory for the bully.

## Girls Aren't Bullies

People tend to think that only boys are bullies and that bullying involves only physical abuse. In fact, bullying is done by both boys and girls, although Olweus reports that boys are more likely to bully. "It should also be reported that bullying with physical means is more common among boys. In contrast, girls often use more subtle and indirect ways of harassment such as slandering, spreading of rumors, and manipulation of friendship relationships (e.g., depriving a girl of her 'best friend')."[6]

The bullying strategies used by females have not been given adequate attention. Depriving students of positive social attachments is one of the cruelest things that can happen to a young person, especially if she is of middle school age. A major developmental task for children of this age is to establish strong peer relationships. There can be long-term ill effects from having those relationships damaged. Therefore, it is extremely important that adults recognize and intervene in these insidious forms of bullying. Adults must set the standard that it is appropriate to choose your own friends but that it is not appropriate to embarrass or humiliate or to undermine others' ability to have friends and belong to peer groups. Students should be taught about this form of bullying so that they, too, recognize it for what it is.

## Bullies Have Low Self-Esteem

Probably the hardest misconception for adults to assimilate is the belief that bullying is fundamentally a problem of low self-esteem. According to Olweus, "There was nothing in the results [of my research] to support the common view; they rather pointed in the opposite direction: The bullies have unusually little anxiety and insecurity. . . . They did not suffer from poor self-esteem."[7] He also found that it was the victims of bullies who most suffered from low self-esteem.

My work with students who bully has led me to conclude that bullies do have a self-esteem problem, but it tends to go in the opposite direction: their self-esteem is overinflated. They are much more likely to suffer from narcissism. They see themselves as superior to others and place the highest value on emotional control. If adults lose control of their emotions when intervening with a bully, that is seen by the bully as a victory. The bully, in contrast, will maintain emotional control to the point of displaying an icy emotional flatness.

## Bullying Is a Learned Behavior

Lastly, many people believe that if someone bullies, he or she will always bully. Olweus's research showed that bullying is a learned pattern of behavior and can be unlearned. He demonstrated that bullying behavior can be interrupted and that students who bully can learn healthier ways of interacting with others.

### Bullying Makes Someone a Bully

It is best to think of bullying as a behavior rather than think of a person who is a bully. Whenever linguistically sensible, I discuss bullying behavior, using the "B-word" as an adjective or a verb. I try to avoid the use of the noun *bully*, and I firmly adhere to this whenever an actual human being is involved. I never refer to a person as a bully. To be a bully is a static condition, whereas behavior is a very changeable thing.

So far we have been talking about bullying as though it were an either-or situation. In fact, it is much more a matter of degree. Almost everyone has, at some time in their lives, committed an act that could be considered bullying. One way that we discover our boundaries is by pushing against them. As children and youth develop, it is most likely that they will cross the line sometime and use their power *over* someone else. After all, that's what bullying is, using your power *over* another. For most of us, this experience doesn't lead to a feeling of satisfaction, so we don't do it again. But we may need to learn that lesson a few times before it becomes set.

## Steps Schools Are Taking to Prevent Bullying

Numerous schools are creating policies that prohibit bullying and are establishing official procedures for addressing incidents that do occur. These policies and procedures are explained to students and given to parents. Some schools are implementing programs that train teachers and teach students about the research findings and work to enhance empathy and delineate a reporting process. Some curricula also contain lessons designed to teach students about tactics they can use to keep themselves safe should they be approached by someone who is attempting to bully them.

Most bullying prevention programs are based on Olweus's findings; however, a few are actually perpetuating the myths and popular misconceptions about bullying. Program content should be carefully evaluated before adoption. Currently, most programs are for K–8; far less has been done for the high school level.

### Conflict Resolution and Bullying Prevention

Conflict resolution and bullying prevention are natural partners. A comprehensive violence prevention plan should include both. Schools that have a solid conflict resolution program in place are ideally positioned to engage in bullying prevention as a next step. Conflict resolution teaches students how to solve problems when power is fairly equal and when both parties have some interest in resolving the conflict. Bullying, however, occurs when one party has more power, has no interest in resolving the problem, and is primarily interested in hurting the other. In these circumstances, conflict resolution techniques are not likely to be effective, so other methods must be in place.

A bullying prevention program should teach students how to distinguish normal peer conflict, which responds well to conflict resolution strategies, from bullying violence, which warrants a different set of strategies. Once students understand which type of conflict they are dealing with, they can decide which strategies to use.

Some of the strategies that children are taught to use in bullying situations are to use humor (get them laughing); agree with them (catch them off guard); call others to help; run away; be assertive; be a broken record (repeat something like "Leave me alone"); refer to school rules; and *always* report the incident to an adult. There are several factors (for example, contextual factors and personality traits) that determine when some strategies are more appropriate than others. For more information, you can consult bullying prevention programs, such as No-Bullying (mentioned earlier) and Bully Proofing Your School.[8]

Researchers Debra Pepler and Wendy Craig of the University of Toronto contend that to be effective in responding to bullying, the targeted person must respond successfully the first time the bullying occurs. If the bully wins the first time, he or she gains power, and the targeted individual is likely to be harassed repeatedly. If, however, the targeted person succeeds *the first time* the bullying occurs, it is unlikely he or she will be targeted again. Therein lies the importance of teaching, and repeatedly practicing, strategies for responding to bullying so that students are prepared to respond the first moment it occurs.

## Restorative Justice and Bullying—Caution Is Needed

For people with a healthy level of empathy development, bullying is an especially offensive behavior. We abhor unfair use of power, whether it involves two toddlers fighting over a toy or world leaders threatening use of weapons of mass destruction. Bullying offends our sense of justice, and we have little tolerance for intervening in it. Older youth want to be able to deal with bullying themselves. They feel that they should be able to figure out the problem without adult intrusion, which they feel usually makes matters worse. For these reasons and others, insistence by professionals in this field that adult intervention is required may be inappropriate for all situations. We want to find a way to touch the hearts of the ones who are bullying, so that they will want to abstain from this behavior in the future.

At first look, restorative justice would appear to be ideally suited to the task. Restorative justice processes are inherently empathy enhancing, which is exactly what is needed in a bullying situation, as we know that empathy tends to be low for those who bully. Restorative justice may be student initiated and student directed, which also solves the problem of too much reliance on adults to resolve the conflict. However, there are some inherent problems with using restorative justice processes for bullying conflicts.

Restorative justice is predicated on people entering the process with an open mind and an open heart. It focuses on enhancing empathy through a heartfelt experience of people relating the ways in which they were harmed by another's actions. When others in the conference, especially the offender, hear the victim and express care for his or her pain, this process goes a long way toward restoring victims. When victims feel that offenders are truly remorseful for the harm they have caused, it helps move them toward forgiveness. Bullies, however, are often not remorseful about their actions, and see themselves as superior to those who show emotions. Bullies are known to use any tactic to gain advantage and to use any process to their own benefit. For these reasons it appears that good restorative justice conferences and bullying are diametrically opposed.

However, as discussed earlier, bullying exists on a continuum from single occurrences to long-standing patterns of behavior, and it is possible that a particular bullying situation might be appropriate for restorative justice methods. The restorative justice practitioner needs to assess the extent of past bullying behavior, consider what has happened to precipitate a change in behavior, determine what evidence of remorse is present, and carefully weigh whether this person can be trusted to participate in good faith. In quality restorative justice processes, participants get "inside information" from victims about their deepest wounds. Bullies excel at deception and manipulation therefore great caution should be taken. They will leave the restorative justice process better equipped to do future harm should they make that choice. If the restorative justice keeper determines that it is safe enough to proceed, steps should be built into the process to check back with victims at specific intervals in the future in ways that are safe for them to be truthful about any subsequent bullying, should it occur.

## Students Reporting Bullying

After the initiation of the No-Bullying Program, a number of schools experienced the same phenomenon: students showed up at the counselor's office telling tearful stories of bullying that they had witnessed. Sometimes the bullying had been going on for many years, yet no reports had been made. Bullies like to have witnesses so that their power can be displayed for others. They may threaten witnesses so as to intimidate them into not reporting the bullying. Witnesses are often fairly normal to high in empathy and are concerned both for the victim and for their own safety. Most say they didn't tell because they were afraid of becoming a target themselves.

These students had experienced years of silence and guilt. They shared the general belief that telling an adult wouldn't help. In fact, many students believe that telling an adult will only make matters worse. Until fairly recently adults have not had good information about what they needed to do. Most would either tell the reporter to avoid the bully, bully the bully, or both. The No-Bullying Program asks an administrator to come to classrooms to assure students that reports of bullying will be taken seriously and held in confidence. We have found that these promises result in reports being made.

Before asking students to report bullying, adults must decide how they are to respond to reports. Many teachers believe they can't discipline a student for behavior they didn't witness themselves. They are reluctant to treat another student's report as more than tattling. In the No-Bullying Program we define the differences between tattling (telling on someone to get him in trouble or to make yourself look good) and reporting (telling an adult when there is a threat to someone's safety). As specific procedures are put in place at their school, all adults who work with children are trained and taught what, specifically, they should do if bullying is reported to them.

A reporting strategy used with No-Bullying as well as other programs is a survey that students complete anonymously. It asks if and where students are bullied or are bullying. Frequency and location of bullying is valuable information that can assist school personnel with supervision.

Olweus's research found that 85 percent of students do not engage in bullying or are not actively bullied. About 15 percent of the school population is in the group of those who bully and those who are their targets.[9] Although we may want the victims to make reports, in fact it is the 85 percent who witness bullying who have both the inner strength to report it and the capacity to create a school norm that disallows it. It is an important strategy of effective anti-bullying programs to engage students as partners in the process of creating a safe school.

Older students sometimes feel they should be able to handle bullying themselves, and they may express sentiments aimed at keeping adults out of the process. That is a risky strategy that can turn into vigilantism. It seems to be both prudent and effective for adults and students to work together to resolve this very insidious problem. Once students understand the risks involved in handling bullying without adult support, they often change their perspective and find ways to partner with adults. This needs to be done carefully so that students' need for independence is supported.

# How Adults Should Intervene in Bullying

In bullying prevention programs, we teach students that all incidents of bullying should be reported to an adult. We therefore need to prepare adults to respond appropriately. Adults need to remember that students who bully are not inherently "bad kids." They, like their victims, need nurture and support and instruction about more appropriate ways of behaving.

## Distinguishing Bullying from Normal Peer Conflict

Adults need to be able to quickly determine if a conflict is a bully conflict that requires adult intervention or a different kind of conflict that the children may be able to solve on their own (or through other conflict resolution methods).

The first thing to consider is the issue of power. If one party to the conflict is clearly more powerful than the other and uses his or her power to dominate the less powerful person, then an adult needs to intervene. Sometimes this is obvious, but at other times it may not be so clear. There are two questions that can help in determining whether to intervene: What is the effect on the victim? and How often is this happening? If a victim is hurt by the event and appears powerless, adults should intervene. Remember that hurt may be physical (harm to one's body or property), emotional (harm to one's self-worth), or social (harm to one's group acceptance). If the harassment or teasing happens repeatedly, then it has crossed the line and is bullying. An adult should intervene. However, consider the case of Luke Woodham, the youth who opened fire in Pearl, Mississippi, killing classmates. Fellow students reported that he had been subjected to years of bullying and had acted as if he were not bothered by it. It is wise to remember that a person may be hurting more than he or she is willing to show, especially in front of peers.

## Establishing Effective Plans for Adult Intervention

The most effective adult intervention plan requires consensus building among school staff to develop a predetermined plan of action that they all agree to use. The following is an example of one such plan:

- First occurrence: intervene and stop the violence. Label the *behavior* as bullying. Discuss with the bullying student, as privately as possible, why bullying is hurtful and not allowed at your school. Get a verbal promise from the student not to do it again. Document the event.

- Second occurrence: intervene and stop the violence. Label the *behavior* as bullying. For a reasonable time period, deny the bullying student access to the activity during which the bullying occurred (for example, loss of recess for a day or two; must have bathroom escort for a week). Contact the bullying student's parent. Document the event.
- Third occurrence: intervene and stop the violence. Label the *behavior* as bullying. Assign the bullying student a "Think About It" worksheet that asks three processing questions about the event: What did you do? What else could you have done? What will you do next time something like this happens? Repeat parent contact. Make referral to a counselor for an educative response. Document the event.
- Fourth occurrence: intervene and stop the violence. Label the *behavior* as bullying. Make referral to administration for disciplinary response. Document the event. (At any level of occurrence, severe acts of bullying may go immediately to a disciplinary response.)
- General intervention guidelines for all situations: stay calm; speak in a firm voice, but don't yell; use nonphysical, nonhostile responses; don't bully the bully.

Adults can also effectively intervene in bullying situations by learning how to identify the typical targets of bullying and helping to comfort those victims.

## Understanding Targets of Bullying

It is quite likely that adults do not clearly understand all the facets of those who are being bullied—the victims or targets. We tend to think of those who are targeted for bullying as people who are small in physical size, shy in disposition, and not very popular with peers. These characteristics may indeed make a person more vulnerable to attack.

Olweus identified another group that is frequently targeted—what he calls *provocative victims*. These victims are commonly misunderstood to be bullies themselves because they may be hyperactive, may pick on other students, and may be disruptive to the classroom environment. The prime indicator that these children are not in fact bullies is that their tactics rarely result in bringing them a satisfying outcome. More often, they misbehave, are caught in the act, and are punished. Bullies, in contrast, are rarely caught in the act or punished. Provocative victims tend to be less able than their peers to exert control over their emotions, which makes them an especially attractive target for bullies who delight in pushing them over the edge and then watching as these victims get blamed for yet another disruption.

### Encouraging Peer Support for Victims of Bullying

Intervention may involve more than directly stopping the conflict in the moment. Children and youth who are targeted for bullying are often those who lack strong affiliation with a peer group. They may lack friendship skills, be predisposed to shyness, be an only child with less experience with other children, or have any number of qualities that have impeded their development of healthy peer relationships. Being a loner, or separated from others, makes someone more vulnerable. Therefore, one of the most important strategies for helping children who are chronically bullied is to assist with the development of peer affiliation.

As a teacher, I could recognize within the first few weeks of school the children in my class who had high levels of empathy. These children wince when an animal is injured in a story; they offer to help others with clean-up tasks; they notice when someone doesn't have a needed pencil and offer to loan one. These children are generally a part of strong peer groups and have a number of friends. I can approach one of these children and ask if he or she has noticed that Sally (an isolated child) is eating alone each day. I then remark, rather casually, that it would be nice if Sally were to be asked to eat with a group of girls who were already friends. Rarely does it fail that this high-empathy child sees to it that Sally doesn't eat alone any more. She helps Sally develop friendships by drawing her into her group.

Though this strategy is more easily used with girls, high-empathy boys, and there are plenty of them, can also be engaged in much the same way. Older students are likely to be more flexible about gender affiliation, and boys or girls can be friends within groups of the opposite sex. This strategy requires relatively little work on the part of the teacher; however, the lifetime effects can be profound for the isolated children who come to our schools each year.

## What Bullying Prevention Might Look Like at the High School Level

I was talking with a group of high school students, and I asked them if they ever saw bullying at their school. They looked at me as if the question were absurd and replied, "Are you kidding? We see it all the time." So I asked what it looked like and requested a specific story. Here's what I was told.

> "Yesterday we were in art class. Before the bell rang this kid, Andrew, got some clay and began to center it on the wheel. This guy came by and knocked it off." I asked if Andrew had protested. "Yeah," they said, "and then the boy picked him up and threw him across the room."

Where was the teacher? "Oh, she was doing hall duty; class hadn't started yet."

I asked how often this kind of thing happened to Andrew and was told that it happened every day. I then asked how long this had been going on and got the most startling answer of all: "Since *kindergarten!*"

Any doubt I may have held that bullying prevention programming was needed at the high school level was dispelled that day. Because this behavior begins so young, it is natural that curriculum developers would begin at the earliest point, and we have done that for many good reasons. But for all the Andrews in the world, it is time that we began to build these programs so that they span all educational levels.

The program information discussed up until this point in the chapter has been related to the No-Bullying Program, which was created for grades K–8. In general, high school programs that focus on developing more positive peer culture are likely to be successful when they use approaches that call for student leadership and involve peer education models. When adults talk to high school students about what their culture is or should be, students are more likely to discount the message as inaccurate or irrelevant than they are when their peers confront the same issues.

So what might a high school program look like? One that I began to work with was developed out of restorative justice principles and was largely student driven. It was called the Student Accountability Board. Where individual students may not be strong enough to take a stand against those who bully and to participate in holding them accountable, a group of students may be. Working under the guidance and with the support of school personnel, students may be able to develop a process that truly holds students accountable to repair the harms their actions have caused.

Patterned after a restorative justice process called the Community Accountability Board, the student version trains a group of students to serve as a type of hearing board that works with students who have committed serious rule violations at school, including bullying. The student who comes before the board is asked to tell his or her story. The board members listen carefully and then consider, along with the student who did the harm, how that person might make reparation to the victim and to the school community. Sometimes it is possible for students to get a clearer truth regarding student misconduct than adults might. With the proper safeguards of some adult involvement, these types of boards hold promise.

Another method that I have seen to be very successful was a teen theater company. This company of young actors developed theater pieces based on their own life experiences and did not shy away from the tough topics. By performing these pieces for school audiences, they broached difficult subjects and provided accurate information on a variety of topics, including sexually transmitted diseases, gender identity, parental abuse, dating violence, and bullying. They were also trained peer counselors and provided support for students from the audience after performances. Many youth confided to them about abuses that they had never discussed with anyone else.

There are a number of approaches that can be successful in combating bullying at the high school level, and I suspect that it would be wise to use several in conjunction. There are some guidelines that are important to remember for working at this age level. First, the students need to have an active role in the process, whatever it is. Peer education is a very powerful model that can be employed in a wide array of applications. Second, adults whom the students trust need to have an ongoing role in the process. Third, all school personnel should be trained in the essential information from research about bullying. Fourth, an anonymous system of reporting needs to be in place to provide a safety mechanism for students, so they will be more willing to come forward with information on bullying.

# Planning for Program Survival

One of the most important things to consider in building a program to last is that it will need to have a broad base of support from school personnel. If it is seen as "just the counselor's program" or "just Ms. Jones's program" it is likely to have a short life span. In a similar fashion, it is important that parents actively support the program, which is usually easy to accomplish with bullying prevention programs. Parents have a lot of concerns about their students' safety at school, and in my experience they are eager to get behind such efforts.

Another very important aspect in sustaining a program is being able to demonstrate its success. Having baseline and comparison data is important for several reasons in addition to getting funding. School personnel are more likely to support a program over time if they see evidence that it is making a positive difference for students. Data you might consider collecting are pre- and posttests of students, such as the "What's Happening" survey that is used in the No-Bullying Program.[10] Keep records of the numbers of anonymous reports that are made. Consider the number and nature of discipline referrals. You may want to look at school attendance data, as truancy is often higher among targets of bullying.

## Getting Parents Engaged

There are a wide range of ways that parents can be involved in these school-based efforts to prevent bullying, but first they need to be well informed themselves. Schools can hold parent talks and evening workshops to ensure that parents have accurate information and do not undermine school efforts by continuing to act according to misguided beliefs about bullying.

Parents may find it important to apply bullying prevention concepts at home as well. At Hillsdale Elementary School in Needham, Massachusetts, teachers presented parents with information about the Easing the Teasing program they were implementing. In the discussion with parents, a surprising fact surfaced. Most students who complained of being targets of bullying said it was their siblings who did the bullying. Parents realized that they could reinforce in the home the material given at school and help decrease bullying behavior in both contexts.

I have participated in some very successful events, such as daylong workshops, that were heavily staffed by parents and other community volunteers. The normal day's schedule was suspended, and all students went to workshops throughout the day. These were actually great fun for the adults and the students, and a good deal of information was covered as a bonus!

The most important thing that parents can do is reinforce the information about bullying that the school is forwarding to the students. They need to know the curriculum or the program and be able to discuss with their children the importance of what is being taught. They need to understand any reporting processes that are in place for students and encourage their children to use them when appropriate. By working together, parents and school personnel can strengthen the safety mechanisms within schools.

## What If the School Isn't Actively Working on Bullying?

If your school is not actively working on bullying, definite action needs to be taken. Armed with information, begin to develop a group of people who are educated on this topic. "Bullying: An Overview for Educators" is a booklet that was written specifically to provide a concise review of pertinent information on this topic.[11] Approach school personnel, beginning with the building administration. Offer to give talks for teachers, and provide good food. After you have told the school administrators of your intention, talk to school board members. Call a reporter from your local newspaper, show him or her what you have learned, and try to find an angle that makes it newsworthy. Tell success stories from other schools. In every way you can, make bullying prevention the talk of the town. Be persistent that this is a real problem and that there are real answers, and simply don't accept "no money," "no time," or "no interest" as a response.

◆ ◆ ◆

Eliminating bullying in a school setting is no small task, but it can be accomplished. It requires the engagement of all the parties in a school, adults and students. Everyone must know, in advance, how they will handle the situation. Adult response that is focused on eliminating bullying in the school setting must be clear and consistent, and sanctions need to be implemented that are increasingly severe. There must be a bottom line that a student—or an adult for that matter—may not hurt others and stay in the school. Such behavior will not be tolerated.

# In Their Own Words

## "It Has Really Helped How Safe We Feel"

*Crest View Elementary School is a neighborhood school serving a cross section of social, economic, and ethnic groups, including a large at-risk and high-needs population. They started a conflict resolution and peer mediation program seven years ago and have just recently implemented a bullying prevention component to the program. Here is what the students and adults said about their bullying prevention efforts.*

*Tye Chait, Gabrielle Williams, Emma Zimmerman, and "Sara Koehler" are a group of fourth and fifth graders.* Immediately they talk about how successful their bullying prevention program was as a result of their peer mediation program. "I think our bullying program is good because I started in kindergarten here and I was bullied by like third graders because we were so little, and then once we got to third grade it got a lot better because we started getting peer mediators and they helped us solve problems," says Gabrielle. Emma explains, "The peer mediators go out at recess and if we see bullying, we go and see what the problem is and we ask and each kid tells their story. We let them try to figure out solutions to their problem."

This explanation sounds like regular issues of peer mediation, and Randy questioned them about what was bullying and what was a regular conflict. It seemed they are familiar with what bullying entailed. "I think a lot of the second graders bully first graders. I know that my little brother who is in first grade gets called names by the second graders because he is not the greatest player in football and so they call him 'pink bunny' and that means something bad. It happens a lot to my brother, and I know a few of his friends get bullied. I think a lot of times it is by older kids. I noticed that it is the kids that aren't as good; they are kind of troublemakers. They are taking out that they are getting mad on little kids who they have control over." Gabrielle offers an explanation about why bullies bully. "I think bullies are hurting inside and they don't know how to express themselves very well and so they take it out on somebody else. That's why bullies do that."

At this elementary school, they are able to successfully mediate these mild or "early formation" types of bullying. However, they find some difference between regular peer mediations and those with bullies. "Sometimes [the bullies] would be stubborn," says Gabrielle. "If it was dangerous or if they were abusing [someone] then they would go to the principal. We would only do it if there was an argument or teasing. But sometimes the bullies won't say everything they did. They will say everything the other person did. So we have to try to put them together and see what happens."

Sara speaks about the importance of having students assist teachers in solving the bullying problem. "I think that our bullying program is really good because there are only so many teachers on the playground and a bunch of kids have problems. I think that if we have peer mediators out there we can help kids solve their problems so it usually won't happen again. But if we just have teachers out there they will usually just 'bench' them or something, so generally they can't help them through the problem."

Gabrielle talks about how the threat of going to the principal finally helped resolve a bullying issue. "We had a problem between two girls, and it was actually just resolved today. It was a monthlong problem. The peer mediators tried all they could to help it and then they finally took it to the principal. It was actually resolved by [the peer mediators] because [the disputants] didn't want to have to go [to the principal's office] again." The case, Emma says, was between two girls who were "sort of friends sometimes, but got into fights when they were in bad moods. Whenever they were in a bad mood they would take it out on each other. They both had family problems. Both of their parents were divorced and one was living with their grandmother off and on." From Emma's point of view, both girls were bullies.

Overall, peer mediation has decreased the amount of bullying on the playground. Says Sara, "I have noticed that when we didn't have peer mediators there would be ongoing bullies. They would just keep being bullies. Now that we have the peer mediators, instead of them just getting benched by a teacher, we can help them see why bullying was bad."

They know that there are things you can do other than mediation if you are being bullied. Says Sara, "One of the things that really is good when you are getting bullied is to ignore them and just walk away. I know one of my brother's friends in second grade has been doing that because he is getting bullied constantly by a third grader. He ignores them and walks away and eventually they seem to be getting tired of it."

Emma talks about the effectiveness of direct communication, as well as its limitations. "The teachers were teaching us to say 'I messages,' like 'I don't like it when you do that, please stop' and to do that at least three times [the broken-record technique]. If they didn't stop then we should go tell a teacher or ask a teacher for help. Then if that teacher didn't do anything about it because they were too busy, [you were supposed to] keep on going to another teacher or adult until you got that problem solved so those bullies wouldn't bully you anymore."

Sara expresses her own issues with being a victim of a bully. "When I was in first grade, I was a tomboy and I got bullied about that. Then when we had peer mediators in third grade, I was really surprised that I wasn't getting bullied at all, and other kids weren't getting bullied either. It has helped a lot."

Have all these efforts made a big difference with bullying? All the children respond with a resounding *yes!*

*Anne Spalding is the PE teacher for the school and has the unique perspective of not only seeing every kid in the school but also coordinating the school's peer mediation program.* She says, "This is my fourth year coaching peer mediators and teaching conflict resolution. I asked one of the students who just came about a month ago about the bullying program, and he said he really likes it here because there is a big difference from his other school. There are more teachers on the playground, there were more teachers that really helped, and the peer mediators and the teacher combination kept the playground a really fun place to be without injuries or bullying."

She, too, recognizes that peer mediators have been able to handle many bullying issues as long as they are trained to handle the special dynamics involved. "I give them strict instructions that if the mediation goes on too long they should take it to the principal. Sometimes the bully has been doing it for many years. They are so darn good at [bullying] that a teacher or administrator [needs to be involved] as the mediator who has really high skills, although I think that some of our [student] mediators are getting there."

Anne continues, "I had a little boy who said that he feels that at our school everybody gets to know each other so well that by the time they get into the upper grades there isn't so much bullying because they have learned not to put each other down. He doesn't think there is much bullying at the upper grades."

She talks about how they had adapted the program to deal with specific bully-victim dynamics. "Years ago kids said that when they told teachers about a bullying situation the teacher would say, 'Go over there and work it out.' Now they feel like the teachers have more information and are really concerned with this bullying issue and taking it seriously."

She concludes by sharing her perspective, developed after being in many different schools. "I personally have worked in a lot of schools in two different school districts. As a PE teacher who sees all the kids, I was overwhelmed by it at first. But at our school, we get so much training in [conflict resolution] that things are so much lighter and my life is so much easier that I can just teach instead of dealing with bullying issues."

*Cindy Monet and Donna Casey are fourth-grade teachers who have been active in the conflict resolution program and, more recently, the bullying prevention component. They admit to being concerned initially about how much time it would take for a classroom teacher.* Says Cindy, "We have been doing conflict mediation for quite some time, but our emphasis on bullying has been during the past couple of years. The program focuses not so much on the bully but on creating the caring community."

Both teachers say that the kids have truly internalized the skills and concepts and that they have seen a noticeable difference at the school. "They have the skills, but sometimes you just have to remind them," says Cindy. "Over the years I have seen so much less conflict on the playground. Now there's not much to do. They pretty much know how to take care of [conflicts and bullying situations]. The program does need to be implemented for a few years before you will probably see a lot of effect from it. But I think the kids are very grateful for it. I have heard the same thing from kids. They say at their old school they felt that they were teased, and here [they] don't feel like that."

Donna adds, "We have the [conflict resolution] pledge all throughout the school, and at the beginning of the year all the kids read it and sign it and then we laminate it in all the classrooms. I will say to a kid [who is bullying], 'You know what, you signed this poster which said that you wouldn't say those words to another person.' The way I see [a difference] in my classroom is that now I am able to put a label on it and say, 'What you just said is what a bully would say; never say that again.' It gives us a kind of vocabulary, and everybody knows that we are all playing by the same rules."

Their program has had the benefit of starting with a strong foundation in conflict resolution skills. Donna shares how this had made a difference. "Conflict resolution is a great place to start because it teaches everyone how to be kind and polite and it teaches them empathy and real people skills. The bullying [prevention strategies] just take it one step farther. Now we are helping kids deal with a person that you really have to stand up to, not just be kind. It was a really good progression for us."

Cindy adds that "the kids are saying to us that kids are reacting to all the years of being bullied." Stories of bullying started emerging that had previously been kept inside, "so we had to look at that [problem] specifically. Even though we have the [violence prevention curriculum] which gives a way of communicating and solving problems, it didn't specifically go after that kid who isn't going to follow the rules and tell them how to handle that person. Now we are taking it one more step in asking, 'How is the whole community going to be handling that instead of the individual? How are we all going to support each other?'"

The school is fortunate in that parents devote time to the program as well. "This year I have two parents who are teaching my lessons," says Donna. "To have parents come gives them buy-in and the kids say, 'Wow, our families are really interested in this too.'"

Overall, their bullying prevention program is just one more aspect of an evolving, comprehensive effort. Says Anne, "I think that we do saturate. These are all pieces of the puzzle that bring it together and make it a nice community, a nice school. I was recently at a meeting with a parent of a new child at our school and the mother said, 'I can't believe this neighborhood, the way that these kids talk to each other. It's so polite and respectful—and they won't put up with bullies.' For me, I think it's because every teacher contributes. Each piece of it, the [conflict resolution curricula], the parent volunteers, the peer mediators, the bullying tapes—without one of those, I don't think this would be as much of a peaceful, calm, wonderful learning environment."

Cindy concludes on a note of realism: "One of the things that I think is really important to remember is that we don't have a utopia here. We still have conflicts and problems. But what we have now are kids able to talk about it. It is something they learn. They have the language. The freedom to say, 'This child did this to me' is always available to them. They don't have to pretend that 'this is a peaceful school, we don't have problems so I can't say anything.' This is a school that talks about their problems and solves them. Really, what we look at is not whether we are the 'perfect school' but whether we are the 'ability-to-problem-solve' school."

This is the pledge that all students at Crest View Elementary sign at the beginning of the school year:

*Conflict Resolution Pledge*

I will pledge to be a part of the solution.

I will eliminate taunting from my own behavior.

I will encourage others to do the same.

I will do my part to make my community a safe place by being more sensitive to others.

I will see the example of a caring individual.

I will eliminate profanity toward others from my language.

I will not let my words or actions hurt others and, if others won't become part of the solution, I will.

*Nevin Platt Middle School is a neighborhood school serving predominantly middle- to upper-class Anglo youth. The school uses a middle school structure in which team-teaching of small groups of students is the norm. In the past five years, the school has developed a unique and very successful bullying prevention program based around the concept of being "put-down free." Lorrie Allen is the counselor who helped start the program as a result of the desperate wish of a student with a disability. Here, she tells the story.* "It was six years ago that one particular student had been dealing with very many put-downs. Over the years, I had been dealing with many other kids, helping them strategize what to do when they got put down. This one physically handicapped student seemed like he was getting it more than anyone else. He was born with his feet going in the wrong direction and fingers that weren't all there. So life was very difficult for him. Ever since the day he was born his parents knew that life in middle school was going to be a hard way to go for him. And lo and behold, it turned out to be true. So there were meetings that we had with his parents and him. We did lots of different strategizing about how he would deal with the problem of getting put down.

"One day after all this work, he came into my office after school and sat down. He had really had it. He was mad. I was out of ideas. I didn't know what else to tell him and didn't know what else to do. All of a sudden I said, 'Why don't you just close your eyes and let's imagine together what a school would be like that you could walk into in the morning and feel safe. A school where you wouldn't have to worry about your clothes or your hair or what kind of job your parents had or how much money you had or how good you were at PE or how well you were able to answer a math question or what race you were or what religion you were.' So we tried to picture that kind of school together for a minute and when he opened his eyes he said, 'I want to go to that school.' It was pretty profound for me, and so we started to talk about it. 'Would we ever be able to create a school like that?' He wasn't sure and I wasn't sure either, so we decided to start talking to other people about whether or not it would ever be possible.

"When we talked to adults, they said, 'Kids can't do it. It is a part of growing up and who they are. They have to put each other down. It is a rite of passage.' Then we began to pull together a group of kids and asked them what they thought. The more we talked to kids the more we discovered that they were sick of [the put-downs]. They didn't like it, they didn't like how it made them feel, and they didn't like watching it. And so that is how our work began. . . .

"The power in what we do is spending time with kids and really talking to them, and finding out what their personal experiences have been and having them share with other students what their personal experiences have been and letting them know that it is not OK to put people down. If you have problems at home or are angry, there are other ways of dealing with it besides giving it away to somebody else in the form of a put-down. Since then, we do different things each year. We evaluate and keep what works. We come up with different ideas. In the first year, we had a committee of kids that met and generated ideas. Even now, if we had a new idea we always run it by kids. A lot of it comes from the kids. . . .

"Kids come forward more now if they see a put-down or if they have been given one. We also really try to get them together with the person who gave them the put-down. Overall, I have had very good luck with it stopping—and there is no retaliation. I tell the kids, 'This is not about getting you in trouble. This is about helping you understand how your words make another person feel.' It is a never-ending battle and we are not perfect. If you are not constantly at it, the kids forget."

She talks about how the program works. "In the beginning of the year, we have groups of eighth graders that come together and share their experiences with sixth graders. Some of their experiences are from elementary school. One example is of this boy who, in elementary school, would get isolated on the playground, and after the weekend, boys would come up to him and ask, 'How many sticks of lard did you eat this weekend?' because he was a little overweight. Painful things like that. Or kids going up to another kid on the playground and calling him a loser for no reason. These eighth graders would still remember how bad the kid who was put down felt and the guilt they have to this day of doing this kind of thing.

"We have training sessions, and then we have panels of five kids that go into each sixth-grade classroom and work for two days with those kids. It is a lot of interactive sharing. We also introduce the sixth graders to a [bullying prevention] strategy, which captures all the different kinds of ways you can react to a put-down. They see it in a lot of different places as well, like the posters all over the hallway walls. The eighth graders make these posters with the sixth graders during those two days and we keep them up around the building.

"When we first started, a kid said the reason why kids put each other down is because they don't know each other. If they only knew each other better then they wouldn't have to put each other down. So we formed groups called 'buddy packs.' They are very powerful because they are cross grade level. Last year we had the whole school do it. We had fifty-two buddy packs and it was a huge effort. We had it every day for a whole week and our schedule was different. It was 'getting to know you' activities along with different activities around put-down strategizing and role playing. Buddy packs were and continue to be really effective.

"Another thing we do is use 'I Will' cards, which came out of the Columbine tragedy. These cards are a commitment that kids make and they keep these cards in their wallet. There are big posters that they all sign as a class. Another activity that has been really helpful is having kids do skits for each other. We had a big incident this year with the seventh grade dealing with the Internet. There was an Internet site called voteforfun.com which seventh graders could access. They used it in a very inappropriate and negative way, like, 'Who has the best boobs in seventh grade?' and those kinds of questions . . . really kind of nasty things. When we did our skits right after this whole thing, you can't believe the kind of sharing that happened in class. Kids admitting, 'I got involved in that and I didn't realize how much it was going to hurt other people.' And apologies and talking about how hurtful things can be.

"Probably another one of the most positive things is that we train kids to go to other elementary schools. The kids love doing that, and what they also learn is that they need to be the role models—that is the whole purpose. They need to come back here and practice what they are preaching. One of the biggest things that we teach kids are things they can do when they see a put-down. You go up to the person who said the put-down and say, 'That is not OK with me.' They don't have to do it in an aggressive way or a bullying kind of way that creates the circle all over again. They can do it in such a way that really lets the other person know it's not OK.

"Each year we survey the kids about the problems they see. We ask them, 'Do you think it's worth it, should we keep trying this year?' Without exception, the kids say we should keep trying. They really have felt that it is worthwhile. There are going to be kids like with any program that are not going to buy in. They are going to think it's stupid. We really try to get those kids to come in. For example, we had an activity several years ago where we included this one kid, and the other kids said, 'Why are you having him come? He is the biggest bully.' We said, 'Think about it for a minute.' And they said, 'Oh yeah, we got it.' At the end of the year we had this huge celebration and this kid was able to stand up and say, 'I used to be a jerk, but I learned that doing and saying those kinds of things is not going to get me more friends.' I could tell you hundreds of experiences like this."

But Lorrie does realize there are some students who are more hardened and are repeat offenders. "When we feel like we have done what we can do, then they go to the assistant principal. But I say to them, 'I am not going to give up on you. I know that you can change this. I know that you don't have to be this way.' We try to talk about what it is that is bothering them because we all know that there is a reason why they are doing it, and we try to address those issues as well."

Has the Put-Down Free program made a difference? Lorrie concludes, "In terms of all of the programs we have done here at this school, this one has the most impact on kids."

*Collette Huen is the other counselor at the school who helps run the program.* "I guess the biggest thing that I have seen is what I call a change in climate, though we are far from perfect. We still deal with kids being put down on a fairly regular basis, but there really is kind of a culture now in this school that it is not cool to put people down. You will overhear kids saying to other kids, 'You can't say that, that's a put-down.' It takes a lot of time, but it is definitely worth it. I am actually a little concerned about next year. The amount of counselor time we are going to have next year is going to be dramatically reduced from what we have had, and I am worried about being able to get all of it done. But it is a very valuable program."

*Cindy Matthew and Ron Lamb are team teachers who each "teach everything" for a group of sixty sixth graders. Both enthusiastically support the program (and the middle school structure that enables them to get to know every student personally), and here they speak about why.* "What I like about the Put-Down Free program at our school is that from the first moment they come to school we begin to develop a common language to talk about hurtful behaviors," says Cindy. "Eighth graders get involved in leadership. We have the whole adult population on the same page about behaviors that are acceptable and not acceptable and strategies that kids can use to deal with bullies."

Ron puts it this way: "I think put-downs and being made fun of is one of the biggest problems that face this age group and is one of the biggest worries of sixth graders when they come in. To come in and know that we have a program in place reassures them. The fact that it is the older kids that really take owner-ship for the program really has an interesting effect. Our former students come in and visit us all the time in our classrooms, and sometimes they come in and they write things on our chalkboard or they will write things on our overhead projec-tor. I really don't pay much attention to it. One time we were going around the room and we were talking about how things were going with our put-down free program and one of the things that was said was how much they liked how the older kids always come in and always write positive messages. The messages say, 'Sixth graders are awesome' or something like that. And I thought, 'That's what they are writing up there' and I didn't even realize it. They are coming in . . . to be nice to the younger kids and trying to set an example for them. The younger kids really notice things like that when it comes from seventh and eighth graders."

Cindy adds, "If you look, there are a very few kids that are the bullies in the school, but what they do is enormously cruel and it is awful and they can make people's lives miserable. What the put-down free program does is that it allows all students to recognize that they can be a part of the solution. We have many stu-dents who would stand up against these bullies, many students who recognize bul-lying and who know whom to turn to get help."

Both teachers recognize the importance of creating a caring classroom com-munity. One of the ways they do that is by writing messages in the morning, posing different questions to them such as, "'Who will you reach out to today, whose life will you make a little bit better today?' Kids love that. We also have Fri-day meetings where kids go around and share compliments and talk about the kindnesses that were given to them or they experienced throughout the week, and it is wonderful. It is not just about stopping bullies. It is about everyone height-ening his or her awareness about becoming a caring person."

Ron adds, "Our program isn't perfect. We tinker with it every year and we get input from the whole building. We tell kids that we are probably not going to have a school that is completely put-down free, but we are trying to work toward that. We continue to try to set that as the ideal where students are going to be able to come to a place where they are not going to be made fun of and they are not going to be bullied. We try to help them to imagine what that would look like and then to figure out what they can do to help them make that a reality. Overall, it is definitely a success. What I have noticed in the past few years is that when our counselors or other adults come into our room and ask the kids, 'Tell me about some of the put-downs that you have been hearing. What has been going on?' there are fewer and fewer hands going up to relate all the stories of put-downs that are going down, because there are fewer and fewer put-downs happening. So we start the year at a better place than we were the year before.

"Sometimes, those kids who are known bullies are asked to be leaders in the put-down free program and to become somebody who goes into the younger grades and says, 'I was one of those kinds of people who used to put other kids down and I did it because . . .' and then tell their story. Often it is because they were insecure. They relate that to the younger kids, and it has so much more credibility especially among their peers because they know that they truly were one of the sources of the problem and now they have become part of the solution. That has a real profound effect."

Cindy mentions that they are using the practice of restorative justice to bring together the offender and the victim of the put-down to make things right. "We involve everyone that was in the circle that could have done something about it, including the person who was the bully, and the victim. In the circle, I see the victim being validated that they did need adult help, instead of being afraid that they told the teacher. I even see ones that were friends with the bully recognizing that they could have done something. Even if the bullies are not changing their behavior, we are frustrating their attempts to do some of the stuff they like to do. It absolutely empowers the victim and the community. To have them suddenly realize, 'I did need adult help with this. This was cruel. It was not just friends in a fight . . . this was bullying' helps them to process what they need to do in the future. It is very empowering."

Says Ron, "We really want to create a climate where those students who are so negative are really in the minority. Then it feels safer for the victims to come forward and say, 'Somebody's doing this to me,' and it becomes much more difficult for somebody to continue to operate in that negative way because the climate and culture of the school is one where people won't stand for that." Says Cindy, "Usually we have the bully tell [the people in the circle] everything they have done, and that is really a difficult thing for them. We are not saying, 'We heard you did this,' but they have to admit what they have done. It is a different type of intervention. And we have them make amends one way or another if they have damaged property. Many times an apology is necessary, but it is not like you can patch everything up again and make it perfect again." But, Ron says, "Oftentimes there are simple things that can be done. Sometimes all the victim wants is an apology and an agreement not to do it again." Cindy adds, "The best situation is when we get the victim, with the support of the adults, to confront the bully and say what is going on that they are not OK with and ask the bully for what they want to have happen and get the bully to agree to that in front of these witnesses. Sometimes it is a bigger forum where we want to involve more teachers and more witnesses. That piece of including witnesses is important for the closet bully—the one who doesn't want anybody to know that he is doing all these things behind the scenes." Both of them have participated in these types of "community conferences." Ron adds, "The fact that we know our students so personally enables us to have a great influence on them."

Ron and Cindy also make the connection in their academic curriculum. "[We weave in bullying issues] into literature. As a matter of fact, the piece we are taking next week [Ray Bradbury's 'All Summer in a Day'] has some major bullying going on." Ron agrees: "There are several stories that I read that involve bullying kinds of situations. It just echoes what we do with the rest of our day. We try to tie in everything that we possibly can." According to Cindy, another one of those ties can be seen with "the peopling of the Americas and witnessing the abuse of power that took place with many ethnic groups." Do students make the connection? "We definitely try to help them make that connection, but sometimes you don't know if they do or if they don't."

So is all this worth it given all the pressures on them to meet academic requirements? Ron says yes. "It is definitely worth it. You can't ignore the social-emotional side of our jobs and of students. It is a part of who they are. We have kids who have been tormented by other students, and they really can't learn because they are so worried about these social-emotional issues, so we have to deal with those things. And by doing that it actually makes our academic teaching even stronger. Ultimately, it just makes your classroom run more smoothly and makes the learning easier for everyone."

Cindy adds, "It doesn't take very much time out of any one day. Occasionally it does when we have to have these pow-wows. But doing all of these preventative things that create community, including classroom meetings, is well worth it."

*Taylor Henry, Carrie Demichaelis, Taylor Schmidt, and Allison Wood are sixth and seventh graders who spoke with great honesty about the program.* "It is a good idea but I don't know if we can make it put-down free totally because I still hear a lot around the school, but I think it is a good idea to keep working on it," says Taylor Henry. Carrie agrees: "It is a really good concept and it is working sort of, but to get everyone to do it is kind of a stretch because there is always going to be people that are going to come up and put you down for whatever reason they have."

Carrie talked about a time when put-downs were dealt with by having to give put-ups. "Someone tried to implement a rule that for every put-down you give, if you get caught by a teacher, you have give them three put-ups. If a person would say, 'You're stupid,' they would then have to say, 'But you are really funny and you are really nice and you are really not stupid,' and it sort of turns it into a joke and it doesn't make the person feel any better." Taylor Henry agrees: "In one of our classes the teacher makes us give five put-ups for every put-down, and it is a total joke."

Clearly, all of them recognize that put-downs are said both in jest and to inflict harm. Like the elementary students at Crest View, all recognize too why people give put-downs. Taylor Henry puts it this way: "I think that they bully people at school just because they have problems at home that they can't deal with." Carrie adds, "People really, really crave the attention that put-downs give them."

Put-downs seem to happen where teachers aren't watching. "Mostly I see it in the locker rooms," says Carrie. "Teachers are probably not going to come to a locker room. In there, people say things like, 'Those shorts are huge, how fat can you be?' The other people laugh and laugh and have fun at one person's expense." Taylor Henry adds, "I see that most put-downs happen on the bus, in the locker room, and at lunch because at lunch there are like no teachers outside until the very end when they whistle us in, and on the bus there is just the bus driver who is focusing on the road, and in the locker room none of the teachers are really there."

"Normally whenever there is a put-down, either physical or verbal, it will be without any supervision," says Carrie, "and that is why the put-down free program is enforced by the kids in the school. Basically the kids are the police, and if there is somebody who is put down you will stand up for them." Taylor Henry agrees: "I think it is a good idea for the kids to do the whole program because if the adults did it all then the kids would be mad at the teachers for doing all the bad stuff. But if it is your friends that are doing it, then maybe they won't be as mad or they won't want to do it anymore." Carrie adds, "If the teachers enforced it then the kids wouldn't much care for that because teachers have more power than the kids. And if a teacher enforced it, then behind their backs the kids would always put people down. In school we are basically machines. We just do what the teacher tells us over and over and over every single day of our lives until the summer. So if a teacher is just telling us to do another thing, it is not going to carry that much weight at all."

Taylor Schmidt builds on this by saying, "The teachers can't watch over you every single minute of the day. They have you for class and then you are out of there and you are in passing period and lunch and stuff, and that is where a lot of the put-downs are. They are not watching us over there. They can't enforce it. We have to." And part of enforcing it is standing up against put-downs—and that isn't easy. "It takes a lot of courage to stand up against a put-down," says Taylor Schmidt, "because it is like one against ten people . . . and they are going to probably start to put you down because you stood up for the person. But you actually feel good after you do it." She concludes, "It will take all the kids standing up for people and stopping put-downs. You have to stand up for people. You have to be the stronger person."

All agree that the school climate has changed a lot from elementary school. "It wasn't all that hard for me to buy into the program," says Carrie. "At first when

I was just coming into Platt I thought it was just a big joke, like, 'This is never going to work, oh my gosh, are they kidding?' Then the counselor started showing us how it worked, and other kids were doing it too and it wasn't that hard." Taylor Schmidt says, "I remember in sixth grade the counselor came in with eighth graders and talked about it and I wanted to do it because I had been put down a lot and I just wanted it to stop." Kelley adds, "I came from an elementary school in a totally different district and back there everywhere you basically turned there would be a put-down. Someone would say something really nasty to you, but when I came to Platt it is like all gone. It is like magic or something."

*Lauren Mangold, Brady Knowles, Lyndsey Fitch, and Andrew Jacquemard are all eighth graders who are now, along with all the other eighth graders, the leaders and role models for the rest of the school. Here they share their thoughts and wisdom after two-and-a-half years with the program.* "I have been here for three years," says Lauren, "so I wouldn't say that there has been a lot of change while I have been at this school. But I had an older brother who went here, and he said that it was a lot worse with put-downs when he was here. Not a lot of kids here are mean to each other. You hear about people putting each other down in other schools and it doesn't really seem to happen here." Others echo this sentiment. Lyndsey says, "I think that the Put-Down Free program has affected our class because in sixth grade there were a lot of put-downs because we were all so new and nobody really knew each other. I think that now we are in eighth grade everybody has just bonded. A lot of people just say hi to random people and everybody is just really nice and they stand up for what is right. So if somebody is being put down because of their religion, I know a lot of people who will stand up and say, 'That is not OK, you need to apologize. This is their religion and you need to respect that.' I think it is really cool how we have come together." Says Andrew, "I think that if you compare our school to other schools, there is a big difference in the amount of put-downs. I am hearing from kids from other schools that they have one or two friends that they only talk to. Here, we are all just one big group."

"I think the Put-Down Free program really makes you think about what you say before you say it," says Lyndsey. "I know I have changed a lot from elementary school because I used to be kind of mean and I was really bossy, and now I think of myself as really nice and I think a lot of times before I speak. I think the program makes kids a lot more aware of how it can hurt people's feelings and what to say and what not to say."

"The eighth graders are kind of like the leaders of the whole Put-Down Free program," says Brady. "In sixth grade, they did a lot of activities with us in coming into our class and teaching us what the Put-Down Free program is and about put-downs and how they make everybody feel and they just kind of made it clear to us that put-downs really were not OK. As we worked from sixth grade up to eighth grade, we played a more active role in the program. This year we are the leaders and we are the ones doing all the activities with the other kids in the school. We are the ones conveying the message that put-downs are not OK." Lauren adds, "You have to be a really good role model because they want to be like you. They really look up to us and we have to really make sure to set a good standard for them so that they can have the same kind of school that we had—or even a better one."

Brady speaks for all when he says, "It really is a student-run program. It is really the students who are out there in the halls and in the classrooms and on the bus because the adults aren't going to be everywhere to say, 'Don't do that.'"

Part of the program connects these eighth graders with elementary school students to teach them about being a put-down free school. "We went to Sanchez Elementary School and we talked to thirty or forty peer mediators and they had no idea what the program was," says Brady. "They knew what a put-down was, but I don't know if they really understood how much a put-down can hurt kids and the ways you can stop the put-downs. We talked to them for an hour about methods they can use to help make their school put-down free. It gave me a sense of accomplishment. It was cool that we could go help someone else see the light. Every kid we talked to said that they wanted them to stop. We just told them how."

Lyndsey talks about how this program has made her look at adults differently. "It makes you feel proud of yourself because I have heard adults say mean things or put other people down. It is kind of sad that adults portray this attitude that adults are so much better than kids. Often kids can do the same roles as adults or even better than adults, yet we are doing a lot of things, like not putting other people down and being nice to a lot of people and they almost don't have the same kind of self-discipline to be nice to everyone and not put down people. A lot of times I think that parents in general look at their kids [from the perspective of an authority who is always right]. I think they should take a step back and look at what they are doing that might influence their kid to do something, like a put-down."

Brady concludes, "I am thankful that we have the put-down free program at our school because it has really helped how safe we feel." Andrew agrees: "I just wish there was a Put-Down Free program in the whole world."

*Mark is an eighth grader who used to use put-downs a lot and bullied others. He changed as a result of the program. Here is what he says.* "When I came in as a sixth grader I was obsessed with giving put-downs. I couldn't stop. Through seventh and eighth grade the program helped me a lot, and now I pretty much have stopped giving put-downs. I really try my hardest not to give them any more. I still get them quite a bit from other kids, but most kids now say to the kids that actually do the put-down, 'Dude, what's the point of it? It is so stupid. You are just being a bigger dork for doing it to them.'

"I stopped because I think I grew up and thought about it a little bit. Other kids are going to be helping me stand up for what I want to happen, what I believe in. So it makes it easier for me to stand up all by myself.

"Once I had to meet with the kid that I had been putting down. That worked because it made me see how it really affected the other person. They often don't want to say how they feel right there because it would make them feel embarrassed. So if they can [say it directly to the] person, the person that did it can look up and say, 'That was pretty stupid, I guess.' It was embarrassing to hear it from the other person.

"I think it is a really good program and that it is really successful. It makes kids feel a lot safer when they come to school. I remember that I used to not want to come to school at all. I think that is one of the reasons I started giving put-downs so much is because other kids were putting me down and to start making myself feel better I wanted to give other kids put-downs. The Put-Down Free program is a lot better for us all."

CHAPTER TWELVE

# R.E.S.P.E.C.T.
## Appreciating and Welcoming Differences

## Priscilla Prutzman

On September 25, 2001, the *New York Times* published a poll about attitudes regarding Arab Americans. The results showed that 50 percent of those polled thought it likely that Arab Americans, Muslims, and immigrants from the Middle East would be singled out unfairly by people in the United States following the events of September 11, 2001.[1] They were not wrong. Since September 11, bias and hate crimes toward these groups have increased.

In the United States and the world, violence based on hate and prejudice is ubiquitous. What can we do to reduce this escalation of violence? What role can bias awareness play in counteracting and preventing violence? What is bias awareness? How does it relate to the larger field of conflict resolution, and what issues emerge in integrating bias awareness into conflict resolution education (CRE)? This chapter will answer some of these questions.

As we become a global society, we live in an increasingly diverse world. Schools where once only one language was spoken may now have as many as 45 different languages used by teachers and students. In New York City, there are over 140 languages spoken. The schools are a microcosm of the city, and it is common for new students not to speak or understand English. Because we are increasingly diverse as a society, it is necessary and pragmatic to move beyond tolerance to welcoming and valuing diversity.

---

Thanks for help with this chapter to Kathleen Cochran, Judith M. Johnson, and Meredith Van Etten.

# Bias Awareness Work

The integration of bias awareness and affirmation into creative conflict resolution is central to the work of Creative Response to Conflict (CRC), where I am director. CRC started in 1972 as Children's Creative Response to Conflict (CCRC) in the multicultural environment of New York City. CRC is known for its CRE programs focused on cooperation, communication, affirmation, conflict resolution, bias awareness, problem solving, and mediation.

Early in our work, many conflicts we saw involved sexism, racism, homophobia, and anti-Semitism. The CCRC program began to treat bias as conflict, teaching responses to bias while at the same time working to create an environment where young people would choose to accept many cultures and appreciate diversity. The theme of bias awareness is an integral element in CRC programs.

## Philosophy of Bias Awareness Work

The philosophy underlying bias awareness work includes several core concepts. First of all, the concept of affirmation is very important. Key affirmations include "We are all special," "We all have unique, positive qualities about ourselves," "Positive feelings engender more positive feelings," and "If we feel positive about ourselves, we are less likely to feel negative toward others." Accordingly, "If we have positive feelings about our culture or cultural background, it is likely that we will have positive feelings about the cultures and cultural backgrounds of others."

Another core concept is that we all have some bias toward others, whether we are aware of it or not. In addition, we have all, at some time, experienced bias against us and this will probably happen to us in the future.

The last principle of bias awareness work is that skills involving communication and conflict resolution are needed in order to effectively respond to bias.

## Guidelines for Bias Awareness Work

In CRC's work, the guideline most often used is, "Everyone has something positive to offer, and everyone respects that person's right to offer something." In bias awareness work, we expand this guideline to include the following principles. First, it is important for all of us to remain open to new ideas, even if these ideas contradict our own. Second, when speaking about bias, it is important to speak from our own experiences, rather than someone else's. It is helpful to encourage participants to begin comments with, "I think," "I believe," "I feel."

Finally, it is important in bias awareness work to help participants feel that they are able to explore in an environment of safety. Confidentiality helps create this safety. Members of groups both large and small are asked to keep all that is said confidential.

In bias awareness work, it is likely that strong feelings will emerge around various issues. Participants are encouraged to learn and grow from these feelings rather than to take stands on individual issues.

## What Does Bias Awareness Work Look Like?

Activities that help us look for the special qualities of each person are central to bias awareness work. Such activities create a foundation for affirming ourselves and others. Other important aspects of anti-bias work include exploring our own and others' cultures, examining ways we have seen and experienced bias, and learning to use communication and conflict resolution skills to develop effective responses to bias.

Often a bias awareness workshop begins with exploring the concept of culture. Bias awareness work often starts by charting and discussing what group members believe culture to be. Next the group might focus on how individuals define their own cultural backgrounds, including what people appreciate about their own cultures and what they find troubling or problematic about them.

Participants then look at different kinds of "isms," including sexism, racism, ageism, classism, anti-Semitism, able-ism, size-ism, and homophobia. Included with these "isms" are other problematic cultural biases, which the group may have experienced as individuals working within the framework of a multicultural environment. The group discusses the various ways that these biases affect the lives of individuals in personal, cultural, and institutional settings.

For many, the discussion of cultural and institutional bias extends their understanding of bias and oppression in significant ways. Many individuals in dominant culture groups think of bias in purely personal terms. They believe that if they harbor no personal hatred, behave respectfully, and have good personal relationships with members of groups who experience discrimination, then they are among the "good people" who are free of bias and prejudice.

Only when they begin to list the cultural and institutional biases that others face do they recognize that they are participants in systems of oppression in which they enjoy advantages at the expense of others. This can motivate participants to become active in working for social justice, rather than being content to be "tolerant" and "nice." Many people are often surprised to see that on a continuum from hate crimes to full appreciation of diversity, tolerance is only somewhere in the middle.

Next, individuals explore the ways that they have personally experienced bias directed against them. The group examines ways of responding to bias, using conflict resolution techniques, both from the perspective of one's own group being attacked and from the perspective of being an ally of a group that is being attacked. An ally is a person of a "power" group (for example, white, male, heterosexual, of medium age) that supports a person of a "nonpower" group (such as a person of color, female, gay, old or young) when she is attacked.

If time allows, participants explore biases that individuals hold against other groups, and discuss the similarities and differences among the various "isms." They may broach the issue of internalized oppression and compare oppressions. They often make presentations about hate crimes and distribute resource lists and materials.

## Early Intervention and Prevention

Since the inception of CRC, it has been CRC's goal to work with children as young as possible, before violence becomes ingrained, so that young people will have the skills to respond to conflict as they get older. The same is true of bias awareness. It is desirable to teach young children bias awareness skills before the layers of bias become part of these young people.

Adults are often surprised to see how far and how quickly elementary students advance in bias awareness work. A few years ago, CRC was asked to further explore bias awareness at a school in Brooklyn, New York. We followed the basic workshop outline described earlier.

A few classes wanted to focus on specific "isms." One of the second-grade classes was particularly interested in sexism. We did a "fishbowl" activity in which girls volunteered to go inside the circle and talk about their experience of being girls, and the boys just listened. Girls talked about not being able to go to as many places, about being excluded from many sports, about being teased by boys. Some girls even talked about what was clearly sexual harassment (being chased, having their skirts lifted up, and so on).

When the boys were inside the circle talking about the experience of being boys, they talked about getting into trouble more often and about not wanting to play with girls. One of the second-grade boys said that he was really glad that he wasn't a girl because girls had such a hard time and because boys gave girls such a hard time.

It was amazing to see the awareness level of these young boys and the degree of empathy that they felt toward the girls. These second graders tended to have little self-consciousness and spoke freely about their experiences. It was surprising to see how clearly the boys understood the unfairness of girls' being treated differently from them and that they could verbalize this oppression so clearly—much more clearly, in fact, than most adult males can.

This group's experience underscores the idea that bias awareness work moves much more slowly with adults than with young people and that young people often are more in touch with their feelings around painful issues than are many adults. This suggests that adults have formed culturally approved biases and have gotten used to them. As more layers of culturally approved biases pile up, adults become numb to them. Thus, when adults do get to work on their own bias, they often move slowly, tentatively, and self-consciously.

In a film by Deborah Chasnoff, *It's Elementary,* children talk about what homophobia is and how it is played out.[2] At one point, one of the children says, "What's the big whoop?" expressing that being lesbian or gay isn't that big a deal and questioning why people are upset about it. Open discussions like this provide an early barrier against biases' developing and escalating.

In one school that has a small African American population, students pointed out that in a corner store the shopkeepers often followed around the students of color. After a bias awareness workshop, a white student went to the store with an African American student and observed the shopkeeper following the African American student around the store. The white student asked the shopkeeper why he was following this student. The shopkeeper looked embarrassed and stopped following the student.

Allied behavior can have a larger social change impact, as demonstrated by an incident in a Montana town where someone threw a cinder block at a house window with a menorah in it. The town got together, and non-Jewish as well as Jewish families put menorahs in their windows, showing support and friendship for the family that had been attacked. This story of standing up to bias is told beautifully in a song by Fred Small called "Not in Our Town, a True Story." The chorus to the song goes like this:

> One moment of conviction, one voice quiet and clear
>
> One act of compassion—it all begins here.
>
> No safety now in Silence, we've got to stand our ground
>
> No hate, no violence not in our town.
>
> FRED SMALL, *ONLY LOVE,* AQUIFER MUSIC

## Bias Awareness Training for Adults

Although we may progress further and faster with young people, bias awareness work with adults is imperative for teachers, parents, aides, bus drivers, and others who work with young people. We don't want young people to learn bias awareness skills only to have them contradicted by the behaviors of adults around them. To support an environment of safety and welcoming for everyone, it is critical that parents and teachers acquire skills to interrupt bias. If bias is not interrupted, it will increase, just as violence will. Yet many adults are either reluctant to address bias or unaware of it when it occurs.

The fact that many adults have become numb to bias is often evident in introductory bias awareness workshops for teachers. When we do the Cultural Go-Around (which consists of asking people to describe their own cultural backgrounds), white Anglo-Saxons often will make the comment, "I feel as if I have no culture." Following this comment, people of color often glare, with some degree of disgust, at the white person who made the comment. The white person is usually confused about the reaction and often does not have the confidence to discuss the issue. The person of color might be thinking something like, "You have no culture? You, who stole my culture, feel you have no culture? You are the culture."

While this conversation doesn't always take place aloud, in essence it has taken place, and it is the type of actual dialogue we need to begin if we are to understand the anger that one group feels toward another and the lack of understanding and knowledge that a member of a dominant group has about a member of a nondominant group. In this case, the white person, a woman, was unaware (until that moment) that she really was part of the dominant culture. She was accepted by it and really did not see what it was, because it was the accepted and acceptable reality.

What is often overlooked (and what we try to work on as a unifying force in our bias awareness work) is that the white woman described here is part of other nonpower, nondominant groups. She is a woman, not a man; she might be old rather than medium aged (old and young people often fall into nonpower groups); she might be lesbian or gay rather than heterosexual; she might be Jewish or Buddhist rather than Christian; she might have a disability or a health problem rather than being "temporarily able bodied." (This last phrase is a powerful example of how at some time in our lives, we all experience being part of a nonpower group. At some time we all get sick, and many of us eventually become disabled.)

This realization gives us something in common and serves as a starting place for bias awareness work. It helps to ward off the "hierarchy of oppression" problem that often separates groups. The "my problem is much worse than your problem" syndrome is what often prevents us from listening to each other's concerns and issues, keeps us separated, and leads to fighting among nonpower groups.

## Essentials of Bias Awareness Work

There are many facets of working with both children and adults on bias awareness. There must be a first step toward awareness, which might come about before or during a training session. Individuals must learn how to interrupt bias when it occurs and discover the value of understanding other people's perspectives.

## A First Step Toward Awareness

A first step toward awareness can be taken because of an actual experience or through exposure to a story or song. The songs described here help us see clearly what the oppression is and give concrete examples of personal and cultural bias. Often we need stories and examples to jump-start our awareness of the oppression that is around us on a daily basis. For instance, in Fred Small's song about a disabled friend visiting a restaurant and experiencing one bias after another, the waiter asks the able-bodied person "What will she have?" rather than asking the disabled person directly, and proceeds to make several disparaging comments about disabilities. Finally, the disabled person says that it would be good to have a ramp so she wouldn't have to come in the back door. The waiter responds that there really isn't much of a need for that because "the handicapped don't come here anyway." The irony and the level of misunderstanding, invisibility, and lack of empathy are the anger-producing elements that cause nonpower group members to become so disgusted with power group members.

In another Fred Small song about a closeted lesbian teacher, the issue of invisibility is visited again. Her coworkers wonder what they are going to do about Annie, because "a pretty girl like her shouldn't be alone" (a heterosexist implication that she should be with a man when she is happily in a relationship with a woman). The song goes on to say that if she plays her cards right and dresses up (the "right" heterosexual way), "she'll find a man to take her home."

Once we get going, it is easy to think of many examples. When asked for examples of oppression that exemplify sexism, groups often brainstorm the following:

Women earn less money than men.

Women can't comfortably go out at night alone.

Women's sports often pay less than men's sports.

In classrooms, boys are often called on more than girls.

In many groups, males talk more than females and are listened to with greater attention.

For racism we often hear these observations:

The income for people of color is less.

There is a huge percentage of people of color in prisons.

The life expectancy of African Americans is considerably lower than for whites.

When an African American male goes into an elevator, he often experiences whites moving away because they assume he is violent.

African Americans are often mistaken for "the hired help."

Youth of color are more readily suspected of stealing than white youth.

For homophobia or heterosexism we often discuss these points:

Gay people can't marry or benefit from a partner's health insurance or transference of a lease or property.

People assume that a person's partner is of the opposite sex.

Many religions prevent lesbians and gays from being religious leaders and, in some cases, exclude them from the religious institutions.

Lesbians and gays cannot be openly so in the military.

These lists are expanded on significantly when participants meet in small groups and focus on one "ism" to come up with many different examples of that kind of bias on personal, cultural, and institutional levels.

Young people readily come up with these examples and with their own "isms," using words such as *sneakerism, clothesism, lookism, size-ism, adultism,* and *language-ism.* These biases are often closely related to put-downs of various kinds that are so common in schools and communities today. In a sense they all relate to a young person's experience with a kind of classism, which is often the hardest "ism" for adults to define or deal with. Classism could include biases related to education, money, appearance, clothing, group or club memberships, or other status symbols.

Young students are often acutely aware of the huge bias against young people (adultism, or assuming everything in the world is best viewed from an adult perspective). This falls under the category of bias against a person because of his or her age, experienced by those who are old or young. Examples young people brainstorm include not being given responsibility; not being taken seriously; not being valued, respected, or even seen; assumptions that they are unable to do certain things; and exclusion from activities because of age.

Young people often bear the brunt of language-ism, an increasing bias in the United States as the country becomes more diverse. Children who have arrived recently to the United States may hear their language mocked. Other students may talk about them in front of them as if they were not there, or speak loudly to them as if they could not hear. Rather than being respected for knowing two languages, they are seen as "second class" or "not very bright."

## Interrupting Bias

In schools and at home, it is clear that if a teacher or parent does not interrupt the bias, adults are essentially teaching the young person that it is all right to make biased comments. If not challenged, bias will not only continue but also escalate, just as it is in the nature of violence to escalate. Hate crimes are on the rise, and most hate crimes seem to be committed by young males who often feel put down themselves. What we often overlook is that conflict resolution skills and positive diversity skills also have the capacity to escalate the more we practice them. The better we get at them, the more they spread to others.

Often we do not respond to a biased comment or incident because we simply do not know what to do. In bias awareness work, conflict resolution and communication skills can be applied to increase our repertoire of positive ways of interrupting and responding to bias. The use of I statements (that is, structuring a response to bias by using the skeleton sentence "I feel _____ when _____ because _____" and filling in the blanks) often is an effective technique when the biased comment is made by someone with whom we are close. Paraphrasing and active listening might be a helpful beginning to try to understand the essence of a person's bias. Offering an alternative to what the person is saying might also be an effective response. Sometimes asking a question concerning the source of information can turn around a biased comment or at least distract the person from continuing the direction of the bias. For example, if someone says, "All pedophiles are gay" (a completely incorrect statement), you could respond with "Where did you hear that?" Or perhaps someone says, "Elderly people shouldn't be allowed to make business decisions because they don't have all their mental abilities." You might answer, "What are you basing that on?" Ignoring the bias, arguing with the person, or making another put-down are all responses that will escalate the bias and the conflict.

We often role-play specific responses with young people and ask them to say what will work for them. As is true of conflict resolution, there is not necessarily one "right" answer that will work for everyone. Instead, we explore many possible responses so that we will have many alternatives to choose from when faced with the reality of a biased comment or incident.

## The Value of Perspective Taking

Being able to understand the point of view of another, or perspective taking, is an important bias awareness skill. In schools, bias awareness work can be integrated with the language arts curriculum by reframing familiar stories such as folk and fairy tales from different points of view. An excellent example of a story with which students readily identify is Leif Fern's *The Maligned Wolf,* the story of Little Red Riding Hood told from the wolf's point of view. As students read the story together, they become aware of a number of bias awareness issues (for example, the perspective of another character in the tale, biases that are commonly held against a group such as wolves, and the interrelationships of the different characters' points of view). Students may be encouraged to rewrite the story from the perspective of another character in the story, such as the grandmother, or rewrite other fairy tales from different points of view.

Point of view, or perspective, may also be illustrated by physically observing scenes from a number of viewpoints or through a variety of viewfinders. The study of optical illusions is also effective in demonstrating the importance of point of view in drawing conclusions and in the development of stereotypes that may lead to biases based on incomplete information.

Understanding point of view is one of the many problem-solving skills related to work in conflict resolution and bias awareness. Other such skills include fluency (generating large numbers of ideas), flexibility (for example, developing new uses for common objects such as a Styrofoam cup), elaboration (adding to or embellishing on ideas), creativity (the origination of new products, ideas, or ways of seeing), tolerance for ambiguity, the ability to see paradox, and many more. All these skills can be worked on within the context of the curriculum and provide a jumping-off place for work on bias issues. When we work on these with students, our goal is that students will be able to use them when they are faced with bias incidents in their everyday lives.

Today many schools promote cross-cultural understanding and appreciation of diverse viewpoints not only through the curriculum but also through clubs and activities aimed specifically at celebrating diversity and working for a more equitable and just society. Students from kindergarten through high school are becoming involved with groups like Kids Kare and Habitat for Humanity. The service learning movement, which has burgeoned since the 1990s, has led to community service becoming required in many high schools, so that students undertake significant service activities and must document and reflect on them as part of their program.

## Age Appropriateness in Bias Awareness

In bias awareness work, it is often surprising to adults how aware young people can be about bias, even children as young as kindergarten age. Every child has experienced bias, if only because they are a young person (adultism/ageism). For very young children, part of bias awareness work is learning the vocabulary of bias awareness, identifying bias, and learning methods of responding to and interrupting bias. Children may be aware that a child is being singled out because of his or her race, gender, or language, but may not yet know the words *racism, sexism,* or *language-ism.* In some cases, children may not be aware that certain biases exist. They may in fact learn the word for a bias before they have witnessed it or experienced it. Although there is a disturbing question in doing this work with young people (Are we teaching them about a new bias?), the development of empathy at an early age far outweighs the danger of children's learning a new bias.

Children often have not yet learned cultural assumptions and biases, so they come to this work in a more open-minded way. Young children can, however, "pick up" the biases of parents, older siblings, and others and may mimic speech and behavior that express bias. Sometimes they may say something they don't fully understand, such as calling someone "gay" as a put-down. It is important to determine what a child is thinking before reacting to what he or she is saying. Asking "What do you mean by that?" may help clarify the situation.

For very young children who are working to develop their gender identity, rigid distinctions about boys and girls can surface: what colors are acceptable for each, what toys and games are appropriate, what kind of pretend play is allowed, and so on. It is important to clarify what children are thinking along these lines and to discuss their ideas, providing examples and personal anecdotes that counter gender stereotypes.

In elementary school, children become more aware of rules and justice issues, of what is fair and unfair. Third and fourth graders can easily see the injustice of bias, prejudice, and discrimination of all kinds. Developing ways of being fair is important at this age.

As they enter adolescence, students often become keenly aware of their world and their place in the world. They are outraged at social injustice and are often eager to be associated with worthwhile causes and efforts. At the same time, this is an age when peer relationships are particularly volatile, and bullying, teasing, and exclusion abound. Consequently, the middle school years are a both promising and challenging time for bias awareness work.

High school students tend to have settled down somewhat from the middle school years and seem more likely to take a "live and let live" attitude. Students often self-identify into different groups (jocks, preppies, nerds, and so on) that may coexist side by side without conflicts. However, sometimes a pecking order develops, with members of "lesser" groups being subjected to exclusion, harassment, and sometimes violence by members of groups that put down other groups. It is particularly important for high schools to have open environments where diversity is welcomed and appreciated. This is an age when hate crimes can happen if the environment does not prevent them.

## Effects of Adult Bias on Children

Bias awareness work can be difficult when parents (and teachers too) carry a specific bias and have taught this bias to children. Even though it is no longer socially acceptable to publicly exhibit racism and sexism, in many places it is still acceptable to exhibit bias against lesbian, gay, bisexual, and transgendered people. Parents often do not want their children exposed to gay issues. The Rainbow Curriculum in the New York City school system was virtually thrown out of the schools because it included gay-friendly books such as *Heather Has Two Mommies.*[3] Since the hate crime murder of Matthew Shepherd, a youth from Laramie, Wyoming, parents cannot deny the dangers of homophobia. Although antigay epithets such as *fag* are still the most common put-downs in schools, reflecting that the society still sees homophobia as acceptable, there is an increasing intolerance toward homophobic acts of violence. CRC has been able to deal with homophobia in elementary schools for many years because we present this bias as related to violence and hate crimes, which most people are opposed to.

## The Importance of Bias Awareness in Bullying Prevention Work

Current interest in bullying has been elevated by school shootings that have promoted the idea that a person who is bullied holds angry feelings inside that can well up and come out in extreme behavior. Investigation of the Columbine tragedy suggests that the students who did the shooting felt as though they were outcasts. Therefore schools and communities want not only to stop bullying before it escalates but also to protect those who are bullied. Recently there has been a growing demand for programs on bullying prevention. There is so much interest in stopping bullying that the topic is now included in many conflict resolution programs, and many programs focus specifically on bullying prevention (see Chapter Eleven).

Bias awareness is extremely important in bullying prevention work, as are conflict resolution skills and assertiveness skills. Many students who are targeted by bullies do not fit in or are "different" in appearance, ethnicity, race, language, or sexual orientation. Studies show that students who are perceived as gay, lesbian, bisexual, or transgendered are at particular risk for bullying and harassment. Interrupting bias and acting as an ally are important skills that can prevent bias-related bullying from escalating into violent incidents and even hate crimes.

# Responding to Tragedy

Since the disaster of September 11, 2001, we have not only seen a need for helping people share their feelings but also found new urgency in recognizing and responding to bias against Arab Americans and Muslim people in particular. It is more important than ever that we teach and practice interrupting bias to prevent the escalation of one of the rapidly growing types of hate crimes. These crimes often spill over to include non-Arab or non-Muslim victims who may often be wrongly perceived to be members of these groups. For instance, Sikhs, who wear turbans, have been targeted, despite the fact that they are neither Arab nor Muslim.

In the weeks following September 11, there were reports of hundreds of hate crimes toward people perceived to have some relationship to the Taliban, who in most cases were not even remotely related to the Taliban.[4] As in the aftermath of the World Trade Center bombing in 1993 and immediately after the Oklahoma City bombing in 1998 (when there was an instantaneous assumption of Arab terrorism), schools with Muslim and Arab American populations are seeing children calling other children "terrorists." We did several workshops for elementary students as young as kindergarten age, practicing ways of interrupting biased comments like this and coming up with alternatives. Getting to this right away had an important impact on the school climate and reduced the number of anti-Arab and anti-Muslim comments in the school and prevented the escalation of hate-related bias.

Learning more about different cultures is another approach to bias awareness, because our biases result from lack of knowledge about a group or culture. After September 11, CRC prepared and distributed a packet of materials that offered helpful resources for parents and teachers, and included websites about the peoples, cultures, religions, geography, history, and politics of the Middle East and South and Central Asia.

Recently at a peace conference presentation on the relationship of bias awareness to conflict resolution, a participant asked if we thought there was an improvement in the number of discrimination and hate crimes. The consensus was that it seems there is some improvement because the president of the United States asks repeatedly that the country not direct any prejudice toward Arab Americans or Muslims. Although there is still much progress to be made, there is a lessening of social acceptance of racist, sexist, homophobic, or other kinds of biased comments, at least in public.

So much conflict is related to cultural difference and misunderstanding. Schools seem to have an increasing commitment to working on bias awareness, and as new parts of conflict resolution emerge (such as anti-bullying work and responses to September 11), bias awareness continues to be an important part of conflict resolution programs.

## Bias Awareness Work Is Ongoing

Work in the areas of cooperation, affirmation, communication, and conflict resolution contributes to creating an environment where diversity is valued, where individuals appreciate their own and others' cultures, and where individuals have the skills to respond to bias effectively. Although students often progress more quickly than adults in bias awareness skills, it is important for all of us, especially educators and parents, to continue to learn more about various cultures, to practice effective responses to bias, and to realize that change won't happen overnight and that we need to be in this work for the long haul.

A few staff development workshops on diversity will not create a welcoming environment. There needs to be a commitment from administration and teachers and parents to continue to work on developing a positive cultural climate in which conflict resolution and mediation skills contribute to interrupting bias and creating positive communities where it seems totally inappropriate to exclude anyone. Our increasingly diverse world makes bias awareness and appreciation of diversity more important than ever.

# In Their Own Words

## "It Made Me Speak Up for Myself and My Culture"

*Boulder High School sits in the heart of a university town. Of all the high schools in the district, it has the greatest amount of diversity. Four years ago, the students began a Multicultural Action Coalition (MAC), and in that time it has grown to include around two hundred students and has been the impetus for an elective class on diversity that is expanding beyond its doors to other high schools in the district. Here is what teachers and students have to say about MAC, the diversity class, and issues of diversity in their school community.*

*Nine MAC students joined Randy for a conversation during their lunch break. They included Michelle Faurot, "Kelsang," Sylvia Mena, and "Tasha," all tenth graders; Jimmy Macias and Katie Dameron, eleventh graders; and "Rosemary," Jacqueline Quesnel, and Nicole Faurot, twelfth graders. They started speaking about how MAC had affected them.* "MAC has affected me by letting me see a bunch of different views of different people and getting to see what they see, not just what I see," says Jimmy. Sylvia adds, "It helps you really focus on what exactly racism and stereotyping are and it helps you understand so you are not just having an assumption. We don't get this in classes, because our teachers may see what is going on, but they don't really do much about it." Says Katie, "I think even in Boulder you get the reversal effect, where people deny that there is any racism to the point that they will blatantly ignore it to convince themselves it is not there. They will avoid doing anything, especially in the classroom setting, because they don't really want to label it and have to say, 'Look, there is racism there.'" Jimmy says, "Basically, [MAC] was created by students for students because there were issues like racism, ageism, and other issues like that around the school."

All participating students in MAC attend the two-and-a-half-day retreat. Says Michelle, "Going on the retreat helped me understand how I could stand up to oppressive comments that I hear people using around the school. I don't do it a ton, but it is an option for me to stand up to people and tell them they shouldn't be saying stuff like that. It made me feel more comfortable doing it. Knowing how many people are in MAC that have taken the training is also helpful because you know that if you say something there is going to be somebody else in the class around you that is going to agree with you." About 200 students have taken the training in a student body of 1,890.

"MAC also really helps people learn how to listen," says Rosemary. "You have to listen to the way that a person feels because you can't really disagree or agree with the way that a person feels. Everybody in MAC gets to say how they feel and everybody listens and that's when the changes really occur, when people listen."

For Jacqueline, it was something else in MAC that made a difference in her life: "The biggest change from MAC is that I was really shy and it made me speak up for myself and my culture. It made me feel proud of who I am and made me feel that being different is a good thing not a bad thing." Tasha agrees: "I got to know a lot more people through MAC retreats and going to the meetings. It makes you interact with more people, and on a different level. You go right to the point instead of saying just hi." Kelsang continues, "We all come together and work together. One thing I learned is how to speak up. Until I joined I did not speak at all but after I got here I opened up to the people."

For Sylvia, "MAC helps increase your perspective through the dyads and discussions. It really helps you see different points of view that you would have never thought of before." Nicole agrees: "I noticed that I never even opened up to diversity before I joined MAC, because I am a white girl and there are so many other people like me that are around me all the time. I am not challenged to go meet people that are different from me or that may have different values or different views on things. Through being in MAC, I have learned so much about myself and my judgments and my biases and how to change that and about other's biases. It is an amazing awakening to the lives of other people."

Katie notices that the problem in school is not the amount of racial conflict but the lack of it. "I think the biggest problem is not the conflict but the lack of conflict, the lack of interaction, the student-motivated segregation. You can walk through the schools and definitely see different areas where people hang out." But Michelle sees improvement. "While there is segregation, I think it is getting better and people are hanging out more together."

Part of the change in school is due to the influence that MAC has had. Says Jacqueline, "We help by going into classrooms and doing stereotype activities. In one activity we did, we had each person wear a label and then they are supposed to plan a dance. . . . They then treat each other according to their label. For the people who are actually involved in it, it changes them." Says Tasha, "It is hard when you grow up with certain people around you and certain influences around you. It is really hard to just let that go. You have certain reactions to say [biased comments]. I will make assumptions about a certain race and I will have to stop myself and say, 'No, that's not right.' My family is like that and I try to tell them, 'You can't do that, because it is not fair to that race,' but they still don't understand. They have already gone for so long with it being comfortable for them to say something like that. But I guess you can keep trying."

Sylvia says, "One thing I learned in MAC is . . . not to yell back at another person but use something more positive." Rosamary agrees: "It is hard to give criticism because otherwise the other person won't listen to you. For people to actually listen, you have to present it in a way that is not offensive when the issue itself is offensive."

"For me," says Michelle, "in my group of friends there's not really racism anymore. Nobody talks like that because we have gotten on each other's cases for saying things like that. But then when I go into class and I get partnered with somebody that I am not really good friends with and don't have a direct influence over, I start hearing it, and it is such a shock to me and I don't really know what to do. I just freeze and say, 'What am I supposed to say?' It has been so long since I have heard a lot of that stuff. In MAC, there really is a ripple effect. It is kind of interesting to see that I have influenced my friends, but there are still ripples out there that I have to get to."

"I moved here from California," says Rosemary, "where there was a lot of segregation and there were a lot of different types of ethnic groups, and I was so shocked when I came here. In California, there was a vast difference between the Mexicans and the Asians. There were gangs and you didn't hang out in high school together. You didn't because of what your ethnicity would say. Here, I was just surprised because I thought that was everywhere, and when I came here I realized it wasn't that way at all." Jacqueline continues, "I moved here from Mexico where I never saw any black person or Asian person or anyone except people like me. I had a PE class where I felt that I was being segregated because of who I was. There was this teacher who really helped me with it. She talked to the class because I started losing my grades. I would be ditching or losing interest in class because I was being put into a situation where I was being left out. I didn't know why they were being like that because I was a human being. Maybe my skin was different but inside we were the same. This teacher talked to them and she made me feel welcome. And MAC helped me to understand who I was."

Two students in the group were in the diversity class, and they spoke about what they liked about it. Says Jimmy, "[The teacher] lets everybody speak. It is not like she is telling us what people feel. She brings in articles and we will have a whole discussion about it. Having everybody discuss in class is really different from other classes, and it helps a lot. Even if you have a whole different perspective, you will hear another's perspective and get everybody's views and then you totally learn everything and it sticks with you." Tasha agrees: "Other classes are boring because you have to do it out of a textbook and listen to the teacher, and nobody really wants to listen to your teacher all the time. When you have more interaction, you want to listen more. I think it is better when you get to hear what other students have to say and hear all the different perspectives and experiences." Rosemary adds, "It is really important to have a class where everybody gets to be heard, where everybody gets to speak."

Jimmy also likes that the teacher for the diversity class "is not better than you. She is learning with us, and we are teaching her, too. The students learn from each other. I think that is the best quality it has."

I asked whether this could happen in other classes too. Tasha said, "In certain curriculum, there is not really room for your thoughts and feelings because you have to focus on certain content. But when it is appropriate, it could be good." Sylvia shares that "the one class that I think you could talk about feelings is history. The history book we have really seems to sugarcoat slavery and the Mexican War. They just say, 'This happened,' but they never seem to tell you what really happened. My teacher tries to show us that perspective. I think we could have more discussions in history, about what your reactions were."

As they got to thinking about this, Rosemary says, "I think that a teacher could have an open discussion in math. A teacher's job is to try to really touch the kids, not just to present the information. Any teacher in any subject could do that. A lot of teachers get into this habit, they almost become like zombies because they seem to lose hope. . . . Textbooks are old and they only represent one side of the story and a lot them are rather biased. I think that teachers need to do the homework that they assign to kids, because numerous times I have found arguments in the book where there will only be one side to the argument. If they would actually go through and do what they are teaching, they could actually teach better."

What would they like to see happen from here? "Everybody should know this stuff," says Jimmy. "We are planning on handing out a survey to get every student's input on unfair rules and any discrimination they experience. We are also planning a silent protest against all forms of oppression to honor those whose voices haven't been heard. By not speaking [in silent protest], you grow individually and you notice things that you don't normally notice."

*Christie Spierns-Smith teaches the diversity class and directs the school's OZONE, which is a designated room and academic and social support structure for at-risk youth.* "The Multicultural Action Coalition has been a very powerful club for the kids, especially for the ones who may feel a little disenfranchised. It is an opportunity to really get to know each other and not just look at each other and say hi. Because of that, it breaks down so many barriers that we all have when we first see somebody and look at their outer skin. Through MAC, not only have very diverse groups gotten together within the school and understood each other, but many projects and other things have come out of the club that have reverberated district wide. Because of this club, about seven of the kids went to our principal last year and said, 'We want to be able to do MAC five days a week, in a classroom setting, and not just meet once or twice a month and have a retreat once a year to talk about these issues.' The principal said, 'How badly do you want this?' And so they advocated for themselves. They had statistics, which they learned in MAC how to do, how to support their causes, how to back it up, how to make it happen within the culture that they are working in. In the end, they got a class approved, called "Understanding Diversity in the United States." It is a five-credit elective class. That just goes to show you the power that comes out of the MAC club because these kids feel empowered. They learn ways to move beyond what they are learning and really put it into action.

"Two years ago, I was trained in equity and diversity at the district level, and it was so powerful to me. I realized then why I was trained as a teacher. So I started seeking out any ways to get involved in the movement, and Daniel [MAC's adult coordinator] invited me to be a support person for the club. My first foray into MAC was to go on a retreat. It was an incredible training situation for the kids, not only for them to get together and start trusting each other and having a working bond within the club, but also to get to know more about themselves—who are they, who do they want to be, how do they relate to the people around them, how is school a vehicle for them or not a vehicle for them. Now I am lucky enough to be teaching the diversity class.

"We have a great mix for the class. We sent a letter home to every parent in many different languages and we capped the class at thirty kids. We were hoping to get fifteen but we ended up with thirty. I can only hope that it is this diverse in the future. The kids are really helping to evaluate the class so that they can help to further design it for the kids to come, so I tell them what pathfinders they are and that they have to make it really meaningful and powerful.

"We talk about all the 'isms' in society and really get into the feeling part of that instead of just defining terms. We define terms so that we are all on the same page, but we specifically get into the feelings of what that means. We have been through a number of different exercises that are very hands-on as far as stereotyping and horizontal and internalized racism. They get to feel what it is really like to be a person in a position of nonpower in our culture. We talk about [readings] that I have pulled from many sources and then they do a dialogue journal based on that reading and how they felt about the concept and whether they agreed or disagreed with the author. The readings go anywhere from immigration issues, to affirmative action issues, to what's in a name, or how people want to identify. We really touch on a myriad of things, but the dialogue journals are unbelievable because these high school kids, many of whom have English as a second language, are reading college-level material, and their analytical skills are unbelievable. They just write ferociously. Where some teachers are having a hard time just getting stuff down from their students, these kids get to tell me how they feel, and it is pretty powerful. And then we process it in class. We talk about where people are coming from and why they feel that way. We talk a lot about things like,

'How do we get along? How do we make this work so we can live together peace-fully together and honor each other?' And that's the bottom line.

"Kids today, to me, are so angry. There is so much pent-up rage and I am not exactly sure where it comes from, but that is something that I work a lot with. When somebody writes or says something that is really filled with anger, we talk a lot about it and try to channel that anger in a way that that person feels em-powered again. We talked a lot at the very beginning—when we were learning to trust each other and learning to talk about some pretty sensitive issues—about the comfort zone, where you are learning stuff that is not particularly new stuff. Then there is the learning edge where you are on the verge of learning something new and it might feel really uncomfortable, and we talk about triggers and the things that put us to the learning edge and how you are going to start being more com-fortable with the learning edge, and even seek out the learning edge.

"In a lot of the readings, we address social justice issues. But we don't just come at it from one point of view, because I want them to get all sides of the story so they can come to their own truth of how they want to move forward with that issue. We talk a lot about the media and whether you have a credible source and how you find out information that you know you can rely on.

"As far as MAC goes, they meet every other week. The kids in it are real pace-setters in this school community. They are the peers that will stand up when some-one says a racist joke. They are the students that, when somebody's getting picked on, will step in the middle of it and defuse it. They are the kids that have felt dis-enfranchised, and they are able to think beyond their own selves and into the future.

"Recently, we had a guest editorial on affirmative action in our school news-paper and the title of the article was 'Don't Hate Me Just Because I'm White.' It was a very anti–affirmative action article. The way it was written was filled with anger and rage about what affirmative action has done to her personally as she has gone out and tried to get into college. The MAC kids just went berserk and very much wanted to address the issue and they marched in, themselves so angry and full of rage. I looked at them and said, 'OK, what are you going to do?' and they organized and they researched and they wrote rebuttals and they were in the next newspaper rebutting the author. But they did it in really productive ways so that not only the author would learn from their point of view but everybody else would learn as well.

"I think there is still a lot of anger around and we have to deal with that con-tinually. But because we are such a diverse population at our high school, we are coming to understand what a positive that is instead of a negative. I think the kids understand that, too. We are seeing our enrollment numbers up from last year, and we directly attribute it to parents who choose the school because it is such a diverse community. We see that again and again on the evaluations.

"It would be unbelievably wonderful if all kids could take this class. We have a superintendent that is very supportive of this effort and we are even aligning this class across the curriculum. Every high school in this district got a [new] position that next year has to go to this class. Now we have aligned this curriculum so that any teacher who has a passion for this can pick it up and use it as their road map. We spent hours making sure that it aligns with language arts and social studies curricula, particularly. That is where we really focus because of the reading and writing component in it. The one thing that I feel very strongly about is that if these kids are going to get empowered not only with their feelings and emotions and how they deal with the conflict, then they have to be able to communicate it. I want them to be really strong readers and writers so that they can continue to find their truth and continue to question and move forward. Any teacher interested in this curriculum can access it through our district, because it is public.

"Overall, I think MAC has been the breeding ground for so many positive things that have happened at this school. It has taken us beyond the Black History Month and into every month as a historical 'moving forward perspective' on how multicultural we are in this country and what we do with that to create a society where we can all get along."

*Daniel Escalante is the adult coordinator for MAC who was hired by the district. He also works for a local nonprofit that provides CRE training.* "MAC came about as a result of some recommendations that were made by a task force on conflict resolution and safety five years ago. It is a student organization that, with district support, hired an adult coordinator. The group formed with the mission of helping to make the high school safer and more welcoming for all students. This was before the bullying programs, the Safe Schools Coalition, and all these other types of programs. The students here wanted to do something different. They were committed to first training themselves and then working to educate other students and members of the high school community—faculty, parents, and administrators. The idea was that if people understood each other better and understood each other's cultures that people would be able to get along better.

"Each year since then we conduct the trainings for students and some faculty, which are generally a day-and-a-half long. Each workshop covers first of all community building, which takes about half a day. There we share our stories with each other, talk about identity, and define some terms like *culture*. We take time to get to know each other better. The second half of the day we look at specifically one form of oppression, which is racism. We tie in other forms of oppression, too. On the second day we focus on homophobia and heterosexism. There we bring in a panel of people who can talk from their own experience. The last part of the training is devoted to action. The idea is that students go through a progression that first looks at themselves, then understanding each other, and then moving on to action. It follows closely the model developed by James Banks of multicultural action. For a lot of students, the training, making a commitment to spreading the word, and being allies is the extent of their involvement. For other students, they get involved in community or school projects. These students present at conferences, like the Peace Leadership conference, the Statewide Parent Coalition conference, the peer counseling conference, and the diversity conference. Every year they present workshops and facilitate discussions. Other students get involved in Reading to End Racism. Some people choose to make classroom presentations. We also cosponsor school events. For example, last year we sponsored a two-and-a-half-hour forum that looked at what people at the school could do to make the high school more welcoming and safer for everybody . . . 'a place for everyone'—that's the school motto.

"Frequently the kids in the cafeteria will sit at different tables according to their group, but what MAC students are trying to do is change that and sit at tables that they wouldn't normally sit at or invite people to sit with them that normally wouldn't. They are trying to break up some of that fragmentation.

"MAC really was the catalyst for getting the class started. The funding that was committed to MAC used to fund a class here called Multicultural Peer Leadership. A lot of the topics of discussion and activities were borrowed from that class. The theory was that with MAC we could reach more students. Instead of twenty students per semester we could reach a couple hundred students. But the idea was that eventually the class would come back. So this last year, MAC made that request and the principal said yes. MAC has been instrumental in getting the class started not only at this high school but also at other district high schools.

"We are now even represented on the governance team. We are infiltrating places where important decisions are made. The governance team is the main decision-making body here at the school. It includes mostly teachers, administrators, a few students from student council, and now someone from MAC. [MAC] students are becoming involved, or infiltrating, student council and other clubs and groups on campus. The term *infiltrating* kind of has a bad connotation in some ways, but once, I asked the superintendent of schools, 'What can we really do to help make positive change in the schools?' and he just said one word . . . he said, 'Infiltrate. Get in there. You have to get people into positions where their voices are heard and represented.' So that has been one of our strategies, [but] still be very connected to MAC so that we have a common vision.

"When we do our trainings and hold our retreat, we do lots of role plays. We spend a lot of time on what to do when prejudice and bias happens and what to do when you see it happening. On this last retreat especially, we talked a lot about conflict resolution skills. We talked about I messages and listening for feelings and needs, and reflective listening, and using that as a way to be allies for each other so that if students hear somebody making a comment like 'That's so gay' or 'spic' or some other derogatory term, then many of the students would feel comfortable knowing what to do or say in that situation. Before, they all said, 'It's really hard, we really don't know what to do. A lot of times it is our friends who are saying this, so we feel awkward saying something about it.' This is taking some time in having an effect on the behavior of a lot of students, but I have seen it. I know that people are working on it. Even at our last meeting I asked them, 'How are things going? Has anyone taken part in any ally activity?' and people would raise their hands and say, 'I tried it and it worked' or 'I tried it and it didn't work' or 'I tried it but I was afraid to.'

"Within MAC, conflict resolution and diversity are very connected. We talk about the basic skills and being sure to express your feelings and your needs. But we also try to encourage the other person to say what it is that they need and find out what kind of resolution they can come to. With the restorative justice model that is trying to get going here, there is some talk about multicultural issues and how they relate to the way we do our conferencing.

"It is my hope that MAC and the class [will] work hand in hand forever. They are kind of like sister and brother because they were born out of the same concern for helping people to understand, as a way of promoting diversity and safety."

# CHAPTER THIRTEEN

# SCHOOL'S OUT
## Time for Fun, Relaxation, and Peaceful Conflict Resolution Education

Sandy Tsubokawa Whittall

When the school bell rings at 3:00, where do the children go, and what do they do? Over 1.7 million children leave school to attend an after-school program while their parents are working. Thousands of these after-school programs are housed in nearby churches, recreation centers, and school cafeterias. In general, after-school programs exist to keep kids safe while parents are at work. In recent years, however, parents, schools, governments, and communities have begun to expect the after-school program to teach the social and emotional skills that schools lack time for during the academic day. Research shows that juvenile crime increases dramatically during the weekday hours of 3:00 to 6:00 P.M. when school is out and adult supervision is not available.[1] The intent of this chapter is to show how conflict resolution strategies can be infused within a quality after-school program.

The first order of business for teaching children and youth the social and emotional skills needed to be successful adults is to create a community of caring among the adults and children involved in the program. Imagine a place for kids to go at 3:00 where they are greeted with a smile and a friendly hello. The children and staff together create an atmosphere of safety and respect. In this community of caring, they may be unrelated but not unattached. Feeling empowered and personally responsible for oneself and others enable children to get along successfully with others at school and at home.

## What's the Mission of the After-School Program?

There are a variety of organizations running after-school programs. Some are grassroots and specific to one school or community; others are part of a national organization. The national organizations running after-school programs might lease, rent, or receive rent-free the use of the school building for the program. They may be related to church, community education, or school district nonprofit community-based organizations; early childhood care and education centers; university cooperative extension education; parks and recreation departments; or youth-serving organizations.

The mission of the organization influences the nature of the after-school conflict resolution program. The organization's values undergird the after-school initiative and its conflict resolution component. For example, among the "scouting programs" of youth-serving organizations, the Camp Fire USA is an organization that works to include all people from all backgrounds to meet the needs of all children. Therefore, it includes conflict resolution training for its staff and volunteers in order to build a sense of community in the programs that include boys and girls of all ages.

However, not all the administrative bodies overseeing the after-school program will include conflict resolution in their curriculum model, so it becomes worth the extra effort to have conversations about the mission of the program and how nonviolent conflict resolution can be taught and valued by the umbrella organization running the program.

## What Do Kids Do at an After-School Program?

Try to remember what it was like to be a kid. Who helped you learn to cross the street, use tools, and learn group games? It was probably a caring, trusted adult who taught you those skills in a loving way. You probably respected that caring adult and beamed with pride when you knew that she respected you as well. But if that adult was not a family member, you may also remember that establishing and building relationships with caring adults was not an easy or accidental process.

How does a group of strangers gain the trust and respect needed to keep everyone safe? Most of the time it is accomplished through caring communication and positive or restorative discipline approaches, inherent in conflict resolution programs. In my experience, conflict resolution skills are best taught by infusing them through activities that kids will find fun and engaging, such as arts, music, literature, games, and regular routines. These activities are a predominant focus of after-school programs, making such programs a wonderful context for conflict resolution education (CRE), a context often unencumbered by the time and content restraints of regular educational environments.

A common practice in the after-school program is to have name tags for children. The tags are worn and magnetized as well. The children move their name tag on a master board to show that they are in attendance and to indicate which area of the school or building they are in at the time. When children come to the after-school program, they check in and have a short period in which they have a snack and engage in self-selected activities. After some individual time, the children usually gather for a group meeting. During this time, some basic ground rules for behavior are developed and then implemented. The rules are simple; they are written down in kid-friendly language on poster board and everyone signs it to signify ownership.

Earlier chapters discussed how important group time can be to establishing a sense of community and connection in a classroom. The same is true for group meetings in after-school programs. Group meeting time is a prime opportunity to begin teaching the skills of conflict resolution. An object such as a glitter wand or stuffed toy can be used to signify who the speaker is. The staff person can teach active listening during group meetings by dividing the group into twos. They may use a listening exercise in which children talk and listen for one minute each. The children then discuss what made them feel respected as a speaker or listener. A few of the pairs can report back to the whole group with their insights. The staff person may summarize the traits of good listeners. Or the group meeting time can be used for role plays that teach conflict resolution. For example, three to four adults and kids role-play for the group using a phrase such as "What are you talking about?" in respectful and disrespectful ways. The group identifies which behaviors the actors portrayed that were respectful or disrespectful.

Group meetings become a process for role-playing conflicts and practicing communication and problem-solving skills. As the adults and children become more caring, the children feel less inhibited about expressing their emotions. Sometimes this means there is more physical conflict, as children have been sitting still in school and need to move and express themselves verbally and physically. A conflict resolution program such as Adventures in Peacemaking can provide an opportunity for the children to learn the skills needed for conflict resolution while playing games that encourage cooperation and the healthy expression of feelings.

## Top Three Reasons to Teach Conflict Resolution in the After-School Program

There are many reasons why we should teach conflict resolution in after-school settings, but three key purposes can be highlighted. First, after-school programs provide for mixed-age grouping and long-term participation. Children are able to get to know each other over time in a casual setting, which helps them develop healthy social and emotional habits. A child may begin the after-school program in kindergarten and continue until the sixth grade, thus having ample time to learn how to accept and celebrate the similarities and differences of the other children attending the program as well as how to resolve the conflicts that inevitably occur. Older children may develop a caretaking orientation to the younger children in the program; younger children may identify role models among the older youth.

Second, after-school programs are an opportunity for daily communication between program staff and parents. When parents drop off and pick up their children, the after-school staff can share information with the parent that helps support a child's self-esteem, conflict resolution skills, and sense of being cared for by loving unrelated adults. Ideally, this connection can supplement relationships the parent has with other caregivers and teachers who are concerned for the well-being of the child. Because the after-school staff sees the child in different situations than a teacher does, their feedback can be very valuable to parents.

Third, after-school programs provide ample time to play and be exposed to a variety of arts, athletics, and other activities that may not be available during the academic day due to the amount of time devoted to academic content curriculum. This may be the greatest strength of the after-school program. The possibilities for integrated learning experiences that engage a number of learning modalities are limited only by the funding, skill, and motivation of the program staff. After-school programs can use various curriculum choices to enhance children's interest. For example, dramatic play can be used to rehearse and stage a peace play for the school and parents. Today's academic curricular demands generally do not allow time for such activities.

## Three Key Areas for Planning Activities

Once an after-school program has decided to infuse CRE within its curriculum, the administrators of the program plan for activities in three key areas: safety and respect, conflict among adults and children, and feelings and ways to express them. Obviously, children need to be physically and emotionally safe in the program. They also need to feel respected by staff and other participants. As is true in the regular classroom, establishing a safe learning environment is the foundation. After-school programs appreciate that conflict is a fact of life. The process of planning for conflict will require effort on the part of everyone connected to the program in order to build a community of belonging that values every individual as unique and special. And, as other authors have mentioned throughout this volume, helping students gain emotional awareness and a comfort with emotional expressions is a critical aspect of developing prosocial skills.

## What's So Special About Combining After-School Programs and CRE?

After-school programs are generally not accountable to an academic curriculum. Therefore, there's time and an opportunity to teach a lesson that will be important as a life skill but may not have the highest priority for a school. The atmosphere in an after-school program is geared to fun and friendships and a relaxed view of lifelong learning. The stage is set to plan, administer, and teach conflict resolution.

Some after-school programs are linked to the school's academic curriculum and provide enriched learning opportunities that support the state academic standards. If this is the case, an ideal opportunity exists to teach conflict resolution through literature. For example, the picture book *The Bracelet*, by Yoshiko Uchida, could be used to discuss friendship and stimulate talk about feelings. Teachers and the after-school staff can plan ways to use picture and chapter books that are not regularly used during the academic day due to time constraints. Collaborative planning of this kind both strengthens programs, and fosters opportunities for children to enjoy books, while discussing the skills needed for peaceful conflict resolution as the characters act out and experience conflict in the story.

Schools and after-school programs can also coordinate their conflict resolution programs. The training, social values, and common vocabulary in both settings help strengthen the learning. The staff coordinator from each program can train about ways to teach that are appropriate to the classroom, the playground, and the after-school program. Parents can receive information from both the academic day school and the after-school program about the importance of nonviolent conflict resolution and ways parents can support what is taught at school.

Family involvement can also be heightened in after-school programs. Parents can be actively engaged in learning about conflict resolution in after-school programs through family fun nights. These are planned by the staff of the after-school program in cooperation with the children. The children cook dinner, invite their parents, and the staff and children play with parents through hands-on learning centers or group noncompetitive games to demonstrate peaceful conflict resolution. Many programs schedule family fun nights once a month or once a quarter depending on the level of parent involvement in the after-school programs.

## How Can Staff Build a Community of Caring in an After-School Program?

For many after-school programs, including Camp Fire USA, which has a specific and broad mission to be inclusive, the initial staff training and orientation to the program includes activities to welcome and familiarize participants with the mission, philosophy, and daily operation of the program. These included "ice-breakers," assessing the strengths of each staff person, and team building. The group sets goals for the program that include conflict resolution skill building for staff and children. Conflict is viewed as a natural part of including diverse people in one program. The first step toward valuing conflict is to spend time letting staff share skills and strategies for conflict resolution that have proven successful for them. Work conflicts will arise among staff in after-school programs, as in all organizations. If staff can plan for ways to resolve their conflicts constructively, they will be better able to model peaceful resolution to conflict.

Assessing the current operation of the after-school program can yield valuable insights into how to plan for CRE. For example, if the review of the program materials shows that there is a lack of toys and that staff routinely intervene in fights over toys, then a plan to purchase more toys could be a major factor in reducing conflict over toys. In addition, this insight suggests that the "toy issue" is a possible topic for a role play or a discussion about constructive conflict management.

The inclusion of a "peace place" in the after-school program helps children resolve conflicts independently. A peace place has two separate purposes, so there are often two different locations for it. First, a peace place is for calming down and getting in touch with your feelings. During a conflict, a child may need to leave the conflict and go someplace to cry, breathe deeply, or redirect some energy away from the conflict. A cozy corner with a rug, pillows, and a mirror and with toys to redirect energy (such as bubbles to blow, koosh balls to toss, or bottles of water to turn over) helps calm kids down. Second, a peace place is for children to negotiate a mutually satisfying resolution of the conflict. The place may have puppets, a sign that has steps to solving problems on it, and chairs to let the kids talk face-to-face. The peace place becomes a self-selected center for children to work out their feelings and conflicts in a way that lets them be in control of the conflict.

Scheduling a time for predictable rituals that acknowledge and accept each person's individuality will help lay a foundation for a caring community. A regular ritual that engages everyone in the program should be a part of every day in the program. For example, it is important to have a gathering time at the beginning or end of the program to show care, concern, and celebration for participants. The activity helps kids and adults feel that they belong. The activity should be special for the group. It could be a song, a chant, a call and response rap, or simply a sharing time.

Playing together is critical to the building of a caring community. Through play the staff and children will laugh and have fun, bridging the gap between children and adults as they engage in fun activities. The organized play needs to be noncompetitive and have a time built in for children to reflect on the feelings and personal learning that are stimulated by noncompetitive play. The playtime needs to be structured to be safe and inclusive so that everyone has a part to play.

## Age-Appropriate CRE Activities in After-School Programs

The conflict resolution skills needed for elementary school children are best taught one-on-one, during group meetings, through cooperative games, stories, music, and art. Programs are generally run as enriched learning or supervisory programs for working parents and paid for by parent fees.

Middle school programs are generally club oriented. The club could be a peer mediator club that is part of the school's peer mediation program or peer counseling program. The clubs are usually scheduled as weekly activities using staff from the school. Youth development organizations such as the YMCA or Boys and Girls Club could easily accommodate a conflict club within their after-school structure.

High school after-school programs are generally geared toward service learning. The service learning might be part of the graduation requirement or a component of the academic curriculum. A conflict club would be a natural link to the school's peer counseling or mediation program. Another component of the program that would be developmentally appropriate for this age would be to train the teens in conflict resolution and have them implement the skills as a service learning project with middle and elementary school students in their after-school programs.

## School's Out

School is over, but the learning continues. The social and emotional skills needed to resolve conflict in nonviolent ways can be taught in the fun, hands-on, multi-age setting of an after-school program. The relaxed atmosphere helps everyone learn to accept and value staff and children just as they are. Through purposeful play, the conflict resolutions skills of communication, cooperation, expression of feelings, appreciation for diversity, and steps for resolving conflicts can be practiced and valued every day from 3:00 P.M. to dinnertime.

# In Their Own Words

## "When the Kids Are Playing, They Are Working as a Team"

*The Adventure Club and Creative Play Centers host twenty-one before- and after-school programs. They serve kindergarten through fifth-grade kids in the second-largest city in Colorado. Most of their sites are inside the elementary schools, so the children are dropped off right at the site before school, and when the bell rings they are released to the school. After school, they come back to the program. The director of the program believes strongly in the importance of teaching conflict resolution skills to the kids in her programs.*

*"Dylan Stone" (age nine), Kayla Booten (nine), Ariel Kerr (nine), Sarah Kampson (eight), Jason Thatcher (ten), Erica Alvarado (eight), and Brianna Hicks (seven) attend the after-school program at the Adventure Club. Here is what they have to say about conflict resolution at the club.* "We work things out mostly by talking," says Dylan, although Kayla differs and says, "Usually if there is a problem, we get separated into different rooms." Says Ariel, "What I do to work out problems, is if a teacher asks me to fix it myself, I ask a friend if they have any solutions. Then, once I do that I will try and think of some way to say I am sorry in a kinder way. Once I am done with that I will try to talk it out with them and see if they will stay calm. Then I spend a week with them and see if we can become friends or something. That usually works. What I do also is if one of my friends gets in a fight with another one of my friends I will ask them what is going on and then I will have the youngest one tell me first. Then I will have the next one tell me. Then I will tell them what they probably did wrong and then tell them why they probably did that." When I asked her how she learned all this, she said, "I have been going here since first grade and I have been spending my summers here and they usually tell us what to do. One teacher always wants us to try to work it out first. Another teacher always asks, 'What's going on?' so I just picked it up. I think it is a pretty peaceful place because we have rules on how to be."

Sarah talks about the sharing circles. "I think we get in circles to help everybody get to know each other and to help us calm down when we need to." Jason adds, "They do the circles because they believe it will calm us down and that it will help us not be so crazy and wild. They ask about how your day was. This center believes in nonviolence and it is a great center to be in. Kids are calm and respectful to each other and are kind to teachers. They are not hitting and punching."

Ariel talks about how much the teachers want the kids to work it out. "After school we have this thing called family talk. If some kids have been mean to each other, [the teacher] tells them what she has been hearing in her office, like name-calling, and she asks them, 'Why are you doing this?' and nobody really raises their hands. Some do and some don't. If they do they usually say, 'This person did this' and then the teacher stops them in the middle and says, 'Why do you think tattle-telling will help? Why don't you just try to work it out first?' What we usually do is if there are two people fighting outside over a tetherball, they sit down and try to work it out if they know what to do. If they don't know what they are going to do, then they ask other people what they think they should do and then those people give them advice and then they work it out so they can show everybody that they can do it."

"It has made a lot of difference," says Jason. "There used to be a lot of fighting and kids picking on other children. Now we don't see that quite as often as we used to see it before. Sometimes they can get out of hand and start arguing and trying to get into a fight over it. Then they usually get a teacher involved and it just turns into a big mess. It doesn't go well. The teacher tries to help you solve the problem and prevent it from ever happening again." Ariel agrees: "I think the best part of it is that kids try to work it out. Sometimes there is a new kid and they are from the Ukraine or something and a teacher tries to give a kid who is doing a few bad things a chance. But if that kid picks up some bad things, [the teacher and student] start talking and then they find another person until they learn the right thing. Then the Ukraine person will help the next person next year because that is how it passes on." Says Jason, "It starts creating kindness for other people. If you are kind to one another and are not violent with each other and use kind words and you keep spreading that on to other people, it could increase and make the world a better place."

Ariel also talks about some of the more traditional means for resolving conflicts at the club. "If we have something going outside and kids are being mean to each other, then we will often come inside and watch a movie until we are calm."

Clearly the norm at the club is to work it out yourself. Erica says, "Kids here try to work it out and if they can't, they get an adult to help. It feels like you are talking to your parents, which is easy. Trying to solve it by yourself is better because you won't be tattle-telling. We feel happy even when we can't solve the problem because we come back to being friends."

But despite the children's eager willingness to resolve conflicts themselves, it seems that some of the kids haven't learned the specific skills for doing so. They have adopted the value of conflict resolution, but have a hard time explaining or using the skill. Erica says, "A lot of teachers say to solve it yourselves and if you can't they will solve it for you and they will make you go to different centers. Most of the times adults solve it because even though people try to get along they still can't do it. . . . They teach us how to work it out, like how to respect and learn how to do things when you can't get along."

Listening to the children here helps us understand what they are capable of and what they need more help with. With a little more negotiation practice, they could become the peacemakers we all dream of.

*Melanie Rush is the executive director of the Adventure Club and Creative Play Centers. She recognizes that her support for conflict resolution may be greater than that of her staff, but she knows it is a process that builds on itself. Randy asked her how conflict resolution is integrated into her programs.*

"I have been in the field for twenty years, and in that time I found that time-outs and traditional discipline strategies weren't meeting the needs of the child. It may have solved the problem in a quick instant for the teacher or the child to re-group for their own self-control, but it wasn't really being productive in other ways. I discovered that learning the social skills was the number one key.

"What we do as far as conflict resolution—and the old-fashioned *discipline* word is totally thrown out—is start with community building. We get the children to cooperate, to respect each other, and to play cooperative games. We do little icebreakers. Children don't turn their brains off when they walk down from the academic school day into our program. They are learning all the time, and part of their learning is social interaction between each other.

"A lot of children don't like to open up at first or don't know how to open up, and we let them take their own time and be at their own pace. When we play games that encourage the children to express their feelings of being sad or happy or frustrated—all those emotions that children have difficulty labeling at that age— we feel like we have a core base started in their social beings. When children talk to each other and communicate with each other and get to know each other, they are less likely to bully or less likely to become a victim because they are a part of a community.

"The way we implement [CRE] is through our activities. Our arts-and-crafts projects start as a group project. We like to do progressive projects, where they start on it one day and finish it on another. The children have conflicts from time to time, but they are more open to communicate with each other—not the tattling and the running to the teacher but working it out together, because they have those communication and social skills building from our circle times and our sharing times and our games. They can go up to their friend and say, 'I really didn't feel good about when you took that marker from me' or 'I don't like the way you cut in front of me.' They can share those feelings with each other before a teacher has to get involved or before they even invite a teacher to get involved. The children all know that they have feelings, their feelings can get hurt, and that it is a safe place to share.

"There are times, and we tell kids, when a teacher needs to get involved. When there is a safety issue or when you feel threatened or you don't feel capable of han-dling it yourself and you want mediation. We really express that 'it is OK' when it is necessary. We also have a cozy corner, which is a quiet center where they can choose to be alone if things have stressed them out or if the school day has been horrendous and they want some alone time. If they are in that cozy corner and someone else wants to come in, they have to ask. The child that is in there first can say, 'No, I want to be alone' or 'Sure, come on in.' We limit two people to that corner and think that children's wishes to be alone should be honored because sometimes our days do get very crazy with hustle and bustle and stresses and we often don't realize that children don't have any alone time. They may be getting nagged at by their parents to do their homework or they are getting nagged at by someone else to wash their hands, or whatever the situation is . . . so it is a calming place for them.

"Sometimes when a child is in a conflict or is having a hard time getting in control of their emotions, we ask them, 'Would you like to go visit the cozy corner and take a break?' Most of the time the children will—if they are aware that their emotions are out of control. In the cozy corner, they can fiddle with the little manipulative things, like bubbles and magic wands that help them be peaceful.

"We have a fish that we pass around during share time, and while they are holding the fish everyone else is respectful until it is their turn to talk. We also have Fred, who is a rubber chicken. They know to respect each other when someone is talking. Then they pass it on to someone who wants to talk. Our sharing time is usually held twice a week . . . and is often held after a big activity or preparing for an activity. Once we teach them, the children will often request the sharing circles.

"We have done a little bit of teaching specific lessons and role playing, but we really don't do it formally. You learn as you go here. When we are mediating between two children, we are showing them and modeling them as we go. We do have some kids who come to this with peer mediation training. The site directors use them and they can be super role models."

Modeling and cooperative game-based learning seem to be their most successful strategies in teaching conflict resolution. With this comes giving students greater "voice and choice," which for some teachers can be hard at first. "A lot of teachers say that it is really difficult to let a child *choose* to participate, because our whole theory is that they *have* to participate. They may think, 'If I have half the class not wanting to participate, what am I going to do with the rest of the class?' But we have found that the more exciting you make an activity, the more they will join the activity. When we have the children choose a variation to the game, then they have buy-in because they have given their input. Decision making and independence are important skills, and the more choices we can give them at a young age, the better they will be at it. They can get so creative doing variations and it often prevents conflicts from happening.

"Giving children the words to use is really such a key, especially with the younger ones. A big part of it is just to help them express. They are becoming more and more verbal, but they still need assistance. We are supposed to be these emotional creatures, but to get our emotions into words is difficult."

Melanie knows the importance of getting buy-in from her directors but also sees certain challenges in the process. "Getting a good base of community is tricky because the director has to have a major buy-in to believe in the program. Everyone who has tried conflict resolution, versus the traditional discipline and the time-out situation—once they have given it a try—sees just how successful it can become, how much simpler and smoother their program runs. But talking them into it and having them buy into it have to come from an internal view. Whether it is through a workshop or an 'ah-ha' moment, they have to make that buy-in. But we have found that the programs that really believe in conflict resolution, the programs that have directors with optimistic attitudes, have far less discipline problems and far more cooperation within the system.

"If you go from one site to another site, depending on who is implementing a conflict resolution program you will see a different amount of change at each site. At the sites that are really committed to the conflict resolution idea, you can see the children interacting with each other in a little different manner. They are a little more respectful to each other; there is a little more sense of community. Any teachers or child-care providers—if they haven't tried it—don't know what they are missing. If you have never tried it or have never been exposed to it, you are not aware of how phenomenal it can make your community building and atmosphere."

*Leslie Parker is an assistant director at the Adventure Club and offers a perspective after having been at the club for only eight months. In this story and in the stories of the kids, you hear how the conflict resolution program is still developing and how kids and adults are working toward true mediation and negotiation.*

"Conflict resolution here is really great. When the kids are playing, they are working as a team. When there is conflict, we sit them both down and talk to them about it and get both sides of the story and not judge them right away. We try to put them in the situation of the other person and ask them how they would feel. Then we tell them, 'You probably should not do that, and in the future you should probably come and tell a teacher because the teacher can handle it.' With the older ones we try to let them work with their peers and sometimes they can help with the resolution. A lot of times it works out really well and they feel like they have a sense of responsibility and respect. We talk to them a lot and try to get to know them well, like the name of their dog or something. It really does work, and you know you can go to that when the kids are really having a problem."

*The Greenwood Athletic Club is located in one of the wealthier neighborhoods in Denver and houses a summer camp program that infuses conflict resolution skills into its everyday activities. This athletic club has some eight to ten thousand members and during the summer hosts up to 125 kids in their day camp. Summer camp serves kids ages five to thirteen; the camp day generally*

*runs from 9 A.M. to 4 P.M. Camp lasts all summer long, which is usually ten or eleven weeks.*
*Karen Van der Wall is the summer camp youth director and speaks here about the program.*

"During summer camp, we use conflict resolution on a daily basis from the first day of camp through the last day of camp. We use things from the *Adventures in Peacemaking* conflict resolution guide, including expression skills, games, and other activities—things that the kids don't realize they are learning. A lot of them are team games. Previous to that when we do our counselor training, we do a lot of those kinds of activities to give them a taste of what those activities should look like.

"On the first day of camp we sit the kids down in a group and tell them that this is one of the things that we are doing in camp. I also advertise it in our brochure and say that conflict resolution is one of our skills that we learn during the summer. Camp is all about life skills, at least here, so we expose them to different life skills and we consider conflict resolution to be one of them.

"Here at summer camp, the conflicts we see are around space—like, 'You put your backpack on my coat' or 'You took something out of my lunch without asking' or 'You are not my friend' or not wanting to be at camp. The other kids will help them with this and will include the kids who don't want to be there anymore. That's really cool to see. They know that they need to take care of themselves and each other.

"If there is something that is going on that is starting to ripple to other people or if the staff feels like the kids are out of control, then we will just stop and say, 'You know, it's chat time, let's throw some stuff out there and get some resolution to what is going on with the group,' and they do and everybody seems to be happy and lifted, and we will move on to something else. But we will stop right then, if it seems to ripple, and use group meetings.

"We have kids come in all different times during the summer so we have to transition them. With the old-timers, it is old hat for them. They will say, 'That's not appropriate; remember we learned that last summer. Remember we have to use our words.' Then they will transition the new kids for that week. We usually do a game or activity each day and then have a reflection on the game, like 'What did it teach you?' so that during the week we can say, 'Remember the game we played the other day?' They learn the language and learn how to be in a cohabitative environment. It's been huge.

"The first year we used it, it wasn't the greatest. There were still some glitches because people didn't have the background in it yet. They didn't think it was a huge thing; they would do it and then not do it. There was not much consistency with it. As the same staff would come back year after year, they would bring those skills that they had learned with the program and then those kids that had already been here would continue on with it. Now we have been doing it for six years.

"I think this work is necessary because it goes along with the forty assets that the school district uses, and we do it because it just makes camp a better place to be. It is safer and it's healthier. It is just something that we believe in as a staff. We have seen some kids come out of their shells—the ones who didn't know how to act around other people or were afraid of confrontation. The shy kids seem to blossom a little bit because of it. Kids also don't have to worry about being in an unsafe environment. Even in this ritzy neighborhood, they still come from un-healthy home lifestyles. For those kids it is even more important because they are seeing [unproductive conflict] at home and they don't know how to deal with it and so they come here and learn how to not be so angry, how not to throw stuff, and hopefully take it back to their siblings. We have a lot of siblings here, so they learn how to deal with each other.

"The people that have been here forever have the language. They don't have to relearn anything. It is something that becomes a part of them, like breathing or eating. The oldest kids that have been in it from the start talk about how when they first started they didn't get it and they didn't understand why we were doing it. As they have gotten older they have the skills background, so when conflict hap-pens, their skills kick in and they say, 'Oh, that's exactly what we have been work-ing on.' It is great to see.

"The old-timers especially will say, 'Now, you know that is not OK. We learned this. We need to work this out.' They don't want the staff to be in it at all. When we go through the program at the beginning, we will be there if we have to be there. Usually that is how it starts. You have to be there to model it. As they go along farther into it, most of the time we don't even know until it is over. They will come up to us and say, 'We just had a conflict and we worked it out and we are friends.' So we say, 'Great, what did you do?' and reflect on it afterwards that way. The brand-new kids need a little more help until they figure it out and the light bulb goes on.

"Some of my staff are younger and still need some of those skills that they didn't get growing up because it is kind of a new thing. So I think it is a good idea for them to have to do it. They are going to have to live together for eleven weeks day in and day out with the same group of people. So I think that it's very healthy for them to have some of that. So I start with them and then we move on to the kids after that. We do a week-and-a-half [staff] training, and a full three days out of that deal with conflict resolution and social and developmental issues with the kids, because if they don't buy into it, then the kids won't buy into it at all.

"In my mind, there isn't any one thing that sticks out as being the best thing to do. I think they need a whole program, whether it is a sit-down individual thing or a group thing or a game thing or any kind of audiovisual. I would hate it to be one piece. They are all different kids and all have different learning styles and they need all the aspects that come with it. I am an endorser for the state for after-school programs and camps. I still see staff intervening and not letting the kids do what they need to do. That's hard for me. It's hard to go into other programs where the kids don't get a chance to do their own thing.

"Even if they are getting it at school, they are living in a different world than we grew up in. So they need a lot of these things, and they are not getting them at home. In whatever extracurricular capacity there is, they need to have some of it because conflict happens with sports, it happens with friends, it happens all the time. I don't think it matters what program you use; I think they all have the same idea. It works for all the kids. It has absolutely changed the way we do things here."

CHAPTER FOURTEEN

# REFLECTIONS ON STORIES OF SUCCESS

## Tricia S. Jones and Randy Compton

L ooking back over the chapters in this book, there is much reason for hope in our future. Although conflict resolution education (CRE) may not provide *the* answer to society's problems, it is undeniable that it provides *an* answer, an important answer. Thus, as we draw this volume to a close, we thought it beneficial to comment on some of the larger lessons that emerged from this book, and some of the things we'd still like to see in terms of developments in the field of CRE.

The message of the volume is clear: CRE and related programs are extremely valuable and should be given the attention and resources they deserve. There are five themes that emerge from previous chapters. Each theme implicates some lessons for the field as well as some longings in terms of what is still needed.

1. CRE offers a way to help schools building safe and caring communities.
2. Recognizing the connections between approaches to CRE helps schools combine approaches and get more out of their synergy.
3. There is a tension between adopting and implementing preprepared (or "canned") programs and focusing on philosophies of CRE, which results in flexible practices.
4. There is a need for better CRE standards and accountability to ensure that CRE is making a difference.
5. Many schools are searching for the best ways to grow and expand their CRE efforts and guarantee their longevity.

## Building Caring Communities

How important is community in schools? What does it take to make a constructive, caring community? How can CRE help in that quest? These are critical questions of our work. They are questions that should define the research, practice, and policy agenda of CRE for the future.

How important is community in schools? From what we have heard from the students and teachers interviewed, it is very important. In the first chapter of this book, we looked at a "day in the life" of a typical middle school student, "Carla." Carla lives in a tough world, with limited connections to other people to make her feel safe and functional, much less nurtured and self-actualizing. Carla is like so many of our children—much more alone than we would like. And when our children turn to potential sources of connection and community, the school is an obvious possibility. But, as we noted earlier, too often our schools aren't given sufficient resources or mandate to provide enough community, enough sense of connection, and enough caring—enough, that is, to compensate for the needs born from our existing social structures and the increasing pressures to perform academically without sufficient concern for our youth's social and emotional intelligence.

Most educators realize that they have the potential to make a "home" for children by building a caring community. One hopes that after reading this book they will have some new ideas about how they can realistically make that happen. We have already acknowledged that classroom and schoolwide practices, and social and emotional learning (SEL), are necessary but not sufficient conditions for creating a caring community. What else does it take? The key skill is *caring*. It may take a teacher like Colleen Conrad at Lincoln Junior High School in Fort Collins, Colorado, who has a mission that students will care for and about each other. Throughout the year, she uses classroom practices, SEL, and curriculum infusion to help students get to know themselves and each other. She helps them see that they can count on her and on each other. By the end of the school year, she has helped them create someplace where they can be themselves and feel safe to experiment and learn in the best meaning of those terms.

Or it may take a Felicia Bruce at Brentwood East Middle School in Long Island, who says "Community is my favorite word." In her work with special education students, she helps them see themselves as capable of being valued and valuable community members. Part of that is teaching them that rewards and punishments are shared in the community. Nicole, one of her students, says, "When we're all in the class and one person is not doing what the rest are doing, the teacher says, 'We're all a community and we all have to work together.'"

It certainly takes an understanding that caring does not come without respect. Priscilla Prutzman, in Chapter Twelve, reminds us of how much disrespect can dominate our schools and how corrosive and interpersonally violent this kind of behavior is for our children. For her and the work of her organization, Creative Response to Conflict, helping students become aware of biases and prejudices they may have and disrespectful behavior they may use is critical to helping students find better ways of being together.

Susan Fountain has worked with many schools to help them develop more positive communities. Having worked with UNICEF, Creative Response to Conflict, and Educators for Social Responsibility, she has considerable experience. She remembers working with one school:

> In [one] class, a student came in the middle of the year, when it's very tough to be accepted. The boy who joined was overweight and was fairly "young" in terms of his social skills. He had considerable learning problems. Other children started to tease and scapegoat him. The parents actually got involved in this as well, even trying to get him removed from the school. This developed into a very bad situation. [We] worked with the class, did a lot of group building and cooperative games to build acceptance, then moved to exercises on inclusion and exclusion. We used an activity in which children close their eyes, get different colored stickers on their foreheads, then open their eyes and have to get into a group with those having the same-colored sticker. Children discussed how they all needed to feel they "belong." After doing this activity several times, we varied it by allowing children who were the forefront of the exclusion to have a "different" sticker, so they could feel what it was like to not "belong." This provoked very deep and honest discussions among the children about exclusion within the class. Then they did role plays about the reasons that children get excluded—gender, wearing glasses, different preferences, like sports or not. They talked about what they could do if they were excluded, or were bystanders seeing someone else excluded.

After consistent work on this issue, the class was able to develop a more positive and nurturing community. But first the students needed to understand their own dynamics of disrespect and agree to disallow that behavior.

Caring also means that you care for those who may not be able to care for themselves. In Chapter Eleven, Beverly B. Title tells us about the extremely important work she and others are doing in anti-bullying programs. When individual students refuse to treat others with respect, it is the responsibility of other members of that community to stand up for those being disrespected. Here Beverly helps us see that adults bear the responsibility for protecting our children even while we are attempting to empower and educate them. We see the links between prejudice, bias, and bullying. When some are allowed to be excluded and disrespected, bullying is more likely.

And caring means accountability. This is the most important message of Chapter Ten, in which Alice Ierley and David Claassen-Wilson explain how restorative justice helps build community in schools by making the offender responsible to the community. This responsibility requires that the offender care for and about the person they've hurt and care for and about the larger community as he or she finds ways of "making it right." The students and teachers of Crested Butte Community School are eloquent in their commentary on how powerful restorative justice processes have been for them in turning their discipline system away from punishment toward responsibility and compassion.

The chapters on anti-bullying and restorative justice remind us that the community we create in school depends on the links we have and can create to healthy external communities. And here is where connection with families of students becomes so crucial. Through positive involvement, parents, guardians, and siblings can help strengthen the school community. Indeed, without family support, these programs can create only a "constructive community on campus." Our interviews also remind us that positive developments in the schools can serve to inspire similar developments outside. For example, the teachers at Hillside Elementary in Needham, Massachusetts, learned that their anti-teasing and anti-bullying program found real resonance with parents who wanted to learn to use these same principles and techniques to reduce sibling teasing and bullying.

Having acknowledged the importance of community and the role of CRE in creating positive community, let's consider some areas where growth is needed. What are some of the things that may prevent CRE from achieving maximum benefit in terms of developing constructive and caring communities?

It would be lovely to have a better understanding of the process through which community develops and is maintained. We have some wonderful insights from the schools we visited, and we have the wisdom of experts in the field, but there is still much to know about how schools with various challenges (in terms of current structures, resource levels, student populations, and so on) can most appropriately begin to build community through CRE.

If students and teachers are not given the necessary skills, they won't be able to build community. Throughout the interviews, students and teachers in schools with restorative justice efforts, anti-bias programs, curriculum infusion, and after-school programs mentioned that more attention to basic skill development would be helpful. This was particularly noted in some of the after-school programs, where several students knew they had to solve problems but said they lacked the skills to be able to do so and didn't think those skills had been provided in the after-school program. Without skills, the students or teachers can envision what a caring community may look like but are unable to "get there." As important as it is to build the vision and align people around the need to achieve the vision, it is also important to give them tools to create that envisioned reality.

And, as we all know, providing those tools forces us to face difficult resource issues. Skill development does not happen overnight. In Chapter Nine, Rachel A. Poliner talks about the learning curve needed for students and teachers to learn new skills. Knowledge is only the first step. Without practice, application, and review, the new skill will not really be learned. Rachel's discussion of curriculum infusion programs also underscores how patient we need to be when asking teachers to develop new teaching skills. The teachers at Pierce Middle School in Milton, Massachusetts, help us appreciate that teaching teachers to infuse CRE effectively is a multiyear process. Once learned, it is a "way of teaching" that permeates the entire educational experience, but that level of mastery is hard won.

An area of connection that can be explored more fruitfully is the link between anti-bullying, bias awareness, and restorative justice programs. Bias and prejudice lie at the heart of exclusion and the destruction of community. Contempt for others may be the most interpersonally violent emotion, with humiliation its hideous consequence. Programs that combat contempt and humiliation are more effective if they combine forces. In general, even with the wonderful work they do, these programs often function as separate entities. Bias awareness programs concentrate on helping people understand operative biases, but usually do not provide resources for how to deal with bullies or how to restore community when contempt or bullying is present. Likewise, anti-bullying programs may discuss sources of bias, but may not help students see deeper issues such as stereotyping, institutionalized racism, and homophobia. Restorative justice programs may not deal with the roots of bias and bullying that underlie specific conflicts. Schools may find they can implement only one program at a time so that they aren't overwhelmed. By recognizing the important connections between programs and enhancing these connections over time, schools can benefit greatly.

It seems appropriate to remember that CRE programs are most successful when adults model constructive conflict management and caring community for children. We don't want to give the impression that community-building efforts are only things that adults should "help students do." It is as important for the adult members of schools and external communities to learn and enact these constructive behaviors for themselves. Schools can examine whether there is exclusion among staff, bullying between teachers (as there often is between adults in the corporate world), staff inability to effectively negotiate their own conflicts, and the like. David Sprague and Lisa Peloquin, the guidance counselor and teacher in Williamsburg, Massachusetts, explained their success in developing constructive community this way: "We don't teach it, we live it." When adults start living the lessons they want their children to learn, amazing things can happen.

## Connections That Empower

The structure of this book assumes, to some extent, that the different types of CRE are unique enough to deserve special and separate attention. Though we agree they are special, we are struck by the connections among all the CRE efforts witnessed throughout this volume. None of the schools we were fortunate enough to visit focus only on one approach to CRE. They have already arrived at the conclusion that if one tool is good, several tools may be better—especially when working with complex issues and complex goals. Here we'd like to articulate some of the connections these schools are enacting that may serve as models for others in similar situations. Some of these connections suggest foundations that educators feel need to be established first. Other connections involve various programs that can link in exciting ways.

Three foundations were evident to the educators we talked to: basic, effective classroom practices; social and emotional learning; and the construction of community in the school and classroom. Not surprisingly, the first two are necessary but not sufficient conditions for the third. Because we've already discussed community, we'll focus on the others.

The importance of basic practices to support effective CRE is striking. In Chapter Three, Carol Miller Lieber reminds us that nothing will happen if the classroom and the school cannot operate with basic practices that provide clarity, direction, and support for a learning initiative that empowers children to "work it out" and participate in making a peaceful school climate. We see Carol's wisdom echoed throughout the book's narratives, but perhaps it is most clearly evidenced in the chapters on negotiation, curriculum integration, and after-school programs. In fact, when doing the interviews, we were struck by how hard it was to decide which portions would go with which chapter. So many examples referred to the importance of co-creating basic rules for school and classroom interaction as a precursor to the success of CRE. We are reminded of one of our colleagues who worked with a troubled school that was looking to use curriculum integration. After meeting with the teachers it became apparent to him that they "needed to build the container first." As he said in one conversation, "If they can't make it a safe place to be, none of this other work will get done." The teachers he was working with realized that, for them, the first hurdle was learning how to institute basic practices that resulted in civil interaction among students. Their insights are shared by many educators we interviewed.

But perhaps the most important foundation is SEL. As Carolyn Saarni suggests, when children develop emotional competence, it is integrally intertwined with the development of conflict competence and social competence.[1] If we want our children to be able to manage conflict effectively, we need to appreciate that conflict is an inherently emotional experience.[2] An emotionally incompetent student cannot be an effective manager of his or her own conflicts and cannot reasonably help others manage their conflicts.

In Chapter Four, Rachael Kessler makes an excellent case for why we should have SEL embedded in any CRE program. The interviews we did with students and teachers resound with testimony to that effect. The students realize how important it is to be able to talk about feelings and have that talk respected and appreciated by others. As Johanna and M.J., the first- and second-grade teachers at the Anne T. Dunphy School articulated, the children need to become comfortable with emotion. Then they can achieve the emotional awareness of both self and others and engage in the kinds of emotional perspective taking and strategic emotional expression that we consider the hallmarks of emotional competence.

Most educators think of SEL as something that should happen in the early elementary grades. And they are right. It should happen there—with gusto. However, the students we talked to from middle schools and high schools across the country are convincing in their support of similar initiatives in their schools. Whether the child is six or sixteen, regular education or "special needs," SEL is necessary if we are to raise youth to be successful in all aspects of their lives.

In addition to the various techniques and materials teachers can use to promote social and emotional development, one of the insights from this book is how valuable the expressive arts can be as a means of conflict discovery. As Sarah Pirtle comments in Chapter Eight, through the arts children of all ages can come to a much deeper awareness of their emotional selves, their emotional reactions to conflict, and their emotional growth through conflict. Throughout the chapters and the accompanying interviews, we heard teachers and students talking about how they used dance, theater, creative writing, music, visual arts, or some combination as a means of learning and living a CRE effort—peer negotiation, peer mediation, bias awareness, anti-bullying. There is such important work still to be done in this area of connection. Zephryn Conte and Russell Brunson, in their interviews, impress us with their work with the Partnership on the Arts and Conflict Resolution Education. But even they would probably agree that we've just begun. The potential is unbounded.

All of the programs discussed in this book may benefit from linkage to peer mediation. Peer mediation is the most prevalent, best known, and best understood form of CRE, as Richard Cohen and Paul I. Kaplan discuss in Chapters Six and Seven. But peer mediation can partner with other CRE efforts in new and exciting ways. Involving peer mediators with bias awareness initiatives, restorative justice, and anti-bullying efforts is full of powerful possibilities. With appropriate guidance, the peer mediators can help manage lower-level conflict involving bias and power abuse. When the conflict may be too intense for mediators to intervene, the mediators can also fulfill other functions, such as providing informal training to children in lower grades, giving presentations on issues, acting as school ambassadors, and serving as "witnesses" (as mentioned in Chapter Six). Peer mediation has natural links to programs that teach basic collaborative negotiation skills to students, as Jennifer K. Druliner and Heather E. Prichard discuss in Chapter Five. In Brentwood East and Brentwood North middle schools, several of the students who had been in the Program for Young Negotiators and had also become peer mediators discussed the natural connections they saw between the programs.

## Preprepared Program- or Philosophy-Based Practices?

There is a serious tension between preprepared programs or curricula that are administered in a lockstep fashion and conflict resolution education initiatives around a basic philosophy or set of principles that allows for flexibility in selecting practices geared to accomplish those objectives. We'll talk about this tension as "program v. practices." In all of the schools we visited, and indeed, in all of the conversations we have had with colleagues, this tension presents itself as a critical challenge facing the field, schools, and practitioners.

Where does this tension come from? Ironically, it comes from an attempt to promote quality conflict resolution education efforts. Unfortunately, it actually may be inhibiting them.

Over the past several years there has been increasing pressure from federal and state governments to use funds to support only "research-proven efforts." This is a laudable goal and one that we support wholeheartedly in terms of the emphasis on efficacy and accountability.

It is important for funders and educators to remember that the emphasis on "research-proven" efforts does not mean they must rely only on canned programs and curricula that can be imported into schools. There can be confusion on the part of educators and administrators when they try to identify which efforts are considered "research proven" in order to secure funding from state and federal agencies.

We urge educators to see the emphasis on research-proven efforts as including both "research-proven programs and research-proven practices." The U.S. Department of Education's Safe and Drug-Free Schools office also encourages this broader thinking in order to support a range of effective conflict resolution education efforts.

In many cases, the research support for successful programs is limited to a specific context of application, yet the assumption is that any school using this program as presented should receive the same benefits. When implemented, the programs may not "perform" as expected because the context in which they are being used is significantly different from the context in which they were tested. Does this mean the programs were poor quality? Not at all; the situation is more analogous to knowing which tool to use when building a house. Using a hammer to saw wood doesn't make the hammer a poor tool. In addition, canned programs can prevent schools from using the wisdom available within their own community. If we believe diversity is a source of strength, it behooves us to encourage schools to develop practices that enhance and appreciate diversity.

All the successful schools we talked with have something in common: none of them used a canned program without adaptation to accomplish their CRE goals. Is this merely a coincidence? No. Several teachers commented that it was a conscious and intentional move on their part not to use a lockstep program, because it simply would not meet the needs of the students and school. Maureen Keeney of the New Castle County Detention Center, a huge fan of the Program for Young Negotiators, argued forcefully that as good as that program is, it cannot be inflexibly applied. It must be tailored to the needs of the students and school. An assistant principal at Pierce Middle School and Carolann Wais of the Laconia School District in New Hampshire, strong proponents for curriculum infusion, know that giving a package of preprepared lessons to teachers may seem helpful but does little to develop their own means of infusion that fit their style and will become a permanent part of their teaching repertoire. Susan Fountain and Priscilla Prutzman, from Creative Response to Conflict, know that a bias awareness initiative is not a set of exercises but a carefully planned intervention and learning experience molded to the issues of the school. We see this theme repeated throughout the narratives in this book. It is a lesson we need to learn as a field.

Although programs and preprepared curricula are valuable tools in a larger effort, they are not sufficient in and of themselves and may have undesired consequences if applied inflexibly. Most successful CRE efforts are the result of careful consideration of the underlying principles and philosophy the school is trying to achieve. This requires the school administrators, teachers, staff, and other stakeholders to identify their educational principles and practices. Once stakeholders can agree to a core set of principles, they can develop an array of techniques and use them as needed and in concert in order to determine the approach that best maximizes the outcome at that time. The experience of the Hannah More School is an excellent example. Their establishment of a peer mediation program for special education students and their current development of a curriculum infusion model exemplify the power of working from a philosophy rather than from a "program" mentality.

Once a school has a clear handle on its guiding philosophy, it is freer to select components of preprepared programs that meet its needs. But in this case, the philosophy leads the program, not vice versa. The builder chooses the hammer not because it's there but because it's needed.

Working from a philosophy also means that the schools can better tailor the effort to fit their needs and expand the effort effectively. If schools isolate programs, seeing each as a separate piece without appreciating their potential interaction, they miss the whole picture, as Gail Alexander from Brentwood North Middle School in Long Island commented. With a philosophy in place, the school can better determine how and when to incorporate a new program into existing efforts.

What are some potentially significant advances in the move toward embracing "philosophy"? The more we can help schools engage in initial dialogues about their underlying philosophy, the more we can avoid implementing programs that are ultimately ineffective. Honest dialogue about needs, interests, and goals should be a mandatory first step in any CRE effort.

We also can learn from our own experiences about what kinds of approaches and combinations work well in the field. This is another form of "research-proven practice." Permutations of programs developed to meet an underlying philosophy may prove useful for others as well as for the initiators. As conflict resolution educators, we should be more diligent about documenting our experiences in thoughtful and rigorous ways so that "evidence" can be shared with the larger community. It is hoped that through these efforts we can help government and funding agencies understand that CRE cannot be a one-size-fits-all strategy.

## Program Standards and Accountability

Some conflict resolution educators complain that schools do not welcome their efforts with open arms. Some of this resistance comes from the lack of a mandate to teach and test these skills. However, it may also be because school administrators have not been given a set of standards by which to assess quality CRE programs. We have certainly heard that comment from administrators and teachers we have worked with. "How do I know this effort will be a quality one? How do I know it will make a difference? How do we set realistic and measurable goals?" And as resources dwindle, these questions are asked more forcefully.

It is incumbent on our professional associations to develop and distribute a set of standards, or at least guidelines, to define components of a quality CRE initiative. This work has already been conducted for SEL programs in the wonderful book *Promoting Social and Emotional Learning: Guidelines for Educators.*[3] The Association for Conflict Resolution has recently issued new standards for CRE. These standards are available on the ACR website, www.acresolution.org/learningcenter.

Schools are forced to speak the language of outcomes. We should realize that this is not going to change. Nor should it change. Outcomes are important. The question is whether the outcomes are appropriately identified and measured. There is a great deal we can do to make sure the outcomes used to assess CRE are valid. Conflict resolution educators should embrace the opportunity to have dialogue about outcomes, to define indices of success, to offer additional means of assessment. Although some schools and practitioners are beginning to do so, we believe that this dialogue should be promoted more widely, perhaps even on a national website such as that of the Association for Conflict Resolution.

One challenge to developing standards is the breadth of the field. As we have discussed, people have differing ideas about how many kinds of programs are included in CRE. In this volume, we can see the breadth and richness of the field. Even the narrower definitions of the field are quite eclectic. The broader the field, the more general the standards needed to cover it. If standards are too general, they lack utility; they provide no real guidance regarding procurement, policy, and implementation decisions.

It makes more sense for members of the CRE field to develop subareas of standards (for example, standards for peer mediation programs, standards for anti-bullying programs, standards for bias awareness programs) and to articulate suggested standards for expanding and integrating a series of efforts in a whole-school or community-linked project (such as those discussed in Chapter Two). A model for the former is the "Standards for Peer Mediation Programs," published by the National Association for Mediation in Education in 1994 and now available on the Association for Conflict Resolution website. Models for a community-linked project are found in Richard Bodine and Donna Crawford's *Handbook of Conflict Resolution Education*[4] and in *Promoting Social and Emotional Learning*, which we've already mentioned.

Identification of standards and outcomes for assessment also can start on a school or district level. For example, let's look at the work currently being done in the Needham School District in Needham, Massachusetts. About a year ago, this school district decided that it wanted to develop a district-wide social and emotional wellness initiative. (This district has five elementary schools, one middle school, and one high school.) Being very wise, the administrators agreed that the first step would be to identify goals of such a program in terms of basic competencies appropriate to each grade level. Over the past year, a select team of teachers and administrators from each school has been meeting and working with a consultant to define these competencies. They started with three core competencies: self-awareness and self-management, social and interpersonal skills, and decision-making skills. They have defined and refined expected outcomes in these areas for K–2, 3–5, 6–8, and 9–12 grade levels. Now that they have identified specific outcomes associated with each competency area, they are reviewing their current curricula and programs to see what needs to be added to provide students with a total social and emotional wellness education. They are also working with an evaluation research consultant to find or develop measures of these specific outcomes.

The educators and administrators of the Needham School District see accountability and assessment as allies, not enemies. They realize that the better they define goals, and outcomes congruent with those goals, the more likely they are to achieve both. They are willing to devote the resources to make this happen in the most productive way.

As the Needham experience and other examples suggest, partnerships between researchers and educators can promote valid assessment. Schools, districts, and professional associations can enlist the aid of researchers to help them operationalize outcomes so that those outcomes can be measured and all interested parties can witness the fruits of educators' and students' efforts.

## How Can We Make CRE Last?

It is frustrating to see educators implement CRE efforts that never become a lasting part of the school. Several authors commented on the challenges of institutionalizing CRE. Many of the teachers and administrators we interviewed gave examples of CRE attempts that flourished for a short time but fell by the wayside after four or five years.

Conflict resolution educators recognize the need to institutionalize their efforts. A more thorough discussion of this issue can be found in a chapter in *Does It Work? The Case for Conflict Resolution Education in Our Nation's Schools.*[5] Examples of effective institutionalization practices are included in volume 19, issue 4 of *Conflict Resolution Quarterly*, the journal of the Association for Conflict Resolution.

Here we offer some insights gained from the interviews conducted for this volume. They show ways in which programs can last and continue to improve.

### Involving Key People in Planning

Most educators can recite the mantra that strategic planning is a key to the success of a new initiative. Those same educators can probably count on one hand the number of effective strategic planning efforts they have witnessed or participated in. It's like dieting. Everybody knows what it really takes to lose weight, but most of us just don't do it. The schools that "do it" make sure that critical stakeholders are involved in making decisions about the CRE efforts and share responsibility for them. In successful cases, administrators are very important in the process. The more administrative support that exists for the program, the better.

## Setting Goals and Objectives

Successful schools, like those in the Needham district, also spend time clarifying what they want to achieve, how they will get there, and how they will know when it happens. They also realize that goals change over time and that what they wanted to accomplish in the past may not be what they want to accomplish now.

## Expanding and Adapting CRE Efforts to Meet Changing Needs

One key to institutionalization is adopting a "growth" frame of mind. If you think in terms of growth and incremental achievement, you automatically think in terms of expansion and flexibility. Schools and the communities they serve are dynamic. CRE efforts must be dynamic as well.

We saw several examples of thoughtful expansion efforts in our interviews. Many schools, such as Lincoln Junior High School in Colorado, started with a peer mediation program, then developed a CRE class (six weeks), and then moved to a curriculum infusion model. The Hannah More School in Maryland began a very successful peer mediation program and is adding a conflict curriculum. Horace Mann Middle School started a peer mediation program and then expanded the kinds of conflicts the program handled, using peer mediation to deal with issues of bullying and bias to improve school culture. Hillside Elementary School began an Easing the Teasing program for students that eventually grew to involve parents and family issues as well. At Coal Creek Elementary School, the peer mediation program may soon expand to include a restorative justice process. Boulder High School had a number of CRE activities but added its Multicultural Action Coalition to meet the students' needs for more bias awareness and cultural sensitivity in the school and added a restorative justice program to deal with the more serious discipline issues in their school.

All of these schools understand that change happens. You can embrace it or be frustrated by it. They see their CRE efforts as works in progress; this philosophy helps make the efforts successful.

## Assessing and Evaluating Your CRE Effort

Successful schools adopt what researchers call an "action research" orientation. They are careful to define what they are looking for. And then they actually look—regularly and carefully—to see whether the CRE effort is doing what it was intended to do. They use this feedback to make improvements in the CRE as the effort unfolds. This approach guarantees a continual monitoring process and program flexibility.

## Listening to Students

Programs that expand based on assessment and evaluation know how to "listen" to information from the school and the surrounding environment. One of the successful strategies we have seen in our work is the importance of listening to the students—the reason the schools exist in the first place.

We cannot overstate the importance of listening to youth when creating, evaluating, and improving programs. They are the ones "working it out," so their feedback is critical. Too often programs are adult centered; when they become student centered, even student driven, there is much more buy-in, not to mention authenticity and freshness. Some of the programs we report in this book came about when adults listened to the students and helped create a program based on students' interests. Having students involved and treating them as empowered partners in CRE fosters responsibility and organizational skills. In our experience, "If they help build it, it will stay."

## Thinking Systemically

Each school is a system unto itself and is embedded in larger systems that influence its nature and direction. Within the school system, a key to successful, lasting CRE is the willingness of administrators to adapt structures to support functions. Two examples come to mind. In Chapter Nine on curriculum infusion, Rachel A. Poliner talked about how schools need to be willing to examine and change structures that make it difficult for teachers to develop infusion skills. The administrators and teachers at Pierce Middle School also explained that one factor in their success with the National Curriculum Integration Project was their willingness to use teaching teams in the same grade in order to provide additional time for meetings and training. The Anne T. Dunphy School provides an excellent example of how looping structures in early elementary grades provide support for SEL programs. Allowing students to stay together for two years with the same teacher means they can build strong relationships and caring community.

Schools can also help their CRE programs last by attending to the links between these efforts and state education standards, as we discussed in Chapter Two. As Carolann Wais, the assistant superintendent of the Administrative School Unit #63, said, "They have to see results. And it's not the administrators, it's the school boards. Because it's the boards that decide what goes into the budget. It will take data and we're learning how to collect that data. You also have to have somebody who's passionate about what they're trying to get. There's got to be the link to student achievement."

At the very least, administrators and teachers should review current structures in terms of how much time teachers have to work with CRE. Something as simple as planning and meeting time can make all the difference to a program's longevity.

## Working Smarter Not Harder

Several times we have mentioned the incredible workload most teachers have and how hard it is for them to add anything to their plate. So if CRE is going to last, it needs to operate on the principle of helping teachers work smarter not harder. All teachers and administrators ask, "How will the teachers fit this in? What are the education pressures? What are the educational incentives? Is this an add-on, or is this part of something more?"

Structural changes can help teachers work smarter, but other methods are also available. Classroom practices, curriculum infusion techniques, and SEL can create not only a caring community in the classroom but also an efficient learning community in the classroom. Once teachers understand how to use these skills, they find they have much less disruption and can spend less time on discipline and more time on content. When they appreciate that curricula can be infused with other information, such as CRE, they begin to see how the same action can have multiple benefits. Once teachers make this move, they can also see the power of integrated education, what can happen when we teach holistically to meet the needs of the whole child.

## Selling the Principles and Practices

Even with all the strategies we've already mentioned, new ideas have to be "sold" to decision makers and those who will be teaching the new material. Whether a conflict resolution program is new or old, decision makers need to be convinced of its benefit if they are to include it in an already full educational agenda. The good news is that proof exists. Those implementing programs need to spend more time spreading this word, and the field should help teachers, practitioners, and program coordinators in that process.

# A Call to Action

We believe that CRE has proven its merit. It is an important answer to society's problems. Thus we'd like to call educators, departments of education, professional associations, and funders to support CRE.

Educators, if you are like your colleagues in this book and have tried CRE, spread the word. Share your experiences with your peers; help them consider how to become involved in CRE. If you have not been involved in CRE, consider how you may take the ideas in this book and put them into practice in your own class. In the appendixes we provide a number of resources that can help you in this exploration.

State and federal departments of education, you have a great deal of influence over whether CRE programs are encouraged and supported. Follow the lead of some state departments of education, such as that of Maine, that have developed learning principles and links to CRE proving how relevant CRE is to many of the learning principles. Once those links are made the superintendents and school boards, as well as teachers and parents, will see the wisdom of adopting these initiatives. At the federal level, a great deal of wonderful work has already been done. We can continue by supporting the process of identifying "research-proven programs" and expanding that to include "research-proven practices."

Professional associations, we encourage you to do as much as possible to promote CRE. You can provide valuable guidance through the development of standards and guidelines, as discussed in an earlier section of this chapter. Through conferences and professional meetings, you can share the experiences, achievements, and research-proven results of CRE with a larger community of educators and practitioners. Through your association publications, you can report on the state of the field and encourage research and practice that will further the ultimate goals of CRE. Your associations can also become more actively involved in policy initiatives by networking with influential groups in education, lobbying for action, and facilitating efforts undertaken by these other groups.

Private and public funders, we encourage you to establish and/or strengthen your funding area for CRE. We already have a large community of skilled service delivery organizations that deserve continued support. However, there are serious needs to fund preservice education programs so that colleges of education can teach new teachers about CRE. This is an area in which the federal government could become very involved. We need funds to support additional research on program development, especially on integrating and expanding CRE efforts. We need funding for research that looks at the long-term impacts of CRE on students and schools. There are many areas to support and funders can easily find a niche in which to make a long-term difference.

If we are to create a society based on the principles of our founders, we need to include in our educational mission the processes of democratic engagement through which kids help make peace in our world. We hope that this book not only educates you on the best practices but also inspires you to take action to promote them.

## In Their Own Words

We offer one last suggestion, for educators in general and those interested in CRE specifically: take time to listen to the stories and strategies of your students. In their words you will hear, as we did, how much they want to have you involved in their lives. How much they long to share what they feel in a place that feels good to them. How much they need their schools to provide the community that is so often lacking outside the school walls. How much they need connection and how much they'd prefer positive connection to the alternative. How much they hope for a bright future and how ready they are to work toward it. And how much they believe CRE can contribute to their lives. In their actions you will find tremendous hope for the future.

# POSTSCRIPT
## The Importance of Supporting Conflict Resolution Education

## Amalia G. Cuervo

In this unique and valuable contribution to the field of conflict resolution education, *Kids Working It Out* authors Tricia S. Jones and Randy Compton provide a powerful and substantive volume on the benefits of working with students to solve problems peacefully.

In recent years, the value of conflict resolution education has been recognized by a number of federal agencies responsible for funding violence prevention and safe school and community initiatives. Among these agencies are the U.S. Department of Justice, the U.S. Department of Education, and the National Endowment for the Arts.

From 1995–2001, the U.S. Department of Justice, Office of Juvenile Justice and Delinquency Prevention (OJJDP) and the U.S. Department of Education, Safe and Drug-Free Schools funded the National Center for Conflict Resolution Education. The Center provided technical assistance and training to schools and published a manual, authored by Donna Crawford and Richard Bodine, called *A Guide to Conflict Resolution Education*. Originally published in 1996, it has recently been updated in 2002. (See Appendix B for information on ordering the publication.) The Center pioneered successfully the use of conflict resolution in secure juvenile justice facilities that resulted in improved organizational climate and reduced tension and conflicts among juveniles. The Center also supported the Peaceable Classroom approach of teaching students the foundation abilities, principles, and problem-solving processes of conflict resolution. These classrooms then become the building blocks of the Peaceable School, a comprehensive whole-school methodology using conflict resolution as a system of managing the entire school environment.

Recognizing the natural affinity between conflict resolution education and the arts, in 1997 the National Endowment for the Arts (NEA) and OJJDP collaborated in developing the Partnership for Conflict Resolution Education in the Arts. This national leadership initiative is designed to strengthen community-based arts programs for youth at risk of drug abuse and violence through professional development workshops on conflict resolution education.

In 1999, the U.S. Department of Justice established an office of Community Dispute Resolution (CDR) to promote and coordinate the use of conflict resolution activities and programs funded by the Department. CDR encourages the use of conflict resolution in a variety of settings, including schools, police, courts, and communities as a means to prevent violence, reduce tensions, and enhance the quality of life.

Under the No Child Left Behind Act of 2001, the U.S. Department of Education legislation for elementary and secondary education includes conflict resolution programs among the list of allowable activities for local educational agencies. However, funding for such programs will be contingent on state and local priorities and how well the CRE programs meet the principles of effectiveness as outlined in the legislation.

Educational standards in today's schools require that students be able to read with understanding, think critically about information, be effective communicators, work collaboratively to problem solve, and make sound decisions. Comprehensive conflict resolution education strategies can provide students with opportunities to learn and practice these critical life skills and thus be more successful in school.

Further research is needed to continue to identify the most effective programs and practices to ensure continued funding. Future support for conflict resolution programs may continue as long as program developers design and implement programs that are based on the best research and knowledge in the field.

Conflict resolution education holds great promise for making our schools and our world a safer, more peaceable place, and schools have the valuable opportunity to be leaders in this important effort of social change. I sincerely hope that local and national governmental and educational agencies support schools in taking up this challenge.

# NOTES

## Foreword

1. "'Fearless' Teacher Halted Killings," *International Herald Tribune*, Apr. 29, 2002, p. 7.

## Chapter One

1. Elkind, D., "The Cosmopolitan School," *Educational Leadership*, 2000–2001, *58*(4), 12–17.
2. Wood, C., *Time to Teach, Time to Learn: Changing the Pace of School*, Greenfield, Mass.: Northeast Foundation for Children, 1999, p. 5.
3. Pipher, M., *The Shelter of Each Other*, New York: Putnam, 1996, p. 76.
4. The Sentencing Project, "Facts About Prisons and Prisoners," [www.sentencingproject.org/brief/brief.htm], Apr. 2002; U.S. Department of Justice, Bureau of Justice Statistics, "Prison Statistics," [www.ojp.usdoj.gov/bjs/prisons.htm], June 30, 2001; Li, Z., "Source of Number of Inmates in China's Prison System?" [www.tibet.ca/wtnarchive/1993/10/14-2_6.html], Oct. 14, 1993; Mosher, S., "Chinese Prison Labor," *Society*, Nov.-Dec. 1991, *29*, 49–59; Butterfield, F., "U.S. Expands Its Lead in the Rate of Imprisonment," *New York Times*, Feb. 11, 1992, p. 16.
5. Center for Media Education, "Children & Television: Frequently Asked Questions," [www.cme.org/children/kids_tv/c_and_t.html], 1997.
6. Silverman, J. G., Raj, A., Mucci, L. A., and Hathaway, J. E., "Dating Violence Against Adolescent Girls and Associated Substance Use, Unhealthy Weight Control, Sexual Risk Behavior, Pregnancy, and Suicidality," *Journal of the American Medical Association*, 2001, *286*(5), 572–579.

7. Center for Defense Information, "Fiscal Year 2002 Budget," [www.cdi.org/issues/budget/fy'02/index.html], 2002.

8. National Center for Education Statistics, "Teachers' Perceptions About Serious Problems in Their Schools, by Type and Control of School: 1990–91 and 1993–94," [nces.ed.gov/pubs2002/digest2001/tables/dt073.asp], May 2002.

9. Elliot, D., Hamburg, B., and Williams, K. (eds.), *Violence in American Schools*, New York: Cambridge University Press, 1999, p. 3.

10. Maine Project Against Bullying, [lincoln.midcoast.com/~wps/against/bullying.html], Apr. 2000. This is a list of facts based on the current research about bullying.

11. Brener, N. D., Simon, T. R., Krug, E. G., and Lowry, R., "Recent Trends in Violence-Related Behaviors Among High School Students in the United States," *Journal of the American Medical Association*, 1999, *282*(5), 440–446.

12. Associated Press, "Report Finds School Crime Declines Slightly," *Boulder Daily Camera*, Nov. 1, 2001, p. 10A.

13. Nelsen, J., *Positive Discipline*, New York: Ballantine, 1996, pp. xi–xiii.

14. Salend, S., *Creating Inclusive Classrooms: Effective and Reflective Practices* (4th ed.), Upper Saddle River, N.J.: Merrill, 2001.

15. Americans for Divorce Reform, "Divorce Rates Marriage Rates—What Happened," www.divorcereform.org/rates.html]; Kreider, R. M., and Fields, J. M., "Number, Timing, and Duration of Marriages and Divorces: 1996," *U.S. Census Bureau Current Population Reports*, Feb. 2002, p. 18.

16. Hersch, P., *A Tribe Apart: A Journey into the Heart of American Adolescence*, New York: Ballantine, 1999.

17. Lapham, L., and others, "School on a Hill: On the Design and Redesign of American Education," *Harper's*, Sept. 2001, *303*(1816), 52.

18. Brendtro, L., Brokenleg, M., and VanBockern, S., *Reclaiming Youth at Risk: Our Hope for the Future*, Bloomington, Ind.: National Educational Service, 1990, pp. 23–25.

19. Brendtro, Brokenleg, and VanBockern, *Reclaiming Youth at Risk*, p. 25.

20. Lapham and others, "School on a Hill," p. 50.

21. Banks, J. A., and Banks, C.A.M., *Multicultural Education: Issues and Perspectives* (2nd ed.), Boston: Allyn & Bacon, 1993.

# Chapter Two

1. Western Justice Foundation, "Transcript of Remarks by Sandra Day O'Connor, Associate Justice, Supreme Court of the United States, on the Occasion of the Dedication Ceremony for the Friends Building of the Western Justice Center Foundation," [www.westernjustice.org/dedication.htm], Feb. 8, 2002.

2. Association for Conflict Resolution, *Recommended Guidelines for Effective CRE Programs in K–12 Classrooms, Schools and School Districts*, Washington, D.C.: Association for Conflict Resolution, 2002.

3. Inger, M., *ERIC Clearinghouse on Urban Education Digest*, June 1991, no. 74 (EDO-UD-89-7).

4. Bodine, R. J., and Crawford, D. K., *The Handbook of Conflict Resolution Education: A Guide to Building Quality Programs in Schools*, San Francisco: Jossey-Bass, 1998.

5. U.S. Department of Education, *Violence and Discipline Problems in U.S. Public Schools 1996–1997*, Washington, D.C.: U.S. Department of Education, 1998.

6. U.S. Department of Education, *Violence and Discipline Problems.*

7. Girard, K., and Koch, S., *Conflict Resolution in the Schools: A Manual for Educators,* San Francisco: Jossey-Bass, 1996.

8. Bodine and Crawford, *Handbook of Conflict Resolution Education,* pp. 55–59.

9. Collaborative for Academic, Social, and Emotional Learning, [www.casel.org], 2002. The website for the Collaborative, also discussed in our Appendixes, provides resources on all aspects of social and emotional learning.

10. Peterson, R., and Skiba, R., "Creating School Climates That Prevent School Violence," *Social Studies,* July-Aug. 2001, *92*(4), 167–175.

11. Ury, W., *The Third Side: Why We Fight and How We Can Stop,* New York: Penguin Books, 2000, p. 7.

12. These statistics are from a Gallup Poll conducted on the Columbine High School massacre, [www.cnn.com/SPECIALS/1998/schools/], May 1999. (Please note that although the Web address shows an incorrect year, the website is correct.)

13. Maine Department of Education, "Learning Results," [www.state.me.us/education/lres/homepage.htm], 2002.

14. Century Middle School, Thornton, Colo., "Challenging Use Minds of Students: Pathway to the Future," "The Eight Student Traits," and "2001/2002 Ends Statements," 2002. These are unpublished documents from Century Middle School. Please contact the Adams-12 School District, Colo.

15. Jones, T. S., and Kmitta, D. (eds.), *Does It Work? The Case for Conflict Resolution Education in Our Nation's Schools,* Washington, D.C.: Conflict Resolution Education Network, 2000.

16. Wiltenberg, M., "Peace Talks," *Christian Science Monitor,* Dec. 4, 2001, *93*(260), 13.

17. U.S. Office of the Surgeon General, *Youth Violence: A Report of the Surgeon General,* Washington, D.C.: U.S. Department of Health and Human Services, 2001, p. 110.

18. U.S. Department of Education, "Creating Safe and Drug-Free Schools: An Action Guide," [www.ed.gov/offices/OESE/SDFS/actguid/index.html], Apr. 1997.

19. U.S. Department of Education, "Safe, Disciplined and Drug-Free Schools Exemplary and Promising Programs List," [www.ed.gov/offices/OERI/ORAD/KAD/expert_panel/drug-free.html], 2002.

20. Jones and Kmitta, *Does It Work?*

21. Sandy, S. V., and Cochran, K., "The Development of Conflict Resolution Skills in Children: Preschool to Adolescence," in M. Deutsch and P. Coleman (eds.), *The Handbook of Conflict Resolution: Theory and Practice* (pp. 316–342), San Francisco: Jossey-Bass, 2001, p. 340.

# Chapter Three

1. Payton, J., Wardlaw, D., Graczyk, P., Bloodworth, M., Tampsett, C., and Weissberg, R., "Social and Emotional Learning: A Framework for Promoting Mental Health and Reducing Risk Behaviors in Children and Youth," *Journal of School Health,* 2000, *70*(5), 179–185.

2. Fernie, D., "Becoming a Student: Messages from First Settings," *Theory into Practice,* Winter 1988, *27*(1), 3–8.

3. Kreidler, W. J., and Furlong, L., *Adventures in Peacemaking,* Cambridge, Mass.: Educators for Social Responsibility, 1996.

4. Poliner, R., and Lieber, C. M., *Building Community Through Student-Staff Orientation, Forums, and Retreats* (working title), Cambridge, Mass.: Educators for Social Responsibility, Fall 2002.

5. Poliner and Lieber, *Building Community Through Student-Staff Orientation, Forums, and Retreats.*

6. Aronson, E., *Nobody Left to Hate: Teaching Compassion After Columbine,* New York: Worth Publishers, 2000.

7. Johnson, D., Johnson, R., and Holubec, E., *Cooperative Learning in the Classroom and School,* Alexandria, Va.: Association for Supervision and Curriculum Development, 1994.

## Chapter Four

1. Goleman, D., *Emotional Intelligence,* New York: Bantam Books, 1995, p. 261.

2. Goleman, *Emotional Intelligence,* pp. 88–89, 283–284.

3. Goleman, *Emotional Intelligence,* p. 14.

4. Brendtro, L., and Long, N., *Rethinking Respect—Reclaiming Children and Youth,* Winter 1996, *4*(4), 2.

5. Pool, C., "Maximizing Learning: A Conversation with Renate Nummela Caine," *Educational Leadership,* 1997, *54*(6), 11–15.

6. Goleman, *Emotional Intelligence,* pp. 86–90.

7. Guidelines on appropriate personal disclosure for teachers can be found at this website: [www.mediatorsfoundation.org/isel/guidelines.html].

8. Brendtro, L., Van Bockern, S., and Clementson, J., "Adult-Wary and Angry: Restoring Social Bonds," *Holistic Education Review,* Mar. 1995, pp. 35–43.

## Chapter Five

1. Johnson, R., and Johnson, D., *Teaching Students to Be Peacemakers,* Edina, Minn.: Interaction, 1995.

2. Fisher, R., Ury, W., and Patton, B., *Getting to Yes: Negotiating Agreement Without Giving In* (2nd ed.), New York: Penguin Books, 1991, p. 5.

3. Bodine, R. J., Crawford, D. K., and Schrumpf, F., *Creating the Peaceable School: A Comprehensive Program for Teaching Conflict Resolution,* Champaign, Ill.: Research Press, 1994, p. 21.

4. Girard, K., and Koch, S., *Conflict Resolution in the Schools: A Manual for Educators,* San Francisco: Jossey-Bass, 1996, p. 36.

5. You can learn about PYN by going to the website of their parent company, SERA Learning, [www.sera.com], 2002.

6. SERA Learning, [www.sera.com], 2002.

7. Fisher, Ury, and Patton, *Getting to Yes.*

8. Porro, B., *Talk It Out: Conflict Resolution in the Elementary Classroom,* Alexandria, Va.: Association for Supervision and Curriculum Development, 1996, p. 2.

9. Johnson and Johnson, *Teaching Students to Be Peacemakers.*

10. Johnson, D., and Johnson, R., "Conflict Resolution and Peer Mediation Programs in Elementary and Secondary Schools: A Review of the Research," *Review of Educational Research,* 1996, *66,* 459–506.

11. Johnson and Johnson, *Teaching Students to Be Peacemakers,* p. 27.

12. Porro, *Talk It Out.*

13. Hocker, J., and Wilmot, W., *Interpersonal Conflict* (3rd ed.), Dubuque, Iowa: Brown, 1991, p. 4.

# Chapter Six

1. In fact, the professional association for the CRE field, now part of the larger Association for Conflict Resolution, was initially called the National Association for Mediation in Education (NAME).
2. There are usually ten to twelve hours of training for elementary students, eighteen to twenty-five hours for middle and high school students.
3. Some schools have used first through third graders as witness/facilitators of classroom-based negotiation processes. Although these student leaders don't take as active a role as mediators, they do play an important role by keeping their peers on task.
4. A small percentage of schools even employ full-time peer mediation coordinators.
5. See Cohen, R., *The School Mediator's Field Guide: Prejudice, Sexual Harassment, Large Groups and Other Daily Challenges*, Watertown, Mass.: School Mediation Associates, 1999, for a detailed analysis of the difficult cases most commonly faced by school-based mediators.

# Chapter Seven

1. The Individuals with Disabilities Education Act Amendments of 1997, "An Overview of the Bill to Provide a Broad Understanding of Some of the Changes in IDEA '97," [www.ed.gov/offices/OSERS/Policy/IDEA/overview.html], Nov. 20, 2001.
2. I conducted the informal survey of National Association of Private Schools for Exceptional Children (NAPSEC) member schools myself, with the help of the executive director of NAPSEC, Sherry Kolbe. We sent questions out by e-mail to all the executive directors and head administrators of private special education schools nationally. The questions were "Does your school have a peer mediation program?" "How long have you had one?" and "Has it been successful?" The e-mail requested a reply to my e-mail address. I received very few responses. This was not a very scientific survey, but I would consider the thinness of the response accurate and indicative of the state of the art of peer mediation nationally in special education schools.

# Chapter Eight

1. Pirtle, S., *Linking Up! Using Music, Movement, and Language Arts to Promote Caring, Cooperation, and Communication*, Cambridge, Mass.: Educators for Social Responsibility, 1998, curriculum materials.
2. For more information about how specific schools developed such assemblies, see Pirtle, S., "Activity Nine: School Celebration—A Weekly Partnership Event," in D. Bucciarelli and S. Pirtle (eds.), *Partnership Education in Action* (pp. 117–119), Tucson, Ariz.: Center for Partnership Studies, 2001; and Pirtle, S., "Social Responsibility Assembly," in *Discovery Time for Cooperation and Conflict Resolution* (pp. 15–16), Nyack, N.Y.: Children's Creative Response to Conflict, 1998.

## Chapter Nine

1. Henkes, K., *Sheila Rae, the Brave*, New York: Mulberry, 1996.
2. Brisson, P., *The Summer My Father Was Ten*, Honesdale, Penn.: Boyds Mills Press, 1999.
3. Polacco, P., *Mrs. Katz and Tush*, New York: Bantam Doubleday Dell, 1992.
4. Aliki, *Marianthe's Story*, New York: Mulberry Books, 1998.
5. Polacco, P., *Thank You, Mr. Falker*, New York: Philomel Books, 1998.
6. Taylor, T., *The Cay*, New York: Avon Books, 1969.
7. Taylor, M., *Roll of Thunder, Hear My Cry*, New York: Puffin Books, 1976.
8. Steinbeck, J., *Of Mice and Men*, New York: Penguin Books, 1937.
9. Hillerman, T., *Sacred Clowns*, New York: HarperCollins, 1993.
10. Greenfield, E., *First Pink Light*, New York: Black Butterfly Press, 1976.
11. Dorris, M., *Morning Girl*, New York: Hyperion, 1992.
12. For the American Revolution lesson by William Galloway, and others, see the website of the National Curriculum Integration Project, [www.ncip.org].
13. Carter, J., *Talking Peace: A Vision for the Next Generation*, New York: Dutton Children's Books, 1993.
14. Mertz, G., and Lieber, C. M., *Conflict in Context: Understanding Local to Global Security*, Cambridge, Mass.: Educators for Social Responsibility, 2000.
15. Poliner, R. A., and Benson, J., *Dialogue: Turning Controversy into Community*, Cambridge, Mass.: Educators for Social Responsibility, 1997.
16. Gross, F. E., Morton, P., and Poliner, R. A., *The Power of Numbers: A Teacher's Guide to Mathematics in a Social Studies Context*, Cambridge, Mass.: Educators for Social Responsibility, 1993.
17. Peterson, B., "Teaching Math Across the Curriculum," *Rethinking Schools*, Fall 1995, *10*(1), 1–4.
18. Ballin, A., Benson, J., and Burt, L., *Trash Conflicts: A Science and Social Studies Curriculum on the Ethics of Disposal*, Cambridge, Mass.: Educators for Social Responsibility, 1993.
19. Sobel, D., *Longitude*, New York: Walker, 1995.
20. dePaola, T., *Oliver Button Is a Sissy*, Orlando: Harcourt Brace, 1979.

## Chapter Ten

1. Zehr, H., *Changing Lenses*, Scottsdale, Penn.: Herald Press, 1990.
2. Umbreit, M. S., Coates, R. B., and Vos, B., *Victim Impact of Restorative Justice Conferencing with Juvenile Offenders*, St. Paul, Minn.: Center for Restorative Justice and Peacemaking, 2000.
3. Briathwaite, J., *Crime, Shame and Reintegration*, Cambridge University Press, 1989.

## Chapter Eleven

1. Brendtro, L., keynote speech at the Colorado School Mediation Project Conference, Denver, June 16, 1999.
2. Olweus, D., *Bullying at School: What We Know and What We Can Do*, Oxford, England: Blackwell, 1993.

3. Title, B., *No-Bullying Program: A Guide for Families* (2nd ed.), Center City, Minn.: Hazelden, 2001, p. 5.

4. Bitney, J., and Title, B., *No-Bullying Program: Preventing Bullying at School Programs* (Director's Manual and K–8 Teacher's Manuals) (2nd ed.), Center City, Minn.: Hazelden, 2001, pp. 7–8.

5. Olweus, *Bullying at School.*

6. Olweus, *Bullying at School*, p. 34.

7. Olwcus, *Bullying at School*, pp. 32 33.

8. Garrity, C., and others, *Bully Proofing Your School*, Longmont, Colo.: Sopris West, 1994.

9. Olweus, *Bullying at School.*

10. Bitney and Title, *No-Bullying Program*, pp. 74–75.

11. Title, B., "Bullying: An Overview for Educators," Center City, Minn.: Hazelden, 1996.

# Chapter Twelve

1. Berke, R., and Elder, J., "Poll Finds Support for War and Fear on Economy," *New York Times*, Sept. 25, 2001, p. A1.

2. Chasnoff, D., and Cohen, H., *It's Elementary*, San Francisco: Women's Educational Media, 1999, video.

3. The Rainbow Curriculum was produced by the Board of Education of the City of New York, 110 Livingston Street, Brooklyn 11201, [www.nycenet.edu].

4. Reports from the American-Arab Anti-Discrimination Committee, [www.adc.org].

# Chapter Thirteen

1. "Fight Crime: Invest in Kids," news release, [www.fightcrime.org/press/backtoschool2001], Sept. 4, 2001.

# Chapter Fourteen

1. Saarni, C., *The Development of Emotional Competence*, New York: Guilford Press, 1999.

2. Jones, T. S., "Emotional Communication in Conflict: Essence and Impact," in W. Eadie and P. Nelson (eds.), *The Language of Conflict and Resolution*, Thousand Oaks, Calif.: Sage, 2000.

3. Elias, M., and others, Association for Supervision and Curriculum Development, *Promoting Social and Emotional Learning: Guidelines for Educators*, Alexandria, Virg.: Association for Supervision and Curriculum Development, 1997.

4. Bodine, R., and Crawford, D., *Handbook of Conflict Resolution Education: A Guide to Building Quality Programs in Schools*, San Francisco: Jossey-Bass, 1998.

5. Jones, T. S., and Kmitta, D. (eds.), *Does It Work? The Case for Conflict Resolution Education in Our Nation's Schools*, Washington, D.C.: Conflict Resolution Education Network, 2000.

# APPENDIX A

## BOOKS, PUBLICATIONS, AND WEBSITES

### After-School Programs

*www.afterschool.gov*   The website of the National Institute on Out-of-School Time at Wellesley College, Wellesley, Mass. The site provides 120 federal funding sources and other resources to support local out-of-school programs.

*www.nsaca.org*   The National School-Age Care Alliance (NSACA) is a national membership organization whose mission is to support quality programs for school-age children and youth in their out-of-school hours.

*www.schoolagenotes.com*   School-Age Notes is a catalogue of resource materials for before- and after-school programs.

*www.mott.org/21.asp*   The Charles Stewart Mott Foundation's 21st Century Community Learning Centers, provides technical assistance to keep schools open as community learning centers.

*www.gse.harvard.edu/~afterschool*   The Program in Afterschool Education and Research (PAER), Harvard Graduate School of Education, is collecting a database of research on after-school programs.

*www.financeproject.org*   The website of the Finance Project, which finances and sustains out-of-school time and community school initiatives.

# Arts and Conflict Education

## General Sources

Brunson, R. *The ART of Peacemaking: Partnership for Conflict Resolution Education in the Arts. Final Report*. Washington, D.C.: National Endowment for the Arts, U.S. Department of Justice, and Office of Juvenile Justice and Delinquency Prevention, 2002.

*www.urbanext.uiuc.edu/conflict*    This website, "Out on a Limb," was developed by Russell Brunson for elementary students to work with graphic arts concepts and conflict resolution education (CRE).

## Peace Theater

Atkins, Greg. *Improv: A Handbook for the Actor*. Portsmouth, N.H.: Heinemann, 1994.

Bey, Theresa M., and Gwendolyn Y. Turner. *Making School a Place of Peace*. Thousand Oaks, Calif.: Corwin Press, 1996.

Bray, Errol. *Playbuilding: A Guide for Group Creation of Plays with Young People*. Portsmouth, N.H.: Heinemann, 1994.

Caruso, Sandra, and Susan Kosoff. *The Young Actor's Book of Improvisation: Dramatic Situations from Shakespeare to Spielberg*. Portsmouth, N.H.: Heinemann, 1998.

Coles, Robert. *The Moral Intelligence of Children: How to Raise a Moral Child*. New York: Plume Book, 1998.

Dee, Peter. *Voices 2000*. Boston: Baker's Plays, 1994.

Goldberg, Andy. *Improv Comedy*. New York: Samuel French Trade, 1991.

Horn, Delton T. *Comedy Improvisation: Exercises and Techniques for Young Actors*. Colorado Springs: Meriwether, 1991.

Inferrere, Gia, and Kelly White. *Spotlight on Character: Plays That Show Character Count*. Torrance, Calif.: Frank Schaffer, 1999.

Spolin, Viola. *Theater Games for the Classroom: A Teacher's Handbook*. Evanston, Ill.: Northwestern University Press, 1986.

Sternberg, Patricia. *Theatre for Conflict Resolution*. Portsmouth, N.H.: Heinemann, 1998.

## Resources for Music and Conflict Discovery

### Picture Books

Hoose, Phillip and Hannah. *Hey, Little Ant*. Berkeley, Calif.: Tricycle Press, 1998. Website with lesson plans: *www.heylittleant.com*.

Morgan, Jennifer. *Born with a Bang: The Universe Tells Our Cosmic Story*. Nevada City, Calif.: Dawn, 2002.

### Early Childhood

Gartrell, Daniel. *A Guidance Approach for the Encouraging Classroom* (2nd ed.). Albany, N.Y.: Delmar, 1998.

Levin, Diane. *Teaching Young Children in Violent Times*. Cambridge, Mass.: Educators for Social Responsibility, 1994.

Pirtle, Sarah. *Linking Up! Using Music, Movement, and Language Arts to Promote Caring, Cooperation and Communication.* Cambridge, Mass.: Educators for Social Responsibility, 1998.

## Resource Book for K–8 Teachers

Pirtle, Sarah. *Discovery Time for Cooperation and Conflict Resolution.* Nyack, N.Y.: Children's Creative Response to Conflict, 1998.

## Resource Books for K–12 Teachers

Bucciarelli, D., and Sarah Pirtle (eds.). *Partnership Education in Action.* Tucson, Ariz.: Center for Partnership Studies, 2001.

Eisler, Riane. *Tomorrow's Children: A Blueprint for Partnership Education in the 21st Century.* Boulder, Colo.: Westview Press, 2000.

## Children's Music Resources

A Gentle Wind. Telephone: (888) FUNSONG. Website: www.gentlewind.com.

The Children's Music Network (CMN). P.O. Box 1341, Evanston, IL 60204. Website: www.cmnonline.org.

## Recordings for Grades K–6

Blue, Bob. "Starting Small." Bob Blue Recordings, 170 E. Hadley Rd. #82, Amherst, MA 01002. E-mail: bblue@k12.oit.umass.edu.

Caduto, Michael. "All One Earth: Songs for the Generations." P.O. Box 1052, Norwich, VT 05055.

Grammer, Red. "Teaching Peace." Red Note Records, 5049 Orangeport, Brewerton, NY 13029.

Hammil, Joanne. "The World's Gonna Listen" and "Pizza Boogie." 70 Capitol St., Watertown, MA 02472.

Harley, Bill. "I'm Gonna Shine: A Gathering of Voices for Freedom." Round River Records, 301 Jacob St., Seekonk, MA 02771.

The Hoose Family. "I Know Math" and "Hey Little Ant." 8 Arlington St., Portland, ME 04101.

McDougall, Eveline. "Amandla: Songs from South Africa." P.O. Box 223, Greenfield, MA 01301.

O'Brien, Bruce. "Love Is in the Middle." 604 Newton St., Eau Claire, WI 54701. Telephone: (715) 832-0721.

Pease, Tom. "Daddy Starts to Dance," "Wobbi Do Wop," and "I'm Gonna Reach." Peaseblossom Music, 6580 County K, Amherst, WI 54406.

Pirtle, Sarah. "Magical Earth," "The Wind Is Telling Secrets," and "Two Hands Hold the Earth." Discovery Center, 63 Main Street, Shelburne Falls, MA 01370.

Ribaudo, Sue, and Paul Lippert. "In the Same Boat." Raspberry Records, 3472 Cornell Place, Cincinnati, OH 45220.

Rogers, Sally. "Piggyback Planet—Songs for the Whole Earth," "Peace by Peace," and "What Can One Little Person Do?" P.O. Box 98, Abington, CT 06230.

Schimmel, Nancy. "All in This Together." 1639 Channing Way, Berkeley, CA 94703.

Stotts, Stuart. "Are We There Yet" and "One Big Dance." 169 Ohio Ave., Madison, WI 53704.

Two of a Kind. "Connections." David and Jenny Heitler-Klevens, 130 W. Nippon, PA 19119.

# Bullying

Leonard, Lana, and Beverly Title. *Victim or Hero? Writing Your Own Life Story* (2nd ed.), 2002. Available from Teaching Peace, P.O. Box 3713, Sedona, AZ 86340. This publication is a sentence completion and personal story–writing workbook that assists adolescents in examining their life choices.

Olweus, Dan. *Bullying at School: What We Know and What We Can Do.* Cambridge, Mass.: Blackwell, 1993.

Title, Beverly, and Lana Leonard. *Civility Rules,* 2000. Available from Teaching Peace, P.O. Box 3713, Sedona, AZ 86340. This publication contains a series of violence prevention activities for school staffs and students, adaptable at all levels, organized by topic: civility, safety, responsibility, tolerance and respect, and restorative discipline.

Title, Beverly. "Bullying: An Overview for Educators." Center City, Minn.: Hazelden, 1996. This booklet provides a concise overview of the basic research on bullying. It is a quick read that introduces the principles of bullying prevention.

*www.bullying.org*   This website is one of the most comprehensive sites available. It provides a thorough list of articles, books, films, legislation, policies, related resources, and research.

*www.teachingpeace.org*   This website offers resource materials and practical advice for educators and parents seeking strategies and techniques to deal with bullying.

*www.crj.anu.edu.au/school.html*   This is the Centre for Restorative Justice at the Research School of Social Sciences, Australian National University. The link is to their Life at School Project. The focus of their research is school bullying.

# Social and Emotional Learning

Goleman, Daniel. *Emotional Intelligence: Why It Can Matter More Than IQ.* New York: Bantam Books, 1995.

Lantieri, Linda (ed.). *Schools with Spirit: Nurturing the Inner Lives of Children and Teachers.* Boston: Beacon Press, 2001.

Elias, Maurice, and others. *Promoting Social and Emotional Learning: Guidelines for Educators.* Washington, D.C.: Association for Supervision and Curriculum Development, 1997.

Kessler, Rachael. *The Soul of Education: Helping Students Find Connection, Compassion and Character at School.* Washington, D.C.: Association for Supervision and Curriculum Development, 2000.

*www.casel.org*   The website of the Collaborative for Academic, Social, and Emotional Learning. For more information about this organization, see the listing in Appendix B.

*www.GLEF.org*   This website of the George Lucas Educational Foundation continues to provide excellent material relevant to social and emotional learning (SEL), and character education. They also have some wonderful new video and CD-ROM resources available, virtually at cost.

*www.nprinc.com*     National Professional Resources is a leading distributor of practical materials for use in SEL, EQ, and character education contexts.

*www.communitiesofhope.org*     This site, sponsored by the Hope Foundation, continues to provide excellent materials for community building and leadership development around SEL and EQ; most important, the organization has Lessons for Life, a wonderful in-service training kit for teacher induction around SEL and character education.

*www.character.org*     This is the Character Education Partnership website, providing a wealth of information and resources about character education programs and materials.

*www.aboutourkids.org*     This website is administered by the New York University Child Study Center and provides a very thorough list of resources concerning SEL programs, materials, and research.

*www.csee.net*     The website of the Center for Social and Emotional Education.

# Peer Mediation

Cohen, Richard. *Students Resolving Conflict: Peer Mediation in Schools.* Glenview, Ill.: Scott, Foresman, 1995.

Schrumpf, Fred, Donna K. Crawford, and Richard J. Bodine. *Peer Mediation: Conflict Resolution in Schools.* Champaign, Ill: Research Press, 1992. Available from the National Center for Conflict Resolution Education.

Cohen, Richard. *The School Mediator's Field Guide: Prejudice, Sexual Harassment, Large Groups and Other Daily Challenges.* Watertown, Mass.: School Mediation Associates, 1999.

*www.nccre.org*     The website of the National Center for Conflict Resolution Education. For more information, see the listing in Appendix B.

*www.schoolmediation.com*     The website of School Mediation Associates. For more information, see the listing in Appendix B.

# General

Kohn, Alfie. *Beyond Discipline: From Compliance to Community.* Alexandria, Va.: Association for Supervision and Curriculum Development, 1996.

Palmer, Parker. *The Courage to Teach: Exploring the Inner Landscape of a Teacher's Life.* San Francisco: Jossey-Bass, 1998.

Lickona, Thomas. *Educating for Character: How Our Schools Can Teach Respect and Responsibility.* New York: Bantam Books, 1991.

Fisher, Roger, and William Ury. *Getting to Yes: Negotiating Agreement Without Giving In.* New York: Penguin Books, 1981.

Faber, Adele, and Elaine Mazlish. *How to Talk So Kids Will Learn.* New York: Avon Books, 1995.

Johnson, David, Roger Johnson, and Edythe Johnson Holubec. *The New Circles of Learning: Cooperation in the Classroom and School.* Alexandria, Va.: Association for Supervision and Curriculum Development, 1994.

Ury, William. *The Third Side: Why We Fight and How We Can Stop.* New York: Penguin Books, 2000.

Wood, Chip. *Time to Teach, Time to Learn.* Greenfield, Mass.: Northeast Foundation for Children, 1999.

Lantieri, Linda, and Janet Patti. *Waging Peace in Our Schools.* Boston: Beacon Press, 1996.

Gossen, Diane Chelsom (ed.). *Restitution: Restructuring School Discipline* (2nd rev. ed.). Chapel Hill, N.C.: New View, 1996.

Jones, Tricia S., and Daniel Kmitta (eds.). *Does It Work? The Case for Conflict Resolution Education in Our Nation's Schools.* Washington, D.C.: Conflict Resolution Education Network, 2000. Available from the Association for Conflict Resolution.

*www.acresolution.org*   The website of the Association for Conflict Resolution. For more information, see the listing in Appendix B.

*www.cde.state.co.us/action/curric/int/teacher.htm*   The website of the Colorado Department of Education program focusing on curriculum integration issues and materials. This site provides excellent materials for teachers. It is also hyperlinked to the National Curriculum Integration Project.

*www.ncip.org*   The website of the National Curriculum Integration Project, developed and administered by the Colorado School Mediation Project. For more information, see the listing in Appendix B.

*www.indiana.edu/~safeschl*   The website of the Safe and Responsive Schools Project at the University of Indiana. This site has a wealth of resources for general CRE.

*www.education.indiana.edu/~cafs*   This website includes *Teacher Talk*, a publication of the Center for Adolescent and Family Studies at Indiana University. The site and publication deal with a variety of topics related to CRE.

*www.coe.ufl.edu/CRPM*   This website is devoted to a project of the University of Florida dealing with development and implementation of CRE and peer mediation for special education students.

*www.abanet.org/dispute*   The website of the American Bar Association Section of Dispute Resolution, which deals generally with conflict management and dispute resolution. They actively support certain CRE programs, such as the Lawyers Adopt-a-School Program.

*www.usdoj.gov/kidspage*   This website of the U.S. Department of Justice provides an overview of several CRE programs, including We Can Work It Out (National Crime Prevention Council), California Lawyers for the Arts (California Bar Association), and the Lawyers Adopt-a-School Program (American Bar Association).

# ORGANIZATIONS AND PROGRAMS

This appendix presents information on several conflict resolution education (CRE) and related organizations, including website information, training materials, and publications from the organizations. The listings are in alphabetical order.

## Association for Conflict Resolution

The Association for Conflict Resolution (ACR), a merged organization of Academy of Family Mediators (AFM), Conflict Resolution Education Network (CREnet), and Society for Professionals in Dispute Resolution (SPIDR), is a professional membership organization representing more than six thousand mediators, arbitrators, educators, and others involved in the field of conflict resolution and collaborative decision making. ACR is dedicated to enhancing the practice and public understanding of conflict resolution through quarterly publications (*Conflict Resolution Quarterly, ACResolution,* and various section newsletters), annual conferences, and a website, and by educating local, state, and federal leaders about policies, practices, and learning opportunities in the field. One of the specific ways that ACR supports CRE is through the work of the Education Section, which has its own newsletter, *The Fourth R.*

ACR has published *Does It Work? The Case for Conflict Resolution Education in Our Nation's Schools,* Tricia S. Jones and Dan Kmitta (eds.), 2000. (It was originally compiled and published by CREnet.) This publication synthesizes current research about CRE and its impact on students, teachers, diverse populations, the CRE institutionalization process, and school and classroom climate. It is available for purchase from ACR.

Sangita Sygdal, COO
Association for Conflict Resolution
1527 New Hamsphire Avenue, NW
Washington, DC 20036
(202) 667-9700
Website: www.acresolution.org
E-mail: info@acresolution.org

# Campus-ADR

Campus-ADR is a Fund for the Improvement of Post-Secondary Education (FIPSE)—a funded conflict resolution clearinghouse for higher education. Unique resources on the website, www.campus-adr.org, include the following:

- Student center, which provides information on academic study options in conflict resolution
- Searchable collection of conflict resolution syllabi
- Current and past issues of the *Conflict Management in Higher Education Report*
- Searchable collection of campus mediation role plays
- Case review forum for anonymous posting of campus mediation cases
- MetaSearch tool linked to all the major dispute resolution databases and indexes on the Web
- Conflict Studies textbook exchange listing service
- Online Program Evaluation Toolkit for campus mediation programs
- Extensive information for instructors developing new Conflict Studies courses

The site was developed by ACR's Education Section cochair, Bill Warters, Wayne State University.

William Warters
Wayne State University
656 West Kirby
Detroit, MI 48202

# Collaborative for Academic, Social and Emotional Learning

The Collaborative for Academic, Social and Emotional Learning (CASEL) is an international network of leading researchers and practitioners in the fields of social and emotional learning (SEL), prevention, positive youth development, character education, and school reform. CASEL has been highly effective as a convening and collaborating organization among researchers, program developers, and educators, as it focuses on many areas of common interest, including program design, evaluation, educator preparation, policy, and advocacy. CASEL's mission is to establish SEL as an integral part of education from preschool through high school. CASEL goals include the following:

- Advance the science of SEL
- Translate scientific knowledge into effective school practices
- Disseminate information about scientifically sound educational strategies and practice

- Enhance training so that educators effectively implement high-quality SEL programs
- Network and collaborate with scientists, educators, advocates, policymakers, and interested citizens to increase coordination of SEL efforts

Several current and recent projects highlight the work of CASEL.

*Teacher preparation for SEL-based instruction:* with support from the Joseph P. Kennedy Jr. Foundation, CASEL and collaborators have developed an SEL 101 course for use in colleges of education. The materials are being pilot tested in seven colleges of education. The materials will be revised and reformatted into twenty-five stand-alone modules on distinct topics that can be infused into existing college of education courses—for example, in classroom management and early childhood development. A dissemination campaign to influence deans and colleges of education to adopt these materials will feature articles and editorials in major professional journals and presentations at professional conferences.

*Educational leadership and SEL:* CASEL has shifted from a primary focus on advancing the science of SEL to engage more directly in work to improve and expand the practice of SEL in schools throughout the country. Partners for Health, Academic, Social, and Emotional Success (PHASES) is a coordinated SEL effort currently conducted in three Chicago elementary schools. PHASES has three major components: (1) school-family partnerships to enhance parents' positive involvement in children's education; (2) classroom-based programming to foster children's social, emotional, and academic competence; and (3) complementary small-group support services for children who are experiencing school and social-emotional adjustment difficulties. Key partners in the PHASES program are CASEL staff, Chicago Public Schools educators, the skilled and nurturing paraprofessionals hired to provide an array of support services to the school communities, the Ounce of Prevention Fund, the University of Illinois at Chicago, the Illinois Department of Human Services, and the Mid-Atlantic Regional Educational Laboratory for Student Success.

*School-family partnerships:* the School-Family Partnership (SFP) project is a collaborative effort by CASEL, the University of Illinois at Chicago, the Mid-Atlantic Regional Educational Laboratory for Student Success (LSS) at Temple University, and parents and teachers at public schools in Chicago and Washington, D.C. For over five years, a team of researchers and practitioners has worked to produce a research-based, step-by-step program that educators can use to increase parent participation in children's education. The teachers' guide, "Enhancing School-Family Partnerships," developed by the SFP team, includes thirty-eight specific goals to promote positive student outcomes through communication and parent involvement at home and school. Each goal is presented along with a rationale and sample materials for easy implementation. The SFP team has also developed a variety of other materials for parents and teachers to facilitate the communication process between home and school (see, for example, the "Partnerships" series). During the first five years of the SFP project, the team developed programming to enhance the academic, social, and emotional competence of kindergarten through fourth-grade children. Currently, the SFP team has begun investigating the area of developmentally appropriate SFP strategies for middle school and high school students and intends to develop materials that educators can use to enhance home-school relationships for older students.

Collaborative for Academic, Social and Emotional Learning
Department of Psychology (MC 285)
University of Illinois at Chicago

1007 West Harrison Street
Chicago, IL 60607
Website: www.casel.org

# Colorado School Mediation Project, Now the School Mediation Center

The School Mediation Center, formerly the Colorado School Mediation Project, provides comprehensive training and support services to school communities interested in utilizing the principles and practices of conflict resolution, SEL, peer mediation, bullying prevention, and restorative justice. The School Mediation Center offers graduate classes, training materials, and conferences to support ongoing programs and teacher education.

## Programs

*Productive Conflict Resolution Program: A Whole School Approach:* a research-based, comprehensive program with eight complementary components designed to build skills and strategies for reducing violence and promoting cooperative and problem-solving behaviors in a caring learning environment.

*Restorative Justice in Schools Program:* an innovative program that seeks to repair the harm done by wrongdoing through face-to-face meetings with those who have been impacted. The program is designed to reduce reliance on suspension, address school and victim safety, and reinforce existing conflict resolution programs.

*Peer Mediation in Schools Program:* a research-based program designed to use peers to help resolve disputes, improve school climate, and address bullying issues early, before they escalate.

*Peace Place Program (K–6):* a classroom-based program that teaches students to solve conflicts through a four-step negotiation process.

*Put Down Free Program:* a newly developed bullying prevention program that is student driven and designed to eliminate put-downs, increase caring communication, and create a positive, caring climate for all.

*National Curriculum Integration Project (NCIP):* an effort devoted to curriculum infusion practices and programs. For more information on the achievements of NCIP, visit the website: www.ncip.org.

## Videos

*Making Things Right: Restorative Justice for School Communities:* an overview of the principles and practices of restorative justice in school settings around the United States, including interviews with teachers, administrators, parents, and students who have been impacted by the process.

*Peer Mediation in Action:* a forty-five-minute video program for students, staff, and parents that shows experienced mediators in action, including a peer mediation group discussing sensitive issues and one of the only teacher-student mediations on video. A fifty-page teacher's guide with valuable background materials, discussion questions, articles, and handouts is included.

*Alternatives to Violence: Conflict Resolution and Mediation:* a two-video set; students learn the value of problem solving and conflict resolution as alternatives to fighting. Includes a teacher's guide and blackline masters.

## Books, Curricula, and Manuals

*Using Stories to Prevent Violence and Promote Cooperation:* a compilation of ten stories from around the world, each with accompanying activities, for use with both primary and secondary students.

*Healing Wounds with Words:* the second volume of the storytelling manual described above. This illustrated version features all new stories and activities for primary and secondary levels.

*Productive Conflict Resolution: A Comprehensive Curriculum and Teacher's Guide for Conflict Resolution Education* (for grades K–2, 3–5, 6–8, and 9–12): a comprehensive set of lessons, integration strategies, background material, and articles for educators, parents, and youth workers.

*Student Mediation Training Manuals:* a comprehensive yet concise resource for training student mediators.

*Coordinator's Student Mediation Training Manuals:* these manuals have all the same resources as the student manuals and in addition include lesson plans and supportive materials for implementing a conflict mediation program in a school.

*Mediation Role Plays:* over twenty different role plays that can be used in trainings, weekly meetings, or classroom lessons; available for elementary, middle, or high school.

*Handouts for Parents:* a collection of thirteen one-page handouts (written by a parent). Reproducible for the whole school.

*Study Circle Articles and Discussion Guide:* a series of stimulating articles dealing with conflict resolution for educators to read and discuss in teams. Includes a manual for discussion leaders and participants.

*Integrating Conflict Resolution into the Curriculum:* provides teachers with examples of how to integrate conflict resolution into social studies, language arts, science, health, and physical education.

## Conferences

*Violence Prevention in School Communities:* for over ten years, this June conference has been a way for educators, practitioners, students, and community members to gather together and discuss positive models for change in the field of violence prevention for schools and communities. The five hundred attendees include teachers, administrators, students, parents, community members, school health personnel, counselors, mediators, the legal community, the law enforcement community, and related professionals.

*Peace Leadership:* a peace conference for youth in the Denver metropolitan area who want to learn more about how they can get involved in building peaceful school communities. In addition to providing a place for discussion, inspiration, and support, the conference offers beginning and advanced training in conflict resolution skills. This October conference is intended for students in grades 4–12, program coordinators, counselors, educators, and parents. Attendance is approximately six hundred.

School Mediation Center, formerly Colorado School Mediation Project
5485 Conestoga Ct., Suite 101
Boulder, CO 80301
(303) 444-7671
Fax: (303) 444-7247
Toll free: (877) 853-5402
Website: www.schoolmediationcenter.org
E-mail: info@schoolmediationcenter.org

# Conflict Resolution Unlimited Institute

Conflict Resolution Unlimited (CRU) Institute provides schoolwide conflict mediation programs for faculty, staff, and parents at elementary, middle, and high schools. The mission of CRU is to teach young people effective, peaceful ways to manage conflict and to develop understanding, respect, and the ability to cooperate within a multicultural world.

## Programs

### Faculty Training

*District training:* CRU trainers travel to your district and provide one- and two-day intensive mediation training workshops for key faculty from multiple schools.

*Regional training:* CRU conducts one- and two-day intensive training programs. The training is open to faculty nationally and internationally. This training enables faculty to learn mediation concepts and skills, understand the whole-school mediation program, and develop methods to teach students these skills.

*Training at your school:* an introductory mini-training or a longer, more intensive training is provided for your entire faculty.

### Student Training

*Peer mediation training:* CRU provides training for students who will act as elementary school conflict managers or as secondary school peer mediators for other students at your school.

*Classroom training:* CRU trainers present conflict mediation concepts and skills to all students in the class. This program emphasizes how students can use mediation approaches in their own lives: how they can "be their own mediator."

*Mediation training for all secondary students:* this multitier program is designed to teach conflict resolution and peer mediation skills to the entire student body. Each year, all new students participate in interactive skill-building training. Students learn how to mediate for others and how to "be their own mediator." Older students serve as mentors for incoming students to train them in the mediation process.

*Cultural Awareness Project (CAP):* this project encourages students to develop sensitivity, respect, understanding, and empathy for cultural differences through a series of directed discussions. The six-session project allows students the opportunity to talk in depth about cultural differences and their impact on everyday interactions. Students examine the nature of put-downs, ridicule, and bullying. They discuss how to create a positive climate at their school. Students gain self-awareness and develop effective ways to interact with a diverse population.

### Parent Training

Two-hour evening sessions introduce parents to the concepts and skills of mediation. Parents are encouraged to bring their children and to practice the mediation process in family role-play groups. Booklets on family problem solving help parents deal with family disputes that occur at home.

## Publications

Kaplan, Nancy. *CRU for Elementary School Conflict Managers.* CRU Institute, 1999. Extensive curriculum manual with over one hundred pages of material, including specific and detailed lesson plans and well-explained training procedures. The manual includes handouts for students, program evaluation forms, and instructions for setting up the program in the school.

Kaplan, Nancy. *CRU for Middle School Peer Mediators.* CRU Institute, 1992–1999. Extensive curriculum manual with over two hundred pages of material, including specific and detailed lesson plans and well-explained training procedures. The manual includes handouts for students, program evaluation forms, and instructions for setting up the program in the school. Includes over forty role plays.

Kaplan, Nancy. *CRU for High School Peer Mediators.* CRU Institute, 1992–1999. Extensive curriculum manual with over two hundred pages of material, including specific and detailed lesson plans and well-explained training procedures. The manual includes handouts for students, program evaluation forms, and instructions for setting up the program in the school. Includes over forty role plays.

Kaplan, Nancy. *CRU for the Classroom: Conflict Resolution Skills for Elementary School Students.* CRU Institute, 1995–1999. A conflict resolution program for the K–6 classroom. Over one hundred pages, the manual includes twelve detailed lesson plans, each twenty to thirty minutes long, and emphasizes negotiation skills and creating an awareness and understanding of the process of mediation.

Kaplan, Nancy. *CRU for Violence Prevention: Mediation Training: Life Skills for the Secondary Classroom.* CRU Institute, 1992–1999. A mediation training program for the middle and high school classroom. Over two hundred pages, the manual includes sixteen detailed lesson plans, each forty-five minutes long, and emphasizes negotiation skills and creating an awareness and understanding of the process of mediation.

Kaplan, Nancy. *Family Problem Solving: Conflict Mediation Training for Parents.* CRU Institute, 1998. A mediation skill training program for parents. Almost one hundred pages, the manual includes four detailed lesson plans, each two hours long. Information covered includes instruction on the mediation process, communication and listening skills, role plays, and running family meetings.

## Videos

Kaplan, Nancy. *Everyday Conflicts, Creative Solutions.* CRU Institute, 1991. Professionally acted dramatization showing how the Conflict Manager process works on the playground. Includes a Leader's Guide, which points out, through an annotated transcript, several mediation skills used in the video.

Kaplan, Nancy. *Rumors, Conflicts, Resolutions.* CRU Institute, 1995. Professionally acted dramatization showing peer mediators helping two high school students resolve a dispute. Includes a Leader's Guide, which points out, through an annotated transcript, several mediation skills used in the video.

Kaplan, Nancy. *Names.* CRU Institute, 1997. Professionally acted dramatization showing how racial and cultural differences can create conflict and how students help other students understand those differences and resolve conflicts through mediation. Includes a Leader's Guide, which points out, through an annotated transcript, several mediation skills used in the video; the guide also provides descriptions of the mediation process, diversity materials, cultural differences and communication exercises, and role plays.

Conflict Resolution Unlimited
845—106th Avenue, NE, Suite 109
Bellevue, WA 98004
Telephone: (206) 451-4015
Toll free: (800) 922-1988
Website: www.cruinstitute.org
E-mail: cru@cruinstitute.org

# Consortium for Appropriate Dispute Resolution in Special Education

The Consortium for Appropriate Dispute Resolution in Special Education (CADRE), the national center on dispute resolution, is funded by the U.S. Department of Education, Office of Special Education Programs. CADRE uses advanced technology as well as traditional means to provide technical assistance to state departments of education on implementation of the mediation requirements under IDEA 1997. CADRE also supports parents, educators, and administrators in benefiting from the full continuum of dispute resolution options that can prevent and resolve conflict and ultimately lead to informed partnerships that focus on results for children and youth.

Consortium for Appropriate Dispute Resolution in Special Education
P.O. Box 51360
Eugene, OR 97405-0906
3411-A Willamette Street
Eugene, OR 97405-5122

Telephone: (541) 686-5060
Fax: (541) 686-5063
TTY: (541) 284-4740
Website: www.directionservice.org/cadre

# Creative Response to Conflict

The mission of Creative Response to Conflict, Inc. (CRC) is to help young people, educators, parents, and others learn creative skills of nonviolent conflict resolution through cooperation, communication, affirmation, problem solving, mediation, and bias awareness. The board and staff of CRC model these approaches and work locally and globally to achieve a nonviolent and just society.

## Services

CRC conducts workshops for people of all ages in conflict resolution, mediation, problem solving, and bias awareness. Workshops can be adapted for specific age groups and to meet specific needs. School-based workshops focus on providing an environment where students and staff can begin looking at new ways to examine conflicts and develop solutions. Specially designed activities help participants see that there are many alternatives to violence.

## Publications and Materials

Prutzman, Priscilla, and others. *The Friendly Classroom for a Small Planet*. The CRC "handbook." Includes the philosophy and insights of CRC and its four themes: communication, affirmation, cooperation, and conflict resolution.

Ni-Azariah, Kinshasha, and others. *A Year of SCRC: 35 Experiential Workshops for the Classroom*. A 105-page book in a loose-leaf format written by members of Students' Creative Response to Conflict, the Cincinnati branch of CRC.

Kreidler, William. *Creative Conflict Resolution: More Than 200 Activities for Keeping Peace in the Classroom K–6*. Over twenty conflict resolution techniques, with examples and worksheets. Discusses how to resolve conflicts with students, parents, administrators, and other teachers.

Williams, Arlene, with a foreword by Priscilla Prutzman. *Tales from the Dragon's Cave: Peacemaking Stories for Everyone*. A collection of fairy tales geared to teaching young children lessons in conflict resolution from a dragon's perspective.

Derman-Sparks, Louise, and the A.B.C. Task Force. *Anti-Bias Curriculum: Tools for Empowering Young Children*. Includes sample dialogues between children and adults; has chapters on gender identity, nonbiased holiday activities, and working with parents.

*CCRC's Friendly Classroom Mediation Manual*. Methods and materials used in CRC mediation training for schoolchildren. Includes mediation scripts, articles, and handouts. Student's packet sold separately.

Schiedewind, Nancy, and Ellen Davidson. *Open Minds to Equality: A Source Book of Learning Activities to Affirm Diversity and Promote Equity* (2nd ed.). A practical resource for multicultural education and social justice.

Pirtle, Sarah. *Discovery Time for Cooperation and Conflict Resolution*. Includes activities on bias awareness and the expressive arts for K–8.

Families Against Violence Advocacy Network. "Families Creating a Circle of Peace." This booklet addresses the concerns of parents, family members, and all committed individuals who wish to take a stand for peace and justice in today's increasingly violent world. It is based on a Family Pledge of Nonviolence and includes forty pages of stories, suggestions, activities, and other resources to help people live each component of the pledge in their day-to-day lives.

Prutzman, Priscilla, Judith M. Johnson, and Susan Fountain. *CCRC'S Friendly Classroom and Communities for Young Children: A Manual of Conflict Resolution Activities and Resources*. A manual for facilitators that contains detailed directions for dozens of activities for those who work with young children, early childhood through primary grades. The activities are arranged by CRC themes. There is a theoretical discussion of issues around each theme.

Creative Response to Conflict, Inc.
Children's Creative Response to Conflict
P.O. Box 271
521 North Broadway
Nyack, NY 10960
Telephone: (845) 353-1796
Fax: (845) 358-4924
E-mail: ccrcnyack@aol.com

# Educators for Social Responsibility

Educators for Social Responsibility (ESR) provides training and staff development in such areas as conflict resolution, SEL, character development, violence prevention, and diversity education. ESR's innovative and practical programs are tailored to match the unique needs of each school, district, or institution and help create safer, more caring, and respectful classroom and school environments.

## Programs

*Resolving Conflict Creatively Program* (K–8): a research-based program in SEL that helps young people develop the skills to reduce violence and prejudice, form caring relationships, and build healthy lives.

*Stories: Exploring Conflict and Character Through Literature and Language Arts* (K–8): *Stories* offers a framework of skills and concepts for integrating social skill development into the language arts curriculum, helping administrators and teachers enhance literacy while creating safe and caring learning communities.

*Partners in Learning* (middle and high school): a program designed to help secondary school communities create a peaceable vision that supports every student's social and emotional well-being and academic achievement.

*Adventures in Peacemaking* (early childhood and after-school): this program provides a wide variety of over one hundred activities, routines, and practices to help children learn cooperation, healthy emotional expression, appreciation for diversity, effective communication, and win-win problem solving.

*Diversity education and social justice workshops* (K–12): ESR's workshops equip educators with multicultural competencies and diverse teaching strategies necessary to help them better serve the social, emotional, and academic needs of all students.

## Publications

Kreidler, William J., and Sandy Tsubokawa Whittall. *Early Childhood Adventures in Peacemaking.* Educators for Social Responsibility, 1999. For preschool–3. This unique guide uses games, music, art, drama, and storytelling to teach young children effective, nonviolent ways to resolve conflicts. This second edition contains sections on developmentally appropriate practice; tips on classroom setup; instructions for incorporating social and emotional skills into daily routines; suggestions for when things don't go as planned; and materials and activities for parents to help reinforce the themes, skills, and concepts of a peaceable program at home.

Kreidler, William J., and Lisa Furlong, with Libby Cowles and IlaSahai Prouty. *Adventures in Peacemaking: A Conflict Resolution Guide for School-Age Programs.* Educators for Social Responsibility, 1996. For grades K–6. Designed to meet the needs of after-school programs, camps, and recreation centers, this guide contains hundreds of hands-on, engaging activities that teach basic conflict resolution skills through cooperative challenges, drama, crafts, music, and even cooking. Also included are easy-to-implement strategies and tips for providers both to reduce conflict in their programs and to intervene effectively when conflict does occur. Adventures in Peacemaking blends ESR's innovative conflict resolution curricula with Project Adventure's activity-based programming.

Kreidler, William J. *Elementary Perspectives: Teaching Concepts of Peace and Conflict.* Educators for Social Responsibility, 1990. For grades K–6. This best-selling curriculum offers more than eighty activities that help teachers and students define peace, explore justice, and learn the value of conflict and its resolution. Students read, write, draw, role-play, sing, and discuss their way through a process that helps them acquire the concrete cooperative and conflict resolution skills needed to become caring and socially responsible citizens.

Kreidler, William J. *Conflict Resolution in the Middle School.* Educators for Social Responsibility, 1997. For grades 6–8. Highly acclaimed, this teacher's guide features twenty-eight skill-building sections to help students address the conflicts that come with adolescence. Included are seven implementation models; sections on creating a classroom for teaching conflict resolution, developing staff and parent support, and assessing student learning; an infusion section, which includes math and science; and a section on adolescent development exploring gender and race.

Kreidler, William J., and Rachel A. Poliner. *Conflict Resolution in the Middle School: Student Workbook and Journal.* Educators for Social Responsibility, 1999. For grades 6–8. This workbook and journal will help deepen students' understanding of conflict, anger management, communication, and appreciating diversity while providing them with practice to strengthen their skills. Vibrantly designed with young adolescents in mind, the workbook includes information handouts and worksheets, journal-writing activities, and self-directed assignments. Through numerous writing activities, students will reflect on issues associated with conflict in their own lives while also learning to be accountable.

Benson, Jeffrey, and Rachel A. Poliner. *Dialogue: Turning Controversy into Community.* Educators for Social Responsibility, 1997. For grades 7–12. Through ten skill-focused chapters, this unique curriculum paints a portrait of nonadversarial dialogue through the story of Centerville, a fictional town caught in a controversy over whether or not to mandate school uniforms. Teachers learn techniques and structures for helping students build such skills as listening, researching issues, understanding and appreciating different perspectives, and creating solutions. Well suited for social studies or English teachers as well as student government and debate team advisers.

Lieber, Carol Miller, with Linda Lantieri and Tom Roderick. *Conflict Resolution in the High School.* Educators for Social Responsibility, 1998. For grades 9–12. This comprehensive, sequenced curriculum will help secondary educators address conflict resolution and problem solving, diversity and intergroup relations, social and emotional development, and building community and creating a peaceable classroom. Includes sections on implementation, assessment, and infusion of conflict resolution throughout a standard curriculum.

Mertz, Gayle, and Carol Miller Lieber. *Conflict in Context: Understanding Local to Global Security.* Educators for Social Responsibility, 2001. For grades 9–12. Current and timely, this new curriculum introduces high school students to the key concepts and skills needed to be responsible citizens. Aided by numerous case studies that are based on actual international issues, students will learn that a complex consideration of security must go beyond military issues to include economics, human rights, and more. Over forty carefully developed lessons stress such skills as researching, mapping, dialogue, critical thinking, and informed analysis.

To learn more about training opportunities, contact ESR at (800) 370-2515, ext. 19, or e-mail to educators@esrnational.org.

Educators for Social Responsibility
23 Garden Street
Cambridge, MA 02138
Telephone: (617) 492-1764
Toll free: (800) 370-2512
Fax: (617) 864-5164
Website: www.esrnational.org

# Environarts

Environarts, Inc., dedicated to the art in creating successful human environments, uses the creative arts (dance, music, theater, and visual arts) to enhance personal growth and promote interpersonal understanding and problem-solving communication. Specializing in SEL and CRE, Environarts has customized programs for organizations nationwide and abroad since 1991, providing transformational workshops, ongoing professional development, and curriculum and training materials appropriate for adult, student, or training-of-trainer applications.

Environarts programs use effective learning technologies that are customized to meet the demands of today's professional and educational challenges. Workshops focus on team building, stress management, emotional literacy (EQ), leadership, performance, and human potential.

Environarts
P.O. Box 2458
Temple, AZ 85280
Telephone: (480) 774-9844
Fax: (480) 858-9757
Website: www.environarts-inc.com

# Good Shepherd Mediation Program

Good Shepherd Mediation Program (GSMP) provides a variety of conflict management and dispute resolution services to the Philadelphia community. Their work in CRE falls into three general areas: peer mediation training, antiviolence education, and Peace Theater.

Peace Theater, developed by GSMP in 1991, is an interactive theater experience designed to "increase the peace" by encouraging children and youth to use communication and problem-solving skills to address interpersonal conflicts as an alternative to physical fighting. Peace Theater introduces conflict resolution concepts to young people ages five to eighteen. It encourages the peaceful resolution of conflict by demonstrating that conflict is normal and that how one responds to conflict may affect the outcome, and by showing how to use communication and problem-solving skills to find win-win solutions to conflict (increase the peace). It helps create an engaging, entertaining, memorable, and *fun* learning experience.

Peace Theater combines improvisational theater and role playing. A role play is a simulation of a real-life situation. The players put themselves in the shoes of the character and react to the situation presented. Peace Theater uses conflict drama to teach communication and conflict resolution skills.

Cheryl Cutrona, Executive Director
Good Shepherd Mediation Program
5356 Chew Avenue
Philadelphia, PA 19138
Telephone: (215) 843-5413
Fax: (215) 843-2080
Website: www.phillymediators.org

# Hannah More School Student Mediation Program

The Hannah More School Student Mediation Program operates within a nonpublic special education middle and high school serving emotionally disturbed, learning disabled, and autistic students and students with behavioral problems.

Paul I. Kaplan, Director of Clinical Services and Coordinator
Hannah More School Student Mediation Program

12039 Reisterstown Road
Reisterstown, MD 21136
Telephone: (410) 526-5000
E-mail: pkaplan@hannahmore.org

# Maine Law and Civics Education

The Maine Law and Civics Education (MLCE) effort is devoted to developing and supporting a variety of programs in CRE. They offer the following programs.

*Bullying Prevention Education Program:* MLCE conducts on-site training for elementary and middle schools in bullying prevention strategies. MLCE advises school administrators on developing an effective schoolwide bullying education program, trains the school's coordinating
committee, conducts staff and parent workshops, and provides curriculum resources and ongoing technical assistance. Training is provided on a fee-for-service basis, partially supported by
grants. Target audience: K–8 schools.

*Conflict management and peer mediation:* MLCE conducts on-site training for staff and students in
conflict management education and peer mediation. MLCE advises school administrators on
developing an effective schoolwide conflict management program, trains the school's coordinating committee, conducts staff workshops, and trains student mediators. Training is provided
on a fee-for-service basis, partially supported by grants. Target audience: K–12 schools.

*Peer Mediation Association of Maine (PM/AM):* PM/AM was formed to improve and advance peer
mediation and conflict management education in Maine schools. Youth mediators, with the
support of their program coordinators and university staff, promote awareness of the benefits
of conflict management, engage in training sessions, and generate support for school-based programs. Regional and statewide conferences are planned and presented by the youth mediators and the university coordinators.

Maine Law and Civics Education
University of Maine Law School
246 Deering Avenue
Portland, ME 04102
Telephone: (207) 780-4159
Website: www.law.usm.maine.edu/mlce
E-mail: pamelaa@usm.maine.edu (for codirector Pamela B. Anderson)
underwd@usm.maine.edu (for codirector Julia M. Underwood)

# Maryland Student Conflict Resolution/Peer Mediation Network

The mission of the Maryland Student Conflict Resolution/Peer Mediation Network is to encourage the development of student conflict resolution and peer mediation programs in Maryland by networking, sharing resources, and providing community education. The network has
the following goals:

- To network (that is, exchange information, approaches, and strategies; share a common vision; consult with people with complementary skills)
- To assist in starting conflict resolution and peer mediation programs
- To "fine-tune" the peer mediation programs
- To develop political clout
- To contribute to the reduction of violence in the community
- To reach out to other organizations (for example, prisons, police, and courts)
- To provide community education about student conflict resolution and peer mediation

Maryland Student Conflict Resolution Peer Mediation Network
12039 Reisterstown Road
Reisterstown, MD 21136
Telephone: (410) 526-5000

# Minnesota Department of Children, Families and Learning

The Minnesota Department of Children, Families and Learning (CFL) provides school districts with assistance in the implementation of restorative practices and classroom management approaches, including training and information on conferencing and circle training. Its monograph, *Restorative Measures: Respecting Everyone's Ability to Resolve Problems*, is available at the CFL website.

Nancy Riestenberg, Prevention Specialist
Minnesota Department of Children, Families and Learning
1500 W. Hwy 36
Roseville, MN 55113
Telephone: (651) 582-8433
Website: cfl.state.mn.us
E-mail: nancy.riestenberg@state.mn.us

# National Association for Community Mediation

The purpose of the National Association for Community Mediation (NAFCM) is to support the maintenance and growth of community-based mediation programs and processes; to present a compelling voice in appropriate legislative, policymaking, professional, and other arenas; and to encourage the development and sharing of resources for these efforts. The NAFCM has the following organizational goals:

- Serve as a national voice and an advocate of community mediation in legislative, policymaking, professional, and other arenas
- Promote the values, understanding, public awareness, and practice of community mediation and collaborative problem solving
- Educate private and public funding sources about the experience, breadth, benefits, and applications of community mediation and develop financial resources for community mediation

- Serve as a national clearinghouse of information on the development and practice of community mediation
- Foster communication and mutual assistance among members in such areas as training, funding, technology, and program and policy development
- Create and maintain a national directory and database for community mediation
- Encourage and promote regional and national collaborative projects among community mediation programs
- Promote and encourage collaboration between community mediation programs and organizations at both the local and national level
- Develop and maintain ties with national, regional, state, and other dispute resolution and related organizations to enhance the growth of community mediation
- Support research, program evaluation, mediation theory development, innovation, and quality in community mediation
- Recognize and celebrate volunteers in community mediation
- Develop local and national community mediation leadership

National Association for Community Mediation
1527 New Hampshire Avenue, NW
Washington, DC 20036
Telephone: (202) 667-9700
Website: www.nafcm.org

# National Center for Conflict Resolution Education

The National Center for Conflict Resolution Education (NCCRE) is dedicated to providing quality professional development services for educators on-site in schools, in school districts, and in partnership with regional and state departments of education. NCCRE's peaceable school, peer mediation, and emotional intelligence institutes offer skill-building training and curriculum resources designed to achieve comprehensive CRE programs in schools.

## Publications

Bodine, Richard J., Donna K. Crawford, and Fred Schrumpf. *Creating the Peaceable School Program Guide: A Comprehensive Program for Teaching Conflict Resolution* (rev. ed.). Champaign, Ill.: Research Press, 2001. Designed for use in upper elementary and middle school grades, this program can also be adapted for younger and older students. Through the conflict resolution strategies of mediation, negotiation, and group problem solving, students learn to recognize, manage, and resolve conflicts in peaceful, noncoercive ways. This guide includes step-by-step teaching procedures; sixty-three learning activities; guidelines for program organization, implementation, and maintenance; sample letters, contracts, and forms; examples of role-play situations; and more.

Bodine, Richard J., Donna K. Crawford, and Fred Schrumpf. *Creating the Peaceable School Student Manual: A Comprehensive Program for Teaching Conflict Resolution* (rev. ed.). Champaign, Ill.: Research Press, 2001. This manual serves as a student workbook and is recommended for each learner participating in the program. It summarizes each important concept: rights and responsibilities, rules, cooperation, conflict, peace and peacemaking, negotiation, mediation, and group problem solving. The manual contains a variety of forms and worksheets designed to reinforce student learning.

Schrumpf, Fred, Donna K. Crawford, and Richard J. Bodine. *Peer Mediation Program Guide: Conflict Resolution in Schools* (rev. ed.). Champaign, Ill.: Research Press, 1996. This widely used resource shows how to design, implement, and operate a successful peer mediation program with students in grades 6–12, placing particular emphasis on social and cultural diversity. It provides step-by-step instructions for staff orientation and training, student orientation, and the selection and training of mediators. Contains thirty activities that prepare student mediators to conduct most mediation requests. Includes numerous reproducible forms.

Schrumpf, Fred, Donna K. Crawford, and Richard J. Bodine. *Peer Mediation Student Manual: Conflict Resolution in Schools* (rev. ed.). Champaign, Ill.: Research Press, 1996. This manual serves as both a workbook and handy reference guide for each student mediator. It covers the program's goals and objectives, the qualities and role of the peer mediator, necessary communication skills, and the six steps in the mediation process. Includes training activities, role-play exercises, worksheets, and sample peer mediation forms.

Bodine, Richard J., and Donna K. Crawford. *Developing Emotional Intelligence: A Guide to Behavior Management and Conflict Resolution in Schools.* Champaign, Ill.: Research Press, 1999. This book is a call to educate rather than control. It shows how to create a noncoercive behavior management program that promotes and supports the development of emotional intelligence. Students will learn to use their emotions intentionally to guide them in making responsible, need-fulfilling choices in such areas as learning, interpersonal relationships, problem solving, and adapting to the complex demands of growth, development, and change. The book concludes with an appendix presenting seven lessons to give students a basic understanding of their behavior—emphasizing that all behavior is purposeful and that all behavior is chosen.

Bodine, Richard J., and Donna K. Crawford. *The Handbook of Conflict Resolution Education: A Guide to Building Quality Programs in Schools.* San Francisco: Jossey-Bass, 1997. CRE is a critical component of comprehensive efforts to prevent violence and reduce crime in schools. This workbook introduces the basic principles of conflict resolution and its application to school settings. It describes the elements of effective conflict resolution programs and gives an overview of the most popular, effective approaches. It also offers step-by-step guidance on planning and implementing a successful conflict resolution program.

## Videos

Bodine, Richard J., and Donna K. Crawford. *Creating the Peaceable School Video.* Champaign, Ill.: Research Press, 1995. This video illustrates the concepts and conflict resolution strategies contained in the *Creating the Peaceable School Program Guide* (described above). A free copy of the guide accompanies the video. The program developers discuss the program's philosophy, background, and objectives. Interviews with students and teachers point out the benefits of the program. The video also features scenes of elementary, middle school, and high school students using mediation, negotiation, and group problem solving. Time: 40 minutes.

Schrumpf, Fred, and Donna K. Crawford. *The Peer Mediation Video: Conflict Resolution in Schools.* Champaign, Ill.: Research Press, 1993. This video program illustrates the concepts and training procedures contained in the peer mediation books described previously. A free copy of the *Peer Mediation Program Guide* accompanies the video. The video includes discussions of the program's objectives and implementation procedures, demonstrations of the six-step mediation process, and videotaped scenes of student training and mediation sessions. The *Peer Mediation Video* is the next best thing to an on-site training presentation by the program developers. Time: 28 minutes.

For more information about books and videos listed here, contact either of the following websites: www.resolutioneducation.com or www.researchpress.com.

National Center for Conflict Resolution Education
Illinois Bar Center
424 S. Second Street
Springfield, IL 62701
Telephone: (217) 523-7056
Website: www.nccre.org
E-mail: info@nccre.org

# New Mexico Center for Dispute Resolution

Founded in 1982, the New Mexico Center for Dispute Resolution (NMCDR) has a rich heritage of building and sustaining peace. NMCDR is an award-winning community mediation agency known for its innovative services and approaches to mediation and dispute resolution. NMCDR provides assistance to educators, youth-serving professionals, organizations, and institutions in the development of mediation and conflict resolution programs in home, school, community, and juvenile justice settings; businesses; faith communities; nonprofit organizations; and government agencies.

New Mexico Center for Dispute Resolution
800 Park Avenue, SW
Albuquerque, NM 87102
Telephone: (505) 247-0571
Toll free: (800) 249-6884
Website: www.nmcdr.org
E-mail: nmcdr@igc.apc.org

# Ohio Commission on Dispute Resolution and Conflict Management

Established in 1989, the Ohio Commission on Dispute Resolution and Conflict Management provides Ohioans with constructive, nonviolent forums, processes, and techniques for resolving disputes. Focused on four program areas—educational institutions, state and local government, courts, and communities—the commission works to positively affect the lives of all Ohio citizens.

The education programs include a variety of resources: grants for the establishment of conflict management programs in K–12 schools, teacher and staff training, materials for helping children cope with terrorism and other trauma, and evaluation and assessment materials.

Maria Mone, Executive Director
Jennifer Batton, Director of Education
Ohio Commission on Dispute Resolution and Conflict Management
77 S. High St., 24th floor
Columbus, OH 43215-6108
Telephone: (614) 644-9275
Fax: (614) 752-9682
Website: www.state.oh.us/cdr

# The Partnership for Conflict Resolution Education in the Arts

The Partnership for Conflict Resolution Education in the Arts (PCREA) recognizes the natural affinity between CRE and the arts. PCREA is a collaboration of the National Endowment for the Arts (NEA) and the Office of Juvenile Justice and Delinquency Prevention (OJJDP) of the U.S. Department of Justice. This national leadership initiative, designed to strengthen community-based arts programs provided for youth at risk for drug abuse and violence, provides training for program administrators, artists, and representatives from collaborating organizations, as well as (in some locations) youth and families served by the program. The training provided through this initiative embraces a threefold purpose:

- To teach artists, program administrators, and staff conflict resolution skills and processes
- To enable arts organizations to infuse conflict resolution principles and processes into the design of their youth programs
- To strengthen the partnerships between arts organizations and community groups that support youth programs.

The following are two examples of PCREA projects:

*ShenanArts Inc., Growing Stages Theatre for Youth, Staunton, Virginia:* as a result of the conflict training provided by the NEA-OJJDP partnership, ShenanArts has developed two programs focused on conflict resolution and peacemaking through the community:

- Peacemakers' Theatre was a ten-week workshop program conducted with three Augusta County High School groups. The schools developed three short one-act pieces on conflict resolution using conflict resolution and transformation as the core of improvisational explorations. The pieces were based on actual incidents at each high school and were performed together as an evening of theater for the public in March 2001. The program is scheduled to continue and expand.
- Silence the Violence was a program commissioned by the United Way of Harrisonburg/Rockingham County to develop a fifty-minute touring piece on the prevention of violence in the community. The finished script has been mounted in a touring production by youth for the community.

*Lane Arts Council, YouthArts, Eugene, Oregon:* the Art of Peacemaking materials and training experience have been a valued and adaptable training development resource. As a result of the conflict resolution training provided by PCREA, the YouthArts program coordinators have infused effective communication and community-building concepts, techniques, and activities into a range of six artist, youth, partner, and broader community workshops held over the past two years. Activities that build skills in effective communication and lead to cooperative problem solving have been especially beneficial to the artists and teen-team assistants working in the Art-Connection summer programs in twelve of the rural Lane County communities.

Lee Kessler, Federal Liaison
National Endowment for the Arts
1100 Pennsylvania Avenue, NW
Washington, DC 20506
Telephone: (202) 682-5400
Website: arts.endow.gov/partner/Conflict.html

# PassageWays Institute

In 1992, Rachael Kessler founded the Institute for Social and Emotional Learning. In 2001, she changed the name to the PassageWays Institute to better reflect its mission, which is

- To broaden awareness among educators, counselors, parents, and youth workers of the need for and nature of spiritual development in children and adolescents
- To provide leadership, coaching, training, curriculum, and staff development that fosters the development of the inner life in schools and after-school programming
- To engage in ongoing research to further expand our understanding of nurturing the inner life in school and in relationship to academics, violence prevention, and character development
- To sponsor programs and activities for youth and their parents

The PassageWays Institute
3833 North 57th Street
Boulder, CO 80301
Telephone: (303) 581-0331
Website: www.mediatorsfoundation.org/isel
E-mail: PassageWaysRK@aol.com

# Program for Young Negotiators

Program for Young Negotiators (PYN), developed by SERA Learning, empowers middle school youth to resolve their problems and conflicts on their own without resorting to violence. By offering negotiation and conflict resolution as a real and compelling alternative to fighting or "giving in," PYN brings a positive, original approach to violence prevention through youth empowerment. PYN

- Improves the participants' ability to talk through disagreements, thus reducing violent conflict
- Aims to teach all youth problem-solving skills rather than teach a core group to mediate as a third party
- Provides the tools for coping with conflicts, solving problems, and achieving goals
- Provides teachers with an opportunity to assess their own conflict management approach
- Adapts to a variety of learning styles

Since 1992, SERA Learning has been a recognized leader in providing educational, juvenile justice, and community-based organizations with life skills programs that are nationally acclaimed and proven to be effective at addressing the needs of youth and young adults ages ten to twenty-four.

SERA Learning teaches adults how to facilitate the Building Personal Power programs with youth and young adults. At the same time, those adults are increasing their own understanding of the programs' concepts and applying them to their own lives. As part of a comprehensive program, SERA Learning offers curriculum, professional development, on-site support, third-party evaluation, and parent components that enable youth to successfully build their own personal power.

Theresa Nguyen
Telephone: (800) 741-9473, ext. 19
E-mail: theresa@sera.com

SERA Learning
2675 Folsom Street, Suite 200
San Francisco, CA 94110
Telephone: (415) 642-2170
Toll free: (800) 741-9473
Fax: (415) 642-3548
Website: www.sera.com

# SaferSanerSchools

SaferSanerSchools is a program of the International Institute for Restorative Practices, which provides training and educational materials on restorative practices in schools. SaferSanerSchools focuses on hands-on, practical strategies that educators can use to respond to difficult students.

SaferSanerSchools
P.O. Box 229
Bethlehem, PA 18016
Telephone: (610) 807-9221
Website: www.safersanerschools.org

# School Mediation Associates

The mission of School Mediation Associates (SMA) is to transform schools into safer, more caring, and more effective institutions. Through its work, SMA

- Encourages young people to become leaders in their schools
- Helps students and educators see conflict as an opportunity for personal and institutional growth
- Teaches students and educators the skills to resolve conflict nonviolently and collaboratively
- Mediates challenging conflicts at educators' request
- Disseminates an approach to problem solving that values diversity and respects differences of opinion

Many thousands of educators, students, and parents have participated in SMA programs since 1984. SMA's services are tailored to meet each school's unique needs. The audience for SMA programs and services include students (grade 4 through college), teachers, administrators, staff, and parents. In some training programs, students and adults are trained together.

## Programs

*Peer mediation training and program implementation* (grade 4 through college): in this popular program pioneered by SMA, a diverse group of student leaders are trained to help their peers resolve a range of interpersonal conflicts, including name-calling, gossip, prejudice, and boyfriend-girlfriend tensions. Mediation sessions are voluntary and confidential. In addition to numerous benefits to school climate and to the students involved, close to 90 percent of mediation sessions result in agreements that resolve the conflict.

*Appreciating Differences workshops* (grade 6 through adult): students and educators explore, and learn to appreciate, their differences on all levels (gender, race, religion, clique, class, ethnic, sexual orientation, and so on). These workshops can be life-changing experiences for participants, who are inspired to work with their peers to erase intolerance and build a safe and caring school community.

*Conflict resolution and mediation training for educators:* ideally, teachers model effective methods of conflict resolution as well as teach them directly to their students. SMA's workshops and training sessions, ranging from two-hour in-service presentations to weeklong workshops, help educators integrate conflict resolution skills into their professional practice and their personal lives.

*Conflict resolution and mediation training for parents:* parents know all too well that conflict can lead to either growth or frustration. SMA's workshop series for parents (usually sponsored by the school) help parents learn skills to resolve conflicts creatively and constructively.

## Publications

Cohen, Richard. *The School Mediator's Field Guide: Prejudice, Sexual Harassment, Large Groups and Other Daily Challenges*. School Mediation Associates, June 1999. An essential resource for every teacher, administrator, counselor, and student who mediates in schools. Learn how to mediate a range of challenging school-based conflicts. Includes case examples and handy checklists for each type of conflict. Both school-based mediators and coordinators of peer mediation programs will refer to this book again and again.

Cohen, Richard. *Students Resolving Conflict: Peer Mediation in Schools*. New York: GoodYear/Addison Wesley, 1995. This book will assist individuals at every level of experience and exposure to peer mediation. Its purpose is to serve as a comprehensive introduction to conflict resolution and peer mediation, a complete technical assistance manual for those involved in the process of implementing a peer mediation program, and a reference work for those who currently operate peer mediation programs. The book includes many tools, such as reproducible program forms, twelve complete conflict resolution lessons, transcripts of peer mediation sessions, and surveys to determine implementation readiness.

School Mediation Associates
134 Standish Road
Watertown, MA 02472
Telephone: (617) 926-0994
Toll free: (800) 833-3318
Website: www.schoolmediation.com
E-mail: sma@schoolmediation.com

# ABOUT THE EDITORS

*Tricia S. Jones* is a professor in the College of Education, Temple University, Philadelphia. Her teaching and research interests are in conflict processes, with special emphasis on emotion in conflict and the development of emotional competence and conflict competence in children. She is the past president (1996–1997) of the International Association of Conflict Management, and has served as a member of both the research and evaluation committee for the National Association for Mediation in Education and the standards committee for the National Institute for Dispute Resolution/Conflict Resolution Education Network. She currently serves as the editor in chief of *Conflict Resolution Quarterly* (formerly *Mediation Quarterly*). Her research and scholarship in conflict resolution education has been funded by the William and Flora Hewlett Foundation, the Surdna Foundation, the United States Information Agency, the State Justice Institute, the Packard Foundation, and the Pennsylvania Commission on Crime and Delinquency. She has published more than forty articles and book chapters on communication and conflict, and coedited the volumes *New Directions on Mediation* (Sage, 1994) and *Does It Work? The Case for Conflict Resolution Education in Our Nation's Schools* (CRENet, 2000); she was the coauthor of *Evaluating Your Conflict Resolution Education Program* (Ohio Department of Education, 2002). She and her husband of twenty-six years, Martin Remland, are the proud parents of Alexander Samuel Remland. She received her Ph.D. in communication from The Ohio State University in 1985.

*Randy Compton* is the executive director of the School Mediation Center (formerly the Colorado School Mediation Project), where he has been helping schools and youth-serving institutions set up conflict resolution, social and emotional learning, peer mediation, and restorative justice programs since 1987. He has served on the standards committee for the National Institute for Dispute Resolution/Conflict Resolution Education Network, which developed recommended guidelines for effective conflict resolution education programs in K–12 classrooms, schools, and districts. Most recently, he has served as the coordinator of the National Curriculum Integration Project, a three-year research project seeking to integrate and infuse conflict resolution into middle school curriculum and culture. He has founded two statewide conferences—the Violence Prevention in School Communities conference and Peace Leadership: A Youth Conference on Peer Mediation and Conflict Management—in addition to authoring numerous articles and curricula for youth. He is married and the father of one beautiful child, Meryl. He holds an M.A. degree (1989) in social conflict from the University of Colorado at Boulder.

# ABOUT THE CONTRIBUTORS

*David Claassen-Wilson* has served as restorative justice coordinator for the School Mediation Center (formerly the Colorado School Mediation Project). He has been working with school districts across Colorado to develop restorative justice programs in schools as alternatives to suspension, expulsion, and police charges. David has a degree in peace studies from Bethel College in Newton, Kansas, and previously served as executive director for the Victim-Offender Reconciliation Program in Boulder, Colorado.

*Richard Cohen* is founder and director of School Mediation Associates, one of the oldest organizations in the world devoted to school-based mediation. He is the author of a number of highly regarded books about peer mediation as well as the free monthly e-newsletter *The School Mediator.* You can find out more about his work at www.schoolmediation.com.

*Amalia G. Cuervo* is a licensed psychotherapist and trained mediator with a small practice in Reston, Virginia, specializing in children and families, coauthor of the award-winning manual, *Toward Better and Safer Schools*, and a member of the board of directors of the Virginia Association of Clinical Counselors. She has worked in the area of school-based prevention for over twenty years as a school counselor and administrator in two school districts and has implemented conflict resolution programs pre-K through high school. Former director of research for the National School Boards Association, and program manager with the U.S. Department of Justice, she is now with the U.S. Department of Education.

*Jennifer K. Druliner* is the education and advocacy manager for the Association for Conflict Resolution (ACR). Previously the associate director of the Conflict Resolution Education Network (CREnet), she holds an M.A. in international peace and conflict resolution from American University in Washington, D.C. While at American University, she participated in a conflict resolution education internship program, partnering with a D.C. high school teacher to infuse conflict resolution into U.S. history classes for ESL students.

*Mark Gerzon,* president of Mediators Foundation since 1985, has worked with school leaders in conflicted communities throughout the United States and in many regions of the world. He has facilitated the bipartisan Congressional Retreats for the U.S. House of Representatives in 1997 and 1999. He is the author of several books including the forthcoming *Leaders Beyond Borders: The Five Values of the Global Revolution.*

*Alice Ierley* is a restorative justice coordinator at the School Mediation Center (formerly the Colorado School Mediation Project) in Boulder. Ierley has been passionately involved in issues related to schools as an attorney, mediator, and trainer and as the parent of two children. Beginning work in mediation in 1994, she has branched out into the restorative justice field over the last three years, pioneering new approaches for schools and communities.

*Paul I. Kaplan* is the director of clinical services at Hannah More School in Reisterstown, Maryland, where he is the coordinator of the student mediation program. Kaplan is also the co-coordinator of the Maryland Student Conflict Resolution/Peer Mediation Network. He is licensed as a certified clinical social worker in Maryland and has experience as a family law attorney and divorce mediator.

*Rachael Kessler* is the director of the PassageWays Institute, where she offers training, consultation, research, and curriculum development to schools, districts, and individual educators and youth development professionals. She is the author of *The Soul of Education: Helping Students Find Connection, Compassion and Character at School,* as well as coauthor of *Promoting Social and Emotional Learning: Guidelines for Educators.* You can reach her at passagewaysrk@aol.com and learn more about her approach at www.mediatorsfoundation.org/isel.

*Carol Miller Lieber,* the secondary program specialist at Educators for Social Responsibility (ESR), is a national leader in integrating principles of prevention, healthy development, and social and emotional learning into everyday practices and policies of middle and high schools. In her thirty-five years as an educator, Lieber has taught students at all grade levels, cofounded an urban secondary school, and served as a university faculty member. Through ESR, she has developed Partners in Learning, an array of programs that help establish safe, caring, and respectful school cultures and classroom learning environments that support healthy development and academic success for all students. She is the author of *Conflict Resolution in the High School, Conflict in Context,* and *Partners in Learning: Personalizing Secondary Classrooms.*

*Sarah Pirtle* is the author of two books for teachers: *Discovery Time for Cooperation and Conflict Resolution* (K–8) and *Linking Up! Using Music, Movement, and Language Arts to Promote Caring, Cooperation, and Communication.* Her young adult novel, *An Outbreak of Peace,* received the Olive Branch Award for outstanding book on world peace. She coedited *Partnership Education in Action.* She has made five children's recordings, including "Two Hands Hold the Earth," which received five national awards. She directs the Discovery Center for Earth-Centered Peace Education, in Shelburne Falls, Massachusetts, and teaches in the Creative Arts in Learning Program of Lesley University.

*Rachel A. Poliner* is an educational consultant working with schools on management, change, and conflict, and on school reforms dealing with social and emotional learning. She works with schools in New England and across the United States, using an approach that spans curriculum and classroom practices, staff development and leadership, and schoolwide programs and climate. Formerly a leader of Educators for Social Responsibility, Poliner was an integral member of the team that helped establish the field of conflict resolution education and, with William J. Kreidler, created the Stories Program: Teaching Conflict and Character Through Literature and Language Arts. A former teacher and director of a nonprofit organization, Poliner is a coauthor of several curricula and an upcoming guide on establishing advisory programs in secondary schools.

*Heather E. Prichard* is a consultant for the Association for Conflict Resolution (ACR) and executive editor of ACR's quarterly magazine, *ACResolution.* Previously the executive director of the Conflict Resolution Education Network (CREnet), she holds an M.A. in international peace and conflict resolution and a certificate in organizational change from American University in Washington, D.C. She is currently working on her Ph.D. in education. Prior to her work with CREnet,

Prichard served as cofounder and director of American University's conflict resolution education internship program (Project PEN), where she designed curricula for high school conflict resolution education programs and courses, and trained over fifty conflict resolution educators to work in public schools.

*Priscilla Prutzman,* cofounder and executive director of Creative Response to Conflict, has an M.A. in communications and media studies from the New School for Social Research and is the author and coauthor of numerous conflict resolution books and articles, including "The Friendly Classroom for a Small Planet" and "Children's Songs for a Friendly Planet." She has received the Margaret Herrman Founders Award from the National Conference on Peacemaking and Conflict Resolution for service to the field, and the Peacemakers Award from the National Peace Foundation.

*Beverly B. Title* has taught at every level from kindergarten through graduate school and is the program developer of the No-Bullying Program. She has helped educators and parents across the country understand bullying and know how to respond appropriately. In addition to being a national consultant and trainer on school violence prevention, she also works with restorative justice as the program manager for the Longmont (Colorado) Community Justice Partnership.

*Sandy Tsubokawa Whittall* is a graduate of San Diego State University and Pacific Oaks College. She has taught every age, from toddlers to adults, but credits her children Zeni and Michi with providing the teachable moments that helped her put theory into practice. She currently works as a consultant to the Colorado Department of Education/Prevention Initiatives, helping improve school-age care in Colorado, and as the program director for Adventures in Peacemaking, for Educators for Social Responsibility in Cambridge, Massachusetts.

# NAME INDEX

## A

Academy of Family Mediators (AFM), 19
Adventure Club and Creative Play Centers, 282–286
Adventures in Peacemaking, 43, 287
Alexander, G., 98, 300
Allen, L., 240–243
Aliki, 181
Alvarado, E., 282–284
Anderson, J., 76–80
Anne T. Dunphy Elementary School (Williamsburg, MA), 156–158, 193–197, 297, 304
Aponte, E., 98–101
Aronson, E., 54
Association for Conflict Resolution (ACR), 19, 301, 325–326; recommended guidelines for CRE, 301

## B

Barnes, A., 105
Benge-Rosson, K., 127–128

Bennington Regional School District (VT), 178
Benson, K., 108
Black, J., 195–196
Bodine, R., 20, 23, 28–29, 90, 301, 305
Booten, K., 282–284
Boston Health Career Academy, 46
Boulder High School (Boulder, CO), 265–273, 303
Bourgeouis, M., 128
Boys and Girls Club, 281
Bradley, H., 123–124
Braithwaite, J., 206
Brendtro, L., 12–13, 65, 222
Brentwood School District (Brentwood, NY), 98–107
Brentwood East Middle School (Brentwood, NY), 98–101, 292, 298
Brentwood North Middle School (Brentwood, NY), 98, 102–107, 298, 300
Brisson, P., 180
Brown, N., 139
Bruce, F., 106–107, 292
Brunson, R., 169–171, 297

Buckland–Shelburne School (MA), 158
Building Bridges program, 158
Bullyproofing Your School program, 226
Burke, K., 76–80
Burman, T. R., 215–216
Byrd, T., 162–163

## C

Caine, R., 67
Calliste, R., 105–107
Camp Fire USA, 276, 279–280
Campus-ADR, 326
Carter, J., 184
Casey, D., 238–240
Cecil, W., 76–80
Center for the Study and Prevention of Violence, 9
Centers for Disease Control, 10
Chait, T., 236–237
Charles, M., 76–80
Chasnoff, D., 255
Chavez, L., 121–123
Claassen–Wilson, D., 20, 24, 294

# SUBJECT INDEX